D1498753

"*Fictions of America* is absolutely essential; what a transformative reading experience. My first reaction upon finishing it: if only I had this extraordinary volume when I was younger. Second reaction: I am so grateful to have it now."
—Junot Díaz, Pulitzer-prize winning author of *The Brief Wondrous Life of Oscar Wao*

"In Baer and Dayal's remarkable new volume...we see collected together for the first time the initial offerings of some of the country's most significant writers. The ensemble reminds us that, our many differences notwithstanding, we are all continually striving, experimenting, smashing shibboleths, and waiting for yet another fresh voice and pioneering talent to make itself known."
—Robert F. Reid-Pharr, Harvard University, author of *Archives of Flesh: Spain, African America, and Post-Humanist Critique*

"A timely reflection on the early American literary imagination, this collection tells new stories of artistic originality through a stunningly diverse array of authors published across three centuries."
—Sarah Rivett, Professor of English and American Studies, Princeton University

"Gathers a fascinating series of texts, some familiar, many not, that does nothing less than uncover a new American literature. This anthology of new beginnings, spanning four centuries, with a superb introduction by the editors, will be essential and eye-opening to students and scholars alike."
—Ross Posnock, Anna S. Garbedian Professor of the Humanities, Columbia University

"Exquisitely edited with judicious selections and expert introductions, Baer and Dayal present in *Fictions of America* a way of reframing the times and timings of American literary history."
—Ivy Wilson, author of *Specters of Democracy: Blackness and the Aesthetics of Nationalism*

"Baer and Dayal have performed an enormous service...by calling attention to an under-examined body of texts, compelling us to rethink our fundamental assumptions about the beginnings of American literature."
—Manu Samriti Chander, Associate Professor of English, Rutgers University–Newark

"Representing a multiplicity of perspectives....this collection is an important chronicle of our complex and varied literary history."
—Wendy Martin, Professor of American Literature & American Studies, Claremont Graduate University

"Here is a rich volume....that will be edifying to students, teachers, and aficionados of the long and turbulent history of American literature."
—Peter Coviello, Professor of English, University of Illinois at Chicago

FICTIONS OF AMERICA

First Warbler Press Edition 2020

First publication information provided on page 323.

Introduction © Ulrich Baer and Smaran Dayal
Selected Additional Readings © Ulrich Baer

ISBN 978-1-7357789-8-3 (paperback)
ISBN 978-1-7357789-9-0 (e-book)

warblerpress.com

Printed in the United States of America. This edition is printed with
chlorine-free ink on acid-free interior paper made from 30% post-consumer
waste recycled material.

FICTIONS OF AMERICA

THE BOOK OF FIRSTS

Edited and Introduced by
ULRICH BAER and SMARAN DAYAL

FOR OUR STUDENTS

CONTENTS

INTRODUCTION

by Ulrich Baer and Smaran Dayal

Phillis Wheatley's 1773 book of poems, *Poems on Various Subjects, Religious and Moral*, is the first known book published by a woman of African descent in America. Wheatley's work is paradigmatic for all of the works collected in this anthology. This project celebrates the pathbreaking contributions of often overlooked literary innovators. Based on the thorough work of countless scholars, writers, and activists, we have gathered the first of various kinds of texts to be published by writers from groups that were not—at the time of publication—recognized, respected, or even seen as fully human by mainstream society. The authors of these texts inaugurated new traditions, adapted conventions to express new things, and expanded the definition of American literature. They also provide evidence of America's commitment to invent "a new and coming civilization," in the words of Ralph Waldo Emerson, which has never been an exclusively political endeavor but also a cultural one. American literature is preoccupied with new beginnings in ways that other traditions are not, simply because America as a cultural project rests on the very idea of a new beginning in particular ways. As indispensable but frequently neglected contributions to our nation's revolutionary effort to imagine and create an unprecedented society, the works gathered in this volume share the quintessential American urge to try the untried, experiment with new ideas, and innovate upon existing conditions. The term "American" here refers to the cultural project of national belonging and democratic representation rather than the state, which did not fully recognize many of the writers here as citizens until long after they had contributed to the national canon. The readings, which are organized chronologically, span the period prior to the United States' independence, because especially during the long nineteenth century America was urgently seeking to inaugurate a new society and culture on its own terms. We include the very first published poems, plays, and novels in America to mark the baseline for this new tradition.

Fiction and poetry are frequently gathered and classified into a mainstream canon that represents a nation's or group's cultural storehouse of memories and knowledge. Nobel laureate Toni Morrison highlighted the importance but also the dangers and consequences of constructing national canons. "Canon debate, whatever the terrain, nature, and range...is the clash of cultures. And *all* of the interests are vested." In assembling *Fictions of America*, we kept Morrison's warning front and center in our minds. This book builds upon other efforts to add more voices to the pantheon of Poe, Hawthorne, Melville, Emerson, Thoreau, Dickinson, and James that constitutes the public idea of America's literary heritage and forms the basis of high school and college reading lists. Each of these writers, Morrison also emphasized, deserves to be read, studied, and debated to understand how our national identity has been shaped. Our book adds to this canon, which has been productively revised for decades already, by gathering for the first time all those poems, plays, stories, and novels that shifted the paradigm of how America represents itself and who can carry out this task.

This book presents works of fiction and poetry, rather than speeches and political essays, because imaginative literature aims not for factual truth alone but for accuracy and authenticity in the telling. It defines literature as works of the imagination that transform the world rather than merely represent it, and that highlight the link between aesthetic and political representation. These texts do not only describe the outside world but activate the power that Phillis Wheatley identifies in a 1773 poem with our capacity to conceive of a new world: "There in one view we grasp the mighty whole, / Or with new worlds amaze th' unbounded soul." Wheatley celebrates the positive liberty of her imagination even when she was denied, as an enslaved person, her physical, political, and legal freedom. *Fictions of America* presents a vanguard of poets and storytellers who understood their work to be more than acts of publishing. These "firsts" often appeared in defiance of social and political attitudes. As such they exemplify the power of the imagination to "grasp...new worlds" and inaugurate a new frame of mind that lets us see both prior and subsequent works, and ourselves, in a different light.

We recognize that the category of a "first" of its kind has been a mark of distinction but can also be deployed to erase earlier cultural works, especially those of Native Americans before the arrival of Europeans and of any culture that does not fit into the paradigm of printed texts. The texts gathered here are "first" only in relation to the particular political entity called the United States. There were many other firsts in the First Nations indigenous to this continent; their priority must be recognized before thinking about who comes first in the context of the United States. While noting this important point, this book presents a fuller understanding of the American canon as originating from a number of "firsts," each of which inaugurated multi-varied, rich traditions.

The category of the "first" is not automatically a marker of uniqueness. Sometimes, to be clear, a text is the first to become publicly available for reasons that have little or nothing to do with its particular merit or relevance, but its survival or discovery is a matter of publishing practices, research priorities, or chance. We regard these texts as openings to explore further readings, either by the same or other authors. Each of them, when considered carefully, harbors tremendous power. In many cases, simply becoming aware of a "first" text and the date of its appearance can re-order our entire conception of the tradition, of American public life, and even of history itself. In this sense, these texts shift the paradigm of what is considered American literature. They modify every text that comes before them and shape our understanding of every subsequent work. They also render moot the claim that including more diverse authors means destroying the canon of America's cultural past. Once works that express the deep and varied roots in our nation's culture are placed next to the texts frequently assigned in high schools and found in major anthologies, we arrive at a deeper and more truthful account of who we have been and who we are as Americans.

Being the first in one's community to break boundaries and accomplish something, like Jupiter Hammon, Phillis Wheatley, Jane Johnston Schoolcraft, John Rollin Ridge, Frances Ellen Watkins Harper, Walt Whitman, María Amparo Ruiz de Burton, S. Alice Callahan, Sui Sin Far, and other trailblazers, is a double-edged distinction. Being the first can be an achievement and also a testament to social exclusion. While paying attention to the first of one's community, identity, or genre corrects a false and incomplete version of American history, placing too much emphasis on this status of being the first can also hide the path that led to this position, and the work done afterwards. The first text of its kind can inaugurate a rich tradition. Fetishizing this status, however, can also cut it off from the cultural context in which it was created. This risk is always present in an anthology, where texts are necessarily abridged and chosen from extensive networks of texts necessary to understand them fully. But the payoff from reading these texts as an essential part of our literary canon is tremendous. They broaden our knowledge of America's efforts to understand itself in moving, dramatic, and thrilling ways.

We were guided by two priorities: artistic originality and first publication of a text by writers once excluded from mainstream culture. Each of these concepts involves newness, both in the sense of literary originality—telling a new story in a new way—and also newness in the sense of being the first text published by a writer in a specific community. Instead of grouping minority writers in thematic clusters, we present a chronology of literary milestones that reveal our nation's cultural past as emerging from multiple tributaries rather than a single stream. Some of the works gathered here, like the poem by Lucy Terry Prince, were first transmitted orally and only later transcribed, or, in the case of George Moses Horton, first memorized and only later published. This book presents many remarkable texts—some available only in rare editions—that have been excluded or overlooked in the study of American literature. Here are excerpts of poems by two con-temporaneous writers:

> Retrospection sadly turned my mind
> To scenes now painted on the map of Time
> Long Past. And as I wandered on, I mused
> On greatness fall'n, beauteous things destroyed;
> When suddenly my footstep paused before
> A mound of moss-grown earth.

***

> I saw in Louisiana a live-oak growing,
> All alone stood it and the moss hung down from the branches,
> Without any companion it grew there uttering joyous leaves of dark
>   green,
> And its look, rude, unbending, lusty, made me think of myself,
> But I wonder'd how it could utter joyous leaves standing alone there
>   without its friend near, for I knew I could not.

Respectively "An Indian's Grave" by John Rollin Ridge, whose Cherokee name is Cheesquatalawny, and Walt Whitman's "I Saw in Louisiana a

Live-Oak Growing" merit close attention for their artistic quality as much as for their role in imagining America for our present time. Yet Ridge's poem is difficult to find, and appears mostly in anthologies devoted to Native American writings, while Whitman's poem is ubiquitous.

In Ridge's poem, both the poet's recollection and progress through the woods are stopped when he stumbles upon the mound. The encounter with an Indian's grave, now overgrown, alters his relation to the past, which the poem recalls for us, and also his progress into the future. This is what artistic greatness means: to claim a new place from which to see connections between past, present and future that had been obscured by conventional ways of looking, with the effect of reshuffling our sense of self. Once we have read Ridge's poem, our understanding of Whitman's effort to sing America into existence, in poems such as "I Saw in Louisiana" and "Starting from Paumanok," the Native name for Whitman's native Long Island, is deepened rather than displaced.

All of the texts in this book accomplish several things at once. They testify to their author's boldness and courage in writing stories and poetry without relying on society or the law to condone, protect, or champion their efforts and status. In doing so they opened doors for other writers who came after them. These stories, poems, and plays also invite today's diverse readers to see themselves in our nation's literature in respectful, dignified, and even heroic poses. Literary critics often disdain a reader's direct identification with fictional characters as a form of simplistic projection. But to encounter one's own likeness, or the fully realized wholeness of someone different from oneself, on the page is a powerful experience that allows us to understand and interpret ourselves and our world. It demonstrates that America has always been comprised of individuals of many different races, genders, and other identities. It asks us to consider the relation between artistic self-presentation and political representation. In certain ways, literary texts can write an individual or community into existence, meaning that they can now be seen and understood in terms set by the author rather than an outside group. If we think of identity only as a political, social, or legal category, we overlook the essential work of language in shaping identity. Finally, these works alter the course of American literature, because it is only from the vantage point of our present moment, when these texts are known, that its history can be told. They have the power to change the very contours of democratic culture.

Our selection is informed by historical research, aided by the diligent work of intrepid and visionary scholars, archivists, activists, artists and writers—often and primarily individuals of color, women, and others belonging to groups not fully recognized in the first decades of American canon-formation and for a long time excluded from various positions of cultural guardianship. They all labored and continue to work with the conviction that uncovering the truth of America's literary past can serve as the basis for building what is right in the future. An honest account of America's literary originality, based on writers who burst through inconceivable odds to make themselves heard, will do much for a more truthful account of what America is and who Americans are today. The point is not to remind us that people of color and women were marginalized in America—this is reliably confirmed by any cursory study of our country's history. The point is to show that the imagination triumphed under extremely adverse and oppressive conditions and that its expression in language is an indispensable step in the achievement of social and political recognition. For long stretches of time, America's rich literary promise was upheld not only in mainstream literature but by poets and writers who in many instances spent part or all of their lives enslaved, were condemned to difficult labor to stay alive, forbidden from learning to read or write, deprived of a formal education, excluded from public venues, or sanctioned in other ways for their mere presence in America.

By matching the idea of literary originality as singularity of cognition, rhetorical skill, and a never completely assimilated strangeness with the presumably more socially oriented idea of "first" employed here, this book invites readers to rethink the categories by which we judge literature as important or negligible, transformative or slight. Is the aesthetic case of "innate quality" made for certain texts really an entirely neutral, objective, and self-evident criterion? Aesthetic achievement means originality of cognitive insight, creative use of linguistic forms, and productive engagement with the available literary and philosophical conventions. But how to define "originality" when there exist no comparable texts? What constitutes a "productive" and successful engagement with the period's formative literary conventions, if those developments explicitly excluded the author's experience in question? Some of the authors in this anthology rely on the conventions of the sentimental novel, for instance, to express experiences and feelings that were considered unthinkable and unmentionable at the time. Some poets employ traditional forms like the sonnet or hymn to express experiences and situations considered beyond the concerns of literary culture at the time. These works are truly original achievements.

Every anthology is the result of numerous decisions and also compromises. We had to make difficult choices about which texts to include, and in many cases chose excerpts that deserve to be read in their entirety. We rely on the most recent scholarship to identify certain texts as "firsts," since their status is debated and might change due to new research. We excluded a vast range of texts not written in English, with the notable exception of poems by Jane Johnston Schoolcraft also published in her native Ojibwe. To produce an accessible book that brings contemporary scholarship to general readers and into classrooms, we rely on categories of genre (chiefly novels, plays, short stories, and poetry) and identity that are in some cases anachronistic for the time of the work's creation. But these categories, for instance "Mexican American," which is not used until some fifty years after María Amparo Ruiz de Burton's novel appears in 1872, or "homosexual," which is invented as a term and social identity decades *after* Cooke and Whitman publish their works, show how literature can precede legal and political recognition. These texts show that American identity and political belonging is bestowed not only by Congress and our courts but enacted via published feats of the imagination that do not depend on laws but shape the political and social categories that emerge much later. Several texts were discovered only recently. While many have appeared in anthologies devoted to specific traditions within American literature, others are still found only in academic editions and specialized journals. We consider them central and essential to the American canon when that canon is defined by a quest for newness, but a newness that does not presume a blank canvas but a network of people shaping this new identity. Each of these texts lets us see the historical connections from our past to our present moment that many Americans have always known about but had to explore outside of public institutions and mainstream anthologies and textbooks. By creating this anthology, we do not intend to upend but to deepen America's sense of history and of itself.

By providing ready access to those first texts that embody and exemplify the true American spirit of innovation, this book celebrates the vitality and courage of those writers still all-too-often relegated to specialized anthologies. The last four decades have seen an enormous expansion of the American literary canon. But no book presents the many astonishing "firsts" in a single, accessible volume. Despite enormous strides in scholarship that have recovered or restored many of these texts to their rightful place, some have remained out of reach for general readers. Instead of erasing our history, *Fictions of America: The Book of Firsts* offers abundant evidence of other imaginations that provide the foundational fictions on which we might build our collective lives today.

ULRICH BAER AND SMARAN DAYAL
New York City, 2020

FICTIONS OF AMERICA

IROQUOIS CREATION MYTH

First Native American creation myth published by a Native author.

This is the earliest extant written account of an American Indian creation myth transcribed by a Native American writer on the North American continent. It was authored in 1816 by John Norton, the son of a Scottish mother and Cherokee father who had been taken as a boy to Scotland by British soldiers after they had destroyed his native town during the French and Indian War (1754–1763). Norton was raised in Scotland, where he enlisted in the army, and was eventually stationed in America. After he left the army, he was adopted into the Mohawk nation where he attained the title of chief. In this role he negotiated with the British Crown and local provincial rulers on behalf of the Mohawks, under the name Teyoninhokarawen. In his one thousand page-long journal, *The Journal of Major John Norton* (1816), he wrote about diplomacy and war to present a more honest account of Indian life and First Nation rights during a time when Indian resistance was framed by many white commentators as illegitimate. He wrote about his father's ancestral Cherokee lands in the American Southeast, which he had visited in 1810 and which flourished until the forced removal and the Trail of Tears, about the Five (and later Six) Nations of the Iroquois (Haudenosaunee) Confederacy, and about the War of 1812 between Great Britain and the United States, which is often considered a turning point for First Nations on the continent.

The creation myth stands out in Norton's primarily documentary and non-fiction journal. It is also referred to as a "earth-diver" story. Many creation stories are transmitted orally and belong to Native Americans according to rules that differ from those of mainstream publishing. These narratives offer a glimpse into the belief systems present before Europeans entered North America. We reprint this version to document one of the first transcribed stories of its kind in North America by a Native author, without suggesting that this text captures the oral tradition of American Indian literature, or that this text is "fictional" in the way that the other literary texts included here are. Rather, it is a powerful act of constitutional storytelling in the mode of religious and national narratives about the origins of peoples, faiths, and humanity as a whole.

The "Earth-Diver" Story [Published 1816]

The tradition of the Nottowegui or Five Nations says, "in the beginning before the formation of the earth; the country above the sky was inhabited by Superior Beings, over whom the Great Spirit presided. His daughter having become pregnant by an illicit connection, he pulled up a great tree by the roots, and threw her through the Cavity thereby formed; but, to prevent her utter destruction, he previously ordered the Great Turtle, to get from the bottom of the waters, some slime on its back, and to wait on the surface of the water to receive her on it. When she had fallen on the back of the Turtle, with the mud she found there, she began to form the earth, and by the time of her delivery had encreased it to the extent of a little island. Her child was a daughter, and as she grew up the earth extended under their hands. When the young woman had arrived at the age of discretion, the Spirits who roved about, in human forms, made proposals of marriage for the young woman: the mother always rejected their offers, until a middle aged man, of a dignified appearance, his bow in his hand, and his quiver on his back, paid his addresses. On being accepted, he entered the house, and seated himself on the berth of his intended spouse; the mother was in a berth on the other side of the fire. She observed that her son-in-law did not lie down all night; but taking two arrows out of his quiver, he put them by the side of his bride: at the dawn of day he took them up, and having replaced them in his quiver, he went out.

"After some time, the old woman perceived her daughter to be pregnant, but could not discover where the father had gone, or who he was. At the time of delivery, the twins disputed which way they should go out of the womb; the wicked one said, let us go out of the side; but the other said, not so, lest we kill our mother; then the wicked one pretending to acquiesce, desired his brother to go out first: but as soon as he was delivered, the wicked one, in attempting to go out at her side, caused the death of his mother.

"The twin brothers were nurtured and raised by their Grandmother; the

eldest was named Teharonghyawago, or the Holder of Heaven; the youngest was called Tawiskaron, or Flinty Rock, from his body being entirely
covered with such a substance. They grew up, and with their bows and
arrows, amused themselves throughout the island, which encreased in
extent, and they were favoured with various animals of Chace. Tawiskaron
was the most fortunate hunter, and enjoyed the favour of his Grandmother.
Teharonghyawago was not so successful in the Chace, and suffered from
their unkindness. When he was a youth, and roaming alone, in melancholy
mood, through the island, a human figure, of noble aspect, appearing to
him, addressed him thus 'My son, I have seen your distress, and heard
your solitary lamentations; you are unhappy in the loss of a mother, in
the unkindness of your Grandmother and brother. I now come to comfort
you, I am your father, and will be your Protector; therefore take courage,
and suffer not your spirit to sink. Take this (giving him an ear of *maize*)
plant it, and attend it in the manner, which I shall direct; it will yield you
a certain support, independent of the Chace, at the same time that it will
render more palatable the viands, which you may thereby obtain. I am the
Great Turtle which supports the earth, on which you move. Your brother's
ill treatment will increase with his years; bear it with patience till the time
appointed, before which you shall hear further.'

"After saying this, and directing him how to plant the corn, he disappeared. Teharonghyawago planted the corn, and returned home. When its
verdant sprouts began to flourish above the ground, he spent his time in
clearing from it all growth of grass and weeds, which might smother it or
retard its advancement while yet in its tender state, before it had acquired
sufficient grandeur to shade the ground. He now discovered that his wicked
brother caught the timid deer, the stately elk with branching horns, and all
the harmless inhabitants of the Forest; and imprisoned them in an extensive
cave, for his own particular use, depriving mortals from having the benefit
of them that was original intended by the Great Spirit. Teharonghyawago
discovered the direction the brother took in conducting these animals captive to the Cave; but never could trace him quite to the spot, as he eluded
his sight with more than common dexterity!

"Teharonghyawago endeavoured to conceal himself on the path that led to
the cave, so that he might follow him imperceptibly; but he found impossible to hide himself from the penetrating Tawiskaron. At length he observed,
that altho' his brother saw, with extraordinary acuteness, every surrounding object, yet he never raised his eyes to look above: Teharonghyawago

then climbed a lofty tree, which grew near to where he thought the place of confinement was situated: in the meantime, his brother passed, searching with his eyes the thickest recesses of the Forest, but never casting a glance above. He then saw his brother take a straight course, and when he was out of sight, Teharonghyawago descended, and came to the Cave, a short time after he had deposited his charge; and finding there an innumerable number of animals confined, he set them free, and returned home.

"It was not long before Tawiskaron, visiting the Cave, discovered that all his captives, which he had taken so much pains to deprive of their liberty, had been liberated: he knew this to be an act of his brother, but dissembling his anger, he meditated revenge, at some future period.

"Teharonghyawago laboured to people the earth with inhabitants, and to found Villages in happy situations, extending the comforts of men. Tawiskaron was equally active in destroying the works his brother had done; and in accumulating every evil in his power on the heads of ill fated mortals. Teharonghyawago saw, with regret, his brother persevere in every wickedness; but waited with patience the result of what his father had told him.

"At one time, being in conversation with his brother, Tawiskaron said 'Brother, what do you think there is on earth, with which you might be killed?' Teharonghyawago replied, 'I know of nothing that could affect my life, unless it be the foam of the billows of the Lake or the downy topped reed.' 'What do you think would take your life?' Tawiskaron answered, 'Nothing except horn or flint.' Here their discourse ended.

"Teharonghyawago returning from hunting, heard a voice singing a plaintive air: he listened and heard it name his Mother, who was killed by Tawiskaron; he immediately hastened towards the spot from whence the voice proceeded, crying, 'Who is that, who dares to name my deceased mother in my hearing?' When he came there, he saw the track of a fawn, which he pursued, without overtaking it, till the autumn, when it dropped its first horns; these he took up, and fixed upon the forked branches of a tree.

"He continued the pursuit seven years; and every autumn, when its horns fell, he picked them up, and placed them as he had done the first. At last, he overtook the deer, now grown to be a stately buck: it begged its life, and said, 'Spare me, and I will give you information that may be of great service to you.' When he had promised it its life, it spoke as follows, 'It was to give you the necessary information that I have been subjected to your pursuit, and that which I shall now tell you was the intended reward of your perseverance and clemency. Your brother, in coming into the world, caused the death of your Mother; if he was then wicked in his infancy, his malice has grown with his stature; he now premeditates evil against you; be therefore on your guard: as soon as he assaults you, exert yourself, and you will overcome him.'

"He returned home; and not long after this adventure, was attacked by his brother. They fought; the one made use of the horn and flint stone which he had provided: the other sought for froth and the reed, which made little impression on the body of Teharonghyawago. They fought a long time, over the whole of the island, until at last Tawiskaron fell under the conquering hand of his brother. According to the varied tones of their voices in the different places through which they passed during the contest, the people, who afterwards sprung up there, spoke different languages."

ANNE BRADSTREET (1612–1672)

First published poet in the North American colonies.

Anne Bradstreet was born Anne Dudley in 1612 in Northamptonshire, England, and married Simon Bradstreet, a graduate of Cambridge University, at the age of sixteen. Her extended family immigrated to America in 1630 as members of the Winthrop Puritan group and settled in the newly-founded town of Ipswich, then in the English settlement of the Massachusetts Bay Colony. Bradstreet and her husband raised eight children and she became one of the first poets to write English verse in the American colonies. Bradstreet wrote many poems during this time that were taken to England and published there in 1650 as her only book under the title *The Tenth Muse, Lately Sprung Up in America*, without her knowledge or approval.

In 1644, the family moved to Andover, also in today's Massachusetts, where Bradstreet lived until her death in 1672. In 1678, *Tenth Muse* was published posthumously in its first American edition and expanded as *Several Poems Compiled with Great Wit and Learning*. Bradstreet's sequence of religious poems entitled *Contemplations* was not published until the middle of the nineteenth century.

Most of Bradstreet's poetry is rooted in the Elizabethan literary tradition of her time and thus marked by musicality, rhetorical sophistication and romantic themes rather than the subjective expression of personal experience found in later, Romantic and modern poetry. Some of her later poems are considered to be more personal, a standard more highly valued by today's readers than by the audiences of her time. She is the first poet to publish poems written in America and possibly the first woman to address the condition of women in colonial America. She was aware that she would not meet with universal approval: "I am obnoxious to each carping tongue/ Who says a needle my hand better fits than a pen."

From THE TENTH MUSE, LATELY SPRUNG UP IN AMERICA [1650]

BEFORE THE BIRTH OF ONE OF HER CHILDREN

All things within this fading world hath end,
Adversity doth still our joys attend;
No ties so strong, no friends so dear and sweet,
But with death's parting blow is sure to meet.
The sentence past is most irrevocable,
A common thing, yet oh, inevitable.
How soon, my Dear, death may my steps attend,
How soon't may be thy lot to lose thy friend,
We are both ignorant, yet love bids me
These farewell lines to recommend to thee,
That when that knot's untied that made us one,
I may seem thine, who in effect am none.
And if I see not half my days that's due,
What nature would, God grant to yours and you;
The many faults that well you know I have
Let be interred in my oblivious grave;
If any worth or virtue were in me,
Let that live freshly in thy memory
And when thou feel'st no grief, as I no harms,
Yet love thy dead, who long lay in thine arms.
And when thy loss shall be repaid with gains
Look to my little babes, my dear remains.
And if thou love thyself, or loved'st me,
These O protect from step-dame's injury.
And if chance to thine eyes shall bring this verse,
With some sad sighs honour my absent hearse;
And kiss this paper for thy love's dear sake,
Who with salt tears this last farewell did take.

THE VANITY OF ALL WORLDLY THINGS

As he said vanity, so vain say I,
Oh! vanity, O vain all under sky;
Where is the man can say, "Lo, I have found
On brittle earth a consolation sound"?

What is't in honor to be set on high?
No, they like beasts and sons of men shall die,
And whilst they live, how oft doth turn their fate;
He's now a captive that was king of late.
What is't in wealth great treasures to obtain?
No, that's but labor, anxious care, and pain.
He heaps up riches, and he heaps up sorrow,
It's his today, but who's his heir tomorrow?
What then? Content in pleasures canst thou find?
More vain than all, that's but to grasp the wind.
The sensual senses for a time they please,
Meanwhile the conscience rage, who shall appease?
What is't in beauty? No that's but a snare,
They're foul enough today, that once were fair.
What is't in flow'ring youth, or manly age?
The first is prone to vice, the last to rage.
Where is it then, in wisdom, learning, arts?
Sure if on earth, it must be in those parts;
Yet these the wisest man of men did find
But vanity, vexation of the mind.
And he that know the most doth still bemoan
He knows not all that here is to be known.
What is it then? To do as stoics tell,
Nor laugh, nor weep, let things go ill or well?
Such stoics are but stocks, such teaching vain,
While man is man, he shall have ease or pain.
If not in honor, beauty, age, nor treasure,
Nor yet in learning, wisdom, youth, nor pleasure,
Where shall I climb, sound, seek, search, or find
That *summum bonum* which may stay my mind?
There is a path no vulture's eye hath seen,
Where lion fierce, nor lion's whelps have been,
Which leads unto that living crystal fount,
Who drinks thereof, the world doth naught account.
The depth and sea have said "'tis not in me,"
With pearl and gold it shall not valued be.
For sapphire, onyx, topaz who would change;
It's hid from eyes of men, they count it strange.

Death and destruction the fame hath heard,
But where and what it is, from heaven's declared;
It brings to honor which shall ne'er decay,
It stores with wealth which time can't wear away.
It yieldeth pleasures far beyond conceit,
And truly beautifies without deceit.
Nor strength, nor wisdom, nor fresh youth shall fade,
Nor death shall see, but are immortal made.
This pearl of price, this tree of life, this spring,
Who is possessed of shall reign a king.
Nor change of state nor cares shall ever see,
But wear his crown unto eternity.
This satiates the soul, this stays the mind,
And all the rest, but vanity we find.

In Memory of My Dear Grandchild Elizabeth Bradstreet, Who Deceased August, 1665 Being a Year and a Half Old

Farewell dear babe, my heart's too much content,
Farewell sweet babe, the pleasure of mine eye,
Farewell fair flower that for a space was lent,
Then ta'en away unto eternity.
Blest babe, why should I once bewail thy fate,
Or sigh the days so soon were terminate;
Sith thou art settled in an everlasting state.
By nature trees do rot when they are grown.
And plums and apples thoroughly ripe do fall,
And corn and grass are in their season mown,
And time brings down what is both strong and tall.
But plants new set to be eradicate,
And buds new blown, to have so short a date,
Is by His hand alone that guides nature and fate.

In Memory of My Dear Grandchild Anne Bradstreet Who Deceased June 20, 1669, Being Three Years and Seven Months Old

With troubled heart and trembling hand I write,
The heavens have changed to sorrow my delight.
How oft with disappointment have I met,

When I on fading things my hopes have set.
Experience might 'fore this have made me wise,
To value things according to their price.
Was ever stable joy yet found below?
Or perfect bliss without mixture of woe?
I knew she was but as a withering flower,
That's here today, perhaps gone in an hour;
Like as a bubble, or the brittle glass,
Or like a shadow turning as it was.
More fool then I to look on that was lent
As if mine own, when thus impermanent.
Farewell dear child, thou ne'er shall come to me,
But yet a little while, and I shall go to thee;
Mean time my throbbing heart's cheered up with this:
Thou with thy Saviour art in endless bliss.

Upon the Burning of Our House
Here Follows Some Verses Upon the Burning of Our House, July 10th. 1666. Copied Out of a Loose Paper.

In silent night when rest I took,
For sorrow near I did not look,
I wakened was with thund'ring noise
And piteous shrieks of dreadful voice.
That fearful sound of "Fire!" and "Fire!"
Let no man know is my Desire.
I, starting up, the light did spy,
And to my God my heart did cry
To straighten me in my Distress
And not to leave me succorless.
Then, coming out, beheld a space
The flame consume my dwelling place.
And when I could no longer look,
I blest His name that gave and took,
That laid my goods now in the dust.
Yea, so it was, and so 'twas just.
It was His own, it was not mine,
Far be it that I should repine;

He might of all justly bereft
But yet sufficient for us left.
When by the ruins oft I past
My sorrowing eyes aside did cast
And here and there the places spy
Where oft I sate and long did lie:
Here stood that trunk, and there that chest,
There lay that store I counted best.
My pleasant things in ashes lie,
And them behold no more shall I.
Under thy roof no guest shall sit,
Nor at thy table eat a bit.
No pleasant talk shall 'ere be told
Nor things recounted done of old.
No Candle e'er shall shine in Thee,
Nor bridegroom's voice e'er heard shall be.
In silence ever shalt thou lie,
Adieu, Adieu, all's vanity.
Then straight I 'gin my heart to chide,
And did thy wealth on earth abide?
Didst fix thy hope on mold'ring dust?
The arm of flesh didst make thy trust?
Raise up thy thoughts above the sky
That dunghill mists away may fly.
Thou hast a house on high erect
Framed by that mighty Architect,
With glory richly furnished,
Stands permanent though this be fled.
It's purchased and paid for too
By Him who hath enough to do.
A price so vast as is unknown,
Yet by His gift is made thine own;
There's wealth enough, I need no more,
Farewell, my pelf, farewell, my store.
The world no longer let me love,
My hope and treasure lies above.

ROBERT HUNTER (1666–1734)

First play written and published in North America.

Androboros was written by Robert Hunter, the British-born governor of the province of New York from 1710 to 1719, and published anonymously in 1714. It is a biting political satire about the New York legislature which blocked many of Hunter's political actions. Like many satirical plays, it was probably intended to be read rather than performed on stage. Unlike other political satires, however, it was written after the events depicted had passed and thus probably not intended to embarrass or expose any individuals directly. It is multilingual, scatological, and rhetorically sophisticated, and in tone perhaps not unrelated to the satires of Jonathan Swift, with whom Hunter maintained a long correspondence.

While the play is highly topical and has had little demonstrable impact on the tradition of American theater, it has been viewed as paving the way to the First Amendment which ensures, in particular, the freedom of political speech from government interference. This link is apparent when reading the play in the context of a celebrated legal case, as Peter A. Davis has recently done. In 1734, a New York-based printer and journalist, John Zenger, was accused of libel by William Cosby, then the royal governor of New York. Lewis Morris, who is presumed to be a co-author of Hunter's play, had pushed Zenger to publish a political broadsheet. As a result, Cosby removed Morris from his position as New York's Chief Justice, thereby putting his speech on trial. Zenger's eventual acquittal became a symbol for the freedom of the press in the United States. The trial, with its antecedent in and direct connection to the play *Androboros* via its co-author, influenced the writing of the First Amendment. (The first staged play in America is the nonextant *Ye Bear and Ye Cubb* by William Darby, presented in Virginia in 1665. The first American play performed by professional actors on an American stage was Thomas Godfrey's *The Prince of Parthia*, in 1767.

Royall Tyler's *The Contrast* was the first comedy by an American staged in America, in 1787.)

From Androboros, A Biographical Farce in Three Acts, viz.
The Senate, The Consistory, and The Apotheosis [1714]

ACT SECOND, SCENE THIRD.

Enter Fizle and Tom of Bedlam.

FIZLE. Gentlemen, I have finish'd the Address. Is it your pleasure that the Clerk read it?

ALL. Ay, Ay.

TOM. *Tom of Bedlam reads.*

To the most Potent Lord *Oinobaros*, Count of *Kynocœmatis*, Baron of *Elaphokardia*, The General Consistory of *New Bethlem* most Humbly Represent, That we your Excellencies ever *Refuted Subjects*.

FIZLE. Devoted Subjects.

TOM OF BEDLAM. Under a deep sense of the manifold *Bastings* we Enjoy'd.

FIZLE. *Blessings*, you Ouph you.

TOM. Blessings we Enjoy'd under your *Wild Administration*.

FIZLE. Mild Administration.

TOM. Mild Administration, find our selves at this time under a *Nonsensical Inclination*.

FIZLE. What's that? Let me see't, *Non-sensical Inclinasion!* It can't be so, It is *Indispensible Obligation*.

TOM. Ay, it should be so.

FIZLE. Write it down so then.

TOM. 'Tis done. Finding our selves under an *Incomprehensible Obstination*.

FLIP. 'Owns'! That's worse than t'other.

TOM. Cry Mercy, That is a blunder, *Indispensible Obligation* to have Recourse to your Excellencies known *Condemnable Opposition* to our Consistory, and all Things Sacred.

FIZLE. I think the Dev'l is in the Fellow. It is *Commendable Disposition*.

TOM. You use so many Long Words, that a Clerk who is not a Scholar may easily mistake one for another. Towards our Consistory; and all things Sacred, Take leave humbly to Represent, That on the *Ev'ning which succeeded the following Day.*

FIZLE. Thou Eternal Dunce! *The Ev'ning which preceded All-hallowday.*

TOM. Which preceded *All-hallowday* some open or secret Enemies to this Consistory broke into our *Cupboard.*

FIZLE. Ward-Robe.

TOM. Wardrobe, taking from thence some Lumber appertaining to the *Chief of our Rogues*, I mean; some Robes appertaining to the Chief of our Number, which they Inhumanely Tore to pieces and Bedaub'd with *Odour.*

MULLIGRUB. Hold! I make Exception to that, for there are sweet Odours as well as sower.

FLIP. 'Slid; 'tis *Ordure, (and not Odour)* which is but another Name for a T—d.

MULLIGRUB. Write it down so then, for a T—is a T—all the world over.

ÆSOP. And the more you stir it, the more 'twill stink. But go on.

TOM. Now tho' we *cannot Possibly Prove*, yet we *Affirm Possitively*, That it is our Keeper.

ÆSOP. How's that?

FIZLE. He reads wrong; it is, *Tho' we cannot Possitively Prove, yet we Affirm,* That *possibly it may be our Keeper.* Go on.

TOM. Our Keeper, or some of his People, who is guilty of this *Facetious Fact.*

FIZLE. Flagitious Fact.

TOM. Flagitious Fact. We further beg leave to Represent, That this Morning in a Collective Body, by a great *Brutality of Noises.*

FIZLE. Plurality of Voices.

TOM. We had declar'd him a *Raskal*, but he had the Impudence to send us packing to our Cells, though we had several *Merduous Matters* under the *Instruction of our Hose.*

MULLIGRUB. Hold! I do not well understand that, Read it again.

FIZLE. He cant read his own Hand; it is *Several Arduous Matters under the Inspection of our House.* Go on.

TOM. Wherefore it is our humble and earnest Supplication, That we may be once more put under your *Wild Distraction.*

FIZLE. Mild Direction.

TOM. Or that of the *Excrement Androboros.*

FIZLE. Excellent *Androboros.*

TOM. That so we may give a *Loose to Our Knavery.*

FIZLE. I'm afraid, Sirrah, you are a Knave; Get loose from out Slavery.

TOM. I'm afraid, Sirrah, you are a Knave; Get loose from our Slavery, and fix a *stolid Security for our Nasty Foundations.*

FIZLE. Is the Dev'l in thee! A solid Foundation for our lasting Security.

TOM. A solid Foundation for our lasting Security. And your Petitioners, *like Asses as they are, in a durty Pound,* shall never cease to *Bray.*

FIZLE. (Raskal! it should be) like as they are in *Duty Bound, shall never cease to pray.* (I could swear he reads thus on purpose.)

ÆSOP. And not be For-sworn. But have you done?

TOM. Yes, an't please your Honors.

FIZLE. Gentlemen, do you approve of this Draught?

ÆSOP. I like it as the Clerk read it.

MULLIGRUB. I approve of all, except the *Ordure* ; I'll have it a T—:

COXCOMB. You'll have it a T—, A T—in your Teeth; it shall stand as it is *Ordure.*

MULLIGRUB. T—d.

DOODLESACK. Ick been on the Cant van de T—d.

BABILARD. Let us Compromise the Matter, and make it *Turdure.*

ALL. Ay, agreed.

ÆSOP. Gentlemen, you have agreed to the Draught of an Address; but what is to be done with it?

COXCOMB. Transmitted to *Oinobaros.*

ÆSOP. For what purpose?

COXCOMB. To ged Rid of our Keeper, and get *Oinobaros* in his room.

ÆSOP. If you should, my mind Forbodes you would repent the Change.

COXCOMB. Why?

ÆSOP. Why! why because a man who could never yet Govern himself, will make but a sorry Governour for others.

COXCOMB. Have a care what you say; That is *Scandalum Magnatum.*

DOODLESACK. Pray, *Mr. Tom.* Wat is dat Lating? Ick forestae't me.

TOM. He say, my Lord is in a very great Post, call'd, *The Scandalum Magnatum.*

DOODLESACK. Is it given him lately.

TOM. No, he has it by inheritance.

ÆSOP. Be advis'd by me; Lay your Address aside, and keep as you are; As for your Keeper, none of you can say that he has done you any harm; and for my part I am convinc'd, that he has done us much good. I must beg leave to tell you a Story.

COXCOMB. Hang you and your Storys; we shan't mind 'em.

ÆSOP. You may give it the same fair play you did to *Mulligrub's* Speech; hear it, tho' you do not mind it. I pray your patience.

> The Frogs, a Factious fickle Race,
> With little Maners, and less Grace,
>   Croak'd for a King so loud,
> That all the Host of Heav'n sate mute
> Nodding to *Jove* to grant their suit,
>   And give 'em what they wou'd.
>
> A King they had, of such a size
> Who's Entry too, made such a Noise,
>   That Ev'ry Neut and Frog
> Affrighted, run to hide their heads;
> Some in the Pool, some 'mongst the Reeds,
>   Like Fools, 'Twas but a Log.
>
> At last, one bolder than the rest,
> Approach'd, and the new Prince Address't,
>   No hurt from thence sustain'd,
> He mock'd his former Fears, and swore
> 'Twas the best stick of Wood that o'er
>   The Marshes ever Reign'd.
>
> Then all the Croaking Crew drew near,
> And in his shade from th' angry Air
>   Were shelter'd safe, and eas'd,
> Nay, more then that, they'd frisk and play
> Upon his back a live long, day,
>   He Undisturb'd and pleas'd.
>
> The Pertest Frog of all the Pack,
> A Toad, some say, his hue was Black;
>   'Tis true; but that's no matter,
> Upon the passive Monarch's head,
> At times would Noxious Venom shed,
>   And both his sides bespatter.
>
> 'Twas That same Frog, the Legends tell,
> Burst when he only meant to swell,

Soon after these Events.
Be that as 'twill, 'twas He that drew
That giddy Senseless Crowd to new
    Sedition and Complaints.

Give us a bustling King, *Dread Sir*!
They cry'd, a King that makes a stir;
    This is not to be mov'd.
Jove heard and gave 'm one, who's care
Was, that they should Obey and Fear,
    No matter how they Lov'd.

It was a *Stork*, who's Law-less Rage
Spar'd neither Sex, Degree nor Age,
    That came within his reach.
And that was great, for whilst his Claws
Ransack'd the Deep, his Vulturs Jaws
    Could wander o'er the Beach.

Then they Implor'd the God to send
From heav'n a Plague, from Hell a Fiend,
    Or any but this Curse.
Peace, cry'd the Monarch of the Gods,
Te Worms; Keep him you have, 'tis odds
    The Next may prove a Worse.

Now If you please, you may put the Question about your Address. I take it to be Log or Stork.

Enter Door-Keeper.

DOOR-KEEPER. Here's a Courier from *Androboros*, just return'd from the Expedition, who desires Admittance.

ÆSOP. It is the most Expeditious Expedition I ever heard of; let us adjourn the Address, and receive the General's Message.

FIZLE. Let him come in.

Enter Messenger.

MESSENGER. The Renown'd *Androboros* with a tender of his hearty Zeal and Affection sends this to the *Consistory*, the Senate being Discontinued.

Delivers a Letter.

FIZLE, *Reads.*

Right Frightful and Formidable, We Greet you Well, And by this Acquaint you, That for many Weighty Considerations Us thereunto moving, We have thought fit to adjourn the Indended [sic] Expedition to a more proper season, because we have, upon due and Mature Examination been fully convinc'd, that the *Mulomachians*, our Reputed Enemies, are in very deed our good and faithful Friends and Allies, who, to remove all Doubts and Scruples, have freely offer'd to Consolidate Consistories with us, as also to divide with us the Commerce of the World, generously resigning and yielding to us that of the two Poles reserving to themselves only what may lie between e'm. They have likewise Condescended that we shall keep some Forts and Holds, which by the Fortune of the War they could not take from us, and have promis'd and engag'd to Raze and Demolish some Places in their Possession to our prejudice, so soon as more Convenient are built in their room and place. You are further to understand, to your Great satisfaction, that this is a Treaty Litteral and Spiritual, so that having two Handles it may be Executed with the greater Facility, or if need be, the One may Execute the other, and so it may Execute it self. Now these Concessions (tho' it be well known that I hate Boasting) having been obtain'd, in a great measure, by the Terror of my Name and Arms, I expect your Thanks. And so we bid you heartily *Farewell. Androboros.*

ÆSOP. Buzzzzz, Hummmmm, Buzzzzz—

FIZLE. What Return shall we give to this Civil and Obliging Message?

ÆSOP. Return him his Letter.

COXCOMB. No, let us vote him Thanks, a Statue and a Triumph!

Enter Keeper.

KEEPER. Be not surpriz'd, I have heard what you are about, and Cordially joyn with you in what you propose, in honour of the Valiant *Androboros,* Having received instructions from my Superiors to use that mighty Man according to his Deserts.

ÆSOP. What! Is our Keeper Mad too?

KEEPER. In the Mean time, all Retire to your respective Apartments, until due Dissposition be made for his Reception.

Exit manent Fizle and Æsop.

LUCY TERRY PRINCE (1724?–1821)

First work of literature by an African American author.

Lucy Terry Prince was born in an unknown location in Africa in circa 1724, kidnapped as a an infant, and sold into slavery around 1730 in Rhode Island. Her owner moved her to the outpost settlement in Deerfield, Massachusetts, where she was converted to Christianity and remained enslaved until she married a free black man named Obijah Prince, who freed her in 1756. They moved to Vermont, where her reputation as a storyteller, orator, and defender of black civil rights grew. Several accounts exist of Terry arguing in a three-hour speech for her son's admission to Williams College after he had served in the War of the American Revolution but was rejected on account of his race. She also presented in a legal case before the Supreme Court, though none of these accounts can be absolutely verified. She died in Vermont in 1821.

The ballad recounts the incident of an Indian ambush of two white families on August 25, 1746, near Deerfield, Massachusetts, in an area called "the Bars" (meaning meadows). The raid occurred eight years before the French and Indian War of 1754–1763, fought by units from the British and French colonies in America and American Indian allies. The poem was probably originally intended to be sung and was preserved in local memory. It was recited by a Deerfield lawyer in 1819 and first published in novelist and biographer Josiah G. Holland's *History of Massachusetts* (1855).

BARS FIGHT [c. 1746]

August 'twas the twenty-fifth,
Seventeen hundred forty-six;
The Indians did in ambush lay,

Some very valiant men to slay,
The names of whom I'll not leave out.
Samuel Allen like a hero fout,
And though he was so brave and bold,
His face no more shalt we behold.
Eleazer Hawks was killed outright,
Before he had time to fight,—
Before he did the Indians see,
Was shot and killed immediately.
Oliver Amsden he was slain,
Which caused his friends much grief and pain.
Simeon Amsden they found dead,
Not many rods distant from his head.
Adonijah Gillett we do hear
Did lose his life which was so dear.
John Sadler fled across the water,
And thus escaped the dreadful slaughter.
Eunice Allen see the Indians coming,
And hopes to save herself by running,
And had not her petticoats stopped her,
The awful creatures had not catched her,
Nor tommy hawked her on the head,
And left her on the ground for dead.
Young Samuel Allen, Oh lack-a-day!
Was taken and carried to Canada.

JUPITER HAMMON (1711–1806)

First published African American poet.

Jupiter Hammon, the first published African American poet, was born into slavery in Lloyd Neck, Long Island, New York in 1711 and spent his entire life enslaved to successive generations of the Lloyd family. Some historians believe that he received tutoring during his childhood alongside his enslaver's children, or that he attended a local religious school. He worked as a clerk and bookkeeper to successive members of the Lloyd family in Long Island and New Haven, Connecticut, converted to Christianity, and probably served as a lay minister to a local Methodist congregation. Hammon published his first work, the broadside poem "An Evening Thought" (also referred to as "An Evening Prayer" and "An Evening's Thought: Salvation by Christ, with Penitential Cries") at the age of forty-nine, in 1760. By then Hammon had already spent half a century in bondage.

Hammon became a prominent member of the African American community and clearly intended his writings to influence fellow African Americans and to win readers for the abolitionist cause. He dedicated a poem to Phillis Wheatley, marking his role in a network of African American writers that used the language of Christianity to express a wide range of experiences and also register resistance to the conditions imposed on them. One of his poems was reprinted in 1787 by a Philadelphia abolitionist society; in the same year Hammon gave a speech to the African Society of New York City titled "An Address to the Negroes in the State of New York." After spending ninety-five years enslaved by the wealthy Lloyd family, Jupiter Hammon was buried in an unmarked grave on the Lloyd estate.

Hammon had no legal standing as a full and free individual, let alone a citizen, in American society until the day of his death in 1806. But of course the first published African American writer knew himself to be so, and was recognized by his own community of Black Americans as the self-directing, rational, complex, and creative individual that he was. While this self-knowledge did not explicitly oppose laws that denied their author's full humanity, his poems can be read in relation to such social and legal conventions. In addition to everything else that they express and convey, Hammon's poems tell us that he thought of himself as a man endowed with the same natural rights as other men when the majority of white America did not believe that, and that his need to express this defining dimension of himself did not require anyone's approval. Imaginative literature is the art of redefining not simply a few things here and there but the entire world as we know it. Read today, Hammon's poems make a mockery of the mindset of his enslavers. They have long been regarded as the source of a literary tradition more powerful than the hypocritical and inhumane laws to which Hammon was subjected.

AN EVENING THOUGHT: SALVATION BY CHRIST,
WITH PENETENTIAL CRIES [1760]

Salvation comes by Christ alone,
    The only Son of God;
Redemption now to every one,
    That love his holy Word.
Dear Jesus we would fly to Thee,
    And leave off every Sin,
Thy tender Mercy well agree;
    Salvation from our King.
Salvation comes now from the Lord,
    Our victorious King.
His holy Name be well ador'd,
    Salvation surely bring.
Dear Jesus give thy Spirit now,
    Thy Grace to every Nation,
That han't the Lord to whom we bow,
    The Author of Salvation.
Dear Jesus unto Thee we cry,
    Give us the Preparation;
Turn not away thy tender Eye;
    We seek thy true Salvation.
Salvation comes from God we know,

The true and only One;
It's well agreed and certain true,
   He gave his only Son.
Lord, hear our penetential Cry:
   Salvation from above;
It is the Lord that doth supply,
   With his Redeeming Love.
Dear Jesus by thy precious Blood,
   The World Redemption have:
Salvation now comes from the Lord,
   He being thy captive slave.
Dear Jesus let the Nations cry,
   And all the People say,
Salvation comes from Christ on high,
   Haste on Tribunal Day.
We cry as Sinners to the Lord,
   Salvation to obtain;
It is firmly fixt his holy Word,
   Ye shall not cry in vain.
Dear Jesus unto Thee we cry,
   And make our Lamentation:
O let our Prayers ascend on high;
   We felt thy Salvation.
Lord turn our dark benighted Souls;
   Give us a true Motion,
And let the Hearts of all the World,
   Make Christ their Salvation.
Ten Thousand Angels cry to Thee,
   Yea louder than the Ocean.
Thou art the Lord, we plainly see;
   Thou art the true Salvation.
Now is the Day, excepted Time;
   The Day of the Salvation;
Increase your Faith, do not repine:
   Awake ye every Nation.
Lord unto whom now shall we go,
   Or seek a safe Abode?
Thou has the Word Salvation too

The only Son of God.
Ho! every one that hunger hath,
    Or pineth after me,
Salvation be thy leading Staff,
    To set the Sinner free.
Dear Jesus unto Thee we fly;
    Depart, depart from Sin,
Salvation doth at length supply,
    The Glory of our King.
Come ye Blessed of the Lord,
    Salvation greatly given;
O turn your Hearts, accept the Word,
    Your Souls are fit for Heaven.
Dear Jesus we now turn to Thee,
    Salvation to obtain;
Our Hearts and Souls do meet again,
    To magnify thy Name.
Come holy Spirit, Heavenly Dove,
    The Object of our Care;
Salvation doth increase our Love;
    Our Hearts hath felt they fear.
Now Glory be to God on High,
    Salvation high and low;
And thus the Soul on Christ rely,
    To Heaven surely go.
Come Blessed Jesus, Heavenly Dove,
    Accept Repentance here;
Salvation give, with tender Love;
    Let us with Angels share.

AN ESSAY ON SLAVERY, WITH SUBMISSION TO DIVINE PROVIDENCE,
KNOWING THAT GOD RULES OVER ALL THINGS [1786]

1

Our forefathers came from africa
tost over the raging main
to a Christian shore there for to stay
and to return again.

2

Dark and dismal was the Day
When slavery began
All humble thoughts were put away
Then slaves were made *by Man.*   *[to]

3

When God doth please for to permit
That slavery should be
It is our duty to submit
Till Christ shall *make us free   *[come again]

4

Come let us join with one consent
With humble hearts *and say   *[to]
For every sin we must repent
And walk in wisdoms way.

5

If we are free *we'll pray to God   *[we will]
If we are slaves the same
*It's firmly fix't in **his word.   *[It is] **[his holy]
Ye shall not pray in vain.

6

Come blessed Jesus in thy Love
And hear thy Children cry
And send them smiles now from above
And grant them Liberty.

7

Tis thou alone can make us free
We are thy subjects two
Pray give up grace to bend a knee
The time we stay below.

8

This unto thee we look for all
Thou art our only King

---

* Denotes alternative reading.

Thou hast the power to save the soul
And bring us flocking in.

9

We come as sinners *unto thee   *[up to]
We know thou hast the word
Come blessed Jesus make us free
And bring us to our God.

10

Although we are in slavery
We will pray unto our God
He hath mercy beyond the sky
Tis in his holy word.

11

Come unto me ye humble souls
Although you live in strife
I keep alive, *I save the soul   [*and]
And give eternal life.

12

To all that do repent of sin
*Be they bond or free   [*Whether]
I am their savior and their king
They must come unto me.

13

Hear the words *now the Lord *   [of]
The call is loud and certain
We must be judged by his word
Without respect of person.

14

Come let us seek his precepts now
And love his holy word
With humble soul we'll surely bow
And wait the great reward.

15

Although we came from africa
We look unto our God

To help with our hearts to sigh and pray
And love his holy word.

16

Although we are in slavery
Bound *by the yoke of Man   *[to]
We must always have a single Eye
And do the best we can.

17

Come let us join with humble voice
Now on the christian shore
If we will have our only choice
Tis Slavery no more.

18

Now let us not repine
And say his wheels are slow
He can fill our hearts with things divine
And give us freedom two.

19

He hath the power all in his hand
And all he doth is right
And if we are tide to yoke of man
We'll pray with all our might. [*We must pray through day and night.]

20

This the State of thousands now
Who are on the christian shore
Forget the Lord to whom we bow
And think of him no more.

21

When shall we hear the joyful sound
Echo the christian shore
Each humble [voice with songs resound]
That Slavery is no more.

22

Then shall we rejoice and sing

Loud praises to our God
Come sweet Jesus heavenly king
Thou art the son *Our Lord.   [*of God]

23

We are thy children blessed Lord
Tho still in Slavery
*We'll seek thy precepts Love thy word   *[We]
Until the day we Die.

24

Come blessed Jesus hear us now
And teach our hearts to pray
And seek the Lord to whom we Bow
Before tribunal day.

25

Now Glory be unto our God
All praise be justly given
Come seek his precepts Love his works
That is the way to Heaven.—

Composed by JUPITER HAMMON
A Negro Man belonging to MR JOHN LLOYD
Queens-Village on Long Island, November 10th 1786

MERCY OTIS WARREN (1728–1814)

First play published by a woman in America.

Mercy Otis Warren was an American poet, dramatist, and historian often considered the first American woman to write primarily for the public rather than herself. Born into a prosperous, politically active New England family, as a girl she received no formal education but studied alongside one of her brothers. In 1754, she married the politically active James Warren, and the couple had five sons. Mercy Warren was close with political leaders of her time and maintained a lifelong correspondence with John Adams, who called her along with his wife "the most accomplished Lady in America." An avid American patriot, she published several plays that satirized fellow citizens sympathetic to the British and denounced British policies and, during the constitutional conventions of the 1780s, *Observations on the new Constitution, and on the Federal and State Conventions*, which opposed ratification of the Constitution without a Bill of Rights. After the Revolutionary War she published two more plays in verse. An important voice in the debates about America's independence, Warren is America's first female historian. She wrote a three-volume *History of the Rise, Progress and Termination of the American Revolution* in 1805, and she is the third woman, after Anne Bradstreet and Phillis Wheatley, to publish a book of poems in America.

The *Adulateur* (1772) is a fierce satire set in a mythical kingdom of Servia with thinly veiled caricatures of real-life political figures. First published in the *Massachussets Spy* newspaper in two installments and anonymously to thwart British retaliation and critics that would focus on the author's gender rather than the play, *The Adulateur* attacked British rule as illegitimate, unjust, and ultimately warranting armed resistance. Rapatio, a haughty, imperious official obviously modeled on Massachusetts's royal governor, Thomas Hutchinson, schemes to destroy his subject's liberties and even kill them to advance his interests. Shortly before its publication, five colonists had been killed by British forces in what became known as the "Boston massacre." In the play, Rapatio orders resisters to be killed. The short play, which was likely read out loud at social gatherings and probably never performed, draws a then-common analogy between the fight for American independence and republican Rome's struggle with tyranny. It foretells the American War of Independence and ends with a prophetic warning.

From THE ADULATEUR, A TRAGEDY, ACTED IN UPPER SERVIA [1772]

ACT I, SCENE I
A street in Servia.
Enter Brutus and Cassius.

BRUTUS:
Is this the once fam'd mistress of the north
The sweet retreat of freedom? Dearly purchas'd!
A clime matur'd with blood; from whose rich soil,
Has sprung a glorious harvest. Oh! my friend,
The change how drear! The sullen ghost of bondage
Stalks full in view—already with her pinions,
She shades the affrighted land—th'insulting soldiers
Tread down our choicest rights; while hoodwink'd justice
Drops her scales, and totters from her basis.
Thus torn with nameless wounds, my bleeding country
Demands a tear—that tear I'll freely give her.
CASSIUS:
Oh! Brutus, our noble ancestors,
Who liv'd for freedom, and for freedom dy'd:
Who scorn'd to roll in affluence, if that state
Was sicken'd over with the dread name of slaves:
Who in this desart stock'd with beasts and men,
Whose untam'd souls breath'd nought but slaughter—
Grasp'd at freedom, and they nobly won it;
Then smil'd and dy'd contented. Should these heroes
Start from their tombs and view their dear possessions,
The price of so much labor, cost and blood,
Gods! What a pang it 'twould cost them; yes, they'd weep,

Nor weep in vain. That good old spirit,
Which warm'd them once, would rouse to noble actions
E're they would *cringe* they'd bathe their swords in blood;
In heaps they'd fall, and on the pile of freedom,
Expire like heroes or they'd save their country.
BRUTUS:
Oh! Cassius, you inspire a noble passion,
It glows within me, and every pulse I feel,
Beats high for glory. I sprang, and Oh! it fires me,
I sprang from men who fought, who bled for freedom:
From men who in the conflict laugh'd at danger;
Struggl'd like patriots, and through seas of blood
Waded to conquest. I'll not disgrace them.
I'll show a spirit worthy of my fire.
Tho' malice dart her stings; tho' poverty
Stares full upon me; though power with all her thundder
Rolls oe'r my head; thy cause my bleeding country
I'll never leave—I'll struggle hard to thee,
And if I perish, perish like a free man.
CASSIUS
You're not alone—there are, I know, ten
Ne'er bow'd the knee to idol power. Repeated insults
Have rous'd the most lethargic. E'en the old man
Whose blood has long creep'd sluggish thro' his veins
Now feels his warmth renew'd, his pulse beat quick,
His eyes dart fire. He grasps his sword.
And calls on youth to aid him.. Yes my son,
My little son, who sportive climbs my knees,
Fondly intreats my aid, and lisps out freedom.
But see our friends—their generous bosoms flow
With manly sentiment. I will accost them.
Patriots hail!

ACT IV, SCENE II
Rapatio's House.
Rapatio alone.

RAPATIO:
O Fortunate!—

Could I have tho't my stars would be so kind
As thus to bring my deep-laid schemes to bear.
Tho' from my youth ambition's path I trod,
Suck'd the contagion from my mother's breast;
The early taint has rankled in my veins;
Despotic rule my first, my sov'reign wish.
Yet to succeed, beyond my sanguine hope,
To quench the generous flame, the ardent love
Of liberty in Servia's free-born sons,
Destroy their boasted rights, and mark them slaves,
To ride triumphant o'er my native land,
And revel on its spoils—But hark!—it groans!
The heaving struggles of expiring freedom!—
Her dying pangs—and I the guilty cause:—
I shudder at the thought—why this confusion?
The phantom conscience, whom I've bid adieu—
Can she return?—O let me, let me fly!
I dare not meet my naked heart alone.
I'll haste for comfort to the busy scenes,
Where fawning courtiers, creatures of my own,
With adulating tongue, midst gaping crouds,
Shall strive to paint me fair—the day is lucky—
The divan meets and Hazelrod presides.
'Tis true in rhetoric he don't excell
Demosthenes, or Cicero of old:
But what of chat, his gratitude to me,
Will animate each period of applause.
I from a fribbling, superficial dabler,
A vain pretender to each learned science,
A poet, preacher, conjurer and quack—
Rear'd the obsequious trifler to my purpose,
Rob'd him in scarlet, dignifi'd the man:
A hecatomb of incense is my due.
How grateful to my ear, these flatt'ring strains!
His fulsome requiems soothe my soul to peace.
Who else wou'd place in such a sacred seat
Credulity inwove with the extremes,
Of servile, weak, implacable and proud.

But see he comes—see that important phiz,
A speech prepar'd, but what I must correct,
If interlarded with profuse encomiums,—
To hold me up the paragon of virtue—
But it may pass—of modern composition,
That's the test—

Enter Hazelrod.

Welcome, my Hazelrod—
My friend, my brother, or still dearer name,
Thou firm abettor of my grand design!
Thou now canst cover what the world call crimes.
We'll then securely crush the scoundrell mob,
And Claudia-like, the citizens ride o'er,
And execute what Nero durst not do.

Hazelrod going hastily off, Rapatio stops him.

I'll call my myrmidons, they shall attend,
Swell the parade with all the venal herd.
Gripeall, that minion of oppressive power,
With simple Dupe, the ready tool of state;
And virtuous Limput perjur'd only once,
Then indispensible to serve a cause
Which truth would ruin; doubtless they'll be there.

Exeunt.

ACT V, SCENE I

Enter Brutus.

BRUTUS:
O my poor country!—
I've wak'd and wept and would have fought for thee,
And emptied every vein, when threatn't ruin.
Lower'd over thy head; but now too late. I fear
The manacles prepar'd by Brundo's hand,
Cruel Rapatio, with more fatal art,
Has fixed, has rivetted beyond redress—
My indignation's rouz'd, my soul disdains,

Nor will I longer stay where poisonous breath
Of sycophants' applause, pollutes the air.
The shameless tyrant snuffs the base perfume;
With unrelenting heart and brazen front
He rears his guilty head amid the fear
Of Servia's virtuous sons, whose latest breath
Shall execrate a wretch, who dare enslave
A generous, free and independent people.
—If, ye pow'rs divine,
Ye mark the movements of this nether world,
And bring them to account—crush, crush these vipers,
Who singl'd out by a community,
To guard their rights—shall for a grasp of oar,
Or paltry office sell them to the foe.

Exit

ACT V, SCENCE III

MARCUS:
Oh no! I scorn it—better live a poor man
And die so too—while virtue and my conscience
Speak peace within. Better, tho' hate and malice
May shoot their shafts against me, better thus
To make my Exit, while the soul with comfort
Reviews the past and smiles upon the future.
BRUTUS:
Yes, Marcus, poverty must be thy fate,
If thou'rt thy country's friend—Think upon it
When I'm gone, as soon perhaps I may be.
Remember it—those men whose crimes now shock,
May close their measures. Yes, the wish'd-for period
May soon arrive, when murders, blood and carnage
Shall crimson all these streets; when this poor country
Shall loose her richest blood, forbid it heaven!
And may these monsters find their glories fade,
Crush'd in the ruins they themselves had made,
While thou, my country, shall again revive,
Shake off misfortune, and through ages live.

See thro' the waste a ray of virtue gleame,
Dispell the shades and brighten all the scene.
Wak'd into life, the blooming forest glows.
And all the desart blossoms as the rose.
From distant lands see virtuous millions fly
To happier climates, and a milder sky,
While on the mind successive pleasures pour,
'Till time expires, and ages are no more.

PHILLIS WHEATLEY (1753?–1784)

First book of poetry published by an African American author.

Phillis Wheatley was born in circa 1753 in either today's Senegal or the Gambia, West Africa, where as a young girl she was captured by slave traders and brought to America in 1761. She was sold to the Wheatley family in Boston, Massachusetts, then a city of less than twenty thousand inhabitants. The Wheatley family taught her to read and write, and she rapidly learned to read the Bible, Greek and Latin classics, and British literature. At age fourteen, Wheatley began to write poetry. She published her first poem in 1767 and quickly gained considerable attention. In 1773, Wheatley visited Great Britain with the Wheatleys' son, where she published her first collection of poetry, *Poems on Various Subjects, Religious and Moral*, the first book written by a Black woman in America. Twelve distinguished Boston dignitaries signed a preface and portrait of Wheatley to prove that the work was indeed written by her. Criticized for presenting Wheatley to London society while still holding her in bondage, the Wheatleys ended her enslavement in 1774, three months before Mrs. Wheatley's death. In 1778, Wheatley married a free Black man, John Peters, with whom she had three children, though none survived. The Peters struggled financially, and she unsuccessfully tried to raise funds for a second book of poetry. Wheatley died in December 1784.

Wheatley's poems follow the neoclassical tradition of British poetry. Many of her poems address renowned figures such as General George Washington, friends, or the emerging United States. Few of her poems touch on the subject of slavery, but closer scrutiny reveals a complex and ingeniously constructed examination of the conditions of her time and its impact in the formal genres available to her. Like other African American writers, Wheatley uses Christianity as the lingua franca with which to criticize the institution of slavery on moral grounds.

From POEMS ON VARIOUS SUBJECTS, RELIGIOUS AND MORAL [1773]

ON BEING BROUGHT FROM AFRICA TO AMERICA

'Twas mercy brought me from my *Pagan* land,
Taught my benighted soul to understand
That there's a God, that there's a *Saviour* too:
Once I redemption neither sought nor knew.
Some view our sable race with scornful eye,
"Their colour is a diabolic dye."
Remember, *Christians*, *Negros*, black as *Cain*,
May be refin'd, and join th' angelic train.

TO THE UNIVERSITY OF CAMBRIDGE, IN NEW ENGLAND

While an intrinsic ardor bids me write,
The muses promise to assist my pen;
'Twas not long since I left my native shore
The land of errors, and *Egyptian* gloom:
Father of mercy, 'twas thy gracious hand
Brought me in safety from those dark abodes.

Students, to you 'tis given to scan the heights
Above, to traverse the ethereal space,
And mark the systems of revolving worlds.
Still more, ye sons of science ye receive
The blissful news by messengers from heav'n,
How *Jesus'* blood for your redemption flows.
See with him hands out-strecht upon the cross;
Immense compassion in his bosom glows;
He hears revilers, nor resents their scorn:
What matchless mercy in the Son of God!
When the whole human race by sin had fall'n,
He deign'd to die that they might rise again,
And share with Him in the sublimest skies,
Life without death, and glory without end.

Improve your privileges while they stay,
Ye pupils, and each hour redeem, that bears
Or good or bad report of you to heav'n.

Let sin, that baneful evil to the soul,
By you be shunn'd, nor once remit your guard;
Suppress the deadly serpent in its egg.
Ye blooming plants of human race divine,
An *Ethiop* tells you 'tis your greatest foe;
Its transient sweetness turns to endless pain,
And in immense perdition sinks the soul.

THOUGHTS ON THE WORKS OF PROVIDENCE

Arise, my soul, on wings enraptur'd, rise
To praise the monarch of the earth and skies,
Whose goodness and beneficence appear
As round its center moves the rolling year,
Or when the morning glows with rosy charms,
Or the sun slumbers in the ocean's arms:
Of light divine be a rich portion lent
To guide my soul, and favor my intend.
Celestial muse, my arduous flight sustain
And raise my mind to a seraphic strain!

Ador'd for ever be the God unseen,
Which round the sun revolves this vast machine,
Though to His eye its mass a point appears:
Ador'd the God that whirls surrounding spheres,
Which first ordain'd that mighty *Sol* should reign
The peerless monarch of th' ethereal train:
Of miles twice forty millions is his height,
And yet his radiance dazzles mortal sight
So far beneath—from him th' extended earth
Vigor derives, and eve'y flow'ry birth:
Vast through her orb she moves with easy grace
Around her *Phoebus* in unbounded space;
True to her course th' impetuous storm derides,
Triumphant o'er the winds, and surging tides.

Almighty, in these wond'rous works of thine,
What *Pow'r*, what *Wisdom*, and what *Goodness* shine?
And are Thy wonders, Lord, by men explor'd,

And yet creating glory unador'd!

Creation smiles in various beauty gay,
While day to night, and night succeeds to day:
That *Wisdom*, which attends *Jehovah's* ways,
Shines most conspicuous in the solar rays:
Without them, destitute of heat and light,
This world would be the reign of endless night:
In their excess how would our race complain,
Abhorring life! how hate its length'ned chain!
From air adust what num'rous ills would rise?
What dire contagion taint the burning skies?
What pestilential vapors, fraught with death,
Would rise, and overspread the lands beneath?

Hail, smiling morn, that from the orient main
Ascending dost adorn the heav'nly plain!
So rich, so various are thy beauteous dies,
That spread through all the circuit of the skies,
That, full of thee, my soul in rapture soars,
And thy great God, the cause of all adores.

O'er beings infinite His love extends,
His *Wisdom* rules them, and His *Pow'r* defends.
When tasks diurnal tire the human frame,
The spirits faint, and dim the vital dame,
Then too that ever active bounty shines,
Which not infinity of space confines.
The sable veil, that *Night* in silence draws,
Conceals effects, but shows the *Almighty Cause*,
Night seals in sleep the wide creation fair,
And all is peaceful but the brow of care.
Again, gay *Phoebus*, as the day before,
Wakes every eye, but what shall wake no more;
Again the face of nature is renewed,
Which still appears harmonious, fair, and good.
May grateful strains salute the smiling morn,
Before its beams the eastern hills adorn!

Shall day to day, and night to night conspire

To show the goodness of the Almighty Sire?
This mental voice shall man regardless hear,
And never, never raise the filial prayer?
To-day, O hearken, nor your folly mourn
For time mispent, that never will return.

But see the sons of vegetation rise,
And spread their leafy banners to the skies.
All-wise Almighty Providence we trace
In trees, and plants, and all the flow'ry race;
As clear as in the nobler frame of man,
All lovely copies of the Maker's plan.
The pow'r the same that forms a ray of light,
That call'd creation from eternal night.
"Let there be light," he said. From his profound
Old *Chaos* heard, and trembled at the sound:
Swift as the word, inspired by power divine,
Behold the light around its maker shine,
The first fair product of th' omnific God,
And now through all his works diffus'd abroad.

As reason's pow'rs by day our God disclose,
So we may trace him in the night's repose:
Say what is sleep? and dreams how passing strange!
When action ceases, and ideas range
Licentious and unbounded o'er the plains,
Where *Fancy's* queen in giddy triumph reigns.
Hear in soft strains the dreaming lover sigh
To a kind fair, or rave in jealousy;
On pleasure now, and now on vengeance bent,
The lab 'ring passions struggle for a vent.
What power, O man! thy *reason* then restores,
So long suspended in nocturnal hours?
What secret hand returns the mental train,
And gives improv'd thine active pow'rs again?
From thee, O man, what gratitude should rise!
And, when from balmy sleep thou op'st thine eyes,
Let thy first thoughts be praises to the skies.
How merciful our God who thus imparts

O'erflowing tides of joy to human hearts,
When wants and woes might be our righteous lot,
Our God forgetting, by our God forgot!

Among the mental pow'rs a question rose,
"What most the image of the Eternal shows?"
When thus to *Reason* (so let *Fancy* rove)
Her great companion spoke, immortal *Love*.

"Say, mighty pow'r, how long shall strife prevail,
And with its murmurs load the whisp'ring gale?
Refer the cause to *Recollection's* shrine,
Who loud proclaims my origin divine,
The cause whence heav'n and earth began to be,
And is not man immortaliz'd by me?
Reason let this most causeless strife subside."
Thus *Love* pronounced, and *Reason* thus replied.

"Thy birth, celestial queen! 'tis mine to own,
In thee resplendent is the Godhead shown;
Thy words persuade, my soul enraptur'd feels
Resistless beauty which thy smile reveals."
Ardent she spoke, and, kindling at her charms,
She clasp'd the blooming goddess in her arms.

Infinite *Love* where'er we turn our eyes
Appears: this ev'ry creature's wants supplies;
This most is heard in *Nature's* constant voice,
This makes the morn, and this the eve rejoice;
This bids the fost'ring rains and dews descend
To nourish all, to serve one gen'ral end,
The good of man: yet man ungrateful pays
But little homage, and but little praise.
To him, whose works array'd with mercy shine,
What songs should rise, how constant, how divine!

To S. M. a Young African Painter, On Seeing His Works

To show the lab'ring bosom's deep intent,
And thought in living characters to paint,

When first thy pencil did those beauties give,
And breathing figures learnt from thee to live,
How did those prospects give my soul delight,
A new creation rushing on my sight?
Still, wond'rous youth! each noble path pursue,
On deathless glories fix thine ardent view:
Still may the painter's and the poet's fire
To aid thy pencil, and thy verse conspire!
And may the charms of each seraphic theme
Conduct thy footsteps to immortal fame!
High to the blissful wonders of the skies
Elate thy soul, and raise thy wishful eyes.
Thrice happy, when exalted to survey
That splendid city, crown'd with endless day,
Whose twice six gates on radiant hinges ring:
Celestial *Salem* blooms in endless spring.
Calm and serene thy moments glide along,
And may the muse inspire each future song!
Still, with the sweets of contemplation bless'd,
May peace with balmy wings your soul invest!
But when these shades of time are chas'd away,
And darkness ends in everlasting day,
On what seraphic pinions shall we move,
And view the landscapes in the realms above?
There shall thy tongue in heav'nly murmurs flow,
And there my muse with heav'nly transport glow:
No more to tell of *Damon's* tender sighs,
Or rising radiance of *Aurora's* eyes,
For nobler themes demand a nobler strain,
And purer language on th' ethereal plain.
Cease, gentle muse! the solemn gloom of night
Now seals the fair creation from my sight.

ON IMAGINATION

Thy various works, imperial queen, we see,
How bright their forms! how deck'd with pomp by thee!
Thy wond'rous acts in beauteous order stand,

And all attest how potent is thine hand.

From *Helicon's* refulgent heights attend,
Ye sacred choir, and my attempts befriend:
To tell her glories with a faithful tongue,
Ye blooming graces, triumph in my song.

Now here, now there, the roving *Fancy* flies,
Till some lov'd object strikes her wand'ring eyes,
Whose silken fetters all the senses bind,
And soft captivity involves the mind.

Imagination! who can sing thy force?
Or who describe the swiftness of thy course?
Soaring through air to find the bright abode,
Th' empyreal palace of the thund'ring God,
We on thy pinions can surpass the wind,
And leave the rolling universe behind:
From star to star the mental optics rove,
Measure the skies, and range the realms above.
There in one view we grasp the mighty whole,
Or with new worlds amaze th' unbounded soul.

Though *Winter* frowns to *Fancy's* raptur'd eyes
The fields may flourish, and gay scenes arise;
The frozen deeps may break their iron bands,
And bid their waters murmur o'er the sands.
Fair *Flora* may resume her fragrant reign,
And with her flow'ry riches deck the plain;
Sylvanus may diffuse his honours round,
And all the forest may with leaves be crown'd:
Show'rs may descend, and dews their gems disclose,
And nectar sparkle on the blooming rose.

Such is thy pow'r, nor are thine orders vain,
O thou the leader of the mental train:
In full perfection all thy works are wrought,
And thine the sceptre o'er the realms of thought.
Before thy throne the subject-passions bow,
Of subject-passions sov'reign ruler thou;

At thy command joy rushes on the heart,
And through the glowing veins the spirits dart.

    Fancy might now her silken pinions try
To rise from earth, and sweep th' expanse on high:
From *Tithon's* bed now might *Aurora* rise,
Her cheeks all glowing with celestial dies,
While a pure stream of light o'erflows the skies.
The monarch of the day I might behold,
And all the mountains tipt with radiant gold,
But I reluctant leave the pleasing views,
Which *Fancy* dresses to delight the *Muse*;
Winter austere forbids me to aspire,
And northern tempests damp the rising fire;
They chill the tides of *Fancy's* flowing sea,
Cease then, my song, cease the unequal lay.

To His Excellency General Washington

Sir. I have taken the freedom to address your Excellency in the enclosed poem, and entreat your acceptance, though I am not insensible of its inaccuracies.

Your being appointed by the Grand Continental Congress to be Generalissimo of the armies of North America, together with the fame of your virtues, excite sensations not easy to suppress. Your generosity, therefore, I presume, will pardon the attempt. Wishing your Excellency all possible success in the great cause you are so generously engaged in. I am,

Your Excellency's most obedient humble servant,

Phillis Wheatley
Providence, Oct. 26, 1775. *

Celestial choir! enthroned in realms of light,
Columbia's scenes of glorious toils I write.
While freedom's cause her anxious breast alarms,
She flashes dreadful in refulgent arms.
See mother earth her offspring's fate bemoan,
And nations gaze at scenes before unknown!

---

* First published in the *Virginia Gazette* in 1776.

See the bright beams of heaven's revolving light
Involved in sorrows and the veil of night!

The goddess comes, she moves divinely fair,
Olive and laurel binds her golden hair:
Wherever shines this native of the skies,
Unnumbered charms and recent graces rise.

Muse! bow propitious while my pen relates
How pour her armies through a thousand gates,
As when Eolus heaven's fair face deforms,
Enwrapped in tempest and a night of storms;
Astonish'd ocean feels the wild uproar,
The refluent surges beat the sounding shore;
Or thick as leaves in Autumn's golden reign,
Such, and so many, moves the warrior's train.
In bright array they seek the work of war,
Where high unfurled the ensign waves in air.
Shall I to Washington their praise recite?
Enough thou know'st them in the fields of fight.
Thee, first in place and honours,—we demand
The grace and glory of thy martial band.
Famed for thy valor, for thy virtues more,
Hear every tongue thy guardian aid implore!

One century scarce perform'd its destined round,
When Gallic powers Columbia's fury found;
And so may you, whoever dares disgrace
The land of freedom's heaven-defended race!
Fix'd are the eyes of nations on the scales,
For in their hopes Columbia's arm prevails.
Anon Britannia droops the pensive head,
While round increase the rising hills of dead.
Ah! cruel blindness to Columbia's state!
Lament thy thirst of boundless power too late.

Proceed, great chief, with virtue on thy side,
Thy ev'ry action let the goddess guide.
A crown, a mansion, and a throne that shine,
With gold unfading, WASHINGTON! be thine.

SAMSON OCCOM (1723–1792)

First published literary work by a Native American author.

Samson Occom was born in 1723 on a Mohegan settlement in present-day Connecticut as the direct descendant of the Mohegan leader, Uncas. He taught himself to read and write as a teenager and converted to Christianity at age eighteen during the Great Awakening. At age twenty, Occom began his studies with Eleazar Wheelock, who later founded Dartmouth College. In 1759, he was ordained a Presbyterian minister. After missionary trips to the Oneida Nation, Occom traveled to England and Scotland from 1766 to 1768 to raise funds for Wheelock's Indian Charity school. Upon his return he discovered that Wheelock had moved the school to New Hampshire as Dartmouth College to educate Anglo-American students. The betrayal ended their association and motivated Occom to become an outspoken advocate for Indian rights.

In 1775 Occom helped found Brothertown, an Indian tribe formed from the Christian Mohegans, Pequots, Narragansetts, Montauks, Tunxis, and Niantics. They settled in Oneida country in upstate New York, where they remained until they were—under threat of removal—forced to relocate to Wisconsin in the 1830s. Occom moved to upstate New York with his family in 1789, serving as minister. He died in 1792.

Occom was, as a tribal leader, an intertribal political figure, and an ordained minister. He is best known today as the author of a short autobiography, written in 1768. In 1774 he published the best-selling *A Sermon Preached at the Execution of Moses Paul, An Indian Who Was Executed at New Haven on the 2nd of September 1772 for the Murder of Mr. Moses Cook, late of Waterbury, on the 7th of December 1771*, which indicts Anglo settler spiritual hypocrisy and pleads for temperance. That year he also published *Sermon at the Execution of Moses Paul and A Choice Collection of Hymns and Spiritual Songs*. He corresponded with Phillis Wheatly, whom he greatly admired, and is considered to have paved the way for other American Indian authors.

From A Choice Collection of Hymns and Spiritual Songs; Intended for the Edification of Sincere Christians, of All Denomiations [1774]

The Sufferings of Christ, or, Throughout the Saviour's Life We Trace

Throughout the Saviour's Life we trace,
Nothing but Shame and deep Disgrace,
No period else is seen;
Till he a spotless Victim fell,
Tasting in Soul a painful Hell,
Caus'd by the Creature's Sin.

On the cold Ground methinks I see
My Jesus kneel, and pray for me;
For this I him adore;
Siez'd with a chilly sweat throughout,
Blood-drops did force their Passage out
Through ev'ry open'd Pore.

A pricking Thorn his Temples bore;
His Back with Lashes all was tore,
Till one the Bones might see;
Mocking, they push'd him here and there,
Marking his Way with Blood and Tear,
Press'd by the heavy Tree.

Thus up the Hill he painful came,
Round him they mock, and make their Game,
At length his Cross they rear;
And can you see the mighty God,
Cry out beneath sin's heavy Load,
Without one thankful Tear?

Thus vailed in Humanity,
He dies in Anguish on the Tree;

What Tongue his Grief can tell?
The shudd'ring Rocks their Heads recline,
The mourning Sun refuse to shine,
When the Creator fell.

Shout, Brethren, shout in songs divine,
He drank the Gall, to give us Wine,
To quench our parching Thirst;
Seraphs advance your Voices higher;
Bride of the Lamb, unite the Choir,
And Laud thy precious Christ.

The Slow Traveller, or, O Happy Souls How Fast You Go

O happy souls how fast you go,
And leave me here behind,
Don't stop for me for now See,
The Lord is just and kind.

Go on, go on, my Soul says go,
And I'll Come after you,
Tho I'm behind, yet I can find,
I'll Sing Hosanna too.

Lord give you strength, that you may run,
And keep your footsteps right,
Tho' fast you go, and I So slow,
You are not out of Sight.

When you get to the Worlds above,
And all his Glory See,
When you get home, Your Journey's done,
Then look you out for me.

For I will come fast as I Can,
A long that way I Stear
Lord give me Strength, I shall at length
Be one amongst you here.

(CHORUS)

There all together we shall be,
Together we will Sing,
Together we will praise our god,
And everlasting King.

A Morning Hymn, or, Now the Shades of Night are Gone

Now the shades of night are gone,
Now the morning light is come;
Lord, we would be thine to-day;
Drive the shades of sin away.

Make our souls as noon-day clear,
Banish every doubt and fear,
In thy vineyard, Lord, today,
We would labor, we would pray.

Keep our haughty passions bound;
Rising up and sitting down;
Going out and coming in,
Keep us safe from every sin.

When our work of life is past,
O receive us then at last;
Labor then will all be o'er,
Night of sin will be no more.

Come All My Young Companions, Come

Come all my Young Companions Come,
And hear me boldly tell,
The wonders of Redeeming Love,
That Sav'd my Soul from Hell.

It was but a few Days ago,
I Saw my awful Case,
Nothing but hell and dark Dispare,
Lay plain before my face.

O then I Viewd the Damned Crew,
Of all the numerous race,

And I of all that went to hell
Deserved the lowest place.

Justice of God So on me lay,
I Could no Comfort find
Till I was Willing to forsake,
And leave all my Sins behind.

The Lord was Strong he bowd my Will,
And made me this to See,
Nothing but Jesus Crusified,
Could Save a wretch like me.

O then I Viewd mount Calvery,
With gods eternal Son,
Who on the Cursed Tree did Die,
For Sins that I had done,

O how Rejoicd I Was to think,
A Saviour I had found,
It turnd my Sorrows into Joy,
To hear the Blessed Sound.

Salvation from my God on high,
So pleasantly did Ring,
It Sot my Soul at Liberty,
To praise my heavenly King,

And while I dwell on Earth below
I'll praise my Jesus here,
And then go to Yonder World
And praise my Jesus there.

And there thro' all Eternity,
In the Sweet Realms above
There I Shall Sing that blessed Song
Free grace and Dying Love.

WILLIAM HILL BROWN (1765–1793)

First novel published in America.

William Hill Brown was born in Boston, the son of Gawen Brown, a noted clockmaker, and Elizabeth Hill Adams Brown. During his short life Brown published a romantic tale, "Harriot, or the Domestic Reconciliation" (1789) a serialized essay, *The Reformer* (1797), essays, poems, and a tragedy, *West Point Preserved* (1797), about the death of a Revolutionary spy. In 1792 he moved to North Carolina to study law with a prominent attorney near a town where his sister had settled. He died of fever in 1793.

He published his two-volume epistolary novel, *The Power of Sympathy; or, The Triumph of Nature* in 1789 anonymously, perhaps because the story was based on a heavily publicized scandal in Boston of a woman who committed suicide after being seduced by her sister's prominent husband. The cautionary tale about the moral corruption of a woman reflects eighteenth century America's preoccupation with the role of women as moral gatekeepers. It centers on a relationship undone by an explosive family secret. The two letters excerpted here are the female protagonist Harriet's reaction to discovering her true relation to her beloved, Harrington, and Harrington's sister's letter about Harriet's subsequent suicide. While clearly indebted to British antecedents, especially Samuel Richardson's popular epistolary novel *Clarrisa* (1748), Brown's work is widely considered the first American novel.

From THE POWER OF SYMPATHY; OR, THE TRIUMPH OF NATURE [1789]

LETTER L.

Harriot to Harrington

BOSTON.

Must I then forget the endearments of the lover, and call you by the name of brother? But does our friendship remain upon this foundation? Is this all that unites us? And has there subsisted nothing more tender—a sentiment more voluntary in our hearts? My feelings affirm that there has. At the hour of our first interview I felt the passion kindle in my breast: Insensible of my own weakness, I indulged its increasing violence and delighted in the flame that fired my reason and my senses. Do you remember our walks, our conversations, our diversions?—The remembrance of these things fill my mind with inconceivable torture—they seem to reproach me with unmerited criminality—I deprecate, I detest all these scenes of gaity and frivolity—yet I have preserved my innocence and my virtue—what then have I to deprecate, what have I to detest?

Alas! how have we been forming schemes of happiness, and mocking our hearts with unsubstantial joys. Farewel! farewel! ye gilded scenes of imagination. How have we been deluded by visionary prospects, and idly dwelt upon that happiness which was never to arrive. How fleeting have been the days that were thus employed!—when anticipation threw open the gates of happiness, and we vainly contemplated the approach of bliss;—when we beheld in reversion, the pleasures of life, and fondly promised ourselves, one day to participate in them;—when we beheld in the magick mirrour of futurity, the lively group of loves that sport in the train of joy. We observed in transports of delight the dear delusion, and saw them, as it were, in bodily form pass in review before us; as the fabled hero views the region of pre-existant spirits, and beholds a race of men yet to be born.

Such was our hope, but even this fairy anticipation was not irrational. We were happy in idea, nor was the reality far behind. And why is the vision vanished? O! I sink, I die, when I reflect—when I find in my *Harrington* a brother—I am penetrated with inexpressible grief—I experience uncommon sensations—I start with horrour at the idea of incest—of ruin—of perdition.

How do I lament this fatal discovery, that includes the termination of a faithful love! I think of him to whom I have resolved to be eternally constant—and ah! how often have I resolved it in my heart. I indulge, in idea, the recollection of his caresses—of his protestations, and of his truth and sincerity—I become lost in a wilderness, and still I travel on, and find myself no nearer an escape. I cherish the dear idea of a lover—I see the danger and do not wish to shun it, because, to avoid it, is to forget it—And can I, at one stroke, erase from my mind the remembrance of all in which my heart used to delight? Ah! I have not the fortitude—I have not the virtue, to "forget myself to marble." On the contrary, I strive no longer to remember our present connexion. I endeavour to forget—I curse the idea of a brother—my hand refuses to trace the word, and yet

    —The name appears
    Already written; blot it out my tears!

Ah, whence this sorrow that invests my soul! This gloom that darkens—this fire of impassioned grief, that involves all my thoughts! why do I rave, and why do I again abandon myself to despair! Come, O *Harrington*! be a friend, a protector, a brother—be him, on whom I could never yet call by the tender, the endearing title of *parent*. I will reverence him in whom all the charities of life are united—I will be dutiful and affectionate to you, and you shall be unto me as a father—I will bend on the knee of respect and love, and will receive your blessing.

Why did you go away so soon? Why leave me when I was incapable of bidding you adieu? When you pressed my cheek with the kiss of love, of fraternal affection, what meant its conscious glow? What meant the ebullition of my veins, the disorder of my nerves, the intoxication of my brain, the blood that mantled in my heart? My hand trembled, and every object seemed to swim before my doubtful view—Amidst the struggle of passion, how could I pronounce the word—how could I call you by the title of brother. True—I attempted to articulate the sound, but it died upon my tongue, and I sank motionless into your arms.

—Allied by birth, and in mind, and similar in age—and in thought still more intimately connected, the sympathy which bound our souls together, at first sight, is less extraordinary. Shall we any longer wonder at its irresistible impulse?—Shall we strive to oppose the *link of nature* that draws us to each other? When I reflect on this, I relapse into weakness and tenderness, and become a prey to warring passions. I view you in two distinct characters: If I indulge the idea of one, the other becomes annihilated, and I vainly imagine I have my choice of a brother or—

I am for a while calm—but alas! how momentary is that calmness; I dwell with rapture on what fancy has represented; but is the choice regulated by virtue? Is it prompted by reason? I recollect myself, and endeavour to rouse my prudence and fortitude; I abhor my conduct, and wish for obscurity and forgetfulness. Who can bear the torment of fluctuating passion? How deplorable is the contest? The head and the heart are at variance, but when Nature pleads, how feeble is the voice of Reason? Yet, when Reason is heard in her turn, how criminal appears every wish of my heart? What remorse do I experience? What horrours surround me? Will my feeble frame, already wasted by a lingering decline, support these evils? Will the shattered, frail bark outride the tempest, and will the waves of affliction beat in vain? Virtue, whose precepts I have not forgotten, will assist me—if not to *surmount,* at least to *suffer* with fortitude and patience.

Oh! I fear, I fear my decaying health—If I must depart, let me beseech you to forget me—I know the strength of your passion, and I dread the fatal consequences my departure may occasion you.

Once more let me intreat you, my dear friend, to arm yourself with every virtue which is capable of sustaining the heaviest calamity. Let the impetuosity of the lover's passion be forgotten in the undisturbed quietness of the brother's affection, and may all the blessings that life can supply be yours—Seek for content, and you will find it, even though we should never meet again in this world.

Adieu!

LETTER LI.

Myra to Mrs. Holmes

BOSTON.

The curtain is dropped, and the scene of life is forever closed—THE LOVELY HARRIOT IS NO MORE.

She is fit to appear in Heaven, for her life was a scene of purity and innocence—If there is any consolation to be felt by a survivor, it is in the reflection of the amiable qualities of the deceased. My heart shall not cease to cherish her idea, for she was beautiful without artifice, and virtuous without affectation.

See! there all pale and dead she lies;
Forever flow my streaming eyes—
There dwelt the fairest—lovliest mind,
    Faith, sweetness, wit together join'd.
Dwelt faith and wit and sweetness there?
O! view the change, and drop a tear.

My brother is exceedingly agitated—He will never support this disastrous stroke—Nothing can attract his attention—nothing allay his grief—but it is the affliction of reason and not of weakness—God grant that it prove not fatal to him.

Adieu!—Adieu!—

SUSANNA ROWSON (1762–1824)

First novel by a woman published in America.

Susanna Rowson was born in Portsmouth, England, to British Royal Navy Lieutenant William Haswell and Susanna Musgrave Haswell, who died from complications of childbirth. Her father left Susanna in England in the care of relatives when he was stationed as a customs officer for the Royal Navy in Massachusetts. Susanna arrived in 1766 in Boston, on a ship that ran aground in Boston harbor where crew and passengers had to be rescued after a harrowing night. Susanna was educated at home alongside several half-siblings from her father's second marriage, to Rachel Woodward. Lieutenant Haswell remained loyal to England during the Revolutionary War. He was placed under house arrest, then forced to surrender his property and move to Hingham where the family lived on the charity of the town. In 1778 they were deported to England. While working as a governess for the children of the Duchess of Devonshire, Susanna wrote poetry, short stories, and novels. In 1786 she published her first novel, *Victoria*, and married William Rowson. He declared bankruptcy in 1792 and the couple started acting in the theater to support themselves. Susanna published a long poem, *A Trip to Parnassus* (1788) and five novels in rapid succession. In 1793 their theater company went to the United States, where Rowson's play *Slaves in Algiers, or A Struggle for Freedom* (1794) was an immediate hit. The Rowsons moved to Boston in 1796, where they acted and Susanna kept publishing plays, novels, poems, and popular songs. In 1797 she retired from acting to open a boarding school, one of the first to offer post-elementary education for girls, for which she wrote popular textbooks in subjects not available to female students such as geography, math, and science. She worked until 1822 as an educator, writer, and editor. She died in Boston on March 2, 1824, one of the most celebrated women in America.

In 1794 she published *Charlotte Temple: A Tale of Truth*, which had been

originally published in England in 1791. It became the first best-selling
novel in the United States, and the country's best-selling book until Harriet
Beecher Stowe's *Uncle Tom's Cabin* in 1852. Charlotte Temple, a naïve
English girl, unwisely elopes to America with a dashing soldier who promises to marry her, is forsaken by him, suffers physical and mental anguish,
and dies after bearing his child. Readers were so enthralled by Rowson's
story of a deceitful British soldier betraying a good woman against the
backdrop of the Revolution that they refused to view it as a work of fiction.
Thousands made pilgrimages to visit a gravestone in New York's Trinity
Church's cemetery that was rumored to be Charlotte Temple's burial place.
The book went through over two hundred editions and was read by as many
as a half-million people, but Rowson did not own the American copyright
and earned little from its bestseller status.

From CHARLOTTE TEMPLE: A TALE OF TRUTH [1794]

CHAPTER I.
A BOARDING SCHOOL.

"ARE YOU FOR a walk," said Montraville to his companion, as they arose
from table; "are you for a walk? or shall we order the chaise and proceed
to Portsmouth?" Belcour preferred the former; and they sauntered out to
view the town, and to make remarks on the inhabitants, as they returned
from church.

Montraville was a Lieutenant in the army: Belcour was his brother officer: they had been to take leave of their friends previous to their departure
for America, and were now returning to Portsmouth, where the troops
waited orders for embarkation. They had stopped at Chichester to dine; and
knowing they had sufficient time to reach the place of destination before
dark, and yet allow them a walk, had resolved, it being Sunday afternoon, to
take a survey of the Chichester ladies as they returned from their devotions.

They had gratified their curiosity, and were preparing to return to the
inn without honouring any of the belles with particular notice, when
Madame Du Pont, at the head of her school, descended from the church.
Such an assemblage of youth and innocence naturally attracted the young
soldiers: they stopped; and, as the little cavalcade passed, almost involuntarily pulled off their hats. A tall, elegant girl looked at Montraville and
blushed: he instantly recollected the features of Charlotte Temple, whom

he had once seen and danced with at a ball at Portsmouth. At that time he thought on her only as a very lovely child, she being then only thirteen; but the improvement two years had made in her person, and the blush of recollection which suffused her cheeks as she passed, awakened in his bosom new and pleasing ideas. Vanity led him to think that pleasure at again beholding him might have occasioned the emotion he had witnessed, and the same vanity led him to wish to see her again.

"She is the sweetest girl in the world," said he, as he entered the inn. Belcour stared. "Did you not notice her?" continued Montraville: "she had on a blue bonnet, and with a pair of lovely eyes of the same colour, has contrived to make me feel devilish odd about the heart."

"Pho," said Belcour, "a musket ball from our friends, the Americans, may in less than two months make you feel worse."

"I never think of the future," replied Montraville; "but am determined to make the most of the present, and would willingly compound with any kind Familiar who would inform me who the girl is, and how I might be likely to obtain an interview."

But no kind Familiar at that time appearing, and the chaise which they had ordered, driving up to the door, Montraville and his companion were obliged to take leave of Chichester and its fair inhabitant, and proceed on their journey.

But Charlotte had made too great an impression on his mind to be easily eradicated: having therefore spent three whole days in thinking on her and in endeavouring to form some plan for seeing her, he determined to set off for Chichester, and trust to chance either to favour or frustrate his designs. Arriving at the verge of the town, he dismounted, and sending the servant forward with the horses, proceeded toward the place, where, in the midst of an extensive pleasure ground, stood the mansion which contained the lovely Charlotte Temple. Montraville leaned on a broken gate, and looked earnestly at the house. The wall which surrounded it was high, and perhaps the Argus's who guarded the Hesperian fruit within, were more watchful than those famed of old.

"'Tis a romantic attempt," said he; "and should I even succeed in seeing and conversing with her, it can be productive of no good: I must of necessity leave England in a few days, and probably may never return; why then should I endeavour to engage the affections of this lovely girl, only to leave her a prey to a thousand inquietudes, of which at present she has no idea? I will return to Portsmouth and think no more about her."

The evening now was closed; a serene stillness reigned; and the chaste Queen of Night with her silver crescent faintly illuminated the hemisphere. The mind of Montraville was hushed into composure by the serenity of the surrounding objects. "I will think on her no more," said he, and turned with an intention to leave the place; but as he turned, he saw the gate which led to the pleasure grounds open, and two women come out, who walked arm-in-arm across the field.

"I will at least see who these are," said he. He overtook them, and giving them the compliments of the evening, begged leave to see them into the more frequented parts of the town: but how was he delighted, when, waiting for an answer, he discovered, under the concealment of a large bonnet, the face of Charlotte Temple.

He soon found means to ingratiate himself with her companion, who was a French teacher at the school, and, at parting, slipped a letter he had purposely written, into Charlotte's hand, and five guineas into that of Mademoiselle, who promised she would endeavour to bring her young charge into the field again the next evening.

CHAPTER II.
DOMESTIC CONCERNS.

MR. TEMPLE WAS the youngest son of a nobleman whose fortune was by no means adequate to the antiquity, grandeur, and I may add, pride of the family. He saw his elder brother made completely wretched by marrying a disagreeable woman, whose fortune helped to prop the sinking dignity of the house; and he beheld his sisters legally prostituted to old, decrepid men, whose titles gave them consequence in the eyes of the world, and whose affluence rendered them splendidly miserable. "I will not sacrifice internal happiness for outward shew," said he: "I will seek Content; and, if I find her in a cottage, will embrace her with as much cordiality as I should if seated on a throne."

Mr. Temple possessed a small estate of about five hundred pounds a year; and with that he resolved to preserve independence, to marry where the feelings of his heart should direct him, and to confine his expenses within the limits of his income. He had a heart open to every generous feeling of humanity, and a hand ready to dispense to those who wanted part of the blessings he enjoyed himself.

As he was universally known to be the friend of the unfortunate, his advice and bounty was frequently solicited; nor was it seldom that he sought out indigent merit, and raised it from obscurity, confining his own expenses within a very narrow compass.

"You are a benevolent fellow," said a young officer to him one day; "and I have a great mind to give you a fine subject to exercise the goodness of your heart upon."

"You cannot oblige me more," said Temple, "than to point out any way by which I can be serviceable to my fellow creatures."

"Come along then," said the young man, "we will go and visit a man who is not in so good a lodging as he deserves; and, were it not that he has an angel with him, who comforts and supports him, he must long since have sunk under his misfortunes." The young man's heart was too full to proceed; and Temple, unwilling to irritate his feelings by making further enquiries, followed him in silence, til they arrived at the Fleet prison.

The officer enquired for Captain Eldridge: a person led them up several pair of dirty stairs, and pointing to a door which led to a miserable, small apartment, said that was the Captain's room, and retired.

The officer, whose name was Blakeney, tapped at the door, and was bid to enter by a voice melodiously soft. He opened the door, and discovered to Temple a scene which rivetted him to the spot with astonishment.

The apartment, though small, and bearing strong marks of poverty, was neat in the extreme. In an arm-chair, his head reclined upon his hand, his eyes fixed on a book which lay open before him, sat an aged man in a Lieutenant's uniform, which, though threadbare, would sooner call a blush of shame into the face of those who could neglect real merit, than cause the hectic of confusion to glow on the cheeks of him who wore it.

Beside him sat a lovely creature busied in painting a fan mount. She was fair as the lily, but sorrow had nipped the rose in her cheek before it was half blown. Her eyes were blue; and her hair, which was light brown, was slightly confined under a plain muslin cap, tied round with a black ribbon; a white linen gown and plain lawn handkerchief composed the remainder of her dress; and in this simple attire, she was more irresistibly charming to such a heart as Temple's, than she would have been, if adorned with all the splendor of a courtly belle.

When they entered, the old man arose from his seat, and shaking Blakeney by the hand with great cordiality, offered Temple his chair; and there being but three in the room, seated himself on the side of his little bed with evident composure.

"This is a strange place," said he to Temple, "to receive visitors of distinction in; but we must fit our feelings to our station. While I am not ashamed to own the cause which brought me here, why should I blush at my situation? Our misfortunes are not our faults; and were it not for that poor girl—"

Here the philosopher was lost in the father. He rose hastily from his seat, and walking toward the window, wiped off a tear which he was afraid would tarnish the cheek of a sailor.

Temple cast his eye on Miss Eldridge: a pellucid drop had stolen from her eyes, and fallen upon a rose she was painting. It blotted and discoloured the flower. "'Tis emblematic," said he mentally: "the rose of youth and health soon fades when watered by the tear of affliction."

"My friend Blakeney," said he, addressing the old man, "told me I could be of service to you: be so kind then, dear Sir, as to point out some way in which I can relieve the anxiety of your heart and increase the pleasures of my own."

"My good young man," said Eldridge, "you know not what you offer. While deprived of my liberty I cannot be free from anxiety on my own account; but that is a trifling concern; my anxious thoughts extend to one more dear a thousand times than life: I am a poor weak old man, and must expect in a few years to sink into silence and oblivion; but when I am gone, who will protect that fair bud of innocence from the blasts of adversity, or from the cruel hand of insult and dishonour."

"Oh, my father!" cried Miss Eldridge, tenderly taking his hand, "be not anxious on that account; for daily are my prayers offered to heaven that our lives may terminate at the same instant, and one grave receive us both; for why should I live when deprived of my only friend."

Temple was moved even to tears. "You will both live many years," said he, "and I hope see much happiness. Cheerly, my friend, cheerly; these passing clouds of adversity will serve only to make the sunshine of prosperity more pleasing. But we are losing time: you might ere this have told me who were your creditors, what were their demands, and other particulars necessary to your liberation."

"My story is short," said Mr. Eldridge, "but there are some particulars which will wring my heart barely to remember; yet to one whose offers of friendship appear so open and disinterested, I will relate every circumstance that led to my present, painful situation. But my child," continued he, addressing his daughter, "let me prevail on you to take this opportunity, while my friends are with me, to enjoy the benefit of air and exercise."

"Go, my love; leave me now; to-morrow at your usual hour I will expect you."

Miss Eldridge impressed on his cheek the kiss of filial affection, and obeyed.

CHAPTER XVIII.
REFLECTIONS.

"AND AM I indeed fallen so low," said Charlotte, "as to be only pitied? Will the voice of approbation no more meet my ear? and shall I never again possess a friend, whose face will wear a smile of joy whenever I approach? Alas! how thoughtless, how dreadfully imprudent have I been! I know not which is most painful to endure, the sneer of contempt, or the glance of compassion, which is depicted in the various countenances of my own sex: they are both equally humiliating. Ah! my dear parents, could you now see the child of your affections, the daughter whom you so dearly loved, a poor solitary being, without society, here wearing out her heavy hours in deep regret and anguish of heart, no kind friend of her own sex to whom she can unbosom her griefs, no beloved mother, no woman of character will appear in my company, and low as your Charlotte is fallen, she cannot associate with infamy."

These were the painful reflections which occupied the mind of Charlotte. Montraville had placed her in a small house a few miles from New-York: he gave her one female attendant, and supplied her with what money she wanted; but business and pleasure so entirely occupied his time, that he had little to devote to the woman, whom he had brought from all her connections, and robbed of innocence. Sometimes, indeed, he would steal out at the close of evening, and pass a few hours with her; and then so much was she attached to him, that all her sorrows were forgotten while blest with his society: she would enjoy a walk by moonlight, or sit by him in a little arbour at the bottom of the garden, and play on the harp, accompanying it with her plaintive, harmonious voice. But often, very often, did he promise to renew his visits, and, forgetful of his promise, leave her to mourn her disappointment. What painful hours of expectation would she pass! She would sit at a window which looked toward a field he used to cross, counting the minutes, and straining her eyes to catch the first glimpse of his person, till blinded with tears of disappointment, she would lean her head on her hands, and give free vent to her sorrows: then catching at some new hope, she would again renew her watchful position, till the shades of evening enveloped every object in a dusky cloud: she would then renew her complaints, and, with a heart bursting with disappointed love and wounded sensibility, retire to a bed which remorse had strewed with thorns, and court in vain that comforter of weary nature (who seldom visits the unhappy) to come and steep her senses in oblivion.

Who can form an adequate idea of the sorrow that preyed upon the mind of Charlotte? The wife, whose breast glows with affection to her husband, and who in return meets only indifference, can but faintly conceive her anguish. Dreadfully painful is the situation of such a woman, but she has many comforts of which our poor Charlotte was deprived. The duteous, faithful wife, though treated with indifference, has one solid pleasure within her own bosom, she can reflect that she has not deserved neglect—that she has ever fulfilled the duties of her station with the strictest exactness; she may hope, by constant assiduity and unremitted attention, to recall her wanderer, and be doubly happy in his returning affection; she knows he cannot leave her to unite himself to another: he cannot cast her out to poverty and contempt; she looks around her, and sees the smile of friendly welcome, or the tear of affectionate consolation, on the face of every person whom she favours with her esteem; and from all these circumstances she gathers comfort: but the poor girl by thoughtless passion led astray, who, in parting with her honour, has forfeited the esteem of the very man to whom she has sacrificed every thing dear and valuable in life, feels his indifference in the fruit of her own folly, and laments her want of power to recall his lost affection; she knows there is no tie but honour, and that, in a man who has been guilty of seduction, is but very feeble: he may leave her in a moment to shame and want; he may marry and forsake her for ever; and should he, she has no redress, no friendly, soothing companion to pour into her wounded mind the balm of consolation, no benevolent hand to lead her back to the path of rectitude; she has disgraced her friends, forfeited the good opinion of the world, and undone herself; she feels herself a poor solitary being in the midst of surrounding multitudes; shame bows her to the earth, remorse tears her distracted mind, and guilt, poverty, and disease close the dreadful scene: she sinks unnoticed to oblivion. The finger of contempt may point out to some passing daughter of youthful mirth, the humble bed where lies this frail sister of mortality; and will she, in the unbounded gaiety of her heart, exult in her own unblemished fame, and triumph over the silent ashes of the dead? Oh no! has she a heart of sensibility, she will stop, and thus address the unhappy victim of folly—

"Thou had'st thy faults, but sure thy sufferings have expiated them: thy errors brought thee to an early grave; but thou wert a fellow-creature—thou hast been unhappy—then be those errors forgotten."

Then, as she stoops to pluck the noxious weed from off the sod, a tear will fall, and consecrate the spot to Charity.

For ever honoured be the sacred drop of humanity; the angel of mercy shall record its source, and the soul from whence it sprang shall be immortal.

My dear Madam, contract not your brow into a frown of disapprobation. I mean not to extenuate the faults of those unhappy women who fall victims to guilt and folly; but surely, when we reflect how many errors we are ourselves subject to, how many secret faults lie hid in the recesses of our hearts, which we should blush to have brought into open day (and yet those faults require the lenity and pity of a benevolent judge, or awful would be our prospect of futurity) I say, my dear Madam, when we consider this, we surely may pity the faults of others.

Believe me, many an unfortunate female, who has once strayed into the thorny paths of vice, would gladly return to virtue, was any generous friend to endeavour to raise and re-assure her; but alas! it cannot be, you say; the world would deride and scoff. Then let me tell you, Madam, 'tis a very unfeeling world, and does not deserve half the blessings which a bountiful Providence showers upon it.

Oh, thou benevolent giver of all good! how shall we erring mortals dare to look up to thy mercy in the great day of retribution, if we now uncharitably refuse to overlook the errors, or alleviate the miseries, of our fellow-creatures.

JANE JOHNSTON SCHOOLCRAFT /
BAMEWAWAGEZHIKAQUAY
(c. 1770–1842)

First work by a Native American woman poet in circulated publication.

Jane Johnston Schoolcraft (her English name) or Bamewawagezhikaquay (her Ojibwe name, meaning "Woman of the Sound the Stars Make Rushing Through the Sky"), was born one of eight children in 1800 in Sault Ste. Marie in today's state of Michigan, then a cross-cultural hub of British, French, Canadian, and American Indian influence. Her mother, Ozhaguscodaywayquay, was born in Chequamegon in the mid 1770s in the northern part of what is now Wisconsin, the daughter of Waubojeeg, a renowned Ojibwe warrior and chief also known for his skills in storytelling and song. Johnston's Irish-born father, John Johnston, was a fur trader who greatly valued books. Jane was educated at home, reading widely and speaking and writing Ojibwe, English, and French. During a brief and difficult time spent with an aunt in Ireland, she may have briefly attended school there. In 1823 she married Henry Rowe Schoolcraft (1793-1864), whom she taught the Ojibwe language and who has become known as the first person to record a large body of American Indian stories. They had three children; but their firstborn, William Henry, died at age two, and one daughter was stillborn. The family lived in a large house befitting Henry's position as the U.S. Indian agent to the Michigan Territory, and Jane traveled several times to New York as well as Detroit. With Jane's assistance Henry self-published *The Literary Voyager, or Muzzeniegun*, which included some of Jane's writings without attribution. When Jane died unexpectedly in 1842, she had written literary prose pieces and poems, only a small number of which had appeared in the handwritten magazine produced by her husband.

She is the first known published American Indian literary writer, the first known Indian woman writer, the first known Indian poet, and the first known poet to write poems in a Native American language. A poet who wrote in at least two languages, navigated several cultures and expressed her pride of belonging to the Ojibwe (Chippewa) people in both English and Ojibwe poems, Jane Johnston Schoolcraft invites us to reconsider existing categories for understanding American and American Indian literacy. Her work has generated lively scholarly debates about the use of sentimental social values and literary conventions as legitimate vs. inauthentic self-expression.

[Language Divine, 1816]

Language divine! Thy aid impart
To breathe the feelings of the heart
That burns with sympathetic woe
For those whose tears incessant flow
Those, to whom fortune now doth prove
A tyrant stern, to him they love.
Sweet charity, now points the way
And I the summons must obey
Quickly thy magic flowers impart,
To soothe the broke and bleeding heart
To lull dispair into a calm
And make my every word a balm
To cheer the agonized breast
And point to heaven—a place of rest.

From The Literary Voyager, or Muzzeniegun [1826]

Pensive Hours

The sun had sunk like a glowing ball,
As lonely I sat in my father's hall;
I walk'd to the window, and musing awhile,
The still, pensive moments I sought to beguile:
Just by me, ran smoothly the dark deep stream,
And bright silver rays on its breast did beam;—
And as with mild luster the vestal orb rose,
All nature betokened a holy repose,

Save the Sound of St. Mary's—that softly and clear
Still fell in sweet murmurs upon my pleas'd ear
Like the murmur of voices we know to be kind,
Or war's silken banners unfurled to the wind,
Now rising, like shouts of the proud daring foe,
Now falling, like whispers congenial and low.
Amidst such a scene, thoughts arose in my mind;
Of my father, far distant—of life, and mankind;
But slowing, receding—with awe most profound
They rested on God, and his works spread around,
Divine meditation!—and tear drops like dew—
Now moisten'd my hand,—for His mercy I knew:
Since even a leaf cannot wither and die,
Unknown to his care, or unseen by his eye;
Oh how much more then, will he hear when we mourn,
And heal the pierced heart that by anguish is torn,
When he sees that the soul to His will loves to bend,
And patiently suffers and waits to the end.
Such thoughts—the lone moments serenely employed,
Creating contentment and peace unalloyed—
Till roused by my harp—which so tremblingly true,
The soft balmy night breeze enchantingly blew,
The sounds to my heart as they vibrated clear,
Thrill'd sweetly and carried the melody tried,
Softer and sweeter the harmony rings,
I fanceyed some spirit was touching the strings,
And answered, or seemed to my hopes, thus to say,
Let thy Soul live in hope, mortal:—watch still and pray.
A holy tranquility spread o'er my mind.
At peace with myself, with my God, and mankind.
I felt that my prayers were heard and approv'd,
For the speedy return of my father beloved;
For the health I so priz'd, but so seldom enjoyed.
That the time yet in store—should be wisely employed.
And my mind ever feel, as I felt at that time,
So pensively joyful, so humbly sublime.—

The Contrast

With pen in hand, I shall contrast,
The present moments with the past
And mark difference, not by grains,
But weighed by feelings, joys and pains.
Calm, tranquil—far from fashion's gaze,
Passed all my earliest, happy days
Sweetly flew the golden hours,
In St. Mary's woodland bowers
Or my father's simple hall,
Oped to whomsoe'er might call
Pains or cares we seldom knew
All the hours so peaceful flew
Concerts sweet we oft enjoyed,
Books our leisure time employed
Friends on every side appeared
From whose minds no ill I feared
If by chance, one gave me pain
The wish to wound me not again
Quick expressed in accents kind
Cast a joy throughout my mind
That, to have been a moment pained,
Seemed like bliss but just attained.
Whene'er in fault, to be reproved,
With gratitude my heart was moved,
So mild and gentle were their words
It seemed as soft as song of birds
For well I knew, that each behest,
Was warmed by love—convincing test.
Thus passed the morning of my days,
My only wish, to gain the praise
Of friends I loved, and neighbours kind,
And keep a calm and heavenly mind.
My efforts, kindly were received,
Nor grieved, nor was myself aggrieved.
But ah! how changed is every scene,
Our little hamlet, and the green,

The long rich green, where warriors played,
And often, breezy elm-wood shade.
How changed, since full of strife and fear,
The world hath sent its votaries here.
The tree cut down—the cot removed,
The cot the simple Indian loved,
The busy strife of young and old
To gain one sordid bit of gold
By trade's o'er done plethoric moil,
And lawsuits, meetings, courts and toil.
Adieu, to days of homebred ease,
When many a rural care could please,
We trim our sail anew, to steer
By shoals we never knew were here,
And with the star flag, raised on high
Discover a new dominion nigh,
And half in joy, half in fear,
Welcome the proud Republic here.

Invocation

*To my Maternal Grand-father on hearing his descent
from Chippewa ancestors misrepresented*

Rise bravest chief! of the mark of the noble deer,
With eagle glance,
Resume thy lance,
And wield again thy warlike spear!
The foes of thy line,
With coward design,
Have dared with black envy to garble the truth,
And stain with a falsehood thy valorous youth.

They say when a child, thou wert ta'en from the Sioux,
And with impotent aim,
To lessen thy fame
Thy warlike lineage basely abuse;
For they know that our band,
Tread a far distant land,

And thou noble chieftain art nerveless and dead,
Thy bow all unstrung, and thy proud spirit fled.
Can the sports of thy youth, or thy deeds ever fade?
Or those e'er forget,
Who are mortal men yet,
The scenes where so bravely thou'st lifted the blade,
Who have fought by thy side,
And remember thy pride,
When rushing to battle, with valour and ire,
Thou saw'st the fell foes of thy nation expire?

Can the warrior forget how sublimely you rose?
Like a star in the west,
When the sun's sunk to rest,
That shines in bright splendour to dazzle our foes?
Thy arm and thy yell,
Once the tale could repel
Which slander invented, and minions detail,
And still shall thy actions refute the false tale.

Rest thou, noblest chief! in thy dark house of clay,
Thy deeds and thy name,
Thy child's child shall proclaim,
And make the dark forests resound with the lay;
Though thy spirit has fled,
To the hills of the dead,
Yet thy name shall be held in my heart's warmest core,
And cherish'd till valour and love be no more.

To the Pine Tree
*On first seeing it
on returning from Europe*

Shing wauk! Shing wauk! Nin ge ik id,
Waish kee wau bum ug, shing wauk
Tuh quish in aun nau aub, ain dak nuk i yaun.
Shing wauk, shing wauk No sa
Shi e gwuh ke do dis au naun
Kau gega way zhau wus co zid.

Mes ah nah, shi egwuh tah gwish en aung
Sin da mik ke aum baun
Kag ait she, ne meen wain dum
Me nah wau, wau bun dah maun
Git yut wi au, wau bun dah maun een
Shing wauk, shing wauk nosa
Shi e gwuh ke do dis au naun.

Ka ween ga go, kau wau bun duh e yun
Tib isht co, izz henau gooz ze no an
Shing wauk wah zhau wush co zid
Ween Ait ah kwanaudj e we we
Kau ge gay wa zhau soush ko zid

Translation

The pine! the pine! I eager cried,
The pine, my father! see it stand,
As first that cherished tree I spied,
Returning to my native land.
The pine! the pine! oh lovely scene!
The pine, that is forever green.

Ah beauteous tree! ah happy sight!
That greets me on my native strand
And hails me, with a friend's delight,
To my own dear bright mother land
Oh 'tis to me a heart-sweet scene,
The pine—the pine! that's ever green.

Not all the trees of England bright,
Not Erin's lawns of green and light
Are half so sweet to memory's eye,
As this dear type of northern sky
Oh 'tis to me a heart-sweet scene,
The pine—the pine! that ever green.

To my ever beloved and lamented Son William Henry

Who was it, nestled on my breast,
"And on my cheek sweet kisses prest"

And in whose smile I felt so blest?
    Sweet Willy.
Who hail'd my form as home I stept,
And in my arms so eager leapt,
And to my bosom joyous crept?
    My Willy.
Who was it, wiped my tearful eye,
And kiss'd away the coming sigh,
And smiling bid me say "good boy"?
    Sweet Willy.
Who was it, looked divinely fair,
Whilst lisping sweet the evening pray'r,
Guileless and free from earthly care?
    My Willy.
Where is that voice attuned to love,
That bid me say "my darling dove"?
But oh! that soul has flown above,
    Sweet Willy.
Whither has fled the rose's hue?
The lilly's whiteness blending grew,
Upon thy cheek—so fair to view.
    My Willy.
Oft have I gaz'd with rapt delight,
Upon those eyes that sparkled bright,
Emitting beams of joy and light!
    Sweet Willy.
Oft have I kiss'd that forehead high,
Like polished marble to the eye,
And blessing, breathed an anxious sigh.
    For Willy.
My son! thy coral lips are pale,
Can I believe the heart-sick tale,
That I, thy loss must ever wail?
    My Willy.
The clouds in darkness seemed to low'r,
The storm has past with awful pow'r,
And nipt my tender, beauteous flow'r!
    Sweet Willy.

But soon my spirit will be free,
And I, my lovely Son shall see,
For God, I know, did this decree!
    My Willy.

RESIGNATION

How hard to teach the heart, opprest with grief;
Amid gay, worldly scenes, to find relief;
And the long cherish'd bliss we had in view,
To banish from the mind where first it grew!
But Faith, in time, can sweetly soothe the soul,
And Resignation hold a mild control;
The mind may then resume a proper tone,
And calmly think on hopes forever flown.

"S"

First published work of fiction by an African American author.

Little is known about the identity of the person who wrote what is considered the first short story by an African American author. The story was serialized in four installments in *Freedom's Journal*, the first African American owned and operated newspaper published in the United States, which appeared out of New York from 1827 to 1829. The paper included news items, political editorials, essays, poems, and several pieces of fiction, many of which were signed only by letters or pseudonyms. Its explicit purpose was to let African Americans participate in public discourse on their own terms: "We wish to plead our own cause. Too long have others spoken for us." Based on this editorial policy, it is assumed that "S" is an African American author. Since "S," the signature used for this story, had appeared in other issues of *Freedom's Journal* under other pieces on topics such as racial equality, African history, and women, some scholars assume that the author was a woman. Other scholars believe that "S" is the pseudonym for Prince Saunders (1775–1839), a diplomat and author who published *Haytian Papers* while an advisor to King Henry I of Haiti, who ruled Haiti as its only monarch from 1807–1811. Others offer the possibility that the story was written by James McCune Smith (1813–1865), an author and physician who was also mentor to Frederick Douglass. The story was redis-covered by pioneering scholar Frances Smith Foster.

The dramatic story tells the tale of a mother with two grown daughters caught in the violence of the Haitian revolution as French troops are trying to put down an insurrection of Black slaves led by Toussaint L'Ouverture, who features in the story. The widowed Madame Paulina, a free woman of color, has raised her daughters out of harm's way thus far, which means she has hidden them away from white men who feel entitled to rape Black women. But when her native village is invaded by French troops, Madame

Paulina must flee the enemy and find safety with the revolutionaries. She procures false papers to secure passage but before she can reach safety, French troops appear. A desperate, on-the-spot decision seems to work when the mother dresses in a French soldier's uniform and presents her daughters as prisoners. Fooling the French troops for a moment, she gains valuable information that can help the revolutionaries. Without her mother's consent, Theresa risks her life to convey this vital information to Toussaint L'Ouverture. Acting against the prevailing ideals of woman-hood and daughterly obedience, Theresa succeeds in breaking through the enemy lines and providing the intelligence to the rebels, thus changing the fate of Haiti's Revolution. But when she seeks her mother and sister, they have vanished. Fearing the worst and thinking that she has sacrificed her family to save her people, the story's heroine despairs, before another turn of events ends the gripping tale.

THERESA: A HAYTIEN TALE [1828]

DURING THE LONG and bloody contest, in St. Domingo, between the white man, who flourished the child of sensuality, rioting on the miseries of his slaves; had the sons of Africa, who, provoked to madness, and armed themselves against French barbarity; Madame Paulina was left a widow, unhappy—unprotected, and exposed to all the horrors of the revolution. Not without much unhappiness, she saw that if she would save her life from the inhumanity of her country's enemy, she must depart from the endeared *village* of her innocent childhood; still dear to her, though now it was become a theatre of many tragic scenes. The once verdant plains, round its environs had been crimsoned with the blood of innocence, and the nature of the times afforded no security to the oppressed natives of Saint Nicholas.

Famine which had usurped the place of plenty and happiness, with her associate security, were banished from the humble dwellings of the injured Haytiens.

After much unpleasant reflections on her pitiable situation, Madame Paulina resolved to address a letter, soliciting the advice of her brother, then at Cape Marie', and at the head of a party of his patriot brethren, who like him, disdained slavery, and were determined to live as free men, or expire in their attempts for liberty and *independence*. But reason had scarce approved this suggestion of her mind, when suddenly she heard a simultaneous volley of musketry, and the appalling roaring of heavy artillery rumbling along the mountain's ridge, like terrifying *thunders*; to this distant warfare, the lapse of fifteen minutes brought a cessation, which announced, that on either side, many that were, had ceased to be. Silence having ensued, there was a stillness in the air. All at Saint Nicholas, desirous to know the issue of the combat, remained in doubtful anxiety.

Each one's heart was the abode of fear and doubt, while the dense smoke, escaping the *despot's* fury, and evading the implacable resentment of those armed in the justice of their cause, was seen to overtop the dusky hills, winding its way upwards in sulphureous columns, as if, to supplicate at the *Eternal's Throne*, and plead the cause of the injured.

The *French* in this combat with the Revolutionists, suffered much, both from the extreme sultriness of the day, and the courage of those with whom they contended; disappointed and harrassed by the Islanders; they thought it a principle of policy, to resort to acts of cruelty; and to intimidate them, resolved, that none of them should be spared; but that the sword should annihilate, or compel them to submit to their wonted degradations; and St. Nicholas was the unfortunate village, first to be devoted to the resentful rage of the cruel enemy. All the natives were doomed to suffer; the mother and the infant that reposed on her bosom, fell by the same sword, while groans of the sick served only as the guides which discovered them to the inhumanity of the inexorable, at whose hands they met a miserable death.

The sun was fast receding to the west, as if ashamed of man's transactions, boasting itself in the dark mantle of twilight, when Gen. Leclerc, fired the few dwellings, then remaining in the village. Misery was now grabbed in her most terrifying robes, and *terror* possessed itself the heart of all, except the *French*, in whose hands were placed the weapons of destruction.

The intelligence of the defeat of the army recently stationed at Cape Marie, reached the ears of the unhappy Paulina, and with horror she heard that her beloved brother in his attempt to regain St. Nicholas, breathed out his valuable life in the cause of freedom, and for his country. But it was now no time to indulge in grief—Safety was the object of the wretched villagers.

To effect an escape from the horrors of this ominous night, was difficult in the extreme; for the passes leading out into the country were all occupied by the enemy's troops, who were not only vigilant, but relentless and cruel. Madame Paulina apprehended her own danger, but her greatest solicitude was for the safety of her daughters, who in the morning of life, were expanding, like the foilages of the rose into elegance and beauty. She had kept them long concealed from the knowledge of the enemy, whose will she knew was their law, and whose law was injustice—the mother's wretchedness, and the daughter's shame and ruin. In happier days, when peace blessed her native island, she had seen a small hut, during a summer's excursion, in an unfrequented spot, in the delightful valley of Vega Real, and on the eastern bank of the beautiful Yuma; and now she resolved if possible, to retreat thither with both her daughters.

Necessity being the source of human inventions, was now ready to commune with her mind on subjects of moment, and to give birth to the events of its decision—and in the midst of the general uproar in which the village now was—The shrieks of the defenceless, the horrible clashing of arms, and the expiring groans of the aged, Paulina hurried herself in the execution of her plans for escaping.

With a feigned passport and letter, she ingeniously contrived to pass out of the village conducting her daughters, like the pious Aeneas, through all the horrors, in which St. Nicholas was now involved.

But though protected by the mantle of night, Madame was hastening on her way to safety and quiet; she frequently would turn her eyes bathed with the dew of sorrow, and heave her farewell sigh towards her ill-fated village; and like Lot when departing out of Sodom, Paulina prayed for mercy for the enemies of her country, and the destroyers of her peace. She and her daughters, driven by cruel ambition, from their peaceful abodes were wretched. Their souls were occupied by fearful doubts and anxiety. Every whisper of the winds among the leaves of the plantain and orange trees, caused her daughters to apprehend the approach of danger, and she to heave the anxious sigh.

The green lizard crossed not the road in the way to its hole, at the noise of the fugitives feet, but they beheld through the shade of the night a body of the enemy; the distant glare of the firefly, was a light which pointed to the enemies camps; while the bat beating the [...] in its nocturnal ranges, often was the false messenger of danger to the fair adventurers. Every *tree* kissed by the zephyrs, that ruffled its leaves, was an army approaching, and in the trunk of every decored mahogany, was seen a *Frenchman* in ambush—not less alarming to the fugitives, were the ripe fruit that frequently fell to the earth. Then having turned into a by-path, Paulina felt herself more secure; and with a soul oppressed with mingled grief and joy, she with maternal affection embraced her daughters, and observed to them, that however just may be the cause which induces us to practice *duplicity*, or the laudable object which gives birth to hypocrisy. Truth alone can make us happy, and prevent the *Internal Judge* of the human mind, filling us with fearful apprehensions, and painting to our imaginations the result which would attend detection.

Morning had just began to peep forth, and the golden rays of the returning sun were seen to burnish the tops of the majestic cibiao mountains, when the bewildered adventurers were suddenly startled by the shrill blast of a bugle; their surprise was not less than their wretchedness, when at no great distance, they beheld approaching them a detachment of the enemy's cavalry. At this unexpected crisis Madame Paulina, overcome with fearful apprehensions, trembled lest she should be wanting in the discharge of her difficult undertaking. But it was now too late; she must either act well her part or be reconducted by the foe to St. Nicholas, and there, after witnessing the destruction of those for whose happiness she was more concerned than for her own, receive a cruel and ignominious death.

The party of horsemen being now very near, she gave some necessary instructions to her daughters, and conducted them onward with no little confidence in her success. The *lieutenant,* by whom the French were commanded, observing her attired in the uniform of a French officer, took her for what she so well affected to be—(a captain of the French army) he made to her the order of the day, and enquired the time she left St. Nicholas, and whether conducting the two prisoners, (for Paulina had the presence of mind to disguise her *daughters* as such) she replied, and taking forth her letter, she handed it to the lieutenant. Succeeding thus far admirably, our adventuress was led to make some enquiries relative to the welfare of the French troops, stationed west of St. Nicholas, and having collected much valuable information, they parted, and Madame Paulina favoured by a ready address, and with much fortitude, escaped death—conducting the dear objects of her tender solicitude far, from the ill-fated village of their infancy.

Being informed by the lieutenant, that at the distance of a few miles, there were encamped a company of the French, she thought it judicious to avoid all public roads, and having turned into a thick grove of the Pimento trees, she proposed to her *daughters* to rest in this spot until darkness again should unfold her mantle.

In this grove of quiet security, the troubled souls of the fugitives ceased partially to be oppressed with fear—the milky juice of the cocoanut allayed their thirst and moistened their parched *lips*, and the delicious orange, and luxurious mango, in spontaneous abundance, yielded a support to their nearly exhausted natures.

Madame Paulina and her daughters were now seated under the shade of a majestic spreading *Guava*. The day was fast declining, and though the heat of July was intensely oppressive; in this secluded spot, the air was rendered fragrant with the variety of arometic shrubs, that grew spontaneously in this grove of peace. The hummingbird skipping capriciously from blossom to blossom, displayed its magnificent plumage, and for a while diverted the minds of the unhappy fugitives from grief and from ominous forbodings; wearied and fatigued by a journey which was not less tiresome than hazardous, their much exhausted natures, were greatly refreshed by the cool breeze which gave to their whole bodies a calm sensation, in which their souls soon participated and Madame and her eldest daughter were now lost in the arms of sleep, the kind restorer of vigour to the minds and bodies of men. All around was now still, save the western woodpecker was heard at times to peck the hollow trunk of some decayed tree, or the distant roaring of heavy cannon, which announced that all creative beings were born to enjoy peace, but man, who stimulated by ambition, is more cruel than the beasts of the forest, which soil he ever renders fertile with the blood of his victims. But Mademoiselle Theresa, the youngest of the three adventurers, greeted not sleep. The vigour of her body was indeed much exhausted, but the emotions of her mind were more active than ever; she saw with the mind's eye the great services which might be rendered to her country; she brought to her imagination the once delightful fields of her native Hayti, now dy'd with the blood of her countrymen in their righteous struggle for liberty and for independence.

Not less did she contemplate the once flourishing plantations ruined and St. Domingo, once the granary of the West Indies, reduced to famine, now the island of misery, and the abode of wretchedness.

It was but the last night, that she witnessed the most terrifying scenes of her life—when the shrieks of her dying friends made her apprehend justly what her own fate must be, should she fail to effect an escape from the village of her happiest days. Theresa thought of the brave St. Clair; she imagined she saw her beloved uncle weltering in his blood, and the barbarous French fixing his venerable head on a pole, and it exposed on a cross road, as the head of a rebel. She shuddered at this thought; her soul was subdued, and the fount of grief issued from her eyes in copious streams, bathing her febrile cheeks with the dews of sorrow. Why, said she, O, my God! hast thou suffered thy creatures to be thus afflicted in all thy spacious earth? Are not we too thy children? And didst thou not cover us with this sable exterior, by which our race is distinguished, and for which they are contemned and ever been cruelly persecuted! O, my God!—my God!—be propitious to the cause of justice—Be near to the Haytiens in their righteous struggle, to obtain those rights which thou hast graciously bestowed on all thy children. Raise up some few of those, who have been long degraded—give to them dominion, and enable them to govern a state of their own—so that the proud and cruel may know that thou art alike the Father of the native of the burning desert, and of the more temperate, region.

It was in the presence of Theresa that the conversation between M. L'Motelle and her heroic mother took place. Madame Paulina, on her part leaving nothing undone, which might serve to accomplish the object for which she had been induced to practice duplicity; M. L'Motelle regarded her for what she really appeared to be; and unhesitatingly spoke of matters concerning the nature of the times; of the military and local situations of the French troops: their condition and strength were topics of interest; and Theresa learned that the distance to the camp of the brave Touissant L'Ouverture, was a single league from the place where he communicated the intelligence. Seeming to be inattentive, she pensively bent her eyes towards the earth, listening the while as he unconsciously developed many military schemes, which were about being executed, and if successful, would, in all probability, terminate in the destruction of the Revolutionists, and, in the final success of the French power in this island. These were invaluable discoveries, and could they be made known in due time to those against whose rights their injustice was intended, it would not fail to give success to Haytien independence, disappoint the arch-enemy, and aid the cause of humanity. But, alas! important as they were to the cause of freedom, by whom shall they be carried.

Who shall reveal them to the Revolutionists: No one interested was near, and they were in the possession of none friendly to the cause of justice, except the three defenceless ones. Theresa herself must be the bearer, or survive only to witness them executed agreeably to the desires of the enemy. In what manner must she act? The salvation of her oppressed country to her, was an object of no little concern; but she also owed a duty to that mother, whose tender solicitude for her happiness, could not be surpassed by any parent, and a sister too, whom she tenderly loved, and whose attachment to her was undivided. Her absence from the grove, she was confidently

assured, would be to them their greatest source of affliction; it would probably terminate the already much exhausted life of her dear mother, and
complete the measure of Amanda's wretchedness. Her own inexperience
in the manner, she should conduct in an affair so important and hazardous, was an obstacle which in connexion with her sense of duty, and care
for her mother's happiness, would deter her from embarking in it. She
paused, then as if aroused by some internal agent, exclaimed, "Oh Hayti!—
be independent, and let Theresa be the unworthy sacrifice offered to that
God, who shall raise his mighty arm in defence of thy injured children. She
drew from her bosom a pencil and wrote on a piece of bark of the Gourd
tree, telling her mother and Amanda, whither she was gone—her errand;
begged that, they would not be unhappy on account of her absence; that
they would remain at their place of peace and quiet, until she should return
to them with an escort, who should conduct them to a safer retreat, and
commit them to the protection of friends. This scroll, Theresa pinned on
her mother's coat, while she and Amanda were yet indulging in repose, and
like an heroine of the age of chivalry, she forsook the grove of Pimento and
hastened on her way to the camp of L'Ouverture. She had scarce reached
the third part of her journey, when her mother dreaming, that one of her
daughters had been borne off by an officer of the enemy, awoke from sleep
and missing Theresa, believed her dream prophetic. It was now that the
keenest anguish filled her soul. Paulina wished not to live. Life to a mother
thus sorely afflicted, is misery—she would go in search of the dear object
of all her affliction, but where, she knew not. Keen is the grief of a mother,
whose child has been forced from her. She is extremely wretched, and her
affliction then, cannot be less severe, than it was when in the anguish and
sorrow of her soul, the dear object of her tenderest solicitude was introduced into the world, to take its station among the Probationers for eternity. Amanda was now awakened by the unhappy and pitiful grief of her
bewildered mother. Hastily she enquired for her sister; Paulina in a burst
of grief and wild despair, told her, she had been borne off while they slept;
with half articulated accents, she related her ominous dream, and the fact
was now realized in her absence from the grove. An icy chillness pervaded
her whole nature—a dark mist covered her eyes—all the objects by which
she was surrounded seemed to recede—her senses were bewildered, and
Amanda, unobserved by her mother, swooned and fell to the earth. But
soon recovering, she beheld the piece of Gourd bark pinned to the skirt
of her mother's coat—she hastened to unpin—it was the hand writing

of Theresa—they read it with avidity—joyful in the happy discovery, the mother and the daughter embraced each other. From neither, words found utterance. Silence was perched upon their tongues, while the tears of mingled joy and sorrow poured from their eyes; The troubles of their souls were greatly subsided, but happiness could not be restored, until the success of Theresa be ascertained, and she again be encircled in their arms.

It was uncertain whether she could in safety reach the camp of the Revolutionists; the roads were at all times travelled by reconnoitering parties of the French; and what would be the fate of the heroic Theresa, if taken by any of them! How cruel would be her usage, particularly, if her intentions and the circumstances, which gave them birth be known. Death inevitable would deprive the world of one so fair, virtuous, and so noble.

Such were the thoughts of the mother and sister of the noble adventuress. But while they were thus grieving, Theresa, favoured by fortune, had safely arrived at the military quarters of the great Toussaint: had communicated to the chieftain the object of her visit to his camp, and was receiving all the distinctions due her exalted virtue, and which her dauntless resolution so justly merited.

The sun was now fast receding behind the lofty Cibao, whose rugged summits in the morning, appeared burnished by its resplendent rays, and darkness was out-stretching here spacious mantle. The orange and citron groves, and all the rich enameled luxuriance of torrid luxuries, now began to wear a sombre aspect, while the chattering Paroquet ceased to imitate man, and disturb the sweets of solitude, with prating garrulity, had retired to her roost on the sturdy logwood. Now it was, that Theresa, under a strong military escort, left the general's camp of hospitality, retracing her steps towards the grove of Pimento, where, at her departure, she left her dear mother and Amanda, enjoying calm repose; seated in a close carriage, her thoughts reverted to the deplorable state of her country; with a prophetic eye she saw the destruction of the French, and their final expulsion from her native island. She entreated the Creator, that he would bless the means, which through her agency, he had been pleased to put in the possession of her too long oppressed countrymen, and that all might be made useful to the cause of freedom. But turning her thoughts toward her mother and sister, Theresa was conscious, that her absence from the grove could not fail to have given them extreme sorrow and unhappiness; her gentle nature recoiled at the recollection, and she gave way to a flood of tears. But recollecting again the important services, she had rendered her aggrieved country and to the Haytien people—the objects which prompted her to disobedience, which induced her to overstep the bounds of modesty, and expose to immediate dangers her life and sex. She felt that her conduct was exculpated, and self-reproach was lost in the consciousness of her laudable efforts to save St. Domingo. Her noble soul re-animated, recovered its wonted calm, as the ocean its quiet motion when the gentle breeze, and the returned sunshine, succeed a tempestuous sky and boisterous winds.

Fated to experience trials, she was now to be made more wretched than ever. St. Lewis was now near the forward progressing company of his brethren in arms. He had been despatched to the Pimento grove, to acquaint Madame Paulina and Amanda of the approach of their dear Theresa. But, alas! by whom, or how was the doleful news to be reported to the heroine? Her mother and sister were not to be found at the place where she had left them: and who shall keep the shocking intelligence from her! Already she saw him approaching; he was now near. She observed the gloomy melancholy, which settled on his brow, that plainly foretold all were not well. She inquired into the result of his journey to the grove, and as an earthquake rends the bosom of the earth, so the intelligence her gentle soul.

"Oh! Theresa!—Theresa!" said she in bitter grief, "thou art the murderer of a mother and a loving sister! Where! where shall I hide me from the displeasure of heaven and the curse of man!—Oh, matricide! matricide! whither shalt thou flee from thy accusing conscience! In life I shall be wretched, and after death, oh! who shall release this soul from the bonds of self-condemnation! Oh my affectionate mother! Hast Theresa rewarded thee thus, for thy tender solicitude for her; was it for this, that thou saved me from the devouring flames of my native St. Nicholas! Was it for this, that thou didst exert all thy ingenuity, and saved me from the uplifted sword of the enemy of St. Domingo!—Oh God! forgive this matricide! Forgive Theresa, who to save her country, sacrificed a mother and a sister—Wretched Amanda! and thrice wretched is thy sister, who devoted thee to misery and death!"

The body of escorts were now arrived at the Pimento grove—Theresa sprang from her carriage; hastened to the place where her mother and sister reposed at her departure. She cried in the anguish of her soul, "My mother, my mother! where art thou!—Come forth—let Theresa embrace thee to her wretched bosom. Come Amanda! dear Amanda, come, and save thy loving sister from black despair!"

"Where, cruel enemy, where have ye conducted them! If ye have murdered my dear mother and sister, let Theresa but embrace their clayey bodies, and while I bless the enemies of the Haytiens!" But her grief was unheard by those, the loss of whom she bitterly deplored; solemn silence occupied the grove, interrupted only by intervals with the moans and sobs of the men of arms, who marked her anguish of soul, and were absorbed into pity. Whither now shall Theresa bend her steps! No kind mother to guide her in life, or affectionate sister, to whom to impart the sorrow of her soul, or participate with in innocent pleasure; friendless and disconsolate, she was now left exposed to many evils, and at a time too when the assiduous care of a mother was most essential in the preservation of her well being. Theresa was on her way back to the camp of the kind Touissant L'Ouverture to claim his fatherly protection, and seek a home in the bosom of those, to whom she had rendered herself dear by her wisdom and virtue. The trampling of many horses was heard rapidly approaching, and bending its way towards the same direction. It was a party of the French troops, and she was now to witness war in all its horrors. The enemy of Haytien freedom was now near. The war trumpet now sounded the terrible blast for the engagement, and the Revolutionists like lions, rushed on to the fight with a simultaneous cry of "Freedom or Death!" The French, great in number, fought in obedience to a cruel master. The Haytiens for liberty and independence, and to obtain their rights of which they long have been unjustly deprived.

The pass between the Mole and the village St. Nicholas, drank up the lives of hundreds in their blood. The French retreated with precipitance, leaving their baggage with their gasping friends, on the spot where victory perched on the standard of freedom: And now the conquerors had began to examine the property deserted by the vanquished. A faint but mournful groan issued from a baggage cart forsaken by the enemy; directed by the light of a flambeau, captain Inginac bent thither his nimble steps. Curiosity is lost in surprise—joy succeeds sorrow—the lost ones are regained. It was Madame Paulina and Amanda, the mother and sister of the unhappy THERESA.

GEORGE MOSES HORTON (1798–after 1867)

First African American to publish a book in the American South.

George Moses Horton was born one of ten children into slavery in Northhampton County, North Carolina. His parents' identities are not known, and his family was divided by their enslavers when he was about fourteen years old. He remained enslaved to three generations of the Horton family. He taught himself to read and around 1815 started charging for made-to-order poems while selling produce in a local market to shoppers and university students who also provided him with books. A group of supporters tried but failed to raise funds to buy Horton's freedom by sponsoring his first book, *The Hope of Liberty. Containing a Number of Poetical Pieces* (1829), transcribed by a local novelist. Horton learned to write in 1832, before North Carolina outlawed teaching Black people to read and write, and paid his owner for free time, during which he wrote poetry and worked as a servant and handyman at the local university. During the 1830s, he married Martha Snipes, an enslaved woman (the marriage was not legally sanctioned or recognized), and they had two children, Free and Rhody. In 1845 he published *The Poetical Works of George M. Horton, The Colored Bard of North Carolina To Which Is Prefixed the Life of the Author Written by Himself* and petitioned unsuccessfully for his release from slavery. After the end of the Civil War, Horton published a collection of poems, *Naked Genius*, several of them about the war. He went to Philadelphia in 1865 or 1866 but became disillusioned when he encountered the segregation and racism of the North. No reliable information exists about his final years. Some biographers claim Horton emigrated to the West African republic of Liberia in 1866 while others say he died in Philadelphia, or in North Carolina in 1880. Horton is the first African American author to publish a book of poetry in its first edition in the United States, fifty years after Phillis Wheatley published her book in London before the nation's founding; the first American to protest his enslavement in verse; and the only enslaved person to publish two books before emancipation and one after. His poems are valued for their subtle rhetoric of protest, remarkable range of topics, and for Horton's creative adaptation of existing literary styles.

From THE HOPE OF LIBERTY [1829] *and* POETICAL WORKS [1845]

ON LIBERTY AND SLAVERY

Alas! and am I born for this,
    To wear this slavish chain?
Deprived of all created bliss,
    Through hardship, toil and pain!

How long have I in bondage lain,
    And languished to be free!
Alas! and must I still complain—
    Deprived of liberty.

Oh, Heaven! and is there no relief
    This side the silent grave—
To soothe the pain—to quell the grief
    And anguish of a slave?

Come Liberty, thou cheerful sound,
    Roll through my ravished ears!
Come, let my grief in joys be drowned,
    And drive away my fears.

Say unto foul oppression, Cease:
    Ye tyrants rage no more,
And let the joyful trump of peace,
    Now bid the vassal soar.

Soar on the pinions of that dove
    Which long has cooed for thee,
And breathed her notes from Afric's grove,
    The sound of Liberty.

Oh, Liberty! thou golden prize,
    So often sought by blood—

We crave thy sacred sun to rise,
    The gift of nature's God:

Bid Slavery hide her haggard face,
    And barbarism fly:
I scorn to see the sad disgrace
    In which enslaved I lie.

Dear Liberty! upon thy breast,
    I languish to respire;
And like the Swan unto her nest,
    I'd to thy smiles retire.

Oh, blest asylum—heavenly balm!
    Unto thy boughs I flee—
And in thy shades the storm shall calm,
    With songs of Liberty!

LOVE

Whilst tracing thy visage I sink in emotion,
    For no other damsel so wond'rous I see;
Thy looks are so pleasing, thy charms so amazing,
    I think of no other, my true-love, but thee.

With heart-burning rapture I gaze on thy beauty,
    And fly like a bird to the boughs of a tree;
Thy looks are so pleasing, thy charms so amazing,
    I fancy no other, my true-love, but thee.

Thus oft in the valley I think, and I wonder
    Why cannot a maid with her lover agree?
Thy looks are so pleasing, thy charms so amazing,
    I pine for no other, my true-love, but thee.

I'd fly from thy frowns with a heart full of sorrow—
    Return, pretty damsel, and smile thou on me;
By every endeavor, I'll try thee forever,
    And languish until I am fancied by thee.

The Slave's Complaint

Am I sadly cast aside,
On misfortune's rugged tide?
Will the world my pains deride
    Forever?

Must I dwell in Slavery's night,
And all pleasure take its flight,
Far beyond my feeble sight,
    Forever?

Worst of all, must Hope grow dim,
And withhold her cheering beam?
Rather let me sleep and dream
    Forever!

Something still my heart surveys,
Groping through this dreary maze;
Is it Hope?—then burn and blaze
    Forever!

Leave me not a wretch confined,
Altogether lame and blind—
Unto gross despair consigned,
    Forever!

Heaven! in whom can I confide?
Canst thou not for all provide?
Condescend to be my guide
    Forever:

And when this transient life shall end,
Oh, may some kind eternal friend
Bid me from servitude ascend,
    Forever!

On Hearing of the Intention of a Gentleman to Purchase the Poet's Freedom

When on life's ocean first I spread my sail,

I then implored a mild auspicious gale;
And from the slippery strand I took my flight,
And sought the peaceful haven of delight.

Tyrannic storms arose upon my soul,
And dreadful did their mad'ning thunders roll;
The pensive muse was shaken from her sphere,
And hope, it vanish'd in the clouds of fear.

At length a golden sun broke thro' the gloom,
And from his smiles arose a sweet perfume—
A calm ensued, and birds began to sing,
And lo! the sacred muse resumed her wing.

With frantic joy she chaunted as she flew,
And kiss'd the clement hand that bore her thro'
Her envious foes did from her sight retreat,
Or prostrate fall beneath her burning feet.

'Twas like a proselyte, allied to Heaven—
Or rising spirits' boast of sins forgiven,
Whose shout dissolves the adamant away
Whose melting voice the stubborn rocks obey.

'Twas like the salutation of the dove,
Borne on the zephyr thro' some lonesome grove,
When Spring returns, and Winter's chill is past,
And vegetation smiles above the blast.

'Twas like the evening of a nuptial pair,
When love pervades the hour of sad despair—
'Twas like fair Helen's sweet return to Troy,
When every Grecian bosom swell'd with joy.

The silent harp which on the osiers hung,
Was then attuned, and manumission sung:
Away by hope the clouds of fear were driven,
And music breathed my gratitude to heaven.

Hard was the race to reach the distant goal,
The needle oft was shaken from the pole;
In such distress, who could forbear to weep?

Toss'd by the headlong billows of the deep!

The tantalizing beams which shone so plain,
Which turn'd my former pleasures into pain—
Which falsely promised all the joys of fame,
Gave way, and to a more substantial flame.

Some philanthropic souls as from afar,
With pity strove to break the slavish bar;
To whom my floods of gratitude shall roll,
And yield with pleasure to their soft control.

And sure of Providence this work begun—
He shod my feet this rugged race to run;
And in despite of all the swelling tide,
Along the dismal path will prove my guide.

Thus on the dusky verge of deep despair,
Eternal Providence was with me there;
When pleasure seemed to fade on life's gay dawn,
And the last beam of hope was almost gone.

DIVISION OF AN ESTATE

It well bespeaks a man beheaded, quite
Divested of the laurel robe of life,
When every member struggles for its base,
The head; the power of order now recedes,
Unheeded efforts rise on ev'ry side,
With dull emotion rolling thro' the brain
Of apprehending slaves. The flocks and herds,
In sad confusion, now run to and fro,
And seem to ask, distressed, the reason why
That they are thus prostrated. Howl, ye dogs!
Ye cattle, low! ye sheep, astonish'd bleat!
Ye bristling swine, trudge squealing thro' the glades,
Void of an owner to impart your food!
Sad horses, lift your heads and neigh aloud,
And caper, frantic, from the dismal scene;
Mow the last food upon your grass clad lea,

And leave a solitary home behind.
In hopeless widowhood, no longer gay,
The trav'ling sun of gain his journey ends;
In unavailing pain; he sets with tears—
A King, sequester'd, sinking from his throne;
Succeeded by a train of busy friends,
Like stars which rise with smiles to mark the flight
Of awful Phoebus to another world.
Stars after stars in fleet succession rise;
Into the wide empire of fortune cleave,
Regardless of the donor of their lamps,
Like heirs forgetful of parental care,
Redound in rev'rence to expiring age.
But soon parental benediction flies
Like vivid meteors in a moment gone,
As though they ne'er had been, but O! the state,
The dark suspense in which poor vassals stand,
Each mind upon the spire of chance hangs, fluctuate;
The day of separation is at hand;
Imagination lifts her gloomy curtain
Like ev'ning's mantle at the flight of day,
Thro' which the trembling pinnacle we spy,
On which we soon must stand with hopeful smiles,
Or apprehending frowns to tumble on
The right or left forever.

On an Old Deluded Suitor

See sad deluded love in years too late,
With tears desponding o'er the tombs of fate;
While dusky evening's veil excludes the light,
Which in the morning broke upon his sight.
He now regrets his vain, his fruitless plan,
And sadly wonders at the faults of man;
'Tis now from beauty's torch he wheels aside,
And strives to soar above affection's tide;
'Tis now that sorrow feeds the worm of pain
With tears which never can the loss regain;

'Tis now he drinks the wormwood and the gall,
And all the sweets of early pleasures pall;
When from his breast the hope of fortune flies,
The songs of transport languish into sighs.
Fond lovely rose that beamed as she blew,
Of all the charms of youth the most untrue;
She with delusive smiles prevail'd to move
This silly heart into the snares of love.
Then like a flower closed against the bee,
Folds her arms and turns her back on me;
When on my fancy's eye her smile she shed,
The torch by which deluded love was led.
Then like a lark from boyhood's maze I soared,
And thus in song her flattering smiles adored;
My heart was then by fondling love betray'd,
A thousand pleasures bloomed but soon to fade;
From joy to joy my heart exulting flew,
In quest of one though fair, yet far from true.

WILLIAM WELLS BROWN (1814?–1884)

First published novel by an African American author.

William Wells Brown was born in approximately 1814 on a Kentucky plantation, the son of an enslaved woman named Elizabeth and her enslaver's cousin. After working for various white men, including a slave trader, to whom he was hired out and eventually sold by his enslaver, Brown escaped from slavery in 1834. He settled in Cincinnati and then Buffalo, where he worked on steamships on Lake Erie and became a paid speaker for an abolitionist society. He published a best-selling autobiography, *Narrative of William W. Brown, a Fugitive Slave, Written by Himself,* in 1847, and represented the American Peace Society at the Paris Peace Congress in 1849. Brown's visibility put him at greater risk even in the North, and he spent three years traveling in Europe, where he wrote and published *Clotel; or, The President's Daughter: A Narrative of Slave Life in the United States* in 1853, about President Jefferson's secret mixed-race daughter and her sale into slavery. The novel appeared in the United States first in serialized form and then several editions. British abolitionists bought Brown's freedom in 1854. He settled in Boston where he worked as a largely self-taught doctor, and published several plays and important historical accounts of Black life in the Americas. Four years after the publication of *Narrative,* in 1857, the United States Supreme Court concluded a ten-year-long legal battle in several courts when it ruled in *Dred Scott vs. Sandford,* also known as the Dred Scott decision, that African Americans were not legally considered American citizens. After the end of the Civil War Brown devoted his life to advocating for Black suffrage and published books about Black life in the South that remain relevant today. He died near Boston in 1884.

Clotel, or, The President's Daughter: A Narrative of Slave Life in the United States was published first in London and then the United States in 1853. It tells the story of the daughters of Jefferson's alleged mistress, Currer, who are sold into slavery where they suffer different fates. Both daughters enter into secret marriages with the men who buy them. They have children who are sold into slavery upon their mother's death, in the case of Clotel's sister, and Clotel's husband legally marries a white woman for political gain. When the lawful wife discovers Clotel and her daughter, she orders Clotel to be sold and turns her husband's daughter into a house servant. Disguised as a man, Clotel tries to rescue her child but is foiled; rather than let herself be captured and enslaved again, she drowns herself in the Potomac, near the White House where her illustrious father served as President. With the novel's melodramatic plot Brown follows the conventions of his time, but we would do well not to dismiss melodrama as superficial. With the help of the genre conventions at his disposal, Brown is able to let his characters speak what had often remained unspeakable in American letters. Employing melodrama lets Brown express the full range of human emotions that mainstream society defined as improper or inappropriate. The hyperbole and rhetorical intensity, which critics sometimes object to as sentimental and melodramatic, allow Brown to reveal the hypocrisy of a social world that considered such expressions impermissible. The institution of slavery produced tremendous suffering, pain, and injustice for black families whose children belonged both to white and Black society.

From CLOTEL; OR, THE PRESIDENT'S DAUGHTER [1853]

CHAPTER I
THE NEGRO SALE

"Why stands she near the auction stand,
    That girl so young and fair?
What brings her to this dismal place,
    Why stands she weeping there?"

WITH THE GROWING population of slaves in the Southern States of America, there is a fearful increase of half whites, most of whose fathers are slaveowners and their mothers slaves. Society does not frown upon the man who sits with his mulatto child upon his knee, whilst its mother stands a slave behind his chair. The late Henry Clay, some years since, predicted that the abolition of Negro slavery would be brought about by the amalgamation of the races. John Randolph, a distinguished slaveholder of Virginia, and a prominent statesman, said in a speech in the legislature of his native state, that "the blood of the first American statesmen coursed through the veins of the slave of the South." In all the cities and towns of the slave states, the real Negro, or clear black, does not amount to more than one in every four of the slave population. This fact is, of itself, the best evidence of the degraded and immoral condition of the relation of master and slave in the United States of America. In all the slave states, the law says:—"Slaves shall be deemed, sold [held], taken, reputed, and adjudged in law to be chattels personal in the hands of their owners and possessors, and their executors, administrators and assigns, to all intents, constructions, and purposes whatsoever. A slave is one who is in the power of a master to whom he belongs. The master may sell him, dispose of his person, his industry, and his labour. He can do nothing, possess nothing, nor acquire anything, but what must belong to his master. The slave is entirely subject to the will of his master, who may correct and chastise him, though not with unusual rigour, or so as to maim and mutilate him, or expose him to the danger of loss of life, or to cause his death. The slave, to remain a slave, must be sensible that there is no appeal from his master." Where the slave is placed by law entirely under the control of the man who claims him, body and soul, as property, what else could be expected than the most depraved social condition? The marriage relation, the oldest and most sacred institution given to man by his Creator, is unknown and unrecognised in the slave laws of the United States. Would that we could say, that the moral and religious teaching in the slave states were better than the laws; but, alas! we cannot. A few years since, some slaveholders became a little uneasy in their minds about the rightfulness of permitting slaves to take to themselves husbands and wives, while they still had others living, and applied to their religious teachers for advice; and the following will show how this grave and important subject was treated:—

"Is a servant, whose husband or wife has been sold by his or her master into a distant country, to be permitted to marry again?"

The query was referred to a committee, who made the following report; which, after discussion, was adopted:—

"That, in view of the circumstances in which servants in this country are placed, the committee are unanimous in the opinion, that it is better to permit servants thus circumstanced to take another husband or wife."

Such was the answer from a committee of the "Shiloh Baptist Association;" and instead of receiving light, those who asked the question were plunged into deeper darkness! A similar question was put to the "Savannah River Association," and the answer, as the following will show, did not materially differ from the one we have already given:—

"Whether, in a case of involuntary separation, of such a character as to preclude all prospect of future intercourse, the parties ought to be allowed to marry again."

Answer:—

"That such separation among persons situated as our slaves are, is civilly a separation by death; and they believe that, in the sight of God, it would be so viewed. To forbid second marriages in such cases would be to expose the parties, not only to stronger hardships and strong temptation, but to church-censure for acting in obedience to their masters, who cannot be expected to acquiesce in a regulation at variance with justice to the slaves, and to the spirit of that command which regulates marriage among Christians. The slaves are not free agents; and a dissolution by death is not more entirely without their consent, and beyond their control than by such separation."

Although marriage, as the above indicates, is a matter which the slave-holders do not think is of any importance, or of any binding force with their slaves; yet it would be doing that degraded class an injustice, not to acknowledge that many of them do regard it as a sacred obligation, and show a willingness to obey the commands of God on this subject. Marriage is, indeed, the first and most important institution of human existence—the foundation of all civilisation and culture—the root of church and state. It is the most intimate covenant of heart formed among mankind; and for many persons the only relation in which they feel the true sentiments of humanity. It gives scope for every human virtue, since each of these is developed from the love and confidence which here predominate. It unites all which ennobles and beautifies life,—sympathy, kindness of will and deed, gratitude, devotion, and every delicate, intimate feeling. As the only asylum for true education, it is the first and last sanctuary of human culture. As husband and wife, through each other become conscious of complete humanity, and every human feeling, and every human virtue; so children, at their first awakening in the fond covenant of love between parents, both of whom are tenderly concerned for the same object, find an image of complete humanity leagued in free love. The spirit of love which prevails between them acts with creative power upon the young mind, and awakens every germ of goodness within it. This invisible and incalculable influence of parental life acts more upon the child than all the efforts of education, whether by means of instruction, precept, or exhortation. If this be a true picture of the vast influence for good of the institution of marriage, what must be the moral degradation of that people to whom marriage is denied? Not content with depriving them of all the higher and holier enjoyments of this relation, by degrading and darkening their souls, the slaveholder denies to his victim even that slight alleviation of his misery, which would result from the marriage relation being protected by law and public opinion. Such is the influence of slavery in the United States, that the ministers of religion, even in the so-called free states, are the mere echoes, instead of the correctors, of public sentiment. We have thought it advisable to show that the present system of chattel slavery in America undermines the entire social condition of man, so as to prepare the reader for the following narrative of slave life, in that otherwise happy and prosperous country.

In all the large towns in the Southern States, there is a class of slaves who are permitted to hire their time of their owners, and for which they pay a high price. These are mulatto women, or quadroons, as they are familiarly known, and are distinguished for their fascinating beauty. The handsomest usually pays the highest price for her time. Many of these women are the favourites of persons who furnish them with the means of paying their owners, and not a few are dressed in the most extravagant manner. Reader, when you take into consideration the fact, that amongst the slave population no safeguard is thrown around virtue, and no inducement held out to slave women to be chaste, you will not be surprised when we tell you that immorality and vice pervade the cities of the Southern States in a manner unknown in the cities and towns of the Northern States. Indeed most of the slave women have no higher aspiration than that of becoming the finely-dressed mistress of some white man. And at Negro balls and parties, this class of women usually cut the greatest figure.

At the close of the year, the following advertisement appeared in a newspaper published in Richmond, the capital of the state of Virginia:—"Notice: Thirty-eight Negroes will be offered for sale on Monday, November 10th, at twelve o'clock, being the entire stock of the late John Graves, Esq. The Negroes are in good condition, some of them very prime; among them are several mechanics, able-bodied field hands, ploughboys, and women with children at the breast, and some of them very prolific in their generating qualities, affording a rare opportunity to any one who wishes to raise a strong and healthy lot of servants for their own use. Also several mulatto girls of rare personal qualities: two of them very superior. Any gentleman or lady wishing to purchase, can take any of the above slaves on trial for a week, for which no charge will be made." Amongst the above slaves to be sold were Currer and her two daughters, Clotel and Althesa; the latter were the girls spoken of in the advertisement as "very superior." Currer was a bright mulatto, and of prepossessing appearance, though then nearly forty years of age. She had hired her time for more than twenty years, during which time she had lived in Richmond. In her younger days Currer had been the housekeeper of a young slaveholder; but of later years had been a laundress or washerwoman, and was considered to be a woman of great taste in getting up linen. The gentleman for whom she had kept house was Thomas Jefferson, by whom she had two daughters. Jefferson being called to Washington to fill a government appointment, Currer was left behind, and thus she took herself to the business of washing, by which means she paid her master, Mr. Graves, and supported herself and two children. At the time of the decease of her master, Currer's daughters, Clotel and Althesa, were aged respectively sixteen and fourteen years, and both, like most of their own sex in America, were well grown. Currer early resolved to bring her daughters up as ladies, as she termed it, and therefore imposed little or no work upon them. As her daughters grew older, Currer had to pay a stipulated price for them; yet her notoriety as a laundress of the first class enabled her to put an extra price upon her charges, and thus she and her daughters lived in comparative luxury. To bring up Clotel and Althesa to attract attention, and especially at balls and parties, was the great aim of Currer. Although the term "Negro ball" is applied to most of these gatherings, yet a majority of the attendants are often whites. Nearly all the Negro parties in the cities and towns of the Southern States are made up of quadroon and mulatto girls, and white men. These are democratic gatherings, where gentlemen, shopkeepers, and their clerks, all appear upon terms of perfect equality. And there is a degree of gentility and decorum in these companies that is not surpassed by similar gatherings of white people in the Slave States. It was at one of these parties that Horatio Green, the son of a wealthy gentleman of Richmond, was first introduced to Clotel. The young man had just returned from college, and was in his twenty-second year. Clotel was sixteen, and was admitted by all to be the most beautiful girl, coloured or white, in the city. So attentive was the young man to the quadroon during the evening that it was noticed by all, and became a matter of general conversation; while Currer appeared delighted beyond measure at her daughter's conquest. From that evening, young Green became the favourite visitor at Currer's house. He soon promised to purchase Clotel, as speedily as it could be effected, and make her mistress of her own dwelling; and Currer looked forward with pride to the time when she should see her daughter emancipated and free. It was a beautiful moonlight night in August, when all who reside in tropical climes are eagerly gasping for a breath of fresh air, that Horatio Green was seated in the small garden behind Currer's cottage, with the object of his affections by his side. And it was here that Horatio drew from his pocket the newspaper, wet from the press, and read the advertisement for the sale of the slaves to which we have alluded; Currer and her two daughters being of the number. At the close of the evening's visit, and as the young man was leaving, he said to the girl, "You shall soon be free and your own mistress."

As might have been expected, the day of sale brought an unusual large number together to compete for the property to be sold. Farmers who make a business of raising slaves for the market were there; slave-traders and speculators were also numerously represented; and in the midst of this throng was one who felt a deeper interest in the result of the sale than any other of the bystanders; this was young Green. True to his promise, he was there with a blank bank check in his pocket, awaiting with impatience to enter the list as a bidder for the beautiful slave. The less valuable slaves were first placed upon the auction block, one after another, and sold to the highest bidder. Husbands and wives were separated with a degree of indifference that is unknown in any other relation of life, except that of slavery. Brothers and sisters were torn from each other; and mothers saw their children leave them for the last time on this earth.

It was late in the day, when the greatest number of persons were thought to be present, that Currer and her daughters were brought forward to the place of sale.—Currer was first ordered to ascend the auction stand, which she did with a trembling step. The slave mother was sold to a trader. Althesa, the youngest, and who was scarcely less beautiful than her sister, was sold to the same trader for one thousand dollars. Clotel was the last, and, as was expected, commanded a higher price than any that had been offered for sale that day. The appearance of Clotel on the auction block created a deep sensation amongst the crowd. There she stood, with a complexion as white as most of those who were waiting with a wish to become her purchasers; her features as finely defined as any of her sex of pure Anglo-Saxon; her long black wavy hair done up in the neatest manner; her form tall and graceful, and her whole appearance indicating one superior to her position. The auctioneer commenced by saying, that "Miss Clotel had been reserved for the last, because she was the most valuable. How much, gentlemen? Real Albino, fit for a fancy girl for any one. She enjoys good health, and has a sweet temper. How much do you say?" "Five hundred dollars." "Only five hundred for such a girl as this? Gentlemen, she is worth a deal more than that sum; you certainly don't know the value of the article you are bidding upon. Here, gentlemen, I hold in my hand a paper certifying that she has a good moral character." "Seven hundred." "Ah; gentlemen, that is something like. This paper also states that she is very intelligent." "Eight hundred." "She is a devoted Christian, and perfectly trustworthy." "Nine hundred." "Nine fifty." "Ten." "Eleven." "Twelve hundred." Here the sale came to a dead stand. The auctioneer stopped, looked around, and began in a rough manner to relate some anecdotes relative to the sale of slaves, which, he said, had come under his own observation. At this juncture the scene was indeed strange. Laughing, joking, swearing, smoking, spitting, and talking kept up a continual hum and noise amongst the crowd; while the slave-girl stood with tears in her eyes, at one time looking towards her mother and sister, and at another towards the young man whom she hoped would become her purchaser. "The chastity of this girl is pure; she has never been from under her mother's care; she is a virtuous creature." "Thirteen." "Fourteen." "Fifteen." "Fifteen hundred dollars," cried the auctioneer, and the maiden was struck for that sum. This was a Southern auction, at which the bones, muscles, sinews, blood, and nerves of a young lady of sixteen were sold for five hundred dollars; her moral character for two hundred; her improved intellect for one hundred; her Christianity for three hundred; and her chastity and virtue for four hundred dollars more. And this, too, in a city thronged with churches, whose tall spires look like so many signals pointing to heaven, and whose ministers preach that slavery is a God-ordained institution! What words can tell the inhumanity, the atrocity, and the immorality of that doctrine which, from exalted office, commends such a crime to the favour of enlightened and Christian people? What indignation from all the world is not due to the government and people who put forth all their strength and power to keep in existence such an institution? Nature abhors it; the age repels it; and Christianity needs all her meekness to forgive it. Clotel was sold for fifteen hundred dollars, but her purchaser was Horatio Green. Thus closed a Negro sale, at which two daughters of Thomas Jefferson, the writer of the Declaration of American Independence, and one of the presidents of the great republic, were disposed of to the highest bidder!

"O God! my every heart-string cries,
　　Dost thou these scenes behold
　In this our boasted Christian land,
　　And must the truth be told?

"Blush, Christian, blush! for e'en the dark,
　　Untutored heathen see
　Thy inconsistency; and, lo!
　　They scorn thy God, and thee!"

CHAPTER XIX

ESCAPE OF CLOTEL

"The fetters galled my weary soul—
　　A soul that seemed but thrown away;
　I spurned the tyrant's base control,
　　Resolved at least the man to play."

No COUNTRY HAS produced so much heroism in so short a time, connected with escapes from peril and oppression, as has occurred in the United States among fugitive slaves, many of whom show great shrewdness in their endeavours to escape from this land of bondage. A slave was one day seen passing on the high road from a border town in the interior of the state of Virginia to the Ohio river. The man had neither hat upon his head or coat upon his back. He was driving before him a very nice fat pig, and appeared to all who saw him to be a labourer employed on an adjoining farm. "No Negro is permitted to go at large in the Slave States without a written pass from his or her master, except on business in the neighbourhood." "Where do you live, my boy?" asked a white man of the slave, as he passed a white house with green blinds. "Jist up de road, sir," was the answer. "That's a fine pig." "Yes, sir, marser like dis choat berry much." And the Negro drove on as if he was in great haste. In this way he and the pig travelled more than fifty miles before they reached the Ohio river. Once at the river they crossed over; the pig was sold; and nine days after the runaway slave passed over the Niagara river, and, for the first time in his life, breathed the air of freedom. A few weeks later, and, on the same road, two slaves were seen passing; one was on horseback, the other was walking before him with his arms tightly bound, and a long rope leading from the man on foot to the one on horseback. "Oh, ho, that's a runaway rascal, I suppose," said a farmer, who met them on the road. "Yes, sir, he bin runaway, and I got him fast. Marser will tan his jacket for him nicely when he gets him." "You are a trustworthy fellow, I imagine," continued the farmer. "Oh yes, sir; marser puts a heap of confidence in dis nigger." And the slaves travelled on. When the one on foot was fatigued they would change positions, the other being tied and driven on foot. This they called "ride and tie." After a journey of more than two hundred miles they reached the Ohio river, turned the horse loose, told him to go home, and proceeded on their way to Canada. However they were not to have it all their own way. There are men in the Free States, and especially in the states adjacent to the Slave States, who make their living by catching the runaway slave, and returning him for the reward that may be offered. As the two slaves above mentioned were travelling on towards the land of freedom, led by the North Star, they were set upon by four of these slave-catchers, and one of them unfortunately captured. The other escaped. The captured fugitive was put under the torture, and compelled to reveal the name of his owner and his place of residence. Filled with delight, the kidnappers started back with their victim. Overjoyed with the prospect of receiving a large reward, they gave themselves up on the third night to pleasure. They put up at an inn. The Negro was chained to the bed-post, in the same room with his captors. At dead of night, when all was still, the slave arose from the floor upon which he had been lying, looked around, and saw that the white men were fast asleep. The brandy punch had done its work. With palpitating heart and trembling limbs he viewed his position. The door was fast, but the warm weather had compelled them to leave the window open. If he could but get his chains off, he might escape through the window to the piazza, and reach the ground by one of the posts that supported the piazza. The sleeper's clothes hung upon chairs by the bed-side; the slave thought of the padlock key, examined the pockets and found it. The chains were soon off, and the Negro stealthily making his way to the window: he stopped and said to himself, "These men are villains, they are enemies to all who like me are trying to be free. Then why not I teach them a lesson?" He then undressed himself, took the clothes of one of the men, dressed himself in them, and escaped through the window, and, a moment more, he was on the high road to Canada. Fifteen days later, and the writer of this gave him a passage across Lake Erie, and saw him safe in her Britannic Majesty's dominions.

We have seen Clotel sold to Mr. French in Vicksburgh, her hair cut short, and everything done to make her realise her position as a servant. Then we have seen her re-sold, because her owners feared she would die through grief. As yet her new purchaser treated her with respectful gentleness, and sought to win her favour by flattery and presents, knowing that whatever he gave her he could take back again. But she dreaded every moment lest the scene should change, and trembled at the sound of every footfall. At every interview with her new master Clotel stoutly maintained that she had left a husband in Virginia, and would never think of taking another. The gold watch and chain, and other glittering presents which he purchased for her, were all laid aside by the quadroon, as if they were of no value to her. In the same house with her was another servant, a man, who had from time to time hired himself from his master. William was his name. He could feel for Clotel, for he, like her, had been separated from near and dear relatives, and often tried to console the poor woman. One day the quadroon observed to him that her hair was growing out again. "Yes," replied William, "you look a good deal like a man with your short hair." "Oh," rejoined she, "I have often been told that I would make a better looking man than a woman. If I had the money," continued she, "I would bid farewell to this place." In a moment more she feared that she had said too much, and smilingly remarked, "I am always talking nonsense." William was a tall, full-bodied Negro, whose very countenance beamed with intelligence. Being a mechanic, he had, by his own industry, made more than what he paid his owner; this he laid aside, with the hope that some day he might get enough to purchase his freedom. He had in his chest one hundred and fifty dollars. His was a heart that felt for others, and he had again and again wiped the tears from his eyes as he heard the story of Clotel as related by herself. "If she can get free with a little money, why not give her what I have?" thought he, and then he resolved to do it. An hour after, he came into the quadroon's room, and laid the money in her lap, and said, "There, Miss Clotel, you said if you had the means you would leave this place; there is money enough to take you to England, where you will be free. You are much fairer than many of the white women of the South, and can easily pass for a free white lady." At first Clotel feared that it was a plan by which the Negro wished to try her fidelity to her owner; but she was soon convinced by his earnest manner, and the deep feeling with which he spoke, that he was honest. "I will take the money only on one condition," said she; "and that is, that I effect your escape as well as my own." "How can that be done?" he inquired. "I will assume the disguise of a gentleman and you that of a servant, and we will take passage on a steamboat and go to Cincinnati, and thence to Canada." Here William put in several objections to the plan. He feared detection, and he well knew that, when a slave is once caught when attempting to escape, if returned is sure to be worse treated than before. However, Clotel satisfied him that the plan could be carried out if he would only play his part.

The resolution was taken, the clothes for her disguise procured, and before night everything was in readiness for their departure. That night Mr. Cooper, their master, was to attend a party, and this was their opportunity. William went to the wharf to look out for a boat, and had scarcely reached the landing ere he heard the puffing of a steamer. He returned and reported the fact. Clotel had already packed her trunk, and had only to dress and all was ready. In less than an hour they were on board the boat. Under the assumed name of "Mr. Johnson," Clotel went to the clerk's office and took a private state room for herself, and paid her own and servant's fare. Besides being attired in a neat suit of black, she had a white silk handkerchief tied round her chin, as if she was an invalid. A pair of green glasses covered her eyes; and fearing that she would be talked to too much and thus render her liable to be detected, she assumed to be very ill. On the other hand, William was playing his part well in the servants' hall; he was talking loudly of his master's wealth. Nothing appeared as good on the boat as in his master's fine mansion. "I don't like dees steam-boats no how," said William; "I hope when marser goes on a journey agin he will take de carriage and de hosses." Mr. Johnson (for such was the name by which Clotel now went) remained in his room, to avoid, as far as possible, conversation with others. After a passage of seven days they arrived at Louisville, and put up at Gough's Hotel. Here they had to await the departure of another boat for the North. They were now in their most critical position. They were still in a slave state, and John C. Calhoun, a distinguished slave-owner, was a guest at this hotel. They feared, also, that trouble would attend their attempt to leave this place for the North, as all persons taking Negroes with them have to give bail that such Negroes are not runaway slaves. The law upon this point is very stringent: all steamboats and other public conveyances are liable to a fine for every slave that escapes by them, besides paying the full value for the slave. After a delay of four hours, Mr. Johnson and servant took passage on the steamer Rodolph, for Pittsburgh. It is usual, before the departure of the boats, for an officer to examine every part of the vessel to see that no slave secretes himself on board. "Where are you going?" asked the officer of William, as he was doing his duty on this occasion. "I am going with marser," was the quick reply. "Who is your master?" "Mr. Johnson, sir, a gentleman in the cabin." "You must take him to the office and satisfy the captain that all is right, or you can't go on this boat." William informed his master what the officer had said. The boat was on the eve of going, and no time could be lost, yet they knew not what to do. At last they went to the office, and Mr. Johnson, addressing the captain, said, "I am informed that my boy can't go with me unless I give security that he belongs to me. "Yes," replied the captain, "that is the law." "A very strange law indeed," rejoined Mr. Johnson, "that one can't take his property with him." After a conversation of some minutes, and a plea on the part of Johnson that he did not wish to be delayed owing to his illness, they were permitted to take their passage without farther trouble, and the boat was soon on its way up the river. The fugitives had now passed the Rubicon, and the next place at which they would land would be in a Free State. Clotel called William to her room, and said to him, "We are now free, you can go on your way to Canada, and I shall go to Virginia in search of my daughter." The announcement that she was going to risk her liberty in a Slave State was unwelcome news to William. With all the eloquence he could command, he tried to persuade Clotel that she could not escape detection, and was only throwing her freedom away. But she had counted the cost, and made up her mind for the worst. In return for the money he had furnished, she had secured for him his liberty, and their engagement was at an end.

After a quick passage the fugitives arrived at Cincinnati, and there separated. William proceeded on his way to Canada, and Clotel again resumed her own apparel, and prepared to start in search of her child. As might have been expected, the escape of those two valuable slaves created no little sensation in Vicksburgh. Advertisements and messages were sent in every direction in which the fugitives were thought to have gone. It was soon, however, known that they had left the town as master and servant; and many were the communications which appeared in the newspapers, in which the writers thought, or pretended, that they had seen the slaves in their disguise. One was to the effect that they had gone off in a chaise; one as master, and the other as servant. But the most probable was an account given by a correspondent of one of the Southern newspapers, who happened to be a passenger in the same steamer in which the slaves escaped, and which we here give:—

"One bright starlight night, in the month of December last, I found myself in the cabin of the steamer Rodolph, then lying in the port of Vicksburgh, and bound to Louisville. I had gone early on board, in order to select a good berth, and having got tired of reading the papers, amused myself with watching the appearance of the passengers as they dropped in, one after another, and I being a believer in physiognomy, formed my own opinion of their characters.

"The second bell rang, and as I yawningly returned my watch to my pocket, my attention was attracted by the appearance of a young man who entered the cabin supported by his servant, a strapping Negro.

"The man was bundled up in a capacious overcoat; his face was bandaged with a white handkerchief, and its expression entirely hid by a pair of enormous spectacles.

"There was something so mysterious and unusual about the young man as he sat restless in the corner, that curiosity led me to observe him more closely.

"He appeared anxious to avoid notice, and before the steamer had fairly left the wharf, requested, in a low, womanly voice, to be shown his berth, as he was an invalid, and must retire early: his name he gave as Mr. Johnson. His servant was called, and he was put quietly to bed. I paced the deck until Tyhee light grew dim in the distance, and then went to my berth.

"I awoke in the morning with the sun shining in my face; we were then just passing St. Helena. It was a mild beautiful morning, and most of the passengers were on deck, enjoying the freshness of the air, and stimulating their appetites for breakfast. Mr. Johnson soon made his appearance, arrayed as on the night before, and took his seat quietly upon the guard of the boat.

"From the better opportunity afforded by daylight, I found that he was a slight build, apparently handsome young man, with black hair and eyes, and of a darkness of complexion that betokened Spanish extraction. Any notice from others seemed painful to him; so to satisfy my curiosity, I questioned his servant, who was standing near, and gained the following information.

"His master was an invalid—he had suffered for a long time under a complication of diseases, that had baffled the skill of the best physicians in Mississippi; he was now suffering principally with the 'rheumatism,' and he was scarcely able to walk or help himself in any way. He came from Vicksburgh, and was now on his way to Philadelphia, at which place resided his uncle, a celebrated physician, and through whose means he hoped to be restored to perfect health.

"This information, communicated in a bold, off-hand manner, enlisted my sympathies for the sufferer, although it occurred to me that he walked rather too gingerly for a person afflicted with so many ailments."

After thanking Clotel for the great service she had done him in bringing him out of slavery, William bade her farewell. The prejudice that exists in the Free States against coloured persons, on account of their colour, is attributable solely to the influence of slavery, and is but another form of slavery itself. And even the slave who escapes from the Southern plantations, is surprised when he reaches the North, at the amount and withering influence of this prejudice. William applied at the railway station for a ticket for the train going to Sandusky, and was told that if he went by that train he would have to ride in the luggage-van. "Why?" asked the astonished Negro. "We don't send a Jim Crow carriage but once a day, and that went this morning." The "Jim Crow" carriage is the one in which the blacks have to ride. Slavery is a school in which its victims learn much shrewdness, and William had been an apt scholar. Without asking any more questions, the Negro took his seat in one of the first-class carriages. He was soon seen and ordered out. Afraid to remain in the town longer, he resolved to go by that train; and consequently seated himself on a goods' box in the luggage van. The train started at its proper time, and all went on well. Just before arriving at the end of the journey, the conductor called on William for his ticket. "I have none," was the reply. "Well, then, you can pay your fare to me," said the officer. "How much is it?" asked the black man. "Two dollars." "What do you charge those in the passenger-carriage?" "Two dollars." "And do you charge me the same as you do those who ride in the best carriages?" asked the Negro. "Yes," was the answer. "I shan't pay it," returned the man. "You black scamp, do you think you can ride on this road without paying your fare?" "No, I don't want to ride for nothing; I only want to pay what's right." "Well, launch out two dollars, and that's right." "No, I shan't; I will pay what I ought, and won't pay any more." "Come, come, nigger, your fare and be done with it," said the conductor, in a manner that is never used except by Americans to blacks. "I won't pay you two dollars, and that enough," said William. "Well, as you have come all the way in the luggage-van, pay me a dollar and a half and you may go." "I shan't do any such thing." "Don't you mean to pay for riding?" "Yes, but I won't pay a dollar and a half for riding up here in the freight-van. If you had let me come in the carriage where others ride, I would have paid you two dollars." "Where were you raised? You seem to think yourself as good as white folks." "I want nothing more than my rights." "Well, give me a dollar, and I will let you off." "No, sir, I shan't do it." "What do you mean to do then, don't you wish to pay anything?" "Yes, sir, I want to pay you the full price." "What do you mean by full price?" "What do you charge per hundred-weight for goods?" inquired the Negro with a degree of gravity that would have astonished Diogenes himself. "A quarter of a dollar per hundred," answered the conductor. "I weigh just one hundred and fifty pounds," returned William, "and will pay you three eighths of a dollar." "Do you expect that you will pay only thirty-seven cents for your ride?" "This, sir, is your own price. I came in a luggage-van, and I'll pay for luggage." After a vain effort to get the Negro to pay more, the conductor took the thirty-seven cents, and noted in his cash-book, "Received for one hundred and fifty pounds of luggage, thirty seven cents." This, reader, is no fiction; it actually occurred in the railway above described.

Thomas Corwin, a member of the American Congress, is one of the blackest white men in the United States. He was once on his way to Congress, and took passage in one of the Ohio river steamers. As he came just at the dinner hour, he immediately went into the dining saloon, and took his seat at the table. A gentleman with his whole party of five ladies at once left the table. "Where is the captain?" cried the man in an angry tone. The captain soon appeared, and it was sometime before he could satisfy the old gent, that Governor Corwin was not a nigger. The newspapers often have notices of mistakes made by innkeepers and others who undertake to accommodate the public, one of which we give below.

On the 6th inst., the Hon. Daniel Webster and family entered Edgartown, on a visit for health and recreation. Arriving at the hotel, without alighting from the coach, the landlord was sent for to see if suitable accommodation could be had. That dignitary appearing, and surveying Mr. Webster, while the hon. senator addressed him, seemed woefully to mistake the dark features of the traveller as he sat back in the corner of the carriage, and to suppose him a coloured man, particularly as there were two coloured servants of Mr. W. outside. So he promptly declared that there was no room for him and his family, and he could not be accommodated there at the same time suggesting that he might perhaps find accommodation at some of the huts up back, to which he pointed. So deeply did the prejudice of looks possess him, that he appeared not to notice that the stranger introduced himself to him as Daniel Webster, or to be so ignorant as not to have heard of such a personage; and turning away, he expressed to the driver his astonishment that he should bring *black* people there for *him* to take in. It was not till he had been repeatedly assured and made to understand that the said Daniel Webster was a real live senator of the United States, that he perceived his awkward mistake and the distinguished honour which he and his house were so near missing.

In most of the Free States, the coloured people are disfranchised on account of their colour. The following scene, which we take from a newspaper in the state of Ohio, will give some idea of the extent to which this prejudice is carried.

"The whole of Thursday last was occupied by the Court of Common Pleas for this county in trying to find out whether one Thomas West was of the VOTING COLOUR, as some had very *constitutional doubts* as to whether his colour was orthodox, and whether his hair was of the official crisp! Was it not a dignified business? Four profound judges, four acute lawyers, twelve grave jurors, and I don't know how many venerable witnesses, making in all about thirty men, perhaps, all engaged in the profound, laborious, and illustrious business, of finding out whether a man who pays tax, works on the road, and is an industrious farmer, has been born according to the republican, Christian constitution of Ohio—so that he can vote! And they wisely, gravely, and 'JUDGMATICALLY' decided that he should not vote! What wisdom—what research it must have required to evolve this truth! It was left for the Court of Common Pleas for Columbian county, Ohio, in the United States of North America, to find out what Solomon never dreamed of—the courts of all civilised, heathen, or Jewish countries, never contemplated. Lest the wisdom of our courts should be circumvented by some such men as might be named, who are so near being born constitutionally that they might be taken for white by sight, I would suggest that our court be invested with SMELLING powers, and that if a man don't exhale the constitutional smell, he shall not vote! This would be an additional security to our liberties."

William found, after all, that liberty in the so-called Free States was more a name than a reality; that prejudice followed the coloured man into every place that he might enter. The temples erected for the worship of the living God are no exception. The finest Baptist church in the city of Boston has the following paragraph in the deed that conveys its seats to pewholders:

"And it is a further condition of these presents, that if the owner or owners of said pew shall determine hereafter to sell the same, it shall first be offered, in writing, to the standing committee of said society for the time being, at such price as might otherwise be obtained for it; and the said committee shall have the right, for ten days after such offer, to purchase said pew for said society, at that price, first deducting therefrom all taxes and assessments on said pew then remaining unpaid. And if the said committee shall not so complete such purchase within said ten days, then the pew may be sold by the owner or owners thereof (after payment of all such arrears) to any one respectable *white person,* but upon the same conditions as are contained in this instrument; and immediate notice of such sale shall be given in writing, by the vendor, to the treasurer of said society."

Such are the conditions upon which the Rowe Street Baptist Church, Boston, disposes of its seats. The writer of this is able to put that whole congregation, minister and all, to flight, by merely putting his coloured face in that church. We once visited a church in New York that had a place set apart for the sons of Ham. It was a dark, dismal looking place in one corner of the gallery, grated in front like a hen-coop, with a black border around it. It had two doors; over one was B. M.—black men; over the other B. W.—black women.

FREDERICK DOUGLASS (1818–1895)

First published novella by an African American author.

Frederick Douglass was born in 1818 into slavery in Maryland, the son of Harriet Bailey, an enslaved Black woman, and an unknown white man. He never learned his actual birthday and endured hunger and cold as a child, especially after his mother's death when he was seven years old. In 1826 he was sent to be the servant of a Baltimore family, where he learned to read, largely by teaching himself. At age twenty, he escaped his life of captivity with the help of his future wife, Anna Murray, a free Black woman, first to New York and then to New Bedford, Massachusetts, in 1838, where he lived undetected. In 1841, at an anti-slavery convention in Nantucket, he was asked to describe his experiences under slavery. His remarks proved so effective that he was hired in a paid position by the Massachusetts Anti-Slavery Society. In 1845 he published his now classic memoir, *Narrative of the Life of Frederick Douglass, an American Slave* (1845), an international bestseller and key text of nineteenth-century American literature. Many of his speeches, essays and other writings crystallize the defining issue of nineteenth-century America as the tension between the Constitution's promise and the reality of slavery. Since the exposure after his book's success created risks of being caught by slave-catchers, Douglass went on a lecture tour in England for two years. Upon his return, he moved to Rochester and embarked on an illustrious career as a newspaper editor, abolitionist, and ultimately the first Black American appointed to high-ranking posts in the U.S. government.

The Heroic Slave is the first and only piece of fiction by Frederick Douglass and is considered the first work of historical fiction and the first novella published by an African American author. Douglass contributed it to a book of anti-slavery testimonies to raise fund for the Rochester Ladies' Anti-Slavery Society, *Autographs for Freedom* (1853), and published it in serialized form in his newspaper, *Frederick Douglass' Paper*. The fifty-page novella tells the heroic story of Madison Washington, who led the nation's most successful and widely known slave revolt in 1841 by taking control of a ship sailing from Virginia to New Orleans. Washington landed the ship in the British-controlled Bahamas where the one hundred and thirty-five enslaved individuals on board found freedom.

From THE HEROIC SLAVE [1853]

PART I.

Oh! child of grief, why weepest thou?
    Why droops thy sad and mournful brow?
Why is thy look so like despair?
    What deep, sad sorrow lingers there?

THE STATE OF Virginia is famous in American annals for the multitudinous array of her statesmen and heroes. She has been dignified by some the mother of statesmen. History has not been sparing in recording their names, or in blazoning their deeds. Her high position in this respect, has given her an enviable distinction among her sister States. With Virginia for his birth-place, even a man of ordinary parts, on account of the general partiality for her sons, easily rises to eminent stations. Men, not great enough to attract special attention in their native States, have, like a certain distinguished citizen in the State of New York, sighed and repined that they were not born in Virginia. Yet not all the great ones of the Old Dominion have, by the fact of their birth-place, escaped undeserved obscurity. By some strange neglect, *one* of the truest, manliest, and bravest of her children,—one who, in after years, will, I think, command the pen of genius to set his merits forth, holds now no higher place in the records of that grand old Commonwealth than is held by a horse or an ox. Let those account for it who can, but there stands the fact, that a man who loved liberty as well as did Patrick Henry,—who deserved it as much as Thomas Jefferson,—and who fought for it with a valor as high, an arm as strong, and against odds as great, as he who led all the armies of the American colonies through the great war for freedom and independence, lives now only in the chattel records of his native State.

Glimpses of this great character are all that can now be presented. He is brought to view only by a few transient incidents, and these afford but partial satisfaction. Like a guiding star on a stormy night, he is seen through the parted clouds and the howling tempests; or, like the gray peak of a menacing rock on a perilous coast, he is seen by the quivering flash of angry lightning, and he again disappears covered with mystery.

Curiously, earnestly, anxiously we peer into the dark, and wish even for the blinding flash, or the light of northern skies to reveal him. But alas! he is still enveloped in darkness, and we return from the pursuit like a wearied and disheartened mother, (after a tedious and unsuccessful search for a lost child,) who returns weighed down with disappointment and sorrow. Speaking of marks, traces, possibles, and probabilities, we come before our readers.

In the spring of 1835, on a Sabbath morning, within hearing of the solemn peals of the church bells at a distant village, a Northern traveller through the State of Virginia drew up his horse to drink at a sparkling brook, near the edge of a dark pine forest. While his weary and thirsty steed drew in the grateful water, the rider caught the sound of a human voice, apparently engaged in earnest conversation.

Following the direction of the sound, he descried, among the tall pines, the man whose voice had arrested his attention. "To whom can he be speaking?" thought the traveller. "He seems to be alone." The circumstance interested him much, and he became intensely curious to know what thoughts and feelings, or, it might be, high aspirations, guided those rich and mellow accents. Tieing his horse at a short distance from the brook, he stealthily drew near the solitary speaker; and, concealing himself by the side of a huge fallen tree, he distinctly heard the following soliloquy:—

"What, then, is life to me? it is aimless and worthless, and worse than worthless. Those birds, perched on yon swinging boughs, in friendly conclave, sounding forth their merry notes in seeming worship of the rising sun, though liable to the sportsman's fowling-piece, are still my superiors. They *live free*, though they may die slaves. They fly where they list by day, and retire in freedom at night. But what is freedom to me, or I to it? I am a *slave*,—born a slave, an abject slave,—even before I made part of this breathing world, the scourge was platted for my back; the fetters were forged for my limbs. How mean a thing am I. That accursed and crawling snake, that miserable reptile, that has just glided into its slimy home, is freer and better off than I. He escaped my blow, and is safe. But here am I, a man,—yes, *a man!*—with thoughts and wishes, with powers and faculties as far as angel's flight above that hated reptile,—yet he is my superior, and scorns to own me as his master, or to stop to take my blows. When he saw my uplifted arm, he darted beyond my reach, and turned to give me battle. I dare not do as much as that. I neither run nor fight, but do meanly stand, answering each heavy blow of a cruel master with doleful wails and piteous cries. I am galled with irons; but even these are more tolerable than the consciousness, the *galling* consciousness of cowardice and indecision. Can it be that I *dare* not run away? *Perish the thought,* I *dare* do any thing which may be done by another. When that young man struggled with the waves *for life,* and others stood back appalled in helpless horror, did I not plunge in, forgetful of life, to save his? The raging bull from whom all others fled, pale with fright, did I not keep at bay with a single pitchfork? Could a coward do that? *No,—no,*—I wrong myself,—I am no coward. *Liberty* I will have, or die in the attempt to gain it. This working that others may live in idleness! This cringing submission to insolence and curses! This living under the constant dread and apprehension of being sold and transferred, like a mere brute, is *too* much for me. I will stand it no longer. What others have done, I will do. These trusty legs, or these sinewy arms shall place me among the free. Tom escaped; so can I. The North Star will not be less kind to me than to him. I will follow it. I will at least make the trial. I have nothing to lose. If I am caught, I shall only be a slave. If I am shot, I shall only lose a life which is a burden and a curse. If I get clear, (as something tells me I shall,) liberty, the inalienable birth-right of every man, precious and priceless, will be mine. My resolution is fixed. *I shall be free.*"

At these words the traveller raised his head cautiously and noiselessly, and caught, from his hiding-place, a full view of the unsuspecting speaker. Madison (for that was the name of our hero) was standing erect, a smile of satisfaction rippled upon his expressive countenance, like that which plays upon the face of one who has but just solved a difficult problem, or vanquished a malignant foe; for at that moment he was free, at least in spirit. The future gleamed brightly before him, and his fetters lay broken at his feet. His air was triumphant.

Madison was of manly form. Tall, symmetrical, round, and strong. In his movements he seemed to combine, with the strength of the lion, a lion's elasticity. His torn sleeves disclosed arms like polished iron. His face was "black, but comely." His eye, lit with emotion, kept guard under a brow as dark and as glossy as the raven's wing. His whole appearance betokened

Herculean strength; yet there was nothing savage or forbidding in his aspect. A child might play in his arms, or dance on his shoulders. A giant's strength, but not a giant's heart was in him. His broad mouth and nose spoke only of good nature and kindness. But his voice, that unfailing index of the soul, though full and melodious, had that in it which could terrify as well as charm. He was just the man you would choose when hardships were to be endured, or danger to be encountered,—intelligent and brave. He had the head to conceive, and the hand to execute. In a word, he was one to be sought as a friend, but to be dreaded as an enemy.

As our traveller gazed upon him, he almost trembled at the thought of his dangerous intrusion. Still he could not quit the place. He had long desired to sound the mysterious depths of the thoughts and feelings of a slave. He was not, therefore, disposed to allow so providential an opportunity to pass unimproved. He resolved to hear more; so he listened again for those mellow and mournful accents which, he says, made such an impression upon him as can never be erased. He did not have to wait long. There came another gush from the same full fountain; now bitter, and now sweet. Scathing denunciations of the cruelty and injustice of slavery; heart-touching narrations of his own personal suffering, intermingled with prayers to the God of the oppressed for help and deliverance, were followed by presentations of the dangers and difficulties of escape, and formed the burden of his eloquent utterances; but his high resolution clung to him,—for he ended each speech by an emphatic declaration of his purpose to be free. It seemed that the very repetition of this, imparted a glow to his countenance. The hope of freedom seemed to sweeten, for a season, the bitter cup of slavery, and to make it, for a time, tolerable; for when in the very whirlwind of anguish,—when his heart's cord seemed screwed up to snapping tension, hope sprung up and soothed his troubled spirit. Fitfully he would exclaim, "How can I leave her? Poor thing! what can she do when I am gone? Oh! oh! 'tis impossible that I can leave poor Susan!"

A brief pause intervened. Our traveller raised his head, and saw again the sorrow-smitten slave. His eye was fixed upon the ground. The strong man staggered under a heavy load. Recovering himself, he argued thus aloud: "All is uncertain here. To-morrow's sun may not rise before I am sold, and separated from her I love. What, then, could I do for her? I should be in more hopeless slavery, and she no nearer to liberty,—whereas if I were free,—my arms my own,—I might devise the means to rescue her."

This said, Madison cast around a searching glance, as if the thought of being overheard had flashed across his mind. He said no more, but, with measured steps, walked away, and was lost to the eye of our traveller amidst the wildering woods.

Long after Madison had left the ground, Mr. Listwell (our traveller) remained in motionless silence, meditating on the extraordinary revelations to which he had listened. He seemed fastened to the spot, and stood half hoping, half fearing the return of the sable preacher to his solitary temple. The speech of Madison rung through the chambers of his soul, and vibrated through his entire frame. "Here is indeed a man," thought he, "of rare endowments,—a child of God,—guilty of no crime but the color of his skin,—hiding away from the face of humanity, and pouring out his thoughts and feelings, his hopes and resolutions to the lonely woods; to him those distant church bells have no grateful music. He shuns the church, the altar, and the great congregation of christian worshippers, and wanders away to the gloomy forest, to utter in the vacant air complaints and griefs, which the religion of his times and his country can neither console nor relieve. Goaded almost to madness by the sense of the injustice done him, he resorts hither to give to his pent up feelings, and to debate with himself the feasibility of plans, plans of his own invention, for his own deliverance. From this hour I am an abolitionist. I have seen enough and heard enough, and I shall go to my home in Ohio resolved to atone for my past indifference to this ill-starred race, by making such exertions as I shall be able to do, for the speedy emancipation of every slave in the land."

[The ship's overseer, Tom Grant, recounts the slave rebellion on the *Creole*.]

"The attack began just about twilight in the evening. Apprehending a squall, I had commanded the second mate to order all hands on deck, to take in sail. A few minutes before this I had seen Madison's head above the hatchway, looking out upon the white-capped waves at the leeward. I think I never saw him look more good-natured. I stood just about midship, on the larboard side. The captain was pacing the quarter-deck on the starboard side, in company with Mr. Jameson, the owner of most of the slaves on board. Both were armed. I had just told the men to lay aloft, and was looking to see my orders obeyed, when I heard the discharge of a pistol on the starboard side; and turning suddenly around, the very deck seemed covered with fiends from the pit. The nineteen negroes were all on deck, with their broken fetters in their hands, rushing in all directions. I put my hand quickly in my pocket to draw out my jack-knife; but before I could draw it, I was knocked senseless to the deck. When I came to myself, (which I did in a few minutes, I suppose, for it was yet quite light,) there was not a white man on deck. The sailors were all aloft in the rigging, and dared not come down. Captain Clarke and Mr. Jameson lay stretched on the quarter-deck,—both dying,—while Madison himself stood at the helm unhurt.

"I was completely weakened by the loss of blood, and had not recovered from the stunning blow which felled me to the deck; but it was a little too much for me, even in my prostrate condition, to see our good brig commanded by a *black murderer*. So I called out to the men to come down and take the ship, or die in the attempt. Suiting the action to the word, I started aft. You murderous villain, said I, to the imp at the helm, and rushed upon him to deal him a blow, when he pushed me back with his strong, black arm, as though I had been a boy of twelve. I looked around for the men. They were still in the rigging. Not one had come down. I started towards Madison again. The rascal now told me to stand back. 'Sir,' said he, 'your life is in my hands. I could have killed you a dozen times over during this last half hour, and could kill you now. You call me a *black murderer*. I am not a murderer. God is my witness that LIBERTY, not *malice*, is the motive for this night's work. I have done no more to those dead men yonder, than they would have done to me in like circumstances. We have struck for our freedom, and if a true man's heart be in you, you will honor us for the deed. We have done that which you applaud your fathers for doing, and if we are murderers, *so were they.*'

"I felt little disposition to reply to this impudent speech. By heaven, it disarmed me. The fellow loomed up before me. I forgot his blackness in the dignity of his manner, and the eloquence of his speech. It seemed as if the souls of both the great dead (whose names he bore) had entered him. To the sailors in the rigging he said: 'Men! the battle is over,—your captain is dead. I have complete command of this vessel. All resistance to my authority will be in vain. My men have won their liberty, with no other weapons but their own BROKEN FETTERS. We are nineteen in number. We do not thirst for your blood, we demand only our rightful freedom. Do not flatter yourselves that I am ignorant of chart or compass. I know both. We are now only about sixty miles from Nassau. Come down, and do your duty. Land us in Nassau, and not a hair of your heads shall be hurt.'

"I shouted, *Stay where you are, men*,—when a sturdy black fellow ran at me with a handspike, and would have split my head open, but for the interference of Madison, who darted between me and the blow. 'I know

what you are up to,' said the latter to me. 'You want to navigate this brig into
a slave port, where you would have us all hanged; but you'll miss it; before
this brig shall touch a slave-cursed shore while I am on board, I will myself
put a match to the magazine, and blow her, and be blown with her, into
a thousand fragments. Now I have saved your life twice within these last
twenty minutes,—for, when you lay helpless on deck, my men were about
to kill you. I held them in check. And if you now (seeing I am your friend
and not your enemy) persist in your resistance to my authority, I give you
fair warning, YOU SHALL DIE.'

"Saying this to me, he cast a glance into the rigging where the ter-
ror-stricken sailors were clinging, like so many frightened monkeys, and
commanded them to come down, in a tone from which there was no
appeal; for four men stood by with muskets in hand, ready at the word of
command to shoot them down.

"I now became satisfied that resistance was out of the question; that my
best policy was to put the brig into Nassau, and secure the assistance of the
American consul at that port. I felt sure that the authorities would enable us
to secure the murderers, and bring them to trial.

"By this time the apprehended squall had burst upon us. The wind
howled furiously,—the ocean was white with foam, which, on account of
the darkness, we could see only by the quick flashes of lightning that darted
occasionally from the angry sky. All was alarm and confusion. Hideous
cries came up from the slave women. Above the roaring billows a succession of heavy thunder rolled along, swelling the terrific din. Owing to the
great darkness, and a sudden shift of the wind, we found ourselves in the
trough of the sea. When shipping a heavy sea over the starboard bow, the
bodies of the captain and Mr. Jameson were washed overboard. For awhile
we had dearer interests to look after than slave property. A more savage
thunder-gust never swept the ocean. Our brig rolled and creaked as if every
bolt would be started, and every thread of oakum would be pressed out of
the seams. To the pumps! to the pumps! I cried, but not a sailor would quit
his grasp. Fortunately this squall soon passed over, or we must have been
food for sharks.

"During all the storm, Madison stood firmly at the helm,—his keen eye
fixed upon the binnacle. He was not indifferent to the dreadful hurricane;
yet he met it with the equanimity of an old sailor. He was silent but not agitated. The first words he uttered after the storm had slightly subsided, were
characteristic of the man. 'Mr. Mate, you cannot write the bloody laws of

slavery on those restless billows. The ocean, if not the land, is free.' I confess, gentlemen, I felt myself in the presence of a superior man; one who, had he been a white man, I would have followed willingly and gladly in any honorable enterprise. Our difference of color was the only ground for difference of action. It was not that his principles were wrong in the abstract; for they are the principles of 1776. But I could not bring myself to recognize their application to one whom I deemed my inferior.

"But to my story. What happened now is soon told. Two hours after the frightful tempest had spent itself, we were plump at the wharf in Nassau. I sent two of our men immediately to our consul with a statement of facts, requesting his interference in our behalf. What he did, or whither he did anything, I don't know; but, by order of the authorities, a company of *black* soldiers came on board, for the purpose, as they said, of protecting the property. These impudent rascals, when I called on them to assist me in keeping the slaves on board, sheltered themselves adroitly under their instructions only to protect property,—and said they did not recognize *persons* as *property*. I told them that by the laws of Virginia and the laws of the United States, the slaves on board were as much property as the barrels of flour in the hold. At this the stupid blockheads showed their *ivory*, rolled up their white eyes in horror, as if the idea of putting men on a footing with merchandise were revolting to their humanity. When these instructions were understood among the negroes, it was impossible for us to keep them on board. They deliberately gathered up their baggage before our eyes, and, against our remonstrances, poured through the gangway,—formed themselves into a procession on the wharf,--bid farewell to all on board, and, uttering the wildest shouts of exultation, they marched, amidst the deafening cheers of a multitude of sympathizing spectators, under the triumphant leadership of their heroic chief and deliverer, MADISON WASHINGTON."

JOHN ROLLIN RIDGE / CHEESQUATALAWNY /
YELLOW BIRD (1827–1867)

First novel published by a Native American author.

John Rollin Ridge, whose Cherokee name was Cheesquatalawny and who
also published as Yellow Bird (the English translation of his Cherokee
name), was born the son of a distinguished family in the Cherokee Nation
in Georgia in 1827. His family gave into pressure from the U.S. government to move west to Indian Territory. In 1839 John witnessed his father's
brutal murder, which haunted him for the rest of his life. He was educated
in Cherokee missionary schools, by a private tutor, and at Great Barrington
Academy in Massachusetts. In 1850 he moved to California during the
Gold Rush, where he worked as a newspaper editor and journalist. Based
on his own background as a committed Democrat in a slaveholding family,
Ridge opposed abolition, President Abraham Lincoln, and the Republicans
during the Civil War, but maintained his support of the Union. After the
end of the Civil War, Ridge led a delegation of Southern Cherokees to rene-
gotiate relations with the federal government in Washington, D.C., hoping
the Cherokee Nation would be admitted as a state of the union. He died in
1878 in California.

In 1854 Ridge published the first known novel by an American Indian
and also the first novel written in California, *The Life and Adventures of
Joaquín Murieta, the Celebrated California Bandit*, which is based on actual
events and claims to be a true account of the folk hero Murieta. In the novel
Ridge portrays the brutality of Anglo Americans who drove California
Mexicans from their land, just as white Americans had pushed Cherokees
from their land during John's childhood. In 1868 his widow published a
collection of his poems as *Poems*; additional poems were recently re-discov-
ered and published by Robert Dale Parker. These poems rival some of the
great nature poems in the Romantic tradition. Like Whitman's poems, they

move beyond the legacy of European Romanticism by juxtaposing evocative descriptions of natural vistas with deep reflections about Americans' particular place in the world.

From THE LIFE AND ADVENTURES OF JOAQUÍN MURIETA THE CELEBRATED CALIFORNIA BANDIT [1854]

I SIT DOWN to write somewhat concerning the life and character of *Joaquín Murieta*, a man as remarkable in the annals of crime as any of the renowned robbers of the Old or New World, who have preceded him; and I do this, not for the purpose of ministering to any depraved taste for the dark and horrible in human action, but rather to contribute my mite to those materials out of which the early history of California shall one day be composed. The character of this truly wonderful man was nothing more than a natural production of the social and moral condition of the country in which he lived, acting upon certain peculiar circumstances favorable to such a result, and, consequently, his individual history is a part of the most valuable history of the State.

There were two Joaquíns, bearing the various surnames of Murieta, O'Comorenia, Valenzuela, Botellier, and Carillo—so that it was supposed there were no less than five sanguinary devils ranging the country at one and the same time. It is now fully ascertained that there were only two, whose proper names were Joaquín Murieta and Joaquín Valenzuela, the latter being nothing more than a distinguished subordinate to the first, who is the Rinaldo Rinaldini of California.

Joaquín Murieta was a Mexican, born in the province of Sonora of respectable parents and educated in the schools of Mexico. While growing up, he was remarkable for a very mild and peaceable disposition, and gave no sign of that indomitable and daring spirit which afterwards characterized him. Those who knew him in his school-boy days speak affectionately of his generous and noble nature at that period of his life and can scarcely credit the fact that the renowned and bloody bandit of California was one and the same being. At an early age of his manhood—indeed, while he was yet scarcely more than a boy—he became tired of the uncertain state of affairs in his own country, the usurpations and revolutions which were of such common occurrence, and resolved to try his fortunes among the American people, of whom he had formed the most favorable opinion from an acquaintance with the few whom he had met in his own native land. The war with Mexico had been fought, and California belonged to the United States. Disgusted with the conduct of his degenerate countrymen and fired with enthusiastic admiration of the American character, the youthful Joaquín left his home with a buoyant heart and full of the exhilarating spirit of adventure. The first that we hear of him in the Golden State is that, in the spring of 1850, he is engaged in the honest occupation of a miner in the Stanislaus placers, then reckoned among the richest portions of the mines. He was then eighteen years of age, a little over the medium height, slenderly but gracefully built, and active as a young tiger. His complexion was neither very dark or very light, but clear and brilliant, and his countenance is pronounced to have been, at that time, exceedingly handsome and attractive. His large black eyes, kindling with the enthusiasm of his earnest nature, his firm and well-formed mouth, his well-shaped head from which the long, glossy, black hair hung down over his shoulders, his silvery voice full of generous utterance, and the frank and cordial bearing which distinguished him made him beloved by all with whom he came in contact. He had the confidence and respect of the whole community around him, and was fast amassing a fortune from his rich mining claim. He had built him a comfortable mining residence in which he had domiciled his heart's treasure—a beautiful Sonorian girl, who had followed the young adventure in all his wanderings with that devotedness of passion which belongs to the dark-eyed damsels of Mexico. It was at this moment of peace and felicity that a blight came over the young man's prospects. The country was then full of lawless and desperate men, who bore the name of Americans but failed to support the honor and dignity of that title. A feeling was prevalent among this class of contempt for any and all Mexicans, whom they looked upon as no better than conquered subjects of the United States, having no rights which could stand before a haughtier and superior race. They made no exceptions. If the proud blood of the Castilians mounted to the cheek of a partial descendant of the Mexiques, showing that he had inherited the old chivalrous spirit of his Spanish ancestry, they looked upon it as a saucy presumption in one so inferior to them. The prejudice of color, the antipathy of races, which are always stronger and bitterer with the ignorant and unlettered, they could not overcome, or if they could, would not, because it afforded them a convenient excuse for their unmanly cruelty and oppression. A band of these lawless men, having the brute power to do as they pleased, visited Joaquín's house and peremptorily bade him leave his claim, as they would allow no

Mexicans to work in that region. Upon his remonstrating against such out-
rageous conduct, they struck him violently over the face, and, being physically superior, compelled him to swallow his wrath. Not content with this,
they tied him hand and foot and ravished his mistress before his eyes. They
left him, but the soul of the young man was from that moment darkened.
It was the first injury he had ever received at the hands of the Americans,
whom he had always hitherto respected, and it wrung him to the soul as a
deeper and deadlier wrong from that very circumstance. He departed with
his weeping and almost heart-broken mistress for a more northern portion
of the mines; and the next we hear of him, he is cultivating a little farm on
the banks of a beautiful stream that watered a fertile valley, far out in the
seclusion of the mountains. Here he might hope for peace—here he might
forget the past, and again be happy. But his dream was not destined to last.
A company of unprincipled Americans—shame that there should be such
bearing the name!—saw his retreat, coveted his little home surrounded by
its fertile tract of land, and drove him from it, with no other excuse than
that he was "an infernal Mexican intruder!" Joaquín's blood boiled in his
veins, but his spirit was still unbroken, nor had the iron so far entered his
soul as to sear up the innate sensitiveness to honor and right which reigned
in his bosom. Twice broken up in his honest pursuit of fortune, he resolved
still to labor on with unflinching brow and with that true *moral* bravery,
which throws its redeeming light forward upon his subsequently dark and
criminal career. How deep must have been the anguish of that young heart
and how strongly rooted the native honesty of his soul, none can know or
imagine but they who have been tried in a like manner. He bundled up his
little movable property, still accompanied by his faithful bosom-friend, and
again started forth to strike once more, like a brave and honest man, for
fortune and for happiness. He arrived at "Murphy's Diggings" in Calaveras
County, in the month of April, and went again to mining, but, meeting
with nothing like his former success, he soon abandoned that business and
devoted his time to dealing "monte," a game which is common in Mexico,
and has been almost universally adopted by gamblers in California. It is
considered by the Mexican in no manner a disreputable employment, and
many well-raised young men from the Atlantic States have resorted to it
as a profession in this land of luck and chances. It was then in much better
odor than it is now, although it is at present a game which may be played
on very fair and honest principles; provided, anything can be strictly honest
or fair which allows the taking of money without a valuable consideration.

It was therefore looked upon as no departure from rectitude on the part of Joaquín, when he commenced the business of dealing "monte." Having a very pleasing exterior and being, despite of all his sorrows, very gay and lively in disposition, he attracted many persons to his table, and won their money with such skill and grace, or lost his own with such perfect good humor that he was considered by all the very beau ideal of a gambler and the prince of clever fellows. His sky seemed clear and his prospects bright, but Fate was weaving her mysterious web around him, and fitting him to be by the force of circumstances what nature never intended to make him.

He had gone a short distance from Murphy's Diggings to see a half-brother, who had been located in that vicinity for several months, and returned to Murphy's upon a horse which his brother had lent him. The animal proved to have been stolen, and being recognized by a number of individuals in town, an excitement was raised on the subject. Joaquín suddenly found himself surrounded by a furious mob and charged with the crime of theft. He told them how it happened that he was riding the horse and in what manner his half-brother had come in possession of it. They listened to no explanation, but bound him to a tree, and publicly disgraced him with the lash. They then proceeded to the house of his half-brother and hung him without judge or jury. It was then that the character of Joaquín changed, suddenly and irrevocably. Wanton cruelty and the tyranny of prejudice had reached their climax. His soul swelled beyond its former boundaries, and the barriers of honor, rocked into atoms by the strong passion which shook his heart like an earthquake, crumbled around him. Then it was that he declared to a friend that he would live henceforth for revenge and that his path should be marked with blood. Fearfully did he keep his promise, as the following pages will show.

It was not long after this unfortunate affair that an American was found dead in the vicinity of Murphy's Diggings, having been cut to pieces with a knife. Though horribly mangled, he was recognized as one of the mob engaged in whipping Joaquín. A doctor, passing in the neighborhood of this murder, was met, shortly afterward, by two men on horseback, who fired their revolvers at him, but, owing to his speed on foot, and the unevenness of the ground, he succeeded in escaping with no further injury than having a bullet shot through his hat within an inch of the top of his head! A panic spread among the rash individuals who had composed that mob, and they were afraid to stir out on their ordinary business. Whenever any one of them strayed out of sight of his camp or ventured to travel on the highway, he was shot down suddenly and mysteriously. Report after report came into the villages that Americans had been found dead on the highways, having been either shot or stabbed, and it was invariably discovered, for many weeks, that the murdered men belonged to the mob who publicly whipped Joaquín. It was fearful and it was strange to see how swiftly and mysteriously those men disappeared. "Murieta's revenge was very nearly complete," said an eyewitness of these events, in reply to an inquiry which I addressed him. "I am inclined to think he *wiped out* the most of those prominently engaged in whipping him."

Thus far, who can blame him? But the iron had entered too deeply in his soul for him to stop here. He had contracted a hatred to the whole American race, and was determined to shed their blood, whenever and wherever an opportunity occurred. It was no time now for him to retrace his steps. He had committed deeds which made him amenable to the law, and his only safety lay in a persistence in the unlawful course which he had begun. It was necessary that he should have horses and that he should have money. These he could not obtain except by robbery and murder, and thus he became an outlaw and a bandit on the verge of his nineteenth year.

The year 1850 rolled away, marked with the eventful history of this young man's wrongs and trials, his bitter revenge on those who had perpetrated the crowning act of his deep injury and disgrace; and, as it closed, it shut him away forever from his peace of mind and purity of heart. He walked forth into the future a dark, determined criminal, and his proud nobility of soul existed only in memory.

It became generally known in 1851 that an organized banditti was ranging the country; but it was not yet ascertained who was the leader. Travelers, laden with the produce of the mines, were met upon the roads by well-dressed men who politely invited them to "stand and deliver"; persons riding alone in the many wild and lonesome regions, which form a large portion of this country, were skillfully noosed with the lasso (which the Mexicans throw with great accuracy, being able thus to capture wild cattle, elk, and sometimes even grizzly bears, upon the plains), dragged from their saddles, and murdered in the adjacent thickets. Horses of the finest mettle were stolen from the ranches, and, being tracked up, were found in the possession of a determined band of men, ready to retain them at all hazards and fully able to stand their ground. The scenes of murder and robbery shifted with the rapidity of lightning. At one time, the northern countries would be suffering slaughters and depredations, at another the southern, and, before one would have imagined it possible, the east and the west, and every point of the compass would be in trouble. There had never been before this, either in '49 or '50, any such as an organized banditti, and it had been a matter of surprise to every one, since the country was so well adapted to a business of this kind—the houses scattered at such distances along the roads, the plains so level and open in which to ride with speed, and the mountains so rugged with their ten thousand fastnesses in which to hide. Grass was abundant in the far-off valleys which lay hidden in the rocky gorges, cool, delicious streams made music at the feet of the towering peaks, or came leaping down in gladness from their sides-game abounded on every hand, and nine unclouded months of the year made a climate so salubrious that nothing could be sweeter than a day's rest under the tall pines or a night's repose under the open canopy of Heaven. Joaquín knew his advantages. His superior intelligence and education gave him the respect of his comrades, and, appealing to the prejudice against the "Yankees," which the disastrous results of the Mexican war had not tended to lessen in their minds, he soon assembled around him a powerful band of his countrymen, who daily increased, as he ran his career of almost magical success. Among the number was Manuel Garcia, more frequently known as "Three-Fingered Jack," from the fact of his having had one of his fingers shot off in a skirmish with an American party during the Mexican war. He was a man of unflinching bravery, but cruel and sanguinary. His form was large and rugged and his countenance so fierce that few liked to look upon it. He was different from his more youthful leader, in possessing nothing of his generous, frank, and cordial disposition, and in being utterly destitute of one merciful trait of humanity. His delight was in murder for its own diabolical sake, and he gloated over the agonies of his unoffending victims. He would sacrifice policy, the safety and interests of the band for the mere gratification of this murderous propensity, and it required all Joaquín's firmness and determination to hold him in check. The history of this monster was well known before he joined Joaquín. He was known to be the same man, who, in 1846, surrounded with his party two Americans, young men by the name of Cowie and Fowler, as they were traveling on the road between Sonoma and Bodega, stripped them entirely naked, and, binding them each to a tree, slowly tortured them to death. He began by throwing knives at their bodies, as if he were practicing at a target; he then cut out their tongues, punched out their eyes with his knife, gashed their bodies in numerous places, and, finally, flaying them alive, left them to die. A thousand cruelties like these had he been guilty of, and, long before Joaquín knew him, he was a hardened experienced, and detestable monster. When it was necessary for the young chief to commit some peculiarly horrible and cold-blooded murder, some deed of hellish ghastliness at which his soul revolted, he deputed this man to do it. And well was it executed, with certainty and to the letter.

An Indian's Grave [1847]

Far in a lonely wood I wandered once,
Where warbling birds of melancholy wing
And music sad, rehearsed their melancholy songs.
All else was silent save the whispering leaves
Strewn by autumnal winds, or here and there
A stream which ever poured a mournful sound
Amid those solitudes so dim, where shadows
Vast and tall, eternal threw their flickering
Darkness. Retrospection sadly turned my mind
To scenes now painted on the map of Time
Long Past. And as I wandered on, I mused
On greatness fall'n, beauteous things destroyed;
When suddenly my footstep paused before
A mound of moss-grown earth. I wondered,
For a while, what mortal here had found
A resting place? But soon I minded me,
That many years agone a noble race
Had roamed these forest-wilds among, and made
These mountain-fastnesses rebound to shouts
Of liberty untamed, and happiness
That knew no bounds. I recollected more,
That, save but a few, they all had fled,
And, fleeing, left some bones behind: The only
Mark that this fair land was once their heritage,
By Nature's gift to her untutored sons.
Then thought I, "This must be the grave of one
Who ranked among the warriors of the
Wilderness!—And when he saw his country

Doomed, his tribe o'erthrown, and his strong arm
Grown weak before his pale-faced foes; and when
He knew the hour was come, in which his soul
Must leave the form it once had moved to noble
Deeds, and travel to the hunting-grounds, where erst
His fathers went, he here had dug his grave,
And, singing wild his death-song to the wind,
Sunk down and died!"

   Sleep on, dark warrior,
Whoe'er thou art! My hand shall not disturb
The slightest stem that takes its nutriment
From thee. The white man's share may plough some other
Mounds where Red men sleep, round which no mourner
Stands in watch to guard the relics of a friend;
But no rude step, and no rude hand shall e'en
Despoil the beauty of this silent spot,
Or sacrilegiously disturb the rest
Of *one* lone Indian form. Sleep on!
The storms that howled around thy head long,
Long ago, and tutored thy stern heart
To agony, have ceased. A thousand cities
Stand, where once thy nation's wigwams stood,—
And num'rous palaces of giant strength
Are floating down the streams where long ago
Thy bark canoe was gliding. All is changed.
Then *sleep* thou on! Perchance that peace, denied
In life, within the lonely grave is found.

REFLECTIONS IRREGULAR [1848]

I cast a backward look—how changed
  The scenes of other days!
I walk, a wearied man, estranged
  From youth's delightful ways.
There in the distance rolleth yet
  That stream whose waves my
Boyish bosom oft has met,

When pleasure lit mine eye.
It rolleth yet, as clear, as bold,
   As pure as it did then;
But I have grown in youth-time old,
   And, mixing now with men,
My sobered eye must not attend
To that sweet stream, my early friend!
The music of its waters clear
Must now but seldom reach my ear,
But murmur on still carelessly
To every heedless passer-by.
How often o'er its rugged cliffs I've strayed,
And gaily listened, as its billows played
Such deep, low music at their base—
And then such brightening thoughts would trace
Upon the tablet of my mind!
Alas, those days have run their race,
Their joys I nowhere now can find.
   I have no time to think
      Of climbing Glory's sunny mount
   I have no time to drink
      At Learning's bubbling fount!
Now corn and potatoes call me
From scenes were wont to enthrall me—
     A weary wight,
     Both day and night
My brain is full of business matters,
     Reality has snatched the light,
     From fancy's hand, that shone so bright,
And tore the dreams she wove, to tatters!

From POEMS [1868]

MOUNT SHASTA

Behold the dread Mt. Shasta, where it stands
Imperial midst the lesser heights, and, like
Some mighty unimpassioned mind, companionless

And cold. The storms of Heaven may beat in wrath
Against it, but it stands in unpolluted
Grandeur still; and from the rolling mists upheaves
Its tower of pride e'en purer than before.
The wintry showers and white-winged tempests leave
Their frozen tributes on its brow, and it
Doth make of them an everlasting crown.
Thus doth it, day by day and age by age,
Defy each stroke of time: still rising highest
Into Heaven!

    Aspiring to the eagle's cloudless height,
No human foot has stained its snowy side;
No human breath has dimmed the icy mirror which
It holds unto the moon and stars and sov'reign sun.
We may not grow familiar with the secrets
Of its hoary top, whereon the Genius
Of that mountain builds his glorious throne!
Far lifted in the boundless blue, he doth
Encircle, with his gaze supreme, the broad
Dominions of the West, which lie beneath
His feet, in pictures of sublime repose
No artist ever drew. He sees the tall
Gigantic hills arise in silentness
And peace, and in the long review of distance
Range themselves in order grand. He sees the sunlight
Play upon the golden streams which through the valleys
Glide. He hears the music of the great and solemn sea,
And overlooks the huge old western wall
To view the birth-place of undying Melody!

    Itself all light, save when some loftiest cloud
Doth for a while embrace its cold forbidding
Form, that monarch mountain casts its mighty
Shadow down upon the crownless peaks below,
That, like inferior minds to some great
Spirit, stand in strong contrasted littleness!
All through the long and Summery months of our
Most tranquil year, it points its icy shaft

On high, to catch the dazzling beams that fall
In showers of splendor round that crystal cone,
And roll in floods of far magnificence
Away from that lone, vast Reflector in
The dome of Heaven.
Still watchful of the fertile
Vale and undulating plains below, the grass
Grows greener in its shade, and sweeter bloom
The flowers. Strong purifier! From its snowy
Side the breezes cool are wafted to the "peaceful
Homes of men," who shelter at its feet, and love
To gaze upon its honored form, aye standing
There the guarantee of health and happiness.
Well might it win communities so blest
To loftier feelings and to nobler thoughts—
The great material symbol of eternal
Things! And well I ween, in after years, how
In the middle of his furrowed track the plowman
In some sultry hour will pause, and wiping
From his brow the dusty sweat, with reverence
Gaze upon that hoary peak. The herdsman
Oft will rein his charger in the plain, and drink
Into his inmost soul the calm sublimity;
And little children, playing on the green, shall
Cease their sport, and, turning to that mountain
Old, shall of their mother ask: "Who made it?"
And she shall answer,—"GOD!"

    And well this Golden State shall thrive, if like
Its own Mt. Shasta, Sovereign Law shall lift
Itself in purer atmosphere—so high
That human feeling, human passion at its base
Shall lie subdued; e'en pity's tears shall on
Its summit freeze; to warm it e'en the sunlight
Of deep sympathy shall fail:
Its pure administration shall be like
The snow immaculate upon that mountain's brow!

The Stolen White Girl

The prairies are broad, and the woodlands are wide
And proud on his steed the wild half-breed may ride,
With the belt round his waist and the knife at his side,
And no white man may claim his beautiful bride.

Though he stole her away from the land of the whites,
Pursuit is in vain, for her bosom delights
In the love that she bears the dark-eyed, the proud,
Whose glance is like starlight beneath a night-cloud.

Far down in the depths of the forest they'll stray,
Where the shadows like night are lingering all day;
Where the flowers are springing up wild at their feet,
And the voices of birds in the branches are sweet.

Together they'll roam by the streamlets that run,
O'ershadowed at times then meeting the sun—
The streamlets that soften their varying tune,
As up the blue heavens calm wanders the moon!

The contrast between them is pleasing and rare;
Her sweet eye of blue, and her soft silken hair,
Her beautiful waist, and her bosom of white
That heaves to the touch with a sense of delight;

His form more majestic and darker his brow,
Where the sun has imparted its liveliest glow—
An eye that grows brighter with passion's true fire,
As he looks on his loved one with earnest desire.

Oh, never let Sorrow's cloud darken their fate,
The girl of the "pale face," her Indian mate!
But deep in the forest of shadows and flowers,
Let Happiness smile, as she wings their sweet hours.

WILLIAM WELLS BROWN (1814?–1884)

First published play by an African American author.

The Escape, the first extant play by an African American playwright (who was already renowned as a writer, memoirist, speaker, and historian) is a five-act comic melodrama marked by dramatic complexity, irony, humor, and deeply rendered characters. It tells the story of Glen and Melinda, an enslaved couple, their brutal treatment at the hands of their highly educated white enslavers, and their final escape to Canada. Set before the abolition of slavery in the Kentucky household of a white doctor and his wife—whose cruelty, venality, and selfishness is cloaked by a veneer of Southern gentility—it is also a moving love story against formidable odds. Based on real-life individuals known to Brown, the main characters are owned by two brothers-in-law, one of whom resents Glen's dignity while the other lusts after Melinda. When Melinda's enslaver tries to rape her, she admits her secret marriage to Glen. The enslaver, Dr. Gaines, orders Glen to be flogged to death, while the doctor's wife, in a jealous rage, tries to force Melinda to drink poison. Glen and Melinda risk a desperate escape. In a meeting house close to the Canadian border, Glen and Melinda are unexpectedly joined by another slave, Cato, who had been loyal to his enslaver but now has abandoned him in the hunt for his valuable slaves. There is a good bit of humor, plenty of suspense, and deftly interwoven information about the legal status of enslaved people who manage to escape but were hunted also in "free" states throughout the entire United States after the Fugitive Slave Act of 1850. Glen and Melinda's courageous "leap for freedom" is ultimately helped by a white abolitionist, but the play centers on two Black people whose moral compass, courage, and love shape the fast-moving plot while society around them seems to leave them few choices. Brown exposes the hypocrisy in individual characters and in the nation's founding texts when, for example, the abolitionist says: "But sir, the Constitution gives me the right to speak my sentiments, at all times and in all places." "We don't care for Constitutions nor nothin' else. We made the Constitution, and we'll break it," is the chilling response.

The play, after dramatically describing the conditions of life under slavery, ends well.

Brown wrote a three-act play, *Experience, or How To Give a Northern Man a Backbone*, in 1856 to vary the genre he used to present his antislavery arguments. He read the play frequently to great effect before large audiences but it is assumed he never intended to publish it. In 1856 he read from *The Leap*, reprinted here, for the first time to the public. The excerpt from *The Leap* here includes Black folk songs, which Brown collected in several other publications, including *The Anti-Slavery Harp; A Collection of Songs for Anti-Slavery Meetings* (1848). A gifted orator, Brown captivated large audiences by reading scenes from his play.

Ira Aldridge, the famous Black actor celebrated by royal courts and audiences in Europe, had adapted a French play, *The Black Doctor*, in 1847, and Victor Séjour's *The Brown Overcoat* was also produced in 1858. The first play by a Black playwright staged in America is probably Henry Brown's *The Drama of King Shotaway* in 1823, of which no text has been found.

From THE ESCAPE; OR, A LEAP FOR FREEDOM [1858]

PLAYWRIGHT'S PREFACE

This play was written for my own amusement, and not with the remotest thought that it would ever be seen by the public eye. I read it privately, however, to a circle of my friends, and through them was invited to read it to a Literary Society. Since then, the drama has been given in various parts of the country. By the earnest solicitation of some in whose judgment I have the greatest confidence, I now present it in a printed form to the public. As I never aspired to be a dramatist, I ask no favor for it, and have little or no solicitude for its fate. If it is not readable, no word of mine can make it so; if it is, to ask a favor for it would be needless.

The main features in the Drama are true. *Glen* and *Melinda* are actual characters, and still reside in Canada. Many of the incidents are drawn from my own experience of eighteen years at the South. The marriage ceremony, as performed in the second act, is still adhered to in many of the Southern States, especially in the farming districts.

The ignorance of the slave, as seen in the case of *Big Sally,* is common wherever chattel slavery exists. The difficulties created in the domestic circle by the presence of beautiful slave women, as found in *Dr. Gaines'* family, is well understood by all who have ever visited the valley of the Mississippi.

The play, no doubt, abounds in defects, but as I was born in slavery, and never had a day's schooling in my life, I owe the public no apology for errors.

W. W. B.

CHARACTERS REPRESENTED

DR. GAINES, *proprietor of the farm at Muddy Creek*
MR. CAMPBELL, *a neighboring slave owner*
REV. JOHN PINCHEN, *a clergyman*
DICK WALKER, *a slave speculator*
Mr. WILDMARSH, *neighbor to Dr. Gaines*
MAJOR MOORE, *a friend of Dr. Gaines*
MR. WHITE, *a citizen of Massachusetts*
BILL JENNINGS, *a slave speculator*
JACOB SCRAGG, *overseer to Dr. Gaines*
MRS. GAINES, *wife of Dr. Gaines*
MR. *and* MRS. NEAL, *and* DAUGHTER, *Quakers, in Ohio*
THOMAS, *Mr. Neal's hired man*
GLEN, *slave of Mr. Hamilton, brother-in-law of Dr. Gaines*
CATO, SAM, SAMPEY (BOB), MELINDA, DOLLY, SUSAN, *and* BIG
SALLY, *slaves of Dr. Gaines*
PETE, NED, BILL, *and* TAPIOCA, *slaves*
OFFICERS, LOUNGERS, BARKEEPER, etc.

ACT ONE
SCENE ONE, *A Sitting-Room.*

Mrs. Gaines, looking at some drawings—Sampey, a white slave, stands behind the lady's chair.

Enter Dr. Gaines, right.

DR. GAINES. Well, my dear, my practice is steadily increasing. I forgot to tell you that neighbor Wyman engaged me yesterday as his family physician; and I hope that the fever and argue, which is now taking hold of the people, will give me more patients. I see by the New Orleans papers that the yellow fever is raging there to a fearful extent. Men of my profession are reaping a harvest in that section this year. I would that we could have a touch of the yellow fever here, for I think I could invent a medicine that would cure it. But the yellow fever is a luxury that we medical men in this climate can't expect to enjoy; yet we may hope for the cholera.

MRS. GAINES Yes, I would be glad to see it more sickly here, so that your business may prosper. But we are always unfortunate. Every body here seems to be in good health, and I am afraid that they'll keep so. However, we must hope for the best. We must trust in the Lord. Providence may possibly send some disease amongst us for our benefit.

Enter Cato, right.

CATO. Mr. Campbell is at de door, massa.
DR. GAINES. Ask him in, Cato.

Enter Mr. Campbell, right.

DR. GAINES. Good morning, Mr. Campbell. Be seated.
MR. CAMPBELL. Good morning, doctor. The same to you, Mrs. Gaines Fine morning, this.
MRS. GAINES. Yes sir; beautiful day.
MR. CAMPBELL. Well, doctor, I've come to engage you for my family physician. I am tired of Dr. Jones. I've lost another very valuable nigger under his treatment; and, as my old mother used to say "change of pastures makes fat calves."
DR. GAINES. I shall be most happy to become your doctor. Of course, you want me to attend to your niggers, as well as to your family?
MR. CAMPBELL. Certainly, sir. I have twenty-three servants. What will you charge me by the year?
DR. GAINES. Of course, you'll do as my other patients do, send your servants to me when they are sick, if able to walk?
MR. CAMPBELL. Oh, yes; I always do that.
DR. GAINES. Then I suppose I'll have to lump it, and say $500 per annum.
MR. CAMPBELL. Well, then, we'll consider that matter settled; and as two of the boys are sick, I'll send them over. So I'll bid you good day, doctor. I would be glad if you could come over some time, and being Mrs. Gaines with you.
DR. GAINES. Yes, I will; and shall be glad if you will pay us a visit, and

bring with you Mrs. Campbell. Come over and spend the day.

MR. CAMPBELL. I will. Good morning, doctor.

Exit Mr. Campbell, right.

DR. GAINES. There, my dear what do you think of that? Five hundred dollars more added to our income. That's patronage worth having! And I am glad to get all the negroes I can to doctor, for Cato is becoming very useful to me in the shop. He can bleed, pull teeth, and do almost anything that the blacks require. He can put up medicine as well as any one. A valuable boy, Cato!

MRS. GAINES. But why did you ask Mr. Campbell to visit you, and to bring his wife? I am sure I would never consent to associate with her, for I understand that she was the daughter of a tanner. You must remember, my dear, that I was born with a silver spoon in my mouth. The blood of the Wyleys runs in my veins. I am surprised that you should ask him to visit you at all; you should have known better.

DR. GAINES. Oh, I did not mean for him to visit me. I only invited him for the sake of compliments, and I think he so understood it; for I should be far from whishing you to associate with Mrs. Campbell. I don't forget, my dear, the family you were raised in, nor do I overlook my own family. My father, you know, fought by the side of Washington, and I hope some day to have a handle to my own name. I am certain Providence intended me for something higher than a medical man. Ah! by-the-by, I had forgotten that I have a couple of patients to visit this morning. I must go at once.

Exit Dr. Gaines, right.

Enter Hannah, left.

MRS. GAINES. Go, Hannah, and tell Dolly to kill a couple of fat pullets, and to put the biscuit to rise. I expect brother Pinchen here this afternoon, and I want everything in order. Hannah, tell Melinda to come here. *(Exit Hannah, left.)* We mistresses do have a hard time in this world; I don't see why the Lord should have imposed such heavy duties on us poor mortals. Well, it can't last always. I long to leave this wicked world, and go home to glory. *(Enter Melinda.)* I am to have company this afternoon, Melinda. I expect brother Pinchen here, and I want everything in order. Got and get one of my new caps, with the lace border, and get out my scalloped-bottomed dimity petticoat, and when you go out, tell Hannah to clean the white-handled knives, and see that not a speck is on them; for I want everything as it should be while brother Pinchen is here.

Exit Mrs. Gaines, left, Melinda, right.

[…]

ACT ONE
SCENE THREE, *A room in the quarters.*

Enter Glen, left.

GLEN. How slowly the time passes away. I've been waiting here two hours, and Melinda has not yet come. What keeps her, I cannot tell. I waited long and late for her last night, and when she approached, I sprang to my feet, caught her in my arms, pressed her to my heart, and kissed away the tears from her moistened cheeks. She placed her trembling hand in mind, and said "Glen, I am yours; I will never be the wife of another." I clasped her to my bosom, and called God to witness that I would ever regard her as a my wife. Old Uncle Joseph joined us in holy wedlock by moonlight; that was the only marriage ceremony. I look upon the vow as ever binding on me, for I am sure that a just God will sanction our union in heaven. Still, this man, who claims Melinda as his property, is unwilling for me to marry the woman of my choice, because he wants her himself. But he shall not have her. What he will say when he finds that we are married, I cannot tell; but I am determined to protect my wife or die. Ah! here comes Melinda.

Enter Melinda, right.

I am glad to see you, Melinda. I've been waiting long, and feared you would not come. Ah! in tears again?

MELINDA. Glen, you are always thinking I am in tears. But what did master say to-day?

GLEN. He again forbade our union.

MELINDA. Indeed! Can he be so cruel?

GLEN. Yes, he can be just so cruel.

MELINDA. Alas! alas! how unfeeling and heartless! But did you appeal to his generosity?

GLEN. Yes, I did; I used all the persuasive powers that I was master of, but to no purpose; he was inflexible. He even offered me a new suit of clothes, if I would give you up; and when I told him that I could not, he said he would flog me to death if I ever spoke to you again.

MELINDA. And what did you say to him?

GLEN. I answered, that, while I loved life better than death, even life itself could not tempt me to consent to a separation that would make life an unchanging curse. Oh, I would kill myself, Melinda, if I thought that, for the sake of life, I would consent to your degradation. No Melinda, I can die, but shall never live to see you the mistress of another man. But, my dear girl, I have a secret to tell you, and no one must know it but you. I will go out and see that no person is within hearing. I will be back soon.

Exit Glen, left.

MELINDA. It is often said that the darkest hour of the night precedes the dawn. It is ever thus with the vicissitudes of human suffering. After the soul has reached the lowest depths of despair, and can no deeper plunge amidst its rolling, fœtid shades, then the reactionary forces of man's nature begin to operate, resolution takes the place of despondency, energy succeeds instead of apathy, and an upward tendency is felt and exhibited. Men then hope against power and smile in defiance of despair. I shall never forget when first I saw Glen. It is now more than a year since he came here with his master, Mr. Hamilton. It was a glorious moonlight night in autumn. The wide and fruitful face of nature was silent and buried in repose. The tall trees on the borders of Muddy Creek waved their leafy branches in the breeze, which was wafted from afar, refreshing over hill and vale, over the rippling water, and the waving corn and wheat fields. The starry sky was studded over with a few light, flitting clouds, while the moon, as if rejoicing to witness the meeting of two hearts that should be cemented by the purest love, sailed triumphantly along among the shifting vapors.

Oh, how happy I have been in my acquaintance with Glen! That he loves me, I do well believe it; that I love him, it is most true. Oh, how I would that those who think the slave incapable of the finer feelings, could only see our hearts, and learn our thoughts,—thoughts that we dare not utter in the presence of our masters! But I fear that Glen will be separated from me, for there is nothing too base and mean for master to do, for the purpose of getting me entirely in his power. But, thanks to Heaven, he does not own Glen, and therefore cannot sell him. Yet he might purchase him from his brother-in-law, so as to send him out of the way. But here comes my husband.

Enter Glen, left.

GLEN. I've been as far as the overseer's house, and all is quiet. Now, Melinda, as you are my wife, I will confide to you a secret. I've long been thinking of making my escape to Canada, and taking you with me. It is true that I don't belong to your master, but he might buy me from Hamilton and then sell me out of the neighborhood.

MELINDA. But we could never succeed in the attempt to escape.

GLEN. We will make the trial, and show that we at least deserve success. There is a slave trader expected here next week, and Dr. Gaines would sell you at once if he knew that we were married. We must get ready and start, and if we can pass the Ohio river, we'll be safe on the road to Canada.

Exit, right.

[...]

ACT THREE
SCENE TWO, *The kitchen—slaves work.*

Enter Hannah, right.

HANNAH. Oh, Cato, do go and tell missis dat you don't want to jump de broomstick wid me,—dat's a good man! Do, Cato; kase I nebber can love you. It was only las week dat massa sold my Sammy, and I don't want any udder man. Do go tell missis dat you don't want me.

CATO. No, Hannah, I ain't a gwine to tell missis no such think, kase I dose want you, and I ain't a-gwine to tell a lie for you ner nobody else. Dar, now you's got it! I don't see why you need to make so much fuss. I is better lookin' den Sam; an' I is a house servant, an' Sam was only a fiel hand; so you ought to feel proud of a change. So go and do a missis tells you.

Exit Hannah, left.

Hannah needn't try to get me to tell a lie; I ain't a-gwine to do it, kase I dose want her, an' I is bin wantin' her dis long time, as' soon as massa sold Sam, I knowed I would get her. By golly, I is gwine to be a married man. Won't I be happy! Now, ef I could only jess run away from ole massa, an' get to Canada wid Hannah, den I'd show 'em who I was. Ah! dat reminds me of my song 'bout ole massa and Canada, an' I'll sing it fer yer. Dis is my moriginal hyme. It comed into my head one night when I was fass asleep under an apple tree, looking up at de moon. Now for my song:—

AIR—*"Dandy Jim"*   *Chorus.*

Come all ye bondmen far and near,
    Let's put a song in massa's ear,
It is a song for our poor race
Who're whipped and trampled with disgrace.

My old massa tells me, Oh,
    This is a land of freedom, Oh;
Let's look about and see if it's so,
Just as massa tells me, Oh.

He tells us of that glorious one,
    I think his name was Washington,
How he did fight for liberty,
To save a threepence tax on tea.

But now we look about and see
    That we poor blacks are not so free;
We're whipped and thrashed about like fools
And have no chance at common schools.

They take our wives, insult and mock,
    And sell our children on the block,
They choke us if we say a word,
And say that "niggers" shan't be heard.

Our preachers, too, with whip and cord,
    Command obedience in the Lord;
They say they learn it from the big book,
But for ourselves, we dare not look.

There is a country far away,
    I think they call it Canada,

And if we reach Victoria's shore,
They say that we are slaves no more.

Now haste, all bondmen, let us go,
    And leave this *Christian* country, Oh;
Haste to the land of the British Queen,
Where whips for negroes are not seen.

Now, if we go, we must take the night,
    And never let them come in sight;
The bloodhounds will be on our track,
And wo to us if they fetch us back.

Now haste all bondmen, let us go,
    And leave this *Christian* country, Oh;
God help us to Victoria's shore
Where we are free and slaves no more!

Enter Mrs. Gaines, left.

MRS. GAINES. Ah! Cato, you're ready, are you? Where is Hannah?

CATO. Yes, missis; I is bin waitin' dis long time. Hannah has bin here tryin' to swade me to tell you dat I don't' want her; but I telled her dat you sed I must jump de broomstick wid her, an' I is gwine to mind you.

MRS. GAINES. That's right, Cato; servants should always mind their masters and mistresses, without asking a question.

CATO. Yes, missis, I allers dose what you and massa tells me, an' axes nobody.

Enter Hannah, right.

MRS. GAINES. Ah! Hannah; come, we are waiting for you. Nothing can be done till you come.

HANNAH. Oh, missis, I don't want to jump de broomstick wid Cato; I can't love him.

MRS. GAINES. Shut up, this moment. Dolly, get the broom. Susan, you take hold of the other end. There, now hold it a little lower—there, a little higher. There, now, that'll do. Now Hannah take hold of Cato's hand. Let Cato take hold of your hand.

HANNAH. Oh, missis do spare me. I don't want to jump de broomstick wid Cato.

MRS. GAINES. Get the cowhide, and follow me to the cellar, and I'll whip you well. I'll let you know how to disobey my orders. Get the cowhide, and follow me to the cellar.

Exit Mrs. Gaines and Hannah, right.

DOLLY. Oh Cato, do go an' tell missis dat you don't want Hannah. Don't you hear how she's whippin her in de cellar? Do do an' tell missis dat you don't want Hannah, and den she'll stop whippin' her.

CATO. No, Dolly, I ain't a-gwine to do no such a thing, kase ef I tell missis dat I don't want Hannah, den missis will whip me; an' I ain't a-gwine to be whipped fer you, ner Hannah, ner nobody else. No, I'll jump de broomstick wid every woman on de place, ef missis wants me to, before I'll be whipped.

DOLLY. Cato, ef I was in Hannah's place, I'd see you in the bottomless pit before I'd live wid you, you great big wall-eyed, empty-headed, knock-kneed fool. You're as mean as your devilish old missis.

CATO. Ef you don't quit dat busin' me, Dolly, I'll tell missis as soon as she comes in, an' she'll whip you, you know she will.

Enter Mrs. Gaines and Hannah, right.
Mrs. Gaines fans herself with her handkerchief, and appears fatigued.

MRS. GAINES. You ought to be ashamed of yourself, Hannah to make me fatigue myself in this way, to make you do your duty. It's very naughty in you, Hannah. Now, Dolly, you and Susan get the broom, and get out in the middle of the room. There, hold it a little lower—a little higher; there, that'll do. Now, remember that this is a solemn occasion; you are going to jump into matrimony. Now, Cato, take hold of Hannah's hand. There, now, why couldn't you let Cato take hold of your hand before? Now get ready, and when I count three, do you jump. Eyes on the *broomstick!* All ready. One, two, three, and over you go. There, now you're husband and wife, and if you don't live happy together, it's your own fault; for I am sure there's nothing to hinder it. Now, Hannah, come up to the house, and I'll give you some whiskey, and you can make some apple toddy, and you and Cato can have a fine time.

Exit Mrs. Gaines and Hannah, left.

DOLLY. I tell you what, Susan, when I get married, I is gwine to have a preacher marry me. I ain't a-gwine to jump de broomstick. Dat will do for fiel' hands, but house servants ought to be 'bove that.

SUSAN. Well, chile, you can't speck any ting else from ole missis. She come from down in Carlina, from 'mong the poor white trash. She don't know any better. You can't speck nothing more dan a jump from a frog. Missis says she is one of de akastocacy; but she ain't no more of an akastocacy dan I is. Missis says she was born wid a silver spoon in her mouf; ef she was, I wish it had a-choked her, dat's what I wish. Missis wanted to make Linda jump de broomstick with Glen, but massa ain't a-gwine to let Linda jump de broomstick wid anybody. He's gwine to keep Linda fer heself.

DOLLY. You know massa took Linda 'way las' night, an' tell missis dat he has sold her and sent her down de river; but I don't b'lieve he has sold her at all. He went ober towards de poplar farm, an' I tink Linda is over dar now. Ef she is dar, missis'll find it out, fer she tell'd massa las' night, dat ef Linda was in de neighborhood, she'd find her.

Exit Dolly and Susan.

[…]

ACT FOUR
SCENE THREE, *Forest at night—large tree.*

Enter Melinda, left.

MELINDA. This is indeed a dark night to be out and alone on this road. But I must find my husband, I must. Poor Glen! if he only knew that I was here, and could get to me, he would. What a curse slavery is! It separates husbands from their wives, and tears mothers from their helpless offspring, and blights all our hopes for this world. I must try to teach Muddy Creek before daylight, and seek out my husband. What's that I hear?—footsteps? I'll get behind this tree.

Enter Glen, right.

GLEN. It is so dark, I'm afraid I've missed the road. Still, this must be the right way to the poplar farm. And if Bob told me the truth, when he said that Melinda was at the poplar farm, I will soon be with her; and if I once get her in my arms, it will be a strong man that shall take her from me. Aye, a dozen strong men shall not be able to wrest her from my arms.

Melinda rushes from behind the tree.

MELINDA. Oh, Glen! It is my husband,—it is!

GLEN. Melinda! Melinda! it is, it is! Oh God! I thank Thee for his manifestation of Thy kindness. Come, come, Melinda, we must go at once to
Canada. I escaped from the overseer, whom Dr. Gaines sent to flog me.
Yes, I struck him over the head with his own club, and I made the wine
flow freely; yet, I pounded his old skillet well for him, and then jumped
out of the window. It was a leap for freedom. Yes, Melinda, it was a leap
for freedom. I've said "master" for the last time. I am free; I'm bound for
Canada. Come, let's be off, at once, for the negro dogs will be put upon
our tracks. Let us once get beyond the Ohio river, and all will be right.

Exit, right.

ROSE TERRY COOKE (1827–1892)

First published lesbian-themed story in America.

Rose Terry Cooke was born into comfortable circumstances in Whethersfield, Connecticut, in 1827 to Henry Wadsworth Terry, who seemed to have lived off his family's money, and Anne Wright Hurlbut, whose father was a shipbuilder who had navigated the globe in a boat. The precoscious Rose moved with her sister Alice and parents to her grandmother's stately home in Hartford at a young age, and grew up surrounding by supportive and doting parents and other relations. She attended Hartford Female Seminary until age sixteen, at which time her father lost some money, changing the family's circumstances. She taught at a church school in Burlington, New Jersey, and returned in 1847 to Hartford where she supported herself financially by writing. Her situation remained precarious when in 1873 she married Rollin H. Cooke, a widower sixteen years her junior. The marriage seems to have been quite happy, although Cooke struggled financially for the rest of her life. She died in 1892, having produced a wide range of popular stories on topics as far-ranging as religion, women's roles, slavery, and modernization that were nonetheless quickly forgotten by a public eager to seize on only a few exemplars of women's writing. Cooke published over one hundred pieces of short fiction in a wide range of respected and popular magazines. Many were subsequently gathered into four book-long collections.

"The Visitation" was published first in July 1858 in *Harper's New Monthly Magazine*. It is a ghost story told by a narrator who lacks confidence to present a neatly arranged and comprehensible tale in the wake of a disturbing event. The event in question is either the narrator's unshakeable, deep love to another woman, that woman's terrible treatment of her (which is never revealed), or the fact that our narrator is now visited by a ghostly "It" who is somehow linked to that woman. The story leaves no doubt that the female narrator is profoundly in love with the resplendent Eleanor, who seems to dazzle everyone who comes in contact with her. This love is at once the most sublime, uplifting, and life-altering experience for our narrator, but also what undoes her. It renders her unfit for marriage to a man and thus shifts into the center of this story the type of deep friendship between women that was immensely popular in fiction at the time. Sexuality and self-understanding were not necessarily linked, and women often lived out their deepest feelings in relationships not with their husbands, who ruled over them in economic and other ways, but with other women. Since "homosexuality" was not invented as a clinical term until many years after this story was published, there has been robust debate over how to classify "My Visitation" and whether to consider it a work of lesbian writing. Many critics decline either to name any single work as the "first" lesbian story, or else they grant this distinction only to later writers, such as Gertrude Stein, whose world is already segmented into heterosexual and homosexual identities. We take the story at face value, even if the period's literature often describes intense friendship in terms that today sound as if they describe romantic and erotic love. There are other potential candidates for a first lesbian-themed story in American letters, but no earlier known story seems to contain "[t]he one present and all-absorbing passion" that haunts and ultimately disqualifies our narrator from heterosexual marriage and love.

My Visitation [1858]

"Is not this she of whom,
When first she came, all flushed you said to me,

***

Now could you share your thought; now should men see
Two women faster welded in one love
Than pairs of wedlock?"

The Princess

IF THIS STORY is incoherent—arranged rather for the writer's thought than for the reader's eye—it is because the brain which dictated it reeled with the sharp assaults of memory, that living anguish that abides while earth passes away into silence; and because the hand that wrote it trembled with electric thrills from a past that can not die, forever fresh in the soul it tested and tortured—powerful after the flight of years as in its first agony, to fill the dim eye with tears, and throb the languid pulses with fresh fever and passion.

Take, then, the record as it stands, and ask not from a cry of mortal pain the liquid cadence and accurate noting of an operatic bravura.

The first time *It* came was in broad day. I was ill, unable to rise; the day was cold; autumnal sunshine, pure and still, streamed through the house and came in at both the south windows of my room, the curtains drawn side to receive it, for the ague of sickness is worse to me than its pain, and not yet had my preparations for winter enabled me to have a fire. Every thing was clear and chill; Aunt Mary, down stairs in the parlor, sat and knitted, as it was her custom to do of an afternoon; Uncle Seth was not at home; the servant had gone to mass, for it was some feast—day of her Church—no sound or echo disturbed the solitude.

There is something peculiar in a silent day of autumn; melancholy pierces its fine sting through the rays of sunshine; sadness cries in the cricket's monotonous voice; separation and death symbolize in the slow leaves that quit the bough reluctantly, and lie down in dust to be over—to rot. I can endure any silence better than this hush of decay; it fills me with preternatural horror; it is as if a tomb opened and breathed out its dank, morbid breath across the murmur of life, to paralyze and to chill.

But that day I had taken refuge from the awe and foreboding, the ticking of the clock, the dust-motes floating on light, the startling crack that now and then a springing board or an ill-hung window made. I had taken a book. I was deep in Shirley ; it excited, it affected me; it is always to me like a brief and voluntary brain-fever to read that book. Jane Eyre is insanity for the time. Villette is like the scarlet fever; it possesses, it chokes, flushes, racks you; it leaves you weak and in vague pain, apprehensive of some bad result; but it was Shirley I read, so forgetting every thing. I am not lonely usually, yet I know when I am alone; there is an indescribable freedom in the sense of solitude, no alien sphere crosses and disturbs mine, no intrusive influence distorts the orbit; I am myself— or I was, then. Presently, as I lay there, the clock struck three. I was to take some potion at that hour. I must rise and get it. I set one foot on the floor, and was putting a shoe upon the other cautiously, when it occurred to me, why was I so careful? and I remembered that it had seemed to me something was on the bed when I moved—my kitten perhaps. I looked, there was nothing there; but I was not alone in the room—there was something else I could not see, I did not hear, but I knew it.

A horror of flesh and sense crept over me; but I was ashamed; I treated it with contempt. Shivering, I walked to the shelf, reached the cup, swallowed my nauseous dose—now tasteless—and went back to bed. It is not worth denying that I trembled. I am a coward. I am always afraid, even when I face the fear; so, shaking, I lay down. My throat was parched, my lips beaded with a sweat of terror, but the consciousness of solitude returned in time to save me from faintness. *It* had gone. And that was the first time.

Here, perhaps, it is best to interpolate my own story, as much of it as is needful to the understanding of this visitation.

I was an orphan, living in the family of my guardian and uncle by marriage, Mr. Van Alstyne. I was not an orphan till fifteen years of happy life at home had fitted me to feel the whole force of such a bereavement. My parents had died within a year of each other, and at the time my story begins I had been ten years under my uncle's roof, He was kind, gentle, generous, and good; all that he could be, not being my father.

It is not necessary to say that I grieved long and deeply over my loss; my nature is intense as well as excitable, and I had no mother. What that brief sentence expresses many will feel; many, more blessed, can not imagine. It is to all meaning enough to define my longing for what I had not, my solitude in all that I had, my eager effort to escape from both longing and solitude.

After I had been a year under my guardian's care, Eleanor Wyse, a far-off cousin of Mr. Van Alstyne, came to board at the house and go to school with me. She was fifteen, I sixteen, but she was far the oldest. In the same family as we were, in the same classes, there were but two ways for us to take, either rivalry or friendship; between two girls of so much individuality there was no neutral ground, and within a month I had decided the matter by falling passionately in love with Eleanor Wyse.

I speak advisedly in the use of that term; no other phrase expresses the blind, irrational, all—enduring devotion I gave to her; no less vivid word belongs to that madness. If I had not been in love with her I should have seen her as I can now—as what she really was; for I believe in physiognomy. I believe that God writes the inner man upon the outer as a restraint upon society; what the moulding of feature lacks, expression, subtle traitor, supplies; and it is only years of repression, of training, of diplomacy, that put the flesh totally in the power of the spirit, and enable man or woman to seem what they are not, what they would be thought.

Eleanor's face was very beautiful; its Greek outline, straight and clear, cut to a perfect contour; the white brow; the long, melancholy eye, with curved, inky lashes; the statuesque head, its undulant, glittering hair bound in a knot of classic severity; the proud, serene mouth, full of carved beauty, opening its scarlet lips to reveal tiny pearlgrains of teeth of that rare delicacy and brilliance that carry a fatal warning; the soft, oval cheek, colorless but not pale, opaque and smooth, betraying Southern blood; the delicate throat, shown whiter under the sweeping shadow and coil of her black-brown tresses; the erect, stately, perfect figure, slight as became her years, but full of strength and promise; all these captivated my intense adoration of beauty. I did not see the label of the sculptor; I did not perceive in that cold, strict chiseling the assertion that its material was marble. I believed the interpretation of its hieroglyphic legend would have run thus: "This is the head of young Pallas; power, intellect, purity are her ægis; the daughter of Jove has not yet tasted passion; virgin, stainless, strong for sacrifice and victory, let the ardent and restless hearts of women seek her to be calmed and taught. *Evoe Athena!*" Nor did I like to see the goddess moved; expression did not become her; the soul that pierced those deep eyes was eager, unquiet, despotic; nothing divine, indeed, yet, in my eyes, it was the unresting, hasting meteor that flashed and faded through mists of earth toward its rest—where I knew not, but its flickering seemed to me atmospheric, not intrinsic.

I looked up to Eleanor with respect as well as fervor. She was full of noble theories. To hear her speak you would have been inwardly shamed by the great and pure thoughts she expressed, the high standard by which she measured all. Truth, disinterestedness, honor, purity, humility, found in her a priestess garmented in candor. If I thought an evil thought, I was thereafter ashamed to see her; if I was indolent or selfish, her presence reproached me; her will, irresistible and mighty, awoke me; if she was kind in speech or act—if she spoke to me caressingly—if she put her warm lips upon my cheek—I was thrilled with joy; her presence affected me, as sunshine does, with a sense of warm life and delight; when we rode, walked, or talked together, I wished the hour eternal; and when she fell into some passion, and burned me with bitter words, stinging me into retort by their injustice, their hard cruelty, it was I who repented—I who humiliated myself—I who, with abundant tears, asked her pardon, worked, plead, prayed to obtain it; and if some spasmodic conscientiousness roused her to excuse herself—to say she had been wrong—my hand closed her lips: I could not hear that:

the fault was mine, mine only. I was glad to be clay as long as she was queen and deity.

I do not think this passion of mine moved Eleanor much. She liked to talk with me; our minds mated, our tastes were alike. I had no need to explain my phrases to her, or to do more than indicate my thoughts; she was receptive and appreciative of thought, not of emotion. Me she never knew. I had no reserve in my nature—none of what is commonly called pride; what I felt I said, to the startling of good usual persons; and because I said it, Eleanor did not think I felt it. To her organization utterance and simplicity were denied; she could not speak her emotions if she would; she would not if she could; and she had no faith in words from others. My demonstrations annoyed her; she could not return them; they could not be ignored; there was a certain spice of life and passion in them that asserted itself poignantly and disturbed her. My services she liked better; yet there was in her the masculine contempt for spaniels; she despised a creature that would endure a blow, mental or physical, without revenging itself; and from her I endured almost any repulse, and forgot it.

She was with us in the house three years, and in that time she learned to love me after a fashion of her own, and I, still blind, adored her more. She found in me a receptivity that suited her, and a useful power of patient endurance. Her will made me a potent instrument. What she wanted she must have, and her want was my law. No time, no pains, no patience were wanting in me to fulfill her ends. I served her truly, and I look back upon it with no regret; futile or fertile, such devotion widens and ripens the soul that it inhabits. No aftershock of anguish can contract the space or undo the maturity; and even in my deepest humiliation before her sublime theories and superhuman ideals I unconsciously grew better myself. A capacity for worship implies much, and results in much.

Yet I think I loved her without much selfishness. I desired nothing better than to see her appreciated and admired. It was inexplicable to me when she was not; and I charged the coolness with which she was spoken of, and the want of enthusiasm for her person and character in general society, to her own starry height above common people, and their infinite distance from her nature.

So these years passed by. We went to school; we finished our school-days; we came out into the world; for, in the mean time, her mother had died, and her father removed to Bangor. She liked the place as a residence, and it had become home to her of late. I hoped it was pleasanter for her to be near me. When Eleanor was about twenty a nephew of Uncle Van Alstyne's came to make us a visit; he was no new acquaintance; he had come often in his boyhood, but since we grew up he had been in college, at the seminary, last in Germany for two years' study, and we did not know him well in his maturer character until this time. Herman Van Alstyne was quiet and plain, but of great capacity; I saw him much, and liked him. Love did not look at us. I was absorbed in Eleanor; so was he; but to her he was of no interest. I think she respected him, but her manner was careless and cold, even neglectful. Herman perceived the repulsion. At first he had taken pains to interest her—to mould her traits—to develop some inner nature in which he had faith; but the stone was intractable; neither ductile nor docile was Pallas; her soul yielded no more to him than the strong sea yields place or submission to the winged wind that smites it in passing.

He was with us three months waiting for a call he said, but stricter chains held him till he broke them with one blow and went to a Western parish.

He had not offered himself to Eleanor and been refused. Wisely he refrained from bringing the matter to a foreknown crisis: he spared himself the pain and Eleanor the regret of a refusal that he regarded truly as certain. I was sorry for the whole affair, for I believed she would scarcely know a better man, but it passed away; I promised to write him when his mother found the correspondence wearying, and we interchanged a few letters at irregular intervals till we met again, letters into which Eleanor's name found no entrance.

Three years after he left I went, early in July, to spend some weeks at the sea-side, for I was not strong; in the last few years my health had failed slowly, but progressively, till I was alarmingly weak and ordered to breathe salt air and use sea-bathing as the best hope of restoration. I do not know why I should reserve the cause of this long languor and sinking: it was nothing wrong in me that I owed it to the breaking of a brief engagement. A young girl, totally inexperienced, I had loved a man and been taught by himself to despise him—a tragedy both trite and sharp; one that is daily reacted, noted, and forgotten by observers, to find a cold record in marble or the catalogues of insane asylums, another perhaps in the eternal calendar of the heavens above. I was too strong in nature to grace either of these mortal lists, and I loved Eleanor too well. I had always loved her more than that man; and when the episode was over, I discovered in myself that I never could have loved any man as I did her, and I went out into the world in this conviction, finding that life had not lost all its charms—that so long as she lived for me

I should neither die nor craze. But the shock and excitement of the affair shattered my nervous system and undermined my health, and the listless, aimless life of a young lady offered no reactive agency to help me: so I went from home to new scenes and fresh atmosphere.

The air of Gloucester Beach strengthened me day by day. The exquisite scenery was a pleasure endless and pure. I asked nothing better than to sit upon some tide-washed rock and watch the creeping waves slide back in half-articulate murmur from the repelling shore, or, eager with the strength of flood, fling themselves, in mock anger, against cliff and crag, only to break in wreaths of silver spray and foam-bellsto glitter and fall in a leap of futile mirth, then rustling in the shingle and sea-weed with vague whispers, that

> "Song half asleep or speech half awake,"

which has lulled so many restless hearts to a momentary quiet, singing them the long lullaby that preludes a longer slumber.

It was excitement enough to walk alone upon the beach when a hot cloudy night drooped over land and sea; when the soft trance and enchantment of summer lulled cloud and wave into stillness absolute and cherishing, when the sole guide I had in that warm gloom was the white edge of surf, and the only sound that smote the quiet, the still-recurring, apprehensive dash, as wave after wave raced, leaped, panted, and hissed after its forerunner.

The Beach House was almost empty at that early season, and I enjoyed all this alone, not without constant yearnings for Eleanor; wanting her, even this scenery lost a charm, and I gave it but faint admiration since I could not see it with her eyes. It must be a very pure love of nature that can exist alone, and without flaw, in the absence of association. The austere soul of the great mother offers no sympathy to the petulant passion or irrational grief of her children. It is only to the heart that has proved itself strong and lofty that her potent and life—giving traits reveal themselves. In this love, as in all others, save only the love of God, the return that is yielded is measured by the power of the adorer, not his want. Truly,

> "Nature never did betray
>   The heart that loved her;"

but she has many and many a time betrayed the partial love—scoffed at the divided worship.

After I had been a fortnight at the Beach, I was joined by Herman Van

Alstyne. He had come on from the West to recruit his own health, suffering from a long intermittent fever, by sea-air; and hearing I was at Gloucester, had come there, and asked my leave to remain, gladly accorded to him. We had always been good friends, and my unspoken sympathy with his liking for, and loss of, Eleanor had established a permanent bond between us. In the constant association into which we were now thrown I learned daily to like him better. He was very weak indeed, quite unable to walk or drive far, and the connection of our families was a sufficient excuse to others for our intimacy. I delighted to offer him any kindness or service in my power, and he repaid me well by the charm of his society.

We spent our mornings always together in some niche of the lofty cliff that towered from the tide below in bare grandeur, reflecting the sun from its abrupt brown crags till every fibre of grass rooted in their crevices grew blanched, and the solitary streamer of bramble or wild creeper became crisp long ere autumn. But this heat was my element; the slow blood quickened in my veins under its vital glow; I felt life stealing back to its deserted and chilly conduits; I basked like a cactus or a lizard into brighter tints and a gayer existence.

There we often sat till noon, talking or silent as we would; for though there was a peculiar charm in the appreciative, thoughtful conversation of Herman Van Alstyne, a better and a rarer trait he possessed in full measure—the power of "a thousand silences."

Or, perhaps, under the old cedars that shed aromatic scents upon the sun-thrilled air, and strewed bits of dry, sturdy leaves upon the short grass that carpeted the summit of the cliff, we preferred shadow to sunshine; and while I rested against some ragged bole, and inhaled all odor and health, he read to me some quaint German story, some incredibly exquisite bit of Tennyson, some sensitively musical passage of Kingsley, or, better and more apt, a song or a poem of Shelley's—vivid, spiritual, supernatural; the ideal of poetry; the leaping flame-tongue of lonely genius hanging in mid-air, self-poised, self-containing, glorious, and unattainable.

I have never known so delicate an apprehension as Mr. Van Alstyne possessed; his nobler traits I was afterward to know—to feel; but now it suited me thoroughly to be so well understood—to feel that I might utter the wildest imagination, or the most unexpected peculiarity of opinion, and never once be asked to explain what I meant—to reduce into social formulas that which was not social but my own. If there is one rest above another to a weary mind it is this freedom from shackles, this consciousness of true response. Never did I perceive a charm in the landscape that he had not noticed before or simultaneously with me; the same felicity of diction or of thought in what we read struck us as with one stroke; we liked the same people, read the same books, agreed in opinion so far as to disagree on and discuss many points without a shadow of impatience or an uncandid expression. We talked together as few men talk—perhaps no women—

> "Talked at large of worldly fate,
> And drew truly every trait"

—but we never spoke of Eleanor.

And so the summer wore on. I perceived a gradual change creep over Herman's manner in its process; he watched me continually. I felt his eyes fixed on me whenever I sat sewing or reading; I never looked up without meeting them. He grew absent and fitful. I did not know what had happened. I accused myself of having pained him. I feared he was ill. I never once thought of the true trouble; and one day it came—he asked me to marry him.

Never was any woman more surprised. I had not thought of the thing. I could not speak at first. I drew from him the hand he attempted to grasp. I did not collect my stricken and ashamed thoughts till, looking up, I saw him perfectly pale, his eyes dark with emotion, waiting, in rigid self-control, for my answer.

I could not, in justice to him or to myself, be less than utterly candid. I told him how much I liked him; how grieved I was that I could have mistaken his feeling for me so entirely; and then I said what I then believed—that I could not marry him—for I had but the lesser part of a heart to give any man. I loved a woman too well to love or to marry. A deep flush of relief crossed his brow.

"Is that the only objection you offer to me?" asked he, calmly.

"It is enough," said I. "If you think that past misery of mine interferes against you, you are in the wrong. I know now that I never loved that man as a woman should love the man she marries, and had I done so, the utter want of respect or trust I feel for him now would have silenced the love forever."

"I did not think of that," said he. "I needed but one assurance—that, except for Miss Wyse, you might have loved me; is it so?"

I could not tell him—I did not know. The one present and all—absorbing passion of my soul was Eleanor; beside her, no rival could enter. I shuddered at the possibility of loving a man so utterly, and then placing myself at his mercy for life, I felt that my safety lay in my freedom from any such tie to Eleanor. She made me miserable often enough as it was; what might she not do were I in her power always? Yet this face of the subject I did not suggest to Mr. Van Alstyne; it was painful enough to be kept to myself. I told him plainly that I could not love another as I did her; that I would not if I could.

He looked at me, not all unmoved, though silently; a gentle shading of something like pity stole across his regard, fixed and keen at first. He neither implored nor deprecated, but lifted my hand reverently to his lips, and said, in a tone of supreme calmness, "I can wait."

I should have combated the hope implied in those words. I was afterward angry with myself for enduring them; but at the moment uncertainty, shaped out of instinct and apprehension, closed my lips; I could not speak, and he left me. I went to my room more moved than I liked to acknowledge; and when he went away the next morning, though I felt the natural relief from embarrassment—knowing that I should not meet him as before—I still missed him, as a part of my daily life.

A month longer at the Beach protracted my stay into autumn; and then, with refreshed health and new strength, I returned home—home! whose chief charm lay in the prospect of seeing Eleanor.

It is true that this hope was not unalloyed. I am possessed of a nature singularly instinctive, and for some weeks past a certain shadow had crept into her letters that pained me. No word or phrase denoted change; but I perceived the uncertain aura, and was irrationally harassed by a trouble too vague for expression.

When I reached Bangor it lay waiting for me sufficiently tangible and legible in the shape of a note from Eleanor.

* * *

And here must I leave a blank. The forgiveness which stirs me to this record refuses to define for alien eyes what that trouble was. All that I can say to justify the extreme and piteous result which followed is, that Eleanor Wyse had utterly, cruelly, and deliberately deceived me; and when it was no longer possible to do so, had been obliged by circumstances to show me what she had done.

Of that day it is best to say but little: the world cracked and reeled under me; I returned from a brief stupor into one bitter, blind tempest of contempt; and in its strength I answered her note concisely and coldly. An hour's time brought me a rejoinder not worth answering, simply perfidious—a regret, "deep and true," that she had been compelled to grieve me, to "reserve" from me any thing.

True! I had believed in truth, in goodness, in disinterested love, in principle; where now were such faiths swept? Verily, over the cliff into the sea! I was morally destroyed; I made shipwreck of myself and my life; my whole soul was a salt raging wave, tideless and foaming, without rest, without intent, without faith or hope in God—for he who loses faith in man loses faith in man's Maker—and this had Eleanor Wyse done for me.

Doubtless, to many, this emotion of mine will seem exaggerated. Let them remember that it was the loss of all that bound to life a lonely, morbid, intense, and excitable woman. Need I say more? If, after many years, with the kind help of nobler men and women, and the great patience of God, I have worn my way, inch by inch, back to some foothold of belief, I feel even yet—in some recoils of memory, some recurring habit of my soul—the reflex influence of those wretched days, months, years, when I suspected every one—"hateful, and hating," of a truth.

Death is hard to bear when its angel breathes upon the face we love, and extinguishes therein the fiery spark of life; but what is death compared to such dissolution as treachery brings? If Eleanor Wyse had died when I loved her and trusted her, I should have gone mourning softly all my days, but not in pain; to find her untrue admitted no remedy, no palliation. Truth was the ruling passion of my mind; that, and nothing else, contented me. Its absence or its loss were the loss and absence of all in those whom I loved; and it was only within a brief time, as years go, that I had grown into the discovery that men are liars in spite of education or policy; what was it, then, to know this of my ideal—of Eleanor?

But let those helpless, miserable weeks go by. If I detail so much as I have, it is to show the reason of my righteous indignation—of my tenacious memory. After a time I supposed that I forgave Eleanor. I thought myself good, most Pharisaically good, to have forgiven such an injury. I made some little comedy of friendship for visible use; I visited her, though not as often as I had done before. I saw her try to supply, with the love of others, the lavish devotion and service I had given her; I saw her fail and suffer in the consciousness of want and dissatisfaction, and, self-righteously, I forgave again! Senseless that I was!—as if forgiveness rankled and grew bitter in one's heart—as if pardon, full and pure, rejoiced in the retributions of this life—fed itself with salt recollections of the past, and evil foreshadowings of the future; as if it could exist without love, without forgetfulness; as if good deeds were its pledge, or good words its seal!

No! I never forgave her. I never forgot one pang she inflicted on me, one untruth she uttered; I never trusted her word or her smile again. I gathered up every circumstance of the past, and hunted it to its source; I discovered that she had not simply deceived but deluded me, and laughed at me in the process.

How my blood boiled over these revelations! how my flesh failed with my heart! Slow, persistent fever gnawed me; my nights were without sleep or rest; my days laggard and delirious. Why I did not go crazy is yet unexplained to myself. I think I did, only that there was a method in my madness that won for it the milder name of nervousness. I was ill—I tottered on the very tempting brink of death, without awe or regret; I made no effort to live, nor any to die, except to pray that I might—the only prayer that ever passed my seared lips. I was sent away from home again; and while I was gone Eleanor married a certain Mr. Mason, of Bangor, and they removed to Illinois—in time, still further West. I was no better for this absence; and, impatient of strangers and intrusive acquaintance, I came home, and, strange as it may seem, I missed Eleanor! Habit is the anchor of half the love in this world, and my habit of loving her survived the love—or held it, perhaps—for I missed her sorrowfully.

I found Herman Van Alstyne at my uncle's when I came, and I was glad—glad of any thing to break the desperate monotony of sorrow. He knew nothing more than everyone knew of this affair, except that he knew me, and from that gathered intuitively a part of the truth; and, by long patience, unwearied and delicate care—watching, waiting, forbearing, and enduring—he brought me nearer a certain degree of calm than I had believed possible, when a sudden summons called him away from Bangor; and it was during his absence that It began to come; as I said in the beginning, more than two years after I had lost Eleanor.

I lay still in my bed on that day of which I had spoken; the long stress of misery that I had undergone in the past years resulted in so much physical exhaustion as to have brought on the exquisite tortures of neuralgia, and it was a sudden access of this chronic rack that to-day held me prisoner. The draught I had taken was an anodyne, and under its influence I fell asleep. I must have slept an hour, when I woke abruptly with a renewed sense of something in the dusk beside me, at my pillow. I screamed as I woke into this terror, and instantly Aunt Mary came in. A cold sigh crossed my

cheek; I shivered with a horror strange and unearthly. Aunt Mary asked if
I had been asleep? I said yes. If I had been dreaming painfully? I did not
answer that. I asked for some water, and getting it she forgot her question;
but I could not bear to be alone. I begged her to sit beside me and to sleep
with me, for I could not endure solitude; perpetual apprehension made me
cringe in every nerve and fibre. I started at the slightest stir of leaf or insect
upon the pane, and the repining autumn wind seemed to come over mile
on mile of graves, bringing thence no mealy scent of white daisies—no
infant-breathing violet odors—no frutescent perfume of sweet-briar, nor
funereal smells of cypress, and plaintive whispers of fir and pine; but wave
after wave of cries from half-free souls; sobbing with dull pain, and moans
of deprecating anguish; a cry that neither heaven nor earth answered, but
which crept—a live desolation—into the ear attent, and the brain morbidly
excited.

Yet gradually this left me. I kept by some kindly human presence all day,
and feared night no more till—

Let me say that all this time I was imperceptibly growing better than I
had been. Hope, the very ministrant of Heaven, was by tiny crevice and
unguarded postern stealing into my heart, though I knew it not, and soft-
ening all my hard thoughts of Eleanor, for I am moved to the outer world
rather by my own moods than theirs; sorrow and pain make me selfish and
unkind; peace, joy, even unconscious hope, expand my love for all mankind. I am better, more tender, more benevolent to others, when I receive
some light and life within.

One night I was all alone; the low, unearthly glimmer of a waning moon
lit the naked earth, a few leaves rustled on the fitful wind that lulled, and
rose, and lulled again, with almost articulate meaning. I lay listening; a long
pause came, of most significant quiet—a faint sigh crossed my brow. *It* was
there beside me!—unseen, unheard, but felt in the secretest recesses of life
and consciousness; a spirit, whereat my marrow curdled, my heart was
constricted, my blood refused to run, my breath failed—fluttered—was it
death? I sprung from my pillow; the presence drew farther away. I could
see nothing, but I felt that something yearning, restless, pained, and sad
regarded me. I began to gather courage. I began to pity a soul that had
cast off life yet could not die to life; and now it drew nearer, as if some
magnetism, born of my kindlier sympathies, melted the barrier between
us, close—closer—till something rustled like a light touch the cover of my
bed, stirred at my ear! Good Heaven! could I bear that? I could not shriek

or cry, I fell forward upon my face. It went, and the wind began its wail; now reproachful sobs filled it: the moon sank, rain gathered overhead, and dripped with sullen persistence all night upon the roof, for all night I heard it.

It is tedious to recount each instance of this visitation. For weeks it staid beside me. I felt it on my bed at night; I felt it by my chair in the day; it swept past me in the garden paths, a cold waft of air; it watched me through the window-blinds; it hung over me sleeping; yet never was I wonted to the presence; every day thrilled me with fresh surprise, and daily it grew, for daily it became more perceivable.

At first I felt only a sense of alien life in a room otherwise solitary; then a breath of air, air from some other sphere than this, penetrative, dark, chilling; then a sound, not of voice, or pulse, but of motion in some inanimate thing, the motion of contact; then came a touch, the gentlest, faintest approach of lips or fingers, I knew not which, to my brow; and last, a growing, gathering, flickering into sight. I saw nothing at first, directly; from the oblique glance that fear impelled I drew an impression of quivering air beside me; then of a shadow, frail and variant; then a shapeless shape of mist, a cloud, dark and portentous and significant; and next those sidelong glances revealed to me an expression; no face, no feature, but, believe it who can, an expression, earnest, melancholy, beseeching; a look that pierced me, that pleaded with my soul's depth, that entreated shelter, succor, consolation, which even in my terror I longed to give.

I might perhaps have suffered physically more than I did from this visiting, but the winged hope of which I spoke before upheld me still, daily, with stronger hands.

Herman had returned to Bangor after a brief absence, and was there still. I could not see him so constantly as I did and refuse my admiration to those traits that ever rule and satisfy me. Mr. Van Alstyne passed with some people for a philosopher, with some for a reformer: there were those who called him singular and self-opinionated; there were others who revered him for his devout nature and stainless life. He was more than any of these, he was a true man: and even in his plain exterior the eye that knew him found a charm peculiar and salient; the deep-sunken, clear, earnest eyes, kindled with a spark of profound depth and meaning; the thin, sharply cut, aquiline outline; the flexible, pure, refined mouth; the bronzed coloring; the overhanging brow—all these wore beauty indefinable, fired by the sweet and vivid smile of the irradiate soul within. In his presence, calm, restful, and strengthening, no subterfuge or evasion could live. He was just, direct, and tenderly strong; it was to him, to him it is, that I owed and owe a new and higher life than I had known before; he saw my sinking and lonely soul, but he saw its self—recuperative power, and with the most delicate and careful tenderness beguiled that motive force into action. He did far more than that; he recalled to me the higher motives that anguish had well—nigh scourged out from my horizon; he taught me as a father teaches his little child a newer trust in the Father of us all. I returned to those divine consolations that he laid before me with a pierced and penitent heart; and in knowing that I was prayed and cared for on earth, I learned anew that God is more tender and more patient than his creatures, and the logic of strong emotion made the truth living and potent. In all this was I drawn toward Herman by the strongest tie that can bind one heart to another—a tie that overarches and outlasts all the fleeting passions of time, for it is the adamantine link of eternity; and had I lost him then, I should have felt for all my life that there was a relation between us, undying and sure, to be renewed and acknowledged at length where such relations respire their native air, where there is neither marrying nor giving in marriage.

But it pleased God that I should live to receive my heart's desire; what began in gratitude ended in love. I might have shrunk from admitting so potent a guest again into my soul, had any other soul sent the messenger thither; but I trusted him when I disbelieved every other creature, and with this trust had crept back to me my faith in God, in good, in life and its ends. Truly, so far as man can do it, he saved my soul alive!

Now it was the early part of December. It was still haunting me. I could see more—eyes, deep and pleading, the outline of a head, pure lineaments, seemed hovering beside me, but if I turned for a direct look they were gone. I did not fear it; my happy faith and Herman shielded me.

The year drew on. The day before Christmas came, still, crisp, but yet warm for its season; no snow shrouded the earth; the far-off sun beamed out benign and pale; the few dry leaves lay quiet as they fell; the firs upon the lawn with curved boughs waited for their ermine, stately and dark. Herman asked me to walk with him. I cloaked and hooded myself, and we went away, away into the deep woods. What we said in that sweet silence of a leafless, sunny forest is known to us two: it is not for you, reader, friendly though you be; it is enough to tell you that I had promised to be his wife, that I was homesick no more.

It was well for me that this happened that day—should I not rather say

God ordered it? —for as ever in this life sorrow tramples upon the foregoing footsteps of joy, so I found upon my return a household in tears. Mr. Mason, Eleanor's husband, had written, at last, two months after it happened, and another month had the letter been in coming—ah! how ever shall I say it? Eleanor was dead! her latest breath had gasped out a cry for me!

If Death is the Spoiler, so is he the Restorer; who shall dare to soil the shroud with any thing but tears? I could do no more but weep; but I mourned for Eleanor again as I had never thought to do; evil, treachery, anguish, and distrust vanished—I remembered only love.

For hours I could not see or speak with Herman, the flood of misery overpowered me; and he too sorrowed, deeply, but serenely. It was late in the evening before I recovered any sort of composure. He sent to my chamber a brief penciled request, and I went down; worn out with weeping, I obeyed like a child. I ate the food he brought me; I drank the restorative draught; quiet, but languid, I laid my head upon his breast, and, held by the firm grasp of his arm, I rested, and he consoled me; a deep and vital draught of peace slaked my soul's feverish thirst. Such peace had I never known, for it was the daughter of experience and trust.

You who, full of youth and its intact passion, give a careless hour to these pages, wonder not that I could find it just to give so noble a man a heart once given and wasted! Know that it is not the flower of any tropic palm that is fit to feed and sustain man, but the ripened clusters of its fruitage—the result of time, and sun, and storm. The first blush, the earliest kiss, the tender and timid glance are sweet indeed; but the true household fire, deep and abiding, is oftenest kindled in the heart matured by passion and by pain, tested in the stress of life, deepened and strengthened by manifold experience; and such a heart receives no unworthy guest, lights its altar—fire for no idol of wood or clay. I felt that I rendered Herman Van Alstyne far nobler and higher homage, that I did him purer justice in loving him now than it had ever been in my power to do before.

First love is a honeyed and dewy romance, fit for novels and school-girls; but of the myriad women who have lived to curse their marriage-day nine-tenths have been those who married in their ignorant girlhood, and married boys.

I have digressed to honor Herman, to vindicate myself. That Christmas-eve I lay sheltered and at rest on his arm, till the toll of midnight rang clear upon my ear. I could forever sing the angels' song now, that for years had been a blank repetition to my wretched and ungodly soul.

"Peace on earth!" was no more a chimera; I knew it at heart. "Good will to men!" that was spontaneous; I loved all in and for one. "Glory to God in the highest!" What did that ask to utter it but a full thankfulness that bore me upward like the flood-tide of a summer sea?

Blessed as I was, my common sense reminded me that it was far into the night, that I ought to sleep; so I said good-night to Herman, and crept with weak steps to my room. I fell asleep to dream of him, of Eleanor, of peace, and I woke into the deep silence that always preceded—*It*.

I woke knowing what stood beside me. Keen starlight pierced the pane, and shed a dim, obscure perception of place and outline over my room. A long, restful, sobbing sigh parted my lips; I perceived *It* was at hand; fear fled; terror died out; I turned my eyes—oh God! it was Eleanor!

Wan—frail—a flowing outline of shadow, but the face in every faultless line and vivid expression; now an expression of intense longing, of wistful prayer, of pleading that would never be denied.

I lifted my heavy arms toward the vision; it swayed and bent above me: the white lips parted; no murmur nor sound clave them, yet they spoke—"Forgive! forgive!"

"Eleanor! Yes love, darling! yes, forever, as I hope to be forgiven!" I cried out aloud. A gleam of rapture and rest relaxed the brow, the sad eyes; love ineffable glowed along each lineament, and transfused to splendor the frigid moulding of snow.

I closed my eyes to crush inward the painful tears, and a touch of lips sealed them with sacred and unearthly repose. I looked again; It had gone forever. The Christmas bells pealed loud and clear for dawn, and my thoughts rung their own joy bells beside the steeple chimes. Herman and Eleanor both loved me—I had forgiven; I was forgiven.

Yet must day and space echo that word once more. Hear me, Eleanor! hear me, from that mystic country where thou hast fled before!

I repeat that forgiveness again. So may Heaven pardon me in the hour of need; so may God look upon me with strong affection in the parting of soul and body, even as I pardon and love thee, Eleanor, with a truth and faith eternal! Thee, forever loved, but, ah! not now forever lost?

HARRIET E. WILSON (1825–1900)

First novel published by an African American woman author.

Harriet E. Wilson (née Adams) was an African American woman born in 1825, in Milford, New Hampshire. Little is known about her life before 1850, when she lived in Milford with a white family, possibly as their indentured servant. In 1851 she married Thomas Wilson, who abandoned Harriet a year later and before the birth of their son George Mason Wilson. Struggling with poverty, Wilson sold hair products in Boston to earn money in order to regain custody of George, who had been placed in a home for poor children. In 1859 she published *Our Nig* at her own expense to supplement her income. Six months later young George died, while a resident of a Milford poor house. After the Civil War, Wilson became a speaker at Spiritualist conventions under the name Dr. Hattie E. Wilson, and in 1870, listed as a white woman in the U.S. Census, she married John Gallatin Robinson in Boston. She earned income as a healer, trance reader, and lecturer, and died in 1900 in Massachusetts.

Our Nig has a plot line familiar from other books, of a woman who strives to preserve her dignity and self-worth in a patriarchal society that leaves poor women few choices for survival but to compromise themselves or marry. The heroine in *Our Nig* faces the additional injustice of racism, especially at the hands of her white mistress. She is clearly modeled on Wilson as a working-class woman in the North where slavery was no longer practiced, but nonetheless continued to have pernicious effects on the lives of free Black people. Love, the key driver in many novels of the time, is here described as "that arbitrary and inexorable tyrant," a startling phrase in a book filled with the heroine's courageous resistance to abuse, unfairness, and hardship. But being hurt by love is an arbitrary matter, meaning it can happen to anyone, while racist and sexist assaults on the main character's well-being are specific to her experience as a Black woman in antebellum

America. *Our Nig* claims its status in American letters by introducing a Black female protagonist who is not only dignified and self-assured but also heroic in ways that had not been encountered on the page before, and by presenting a plot that creatively adapts the conventions of the sentimental novel and the slave narrative to say something new. *Our Nig* became a widely discussed and controversial narrative in its time but had been largely overlooked until the book was rediscovered in 1982 by the literary scholar Henry Louis Gates, Jr.

From OUR NIG; OR, SKETCHES FROM THE LIFE OF A FREE BLACK, IN A TWO-STORY WHITE HOUSE, NORTH [1859]

PREFACE.

In offering to the public the following pages, the writer confesses her inability to minister to the refined and cultivated, the pleasure supplied by abler pens. It is not for such these crude narrations appear. Deserted by kindred, disabled by failing health, I am forced to some experiment which shall aid me in maintaining myself and child without extinguishing this feeble life. I would not from these motives even palliate slavery at the South, by disclosures of its appurtenances North. My mistress was wholly imbued with *Southern* principles. I do not pretend to divulge every transaction in my own life, which the unprejudiced would declare unfavorable in comparison with treatment of legal bondmen; I have purposely omitted what would most provoke shame in our good anti-slavery friends at home.

My humble position and frank confession of errors will, I hope, shield me from severe criticism. Indeed, defects are so apparent it requires no skilful hand to expose them.

I sincerely appeal to my colored brethren universally for patronage, hoping they will not condemn this attempt of their sister to be erudite, but rally around me a faithful band of supporters and defenders.

H. E. W.

CHAPTER 1
MAG SMITH, MY MOTHER.

Oh, Grief beyond all other griefs, when fate
First leaves the young heart lone and desolate

In the wide world, without that only tie
For which it loved to live or feared to die;
Lorn as the hung-up lute, that ne'er hath spoken
Since the sad day its master-chord was broken!
—MOORE.

LONELY MAG SMITH! See her as she walks with downcast eyes and heavy heart. It was not always thus. She *had* a loving, trusting heart. Early deprived of parental guardianship, far removed from relatives, she was left to guide her tiny boat over life's surges alone and inexperienced. As she merged into womanhood, unprotected, uncherished, uncared for, there fell on her ear the music of love, awakening an intensity of emotion long dormant. It whispered of an elevation before unaspired to; of ease and plenty her simple heart had never dreamed of as hers. She knew the voice of her charmer, so ravishing, sounded far above her. It seemed like an angel's, alluring her upward and onward. She thought she could ascend to him and become an equal. She surrendered to him a priceless gem, which he proudly garnered as a trophy, with those of other victims, and left her to her fate. The world seemed full of hateful deceivers and crushing arrogance. Conscious that the great bond of union to her former companions was severed, that the disdain of others would be insupportable, she determined to leave the few friends she possessed, and seek an asylum among strangers. Her offspring came unwelcomed, and before its nativity numbered weeks, it passed from earth, ascending to a purer and better life.

"God be thanked," ejaculated Mag, as she saw its breathing cease; "no one can taunt *her* with my ruin."

Blessed release! may we all respond. How many pure, innocent children not only inherit a wicked heart of their own, claiming life-long scrutiny and restraint, but are heirs also of parental disgrace and calumny, from which only long years of patient endurance in paths of rectitude can disencumber them.

Mag's new home was soon contaminated by the publicity of her fall; she had a feeling of degradation oppressing her; but she resolved to be circumspect, and try to regain in a measure what she had lost. Then some foul tongue would jest of her shame, and averted looks and cold greetings disheartened her. She saw she could not bury in forgetfulness her misdeed, so she resolved to leave her home and seek another in the place she at first fled from.

Alas, how fearful are we to be first in extending a helping hand to those who stagger in the mires of infamy; to speak the first words of hope and warning to those emerging into the sunlight of morality! Who can tell what numbers, advancing just far enough to hear a cold welcome and join in the reserved converse of professed reformers, disappointed, disheartened, have chosen to dwell in unclean places, rather than encounter these "holier-than-thou" of the great brotherhood of man!

Such was Mag's experience; and disdaining to ask favor or friendship from a sneering world, she resolved to shut herself up in a hovel she had often passed in better days, and which she knew to be untenanted. She vowed to ask no favors of familiar faces; to die neglected and forgotten before she would be dependent on any. Removed from the village, she was seldom seen except as upon your introduction, gentle reader, with down-cast visage, returning her work to her employer, and thus providing herself with the means of subsistence. In two years many hands craved the same avocation; foreigners who cheapened toil and clamored for a livelihood, competed with her, and she could not thus sustain herself. She was now above no drudgery. Occasionally old acquaintances called to be favored with help of some kind, which she was glad to bestow for the sake of the money it would bring her; but the association with them was such a pain-ful reminder of by-gones, she returned to her hut morose and revengeful, refusing all offers of a better home than she possessed. Thus she lived for years, hugging her wrongs, but making no effort to escape. She had never known plenty, scarcely competency; but the present was beyond compari-son with those innocent years when the coronet of virtue was hers.

Every year her melancholy increased, her means diminished. At last no one seemed to notice her, save a kind-hearted African, who often called to inquire after her health and to see if she needed any fuel, he having the responsibility of furnishing that article, and she in return mending or making garments.

"How much you earn dis week, Mag?" asked he one Saturday evening.

"Little enough, Jim. Two or three days without any dinner. I washed for the Reeds, and did a small job for Mrs. Bellmont; that's all. I shall starve soon, unless I can get more to do. Folks seem as afraid to come here as if they expected to get some awful disease. I don't believe there is a person in the world but would be glad to have me dead and out of the way."

"No, no, Mag! don't talk so. You shan't starve so long as I have barrels to hoop. Peter Greene boards me cheap. I'll help you, if nobody else will."

A tear stood in Mag's faded eye. "I'm glad," she said, with a softer tone than before, "if there is *one* who isn't glad to see me suffer. I b'lieve all Singleton wants to see me punished, and feel as if they could tell when I've been punished long enough. It's a long day ahead they'll set it, I reckon."

After the usual supply of fuel was prepared, Jim returned home. Full of pity for Mag, he set about devising measures for her relief. "By golly!" said he to himself one day—for he had become so absorbed in Mag's interest that he had fallen into a habit of musing aloud—"By golly! I wish she'd *marry* me."

"Who?" shouted Pete Greene, suddenly starting from an unobserved corner of the rude shop.

"Where you come from, you sly nigger!" exclaimed Jim.

"Come, tell me, who is't?" said Pete; "Mag Smith, you want to marry?"

"Git out, Pete! and when you come in dis shop again, let a nigger know it. Don't steal in like a thief."

Pity and love know little severance. One attends the other. Jim acknowledged the presence of the former, and his efforts in Mag's behalf told also of a finer principle.

This sudden expedient which he had unintentionally disclosed, roused his thinking and inventive powers to study upon the best method of introducing the subject to Mag.

He belted his barrels, with many a scheme revolving in his mind, none of which quite satisfied him, or seemed, on the whole, expedient. He thought of the pleasing contrast between her fair face and his own dark skin; the smooth, straight hair, which he had once, in expression of pity, kindly stroked on her now wrinkled but once fair brow. There was a tempest gathering in his heart, and at last, to ease his pent-up passion, he exclaimed aloud, "By golly!" Recollecting his former exposure, he glanced around to see if Pete was in hearing again. Satisfied on this point, he continued: "She'd be as much of a prize to me as she'd fall short of coming up to the mark with white folks. I don't care for past things. I've done things 'fore now I's 'shamed of. She's good enough for me, any how."

One more glance about the premises to be sure Pete was away.

The next Saturday night brought Jim to the hovel again. The cold was fast coming to tarry its apportioned time. Mag was nearly despairing of meeting its rigor.

"How's the wood, Mag?" asked Jim.

"All gone; and no more to cut, any how," was the reply.

"Too bad!" Jim said. His truthful reply would have been, I'm glad.

"Anything to eat in the house?" continued he.

"No," replied Mag.

"Too bad!" again, orally, with the same *inward* gratulation as before.

"Well, Mag," said Jim, after a short pause, "you's down low enough. I don't see but I've got to take care of ye. 'Sposin' we marry!"

Mag raised her eyes, full of amazement, and uttered a sonorous "What?" Jim felt abashed for a moment. He knew well what were her objections.

"You's had trial of white folks any how. They run off and left ye, and now none of 'em come near ye to see if you's dead or alive. I's black outside, I know, but I's got a white heart inside. Which you rather have, a black heart in a white skin, or a white heart in a black one?"

"Oh, dear!" sighed Mag; "Nobody on earth cares for *me*—"

"I do," interrupted Jim.

"I can do but two things," said she, "beg my living, or get it from you."

"Take me, Mag. I can give you a better home than this, and not let you suffer so."

He prevailed; they married. You can philosophize, gentle reader, upon the impropriety of such unions, and preach dozens of sermons on the evils of amalgamation. Want is a more powerful philosopher and preacher. Poor Mag. She has sundered another bond which held her to her fellows. She has descended another step down the ladder of infamy.

CHAPTER II.
MY FATHER'S DEATH.

Misery! we have known each other,
Like a sister and a brother,
Living in the same lone home
Many years—we must live some
Hours or ages yet to come.
—Shelley.

Jim, proud of his treasure,—a white wife,—tried hard to fulfil his promises; and furnished her with a more comfortable dwelling, diet, and apparel. It was comparatively a comfortable winter she passed after her marriage. When Jim could work, all went on well. Industrious, and fond of Mag, he was determined she should not regret her union to him. Time levied an additional charge upon him, in the form of two pretty mulattos, whose infantile pranks amply repaid the additional toil. A few years, and a severe cough and pain in his side compelled him to be an idler for weeks together, and Mag had thus a reminder of by-gones. She cared for him only as a means to subserve her own comfort; yet she nursed him faithfully and true to marriage vows till death released her. He became the victim of consumption. He loved Mag to the last. So long as life continued, he stifled his sensibility to pain, and toiled for her sustenance long after he was able to do so.

A few expressive wishes for her welfare; a hope of better days for her; an anxiety lest they should not all go to the "good place"; brief advice about their children; a hope expressed that Mag would not be neglected as she used to be; the manifestation of Christian patience; these were *all* the legacy of miserable Mag. A feeling of cold desolation came over her, as she turned from the grave of one who had been truly faithful to her.

She was now expelled from companionship with white people; this last step—her union with a black—was the climax of repulsion.

Seth Shipley, a partner in Jim's business, wished her to remain in her present home; but she declined, and returned to her hovel again, with obstacles threefold more insurmountable than before. Seth accompanied her, giving her a weekly allowance which furnished most of the food necessary for the four inmates. After a time, work failed; their means were reduced.

How Mag toiled and suffered, yielding to fits of desperation, bursts of anger, and uttering curses too fearful to repeat. When both were supplied with work, they prospered; if idle, they were hungry together. In this way their interests became united; they planned for the future together. Mag had lived an outcast for years. She had ceased to feel the gushings of penitence; she had crushed the sharp agonies of an awakened conscience. She had no longings for a purer heart, a better life. Far easier to descend lower. She entered the darkness of perpetual infamy. She asked not the rite of civilization or Christianity. Her will made her the wife of Seth. Soon followed scenes familiar and trying.

"It's no use," said Seth one day, "we must give the children away, and try to get work in some other place."

"Who'll take the black devils?" snarled Mag.

"They're none of mine," said Seth, "what you growling about?"

"Nobody will want any thing of mine, or yours either," she replied.

"We'll make 'em, p'r'aps," he said. "There's Frado's six years old, and pretty, if she is yours, and white folks'll say so. She'd be a prize somewhere," he continued, tipping his chair back against the wall, and placing his feet upon the rounds, as if he had much more to say when in the right position.

Frado, as they called one of Mag's children, was a beautiful mulatto, with long, curly black hair, and handsome, roguish eyes, sparkling with an exuberance of spirit almost beyond restraint.

Hearing her name mentioned, she looked up from her play, to see what Seth had to say of her.

"Wouldn't the Bellmonts take her?" asked Seth.

"Bellmonts?" shouted Mag. "His wife is a right she-devil! and if—"

"Hadn't they better be all together?" interrupted Seth, reminding her of a like epithet used in reference to her little ones.

Without seeming to notice him, she continued, "She can't keep a girl in the house over a week; and Mr. Bellmont wants to hire a boy to work for him, but he can't find one that will live in the house with her; she's so ugly, they can't."

"Well, we've got to make a move soon," answered Seth; "if you go with me, we shall go right off. Had you rather spare the other one?" asked Seth, after a short pause.

"One's as bad as t'other," replied Mag. "Frado is such a wild, frolicky thing, and means to do jest as she's a mind to; she won't go if she don't want to. I don't want to tell her she is to be given away."

"I will," said Seth. "Come here, Frado?"

The child seemed to have some dim foreshadowing of evil, and declined.

"Come here," he continued; "I want to tell you something."

She came reluctantly. He took her hand and said: "We're going to move, by-'m-bye; will you go?"

"No!" screamed she; and giving a sudden jerk which destroyed Seth's equilibrium, left him sprawling on the floor, while she escaped through the open door.

"She's a hard one," said Seth, brushing his patched coat sleeve. "I'd risk her at Bellmont's."

They discussed the expediency of a speedy departure. Seth would first seek employment, and then return for Mag. They would take with them what they could carry, and leave the rest with Pete Greene, and come for them when they were wanted. They were long in arranging affairs satisfactorily, and were not a little startled at the close of their conference to find Frado missing. They thought approaching night would bring her. Twilight passed into darkness, and she did not come. They thought she had understood their plans, and had, perhaps, permanently withdrawn. They could not rest without making some effort to ascertain her retreat. Seth went in pursuit, and returned without her. They rallied others when they discovered that another little colored girl was missing, a favorite playmate of Frado's. All effort proved unavailing. Mag felt sure her fears were realized, and that she might never see her again. Before her anxieties became realities, both were safely returned, and from them and their attendant they learned that they went to walk, and not minding the direction soon found themselves lost. They had climbed fences and walls, passed through thickets and marshes, and when night approached selected a thick cluster of shrubbery as a covert for the night. They were discovered by the person who now restored them, chatting of their prospects, Frado attempting to banish the childish fears of her companion. As they were some miles from home, they were kindly cared for until morning. Mag was relieved to know her child was not driven to desperation by their intentions to relieve themselves of her, and she was inclined to think severe restraint would be healthful.

The removal was all arranged; the few days necessary for such migra-tions passed quickly, and one bright summer morning they bade farewell to their Singleton hovel, and with budgets and bundles commenced their weary march. As they neared the village, they heard the merry shouts of children gathered around the school-room, awaiting the coming of their teacher.

"Halloo!" screamed one, "Black, white and yeller!" "Black, white and yeller," echoed a dozen voices.

It did not grate so harshly on poor Mag as once it would. She did not even turn her head to look at them. She had passed into an insensibility no childish taunt could penetrate, else she would have reproached herself as she passed familiar scenes, for extending the separation once so easily annihilated by steadfast integrity. Two miles beyond lived the Bellmonts, in a large, old fashioned, two-story white house, environed by fruitful acres, and embellished by shrubbery and shade trees. Years ago a youthful couple consecrated it as home; and after many little feet had worn paths to favorite fruit trees, and over its green hills, and mingled at last with brother man in the race which belongs neither to the swift or strong, the sire became grey-haired and decrepit, and went to his last repose. His aged consort soon followed him. The old homestead thus passed into the hands of a son, to whose wife Mag had applied the epithet "she-devil," as may be remembered. John, the son, had not in his family arrangements departed from the exam-ple of the father. The pastimes of his boyhood were ever freshly revived by witnessing the games of his own sons as they rallied about the same goal his youthful feet had often won; as well as by the amusements of his daughters in their imitations of maternal duties.

At the time we introduce them, however, John is wearing the badge of age. Most of his children were from home; some seeking employment; some were already settled in homes of their own. A maiden sister shared with him the estate on which he resided, and occupied a portion of the house.

Within sight of the house, Seth seated himself with his bundles and the child he had been leading, while Mag walked onward to the house leading Frado. A knock at the door brought Mrs. Bellmont, and Mag asked if she would be willing to let that child stop there while she went to the Reed's house to wash, and when she came back she would call and get her. It seemed a novel request, but she consented. Why the impetuous child entered the house, we cannot tell; the door closed, and Mag hastily departed. Frado waited for the close of day, which was to bring back her mother. Alas! it never came. It was the last time she ever saw or heard of her mother.

CHAPTER XII.
THE WINDING UP OF THE MATTER.

Nothing new under the sun.
—Solomon.

A FEW YEARS ago, within the compass of my narrative, there appeared often in some of our New England villages, professed fugitives from slavery, who recounted their personal experience in homely phrase, and awakened the indignation of non-slaveholders against brother Pro. Such a one appeared in the new home of Frado; and as people of color were rare there, was it strange she should attract her dark brother; that he should inquire her out; succeed in seeing her; feel a strange sensation in his heart towards her; that he should toy with her shining curls, feel proud to provoke her to smile and expose the ivory concealed by thin, ruby lips; that her sparkling eyes should fascinate; that he should propose; that they should marry? A short acquaintance was indeed an objection, but she saw him often, and thought she knew him. He never spoke of his enslavement to her when alone, but she felt that, like her own oppression, it was painful to disturb oftener than was needful.

He was a fine, straight negro, whose back showed no marks of the lash, erect as if it never crouched beneath a burden. There was a silent sympathy which Frado felt attracted her, and she opened her heart to the presence of love—that arbitrary and inexorable tyrant.

She removed to Singleton, her former residence, and there was married. Here were Frado's first feelings of trust and repose on human arm. She realized, for the first time, the relief of looking to another for comfortable support. Occasionally he would leave her to "lecture."

Those tours were prolonged often to weeks. Of course he had little spare money. Frado was again feeling her self-dependence, and was at last compelled to resort alone to that. Samuel was kind to her when at home, but made no provision for his absence, which was at last unprecedented.

He left her to her fate—embarked at sea, with the disclosure that he had never seen the South, and that his illiterate harangues were humbugs for hungry abolitionists. Once more alone! Yet not alone. A still newer companionship would soon force itself upon her. No one wanted her with such prospects. Herself was burden enough; who would have an additional one?

The horrors of her condition nearly prostrated her, and she was again thrown upon the public for sustenance. Then followed the birth of her child. The long absent Samuel unexpectedly returned, and rescued her from charity. Recovering from her expected illness, she once more commenced toil for herself and child, in a room obtained of a poor woman, but with better fortune. One so well known would not be wholly neglected. Kind friends watched her when Samuel was from home, prevented her from suffering, and when the cold weather pinched the warmly clad, a kind friend took them in, and thus preserved them. At last Samuel's business became very engrossing, and after long desertion, news reached his family that he had become a victim of yellow fever, in New Orleans.

So much toil as was necessary to sustain Frado, was more than she could endure. As soon as her babe could be nourished without his mother, she left him in charge of a Mrs. Capon, and procured an agency, hoping to recruit her health, and gain an easier livelihood for herself and child. This afforded her better maintenance than she had yet found. She passed into the various towns of the State she lived in, then into Massachusetts. Strange were some of her adventures. Watched by kidnappers, maltreated by professed abolitionists, who didn't want slaves at the South, nor niggers in their own houses, North. Faugh! to lodge one; to eat with one; to admit one through the front door; to sit next one; awful!

Traps slyly laid by the vicious to ensnare her, she resolutely avoided. In one of her tours, Providence favored her with a friend who, pitying her cheerless lot, kindly provided her with a valuable recipe, from which she might herself manufacture a useful article for her maintenance. This proved a more agreeable, and an easier way of sustenance.

And thus, to the present time, may you see her busily employed in preparing her merchandise; then sallying forth to encounter many frowns, but some kind friends and purchasers. Nothing turns her from her steadfast purpose of elevating herself. Reposing on God, she has thus far journeyed securely. Still an invalid, she asks your sympathy, gentle reader. Refuse not, because some part of her history is unknown, save by the Omniscient God. Enough has been unrolled to demand your sympathy and aid.

Do you ask the destiny of those connected with her *early* history? A few years only have elapsed since Mr. and Mrs. B. passed into another world. As age increased, Mrs. B. became more irritable, so that no one, even her own children, could remain with her; and she was accompanied by her husband to the home of Lewis, where, after an agony in death unspeakable, she passed away. Only a few months since, Aunt Abby entered heaven. Jack and his wife rest in heaven, disturbed by no intruders; and Susan and her child are yet with the living. Jane has silver locks in place of auburn tresses, but she has the early love of Henry still, and has never regretted her exchange of lovers. Frado has passed from their memories, as Joseph from the butler's, but she will never cease to track them till beyond mortal vision.

FRANCES ELLEN WATKINS HARPER (1825–1911)

First short story published by an African American woman author.

Frances Ellen Watkins Harper was born in 1825 in Baltimore, the only child of free African American parents. An aunt and uncle, Harriet and William Watkins, raised her after her mother died when she was three years old. She attended the Academy for Negro Youth, a school run by her uncle, until the age of thirteen, and then worked in a Quaker household, where she had access to a wide range of literature. After teaching in Ohio and Pennsylvania, she became a traveling speaker for the abolitionist cause. In 1860 she married Fenton Harper, already father to three children of his own, and together they had a daughter. After her husband's death in 1864, Harper continued to support her family through speaking engagements. She was superintendent of the Colored Section of the Philadelphia and Pennsylvania Women's Christian Temperance Union, a member of the American Women's Suffrage Association, and director of the American Association of Colored Youth. As a lecturer and author, Harper was a household name in the nineteenth century alongside luminaries such as Elizabeth Cady Stanton and Frederick Douglass. She debated the latter while advocating for Black women's right to vote. Today she is celebrated as one of the key authors and activists of her time. Not only was she the first African American woman to publish a signed short story, but as an influential abolitionist, suffragist, author, and journalist she co-founded the National Association of Colored Women's Clubs.

One of the most prolific African American writers during the nineteenth century, Harper published many collections of poetry, several of which were enormously popular. She also published at least four novels, including *Iola Leroy* (1892), essays, and articles. Her short story "The Two Offers" was credited to Frances Ellen Watkins and published in two installments in 1859 in the newly founded *Anglo-African Magazine*. "The Two Offers" presents two female cousins deliberating on a marriage proposal at a time when marriage could mean either an escape from poverty and oppression or the beginning of another type of dependency; and not getting married could also condemn a woman to loneliness and misery. The story examines the possibility of women's independence and counters the idea that romantic attraction or money should decide marriage and delimit a woman's life.

Harper's poem "Learning to Read" is set after the Civil War and Emancipation and published in 1872 as part of her enormously popular *Sketches of Southern Life*. The poem's speaker, Aunt Chloe, an African American woman, had been prohibited by white slaveholders to read and write and is now discouraged from learning to do so by her own people: "And said there is no use trying, / Oh! Chloe, you're too late; / But as I was rising sixty, / I had no time to wait." The poem's final stanza celebrates the woman speaker's newfound independence from both white and Black society. Several decades before Virginia Woolf would demand for every woman a "room of her own," Harper called for "[A] little cabin / A place to call my own." If Harper had aimed to make a political or legal statement, which she did elsewhere, this final stanza would not be needed. It testifies to her—and every human being's—urge to speak and to imagine life on her own terms instead of those given, or withheld, by society.

In contrast, "The Two Offers" does not address slavery, freedom, or political rights, and does not mention the main figure's racial identity, which readers could assume from the place of publication. Harper's lectures and other writings that explicitly address race constitute one dimension of her interventions into American society; her fiction and poetry—no less significant—constitute another by testifying to her literary prowess and the audacity of her imagination.

The Two Offers [1859]

"What is the matter with you, Laura, this morning? I have been watching you this hour, and in that time you have commenced a half dozen letters and torn them all up. What matter of such grave moment is puzzling your dear little head, that you do not know how to decide?"

"Well, it is an important matter: I have two offers for marriage, and I do not know which to choose."

"I should accept neither, or to say the least, not at present."

"Why not?"

"Because I think a woman who is undecided between two offers, has not love enough for either to make a choice; and in that very hesitation, indecision, she has a reason to pause and seriously reflect, lest her marriage, instead of being an affinity of souls or a union of hearts, should only be a mere matter of bargain and sale, or an affair of convenience and selfish interest."

"But I consider them both very good offers, just such as many a girl would gladly receive. But to tell you the truth, I do not think that I regard either as a woman should the man she chooses for her husband. But then if I refuse, there is the risk of being an old maid, and that is not to be thought of."

"Well, suppose there is, is that the most dreadful fate that can befall a woman? Is there not more intense wretchedness in an ill-assorted marriage—more utter loneliness in a loveless home, than in the lot of the old maid who accepts her earthly mission as a gift from God, and strives to walk the path of life with earnest and unfaltering steps?"

"Oh! what a little preacher you are. I really believe that you were cut out for an old maid; that when nature formed you, she put in a double portion of intellect to make up for a deficiency of love; and yet you are kind and affectionate. But I do not think that you know anything of the grand, over-mastering passion, or the deep necessity of woman's heart for loving."

"Do you think so?" resumed the first speaker; and bending over her work she quietly applied herself to the knitting that had lain neglected by her side, during this brief conversation; but as she did so, a shadow flitted over her pale and intellectual brow, a mist gathered in her eyes, and a slight quivering of the lips, revealed a depth of feeling to which her companion was a stranger.

But before I proceed with my story, let me give you a slight history of the speakers. They were cousins, who had met life under different auspices. Laura Lagrange, was the only daughter of rich and indulgent parents, who had spared no pains to make her an accomplished lady. Her cousin, Janette Alston, was the child of parents, rich only in goodness and affection. Her father had been unfortunate in business, and dying before he could retrieve his fortunes, left his business in an embarrassed state. His widow was unacquainted with his business affairs, and when the estate was settled, hungry creditors had brought their claims and the lawyers had received their fees, she found herself homeless and almost penniless, and she who had been sheltered in the warm clasp of loving arms, found them too powerless to shield her from the pitiless pelting storms of adversity. Year after year she struggled with poverty and wrestled with want, till her toil-worn hands became too feeble to hold the shattered chords of existence, and her tear-dimmed eyes grew heavy with the slumber of death. Her daughter had watched over her with untiring devotion, had closed her eyes in death, and gone out into the busy, restless world, missing a precious tone from the voices of earth, a beloved step from the paths of life. Too self reliant to depend on the charity of relations, she endeavored to support herself by her own exertions, and she had succeeded. Her path for a while was marked with struggle and trial, but instead of uselessly repining, she met them bravely, and her life became not a thing of ease and indulgence, but of conquest, victory, and accomplishments. At the time when this conversation took place, the deep trials of her life had passed away. The achievements of her genius had won her a position in the literary world, where she shone as one of its bright particular stars. And with her fame came a competence of worldly means, which gave her leisure for improvement, and the riper development of her rare talents. And she, that pale intellectual woman, whose genius gave life and vivacity to the social circle, and whose presence threw a halo of beauty and grace around the charmed atmosphere in which she moved, had at one period of her life, known the mystic and solemn strength of an all-absorbing love. Years faded into the misty past, had seen the kindling of her eye, the quick flushing of her cheek, and the wild throbbing of her heart, at tones of a voice long since hushed to the stillness of death. Deeply, wildly, passionately, she had loved. Her whole life seemed like the pouring out of rich, warm and gushing affections. This love quickened her talents, inspired her genius, and threw over her life a tender and spiritual earnestness. And then came a fearful shock, a mournful waking from that "dream of beauty and delight." A shadow fell around her path; it came between her and the object of her heart's worship; first a few cold words, estrangement, and then a painful separation; the old story of woman's pride—digging the sepulchre of her happiness, and then a new-made grave, and her path over it to the spirit world; and thus faded out from that young heart her bright, brief and saddened dream of life. Faint and spirit-broken, she turned from the scenes associated with the memory of the loved and lost. She tried to break the chain of sad associations that bound her to the mournful past; and so, pressing back the bitter sobs from her almost breaking heart, like the dying dolphin, whose beauty is born of its death anguish, her genius gathered strength from suffering and wondrous power and brilliancy from the agony she hid within the desolate chambers of her soul. Men hailed her as one of earth's strangely gifted children, and wreathed the garlands of fame for her brow, when it was throbbing with a wild and fearful unrest. They breathed her name with applause, when through the lonely halls of her stricken spirit, was an earnest cry for peace, a deep yearning for sympathy and heart-support.

But life, with its stern realities, met her; its solemn responsibilities confronted her, and turning, with an earnest and shattered spirit, to life's duties and trials, she found a calmness and strength that she had only imagined in her dreams of poetry and song. We will now pass over a period of ten years, and the cousins have met again. In that calm and lovely woman, in whose eyes is a depth of tenderness, tempering the flashes of her genius, whose looks and tones are full of sympathy and love, we recognize the once smitten and stricken Janette Alston. The bloom of her girlhood had given way to a higher type of spiritual beauty, as if some unseen hand had been polishing and refining the temple in which her lovely spirit found its habitation; and this had been the fact. Her inner life had grown beautiful, and it was this that was constantly developing the outer. Never, in the early flush of womanhood, when an absorbing love had lit up her eyes and glowed in her life, had she appeared so interesting as when, with a countenance which seemed overshadowed with a spiritual light, she bent over the death-bed of a young woman, just lingering at the shadowy gates of the unseen land.

"Has he come?" faintly but eagerly exclaimed the dying woman. "Oh! how I have longed for his coming, and even in death he forgets me."

"Oh, do not say so, dear Laura, some accident may have detained him," said Janette to her cousin; for on that bed, from whence she will never rise, lies the once-beautiful and lighthearted Laura Lagrange, the brightness of whose eyes has long since been dimmed with tears, and whose voice had become like a harp whose every chord is turned to sadness—whose faintest thrill and loudest vibrations are but the variations of agony. A heavy hand was laid upon her once warm and bounding heart, and a voice came whispering through her soul, that she must die. But, to her, the tidings was a message of deliverance—a voice, hushing her wild sorrows to the calmness of resignation and hope. Life had grown so weary upon her head—the future looked so hopeless—she had no wish to tread again the track where thorns had pierced her feet, and clouds overcast her sky; and she hailed the coming of death's angel as the footsteps of a welcome friend. And yet, earth had one object so very dear to her weary heart. It was her absent and recreant husband; for, since that conversation, she had accepted one of her offers, and become a wife. But, before she married, she learned that great lesson of human experience and woman's life, to love the man who bowed at her shrine, a willing worshipper. He had a pleasing address, raven hair, flashing eyes, a voice of thrilling sweetness, and lips of persuasive eloquence; and being well versed in the ways of the world, he won his way to her heart, and she became his bride, and he was proud of his prize. Vain and superficial in his character, he looked upon marriage not as a divine sacrament for the soul's development and human progression, but as the title-deed that gave him possession of the woman he thought he loved. But alas for her, the laxity of his principles had rendered him unworthy of the deep and undying devotion of a pure-hearted woman; but, for awhile, he hid from her his true character, and she blindly loved him, and for a short period was happy in the consciousness of being beloved; though sometimes a vague unrest would fill her soul, when, overflowing with a sense of the good, the beautiful, and the true, she would turn to him, but find no response to the deep yearnings of her soul—no appreciation of life's highest realities—its solemn grandeur and significant importance. Their souls never met, and soon she found a void in her bosom, that his earth-born love could not fill. He did not satisfy the wants of her mental and moral nature—between him and her there was no affinity of minds, no intercommunion of souls.

Talk as you will of woman's deep capacity for loving, of the strength of her affectional nature. I do not deny it; but will the mere possession of any human love, fully satisfy all the demands of her whole being? You may paint her in poetry or fiction, as a frail vine, clinging to her brother man for support, and dying when deprived of it; and all this may sound well enough to please the imaginations of school-girls, or love-lorn maidens. But woman—the true woman—if you would render her happy, it needs more than the mere development of her affectional nature. Her conscience should be enlightened, her faith in the true and right established, scope given to her Heaven-endowed and God-given faculties. The true aim of female education should be not a development of one or two, but all the faculties of the human soul, because no perfect womanhood is developed by imperfect culture. Intense love is often akin to intense suffering, and to trust the whole wealth of a woman's nature on the frail bark of human love, may often be like trusting a cargo of gold and precious gems, to a bark that has never battled with the storm, or buffeted the waves. Is it any wonder, then, that so many life-barks go down, paving the ocean of time with precious hearts and wasted hopes? that so many float around us, shattered and dismasted wrecks? that so many are stranded on the shoals of existence, mournful beacons and solemn warnings for the thoughtless, to whom marriage is a careless and hasty rushing together of the affections? Alas that an institution so fraught with good for humanity should be so perverted, and that state of life, which should be filled with happiness, become so replete with misery. And this was the fate of Laura Lagrange. For a brief period after her marriage her life seemed like a bright and beautiful dream, full of hope and radiant with joy. And then there came a change—he found other attractions that lay beyond the pale of home influences. The gambling saloon had power to win him from her side, he had lived in an element of unhealthy and unhallowed excitements, and the society of a loving wife, the pleasures of a well-regulated home, were enjoyments too tame for one who had vitiated his tastes by the pleasures of sin. There were charmed houses of vice, built upon dead men's loves, where, amid the flow of song, laughter, wine, and careless mirth, he would spend hour after hour, forgetting the cheek that was paling through his neglect, heedless of the tear-dimmed eyes, peering anxiously into the darkness, waiting, or watching his return.

The influence of old associations was upon him. In early life, home had been to him a place of ceilings and walls, not a true home, built upon goodness, love and truth. It was a place where velvet carpets hushed its tread, where images of loveliness and beauty invoked into being by painter's art and sculptor's skill, pleased the eye and gratified the taste, where magnificence surrounded his way and costly clothing adorned his person; but it was not the place for the true culture and right development of his soul. His father had been too much engrossed in making money, and his mother in spending it, in striving to maintain a fashionable position in society, and shining in the eyes of the world, to give the proper direction to the character of their wayward and impulsive son. His mother put beautiful robes upon his body, but left ugly scars upon his soul; she pampered his appetite, but starved his spirit. Every mother should be a true artist, who knows how to weave into her child's life images of grace and beauty, the true poet capable of writing on the soul of childhood the harmony of love and truth, and teaching it how to produce the grandest of all poems—the poetry of a true and noble life. But in his home, a love for the good, the true and right, had been sacrificed at the shrine of frivolity and fashion. That parental authority which should have been preserved as a string of precious pearls, unbroken and unscattered, was simply the administration of chance. At one time obedience was enforced by authority, at another time by flattery and promises, and just as often it was not enforced at all. His early associations were formed as chance directed, and from his want of home-training, his character received a bias, his life a shade, which ran through every avenue of his existence, and darkened all his future hours. Oh, if we would trace the history of all the crimes that have o'ershadowed this sin-shrouded and sorrow-darkened world of ours, how many might be seen arising from the wrong home influences, or the weakening of the home ties. Home should always be the best school for the affections, the birthplace of high resolves, and the altar upon which lofty aspirations are kindled, from whence the soul may go forth strengthened, to act its part aright in the great drama of life with conscience enlightened, affections cultivated, and reason and judgment dominant. But alas for the young wife. Her husband had not been blessed with such a home. When he entered the arena of life, the voices from home did not linger around his path as angels of guidance about his steps; they were not like so many messages to invite him to deeds of high and holy worth. The memory of no sainted mother arose between him and deeds of darkness; the earnest prayers of no father arrested him in his downward course: and before a year of his married life had waned, his young wife had learned to wait and mourn his frequent and uncalled-for absence. More than once had she seen him come home from his midnight haunts, the bright intelligence of his eye displaced by the drunkard's stare, and his manly gait changed to the inebriate's stagger; and she was beginning to know the bitter agony that is compressed in the mournful words, a drunkard's wife. And then there came a bright but brief episode in her experience; the angel of life gave to her existence a deeper meaning and loftier significance; she sheltered in the warm clasp of her loving arms, a dear babe, a precious child, whose love filled every chamber of her heart, and felt the fount of maternal love gushing so new within her soul. That child was hers. How overshadowing was the love with which she bent over its helplessness, how much it helped to fill the void and chasms in her soul. How many lonely hours were beguiled by its winsome ways, its answering smiles and fond caresses. How exquisite and solemn was the feeling that thrilled her heart when she clasped the tiny hands together and taught her dear child to call God "Our Father."

What a blessing was that child. The father paused in his headlong career, awed by the strange beauty and precocious intellect of his child; and the mother's life had a better expression through her ministrations of love. And then there came hours of bitter anguish, shading the sunlight of her home and hushing the music of her heart. The angel of death bent over the couch of her child and beaconed it away. Closer and closer the mother strained her child to her wildly heaving breast, and struggled with the heavy hand that lay upon its heart. Love and agony contended with death, and the language of the mother's heart was,

"Oh, Death, away! that innocent is mine;
 I cannot spare him from my arms
To lay him, Death, in thine.
I am a mother,
Death; I gave that darling birth
I could not bear his lifeless limbs
 Should moulder in the earth."

But death was stronger than love and mightier than agony and won the child for the land of crystal founts and deathless flowers, and the poor, stricken mother sat down beneath the shadow of her mighty grief, feeling as if a great light had gone out from her soul, and that the sunshine had suddenly faded around her path. She turned in her deep anguish to the father of her child, the loved and cherished dead. For awhile his words were kind and tender, his heart seemed subdued, and his tenderness fell upon her worn and weary heart like rain on perishing flowers, or cooling waters to lips all parched with thirst and scorched with fever; but the change was evanescent, the influence of unhallowed associations and evil habits had vitiated and poisoned the springs of his existence. They had bound him in their meshes, and he lacked the moral strength to break his fetters, and stand erect in all the strength and dignity of a true manhood, making life's highest excellence his ideal, and striving to gain it.

And yet moments of deep contrition would sweep over him, when he would resolve to abandon the wine-cup forever, when he was ready to forswear the handling of another card, and he would try to break away from the associations that he felt were working his ruin; but when the hour of temptation came his strength was weakness, his earnest purposes were cobwebs, his well-meant resolutions ropes of sand, and thus passed year after year of the married life of Laura Lagrange. She tried to hide her agony from the public gaze, to smile when her heart was almost breaking. But year after year her voice grew fainter and sadder, her once light and bounding step grew slower and faltering. Year after year she wrestled with agony, and strove with despair, till the quick eyes of her brother read, in the paling of her cheek and the dimming eye, the secret anguish of her worn and weary spirit. On that wan, sad face, he saw the death-tokens, and he knew the dark wing of the mystic angel swept coldly around her path. "Laura," said her brother to her one day, "you are not well, and I think you need our mother's tender care and nursing. You are daily losing strength, and if you will go I will accompany you." At first, she hesitated, she shrank almost instinctively from presenting that pale sad face to the loved ones at home. That face was such a tell-tale; it told of heart-sickness, of hope deferred, and the mournful story of unrequited love. But then a deep yearning for home sympathy woke within her a passionate longing for love's kind words, for tenderness and heart-support, and she resolved to seek the home of her childhood and lay her weary head upon her mother's bosom, to be folded again in her loving arms, to lay that poor, bruised and aching heart where it might beat and throb closely to the loved ones at home. A kind welcome awaited her. All that love and tenderness could devise was done to bring the bloom to her cheek and the light to her eye; but it was all in vain; her's was a disease that no medicine could cure, no earthly balm would heal. It was a slow wasting of the vital forces, the sickness of the soul. The unkindness and neglect of her husband, lay like a leaden weight upon her heart, and slowly oozed way its life-drops. And where was he that had won her love, and then cast it aside as a useless thing, who rifled her heart of its wealth and spread bitter ashes upon its broken altars? He was lingering away from her when the death-damps were gathering on her brow, when his name was trembling on her lips! lingering away! when she was watching his coming, though the death films were gathering before her eyes, and earthly things were fading from her vision. "I think I hear him now," said the dying woman, "surely that is his step;" but the sound died away in the distance. Again she started from an uneasy slumber, "That is his voice! I am so glad he has come." Tears gathered in the eyes of the sad watchers by that dying bed, for they knew that she was deceived. He had not returned. For her sake they wished his coming. Slowly the hours waned away, and then came the sad, soul-sickening thought that she was forgotten, forgotten in the last hour of human need, forgotten when the spirit, about to be dissolved, paused for the last time on the threshold of existence, a weary watcher at the gates of death. "He has forgotten me," again she faintly murmured, and the last tears she would ever shed on earth sprung to her mournful eyes, and clasping her hands together in silent anguish, a few broken sentences issued from her pale and quivering lips. They were prayers for strength and earnest pleading for him who had desolated her young life, by turning its sunshine to shadows, its smiles to tears. "He has forgotten me," she murmured again, "but I can bear it, the bitterness of death is passed, and soon I hope to exchange the shadows of death for the brightness of eternity, the rugged paths of life for the golden streets of glory, and the care and turmoils of earth for the peace and rest of heaven." Her voice grew fainter and fainter, they saw the shadows that never deceive flit over her pale and faded face, and knew that the death angel waited to soothe their weary one to rest, to calm the throbbing of her bosom and cool the fever of her brain. And amid the silent hush of their grief the freed spirit, refined through suffering, and brought into divine harmony through the spirit of the living Christ, passed over the dark waters of death as on a bridge of light, over whose radiant arches hovering angels bent. They parted the dark locks from her marble brow, closed the waxen lids over the once bright and laughing eye, and left her to the dreamless slumber of the grave. Her cousin turned from that death-bed a sadder and wiser woman. She resolved more earnestly than ever to make the world better by her example, gladder by her presence, and to kindle the fires of her genius on the altars of universal love and truth. She had a higher and better object in all her writings than the mere acquisition of gold, or acquirement of fame. She felt that she had a high and holy mission on the battle-field of existence, that life was not given her to be frittered away in nonsense, or wasted away in trifling pursuits. She would willingly espouse an unpopular cause but not an unrighteous one. In her the down-trodden slave found an earnest advocate; the flying fugitive remembered her kindness as he stepped cautiously through our Republic, to gain his freedom in a monarchial land, having broken the chains on which the rust of centuries had gathered. Little children learned to name her with affection, the poor called her blessed, as she broke her bread to the pale lips of hunger. Her life was like a beautiful story, only it was clothed with the dignity of reality and invested with the sublimity of truth. True, she was an old maid. No husband brightened her life with his love, or shaded it with his neglect. No children nestling lovingly in her arms called her mother. No one appended Mrs. to her name; she was indeed an old maid, not vainly striving to keep up an appearance of girlishness, when departed was written on her youth. Not vainly pining at her loneliness and isolation: the world was full of warm, loving hearts, and her own beat in unison with them. Neither was she always sentimentally sighing for something to love, objects of affection were all around her, and the world was not so wealthy in love that it had no use for her's; in blessing others she made a life and benediction, and as old age descended peacefully and gently upon her, she had learned one of life's most precious lessons, that true happiness consists not so much in the fruition of our wishes as in the regulation of desires and the full development and right culture of our whole natures.

LEARNING TO READ [1859]

Very soon the Yankee teachers
    Came down and set up school;
But, oh! how the Rebs did hate it,—
    It was agin' their rule.

Our masters always tried to hide
    Book learning from our eyes;
Knowledge did'nt agree with slavery—
    'Twould make us all too wise.

But some of us would try to steal
    A little from the book.
And put the words together,
    And learn by hook or crook.

I remember Uncle Caldwell,
Who took pot-liquor fat
And greased the pages of his book,
    And hid it in his hat.

And had his master ever seen
    The leaves upon his head,
He'd have thought them greasy papers,
    But nothing to be read.

And there was Mr. Turner's Ben,
    Who heard the children spell,
And picked the words right up by heart,
    And learned to read 'em well.

Well, the Northern folks kept sending

The Yankee teachers down;
And they stood right up and helped us,
    Though Rebs did sneer and frown.

And, I longed to read my Bible,
    For precious words it said;
But when I begun to learn it,
    Folks just shook their heads,

And said there is no use trying,
    Oh! Chloe, you're too late;
But as I was rising sixty,
    I had no time to wait.

So I got a pair of glasses,
    And straight to work I went,
And never stopped till I could read
    The hymns and Testament.

Then I got a little cabin—
    A place to call my own—
And I felt independent
    As the queen upon her throne.

MARTIN DELANY (1812–1885)

First published work of fantasy fiction by an African American author.

Martin Robinson Delany was born in 1812, a free person of color to an enslaved father and free Black mother in Charles Town, now West Virginia. His mother moved the family to Pennsylvania to escape Southern conditions and educate her children during a time when teaching Black people to read and write was illegal in Virginia. Delany worked as a laborer and barber, and apprenticed to be a doctor (physicians were not licensed officially at the time). In 1843 he married Catherine A. Richards, and they had eleven children, of which seven survived to adulthood. In 1850 Harvard Medical School dismissed Delany and the two other enrolled Black students because white students protested their presence. Delany increasingly doubted the possibility of Black liberation in a racist society. He was co-editor, with Frederick Douglass, of the *North Star* newspaper but supported Black emigration from America to Africa rather than Douglass's assimilationist program. In 1856 he moved to Canada and traveled to Liberia to make concrete plans for Black Americans to emigrate there. During the Civil War he raised thousands of troops for the Union States Colored Troops and in 1865 convinced President Lincoln to form a Black unit, making him the first African American field grade officer in the U.S. Army. After the war he moved to South Carolina where he unsuccessfully ran for Lieutenant Governor but was active in political life while running a land and brokerage business.

Blake was published in two parts: the first by the *Anglo-African Magazine* (AAM) in 1859, and the second by the *Weekly Anglo-African Magazine* (WAA) in 1861-62, the earlier part of the American Civil War. The serial novel in book form has been published incomplete as there are no extant copies of the May 1862 issues, which probably contain the final chapters. The novel was a response to Harriet Beecher Stowe's best-selling *Uncle Tom's*

Cabin (1855), which portrayed enslaved people as generally passive. The novel recounts an enslaved man's escape from a Southern plantation and subsequent efforts to unite the enslaved and free Black populations in the quest for freedom. It imagines a global slave insurrection and a pan-Africanist movement, which makes it the first book of African American utopian fiction. Long overlooked, *Blake* drew renewed attention in the 1960s because the novel imagines Black liberation on Black terms rather than making freedom dependent on criteria established and respected by white society.

From BLAKE; OR, THE HUTS OF AMERICA: A TALE OF THE MISSISSIPPI VALLEY, THE SOUTHERN UNITED STATES, AND CUBA [1859]

CHAPTER 1

THE PROJECT

By myself, the Lord of Ages,
I have sworn to right the wrong;
I have pledged my hard unbroken
For the weak against the strong.
—HARRIET BEECHER STOWE

ON ONE OF those exciting occasions during a contest for the presidency of the United States, a number of gentlemen met in the city of Baltimore. They were few in number, and appeared little concerned about the affairs of the general government. Though men of intelligence, their time and attention appeared to be entirely absorbed in an adventure of self-interest. They met for the purpose of completing arrangements for refitting the old ship "Merchantman," which then lay in the harbor near Fell's Point. Colonel Stephen Franks, Major James Armsted, Captain Richard Paul, and Captain George Royer composed those who represented the American side—Captain Juan Garcia and Captain Jose Castello, those of Cuban interest.

Here a conversation ensued upon what seemed a point of vital importance to the company; it related to the place best suited for the completion of their arrangements. The Americans insisted on Baltimore as affording the greatest facilities, and having done more for the encouragement and protection of the trade than any other known place, whilst the Cubans, on the other side, urged their objections on the ground that the continual increase of liberal principles in the various political parties, which were fast ushering into existence, made the objection beyond a controversy. Havana was contended for as a point best suited for adjusting their arrangements, and that too with many apparent reasons; but for some cause, the preference for Baltimore prevailed.

Subsequently to the adjustment of their affairs by the most complete arrangement for refitting the vessel, Colonel Franks took leave of the party for his home in the distant state of Mississippi.

CHAPTER 2
COLONEL FRANKS AT HOME

ON THE RETURN of Colonel Stephen Franks to his home at Natchez, he met there Mrs. Arabella, the wife of Judge Ballard, an eminent jurist of one of the Northern States. She had arrived but a day before him, on a visit to some relatives, of whom Mrs. Franks was one. The conversation, as is customary on the meeting of Americans residing in such distant latitudes, readily turned on the general policy of the country.

Mrs. Ballard possessed the highest intelligence, and Mrs. Maria Franks was among the most accomplished of Southern ladies.

"Tell me, Madam Ballard, how will the North go in the present issue?" enquired Franks.

"Give yourself no concern about that, Colonel," replied Mrs. Ballard, "you will find the North true to the country."

"What you consider true, may be false—that is, it might be true to you, and false to us," continued he.

"You do not understand me, Colonel," she rejoined, "we can have no interests separate from yours; you know the time-honored motto, 'united we stand,' and so forth, must apply to the American people under every policy in every section of the Union."

"So it should, but amidst the general clamor in the contest for ascendancy, may you not lose sight of this important point?"

"How can we? You, I'm sure, Colonel, know very well that in our country commercial interests have taken precedence of all others, which is a sufficient guarantee of our fidelity to the South."

"That may be, madam, but we are still apprehensive."

"Well, sir, we certainly do not know what more to do to give you assurance of our sincerity. We have as a plight of faith yielded Boston, New York, and Philadelphia—the intelligence and wealth of the North—in carrying out the Compromise measures for the interests of the South; can we do more?"

"True, Madam Ballard, true! I yield the controversy. You have already done more than we of the South expected. I now remember that the Judge himself tried the first case under the Act, in your city, by which the measures were tested."

"He did, sir, and if you will not consider me unwomanly by telling you, desired me, on coming here, to seek every opportunity to give the fullest assurance that the judiciary are sound on that question. Indeed, so far as an individual might be concerned, his interests in another direction—as you know—place him beyond suspicion," concluded Mrs. Ballard.

"I am satisfied, madam, and by your permission, arrest the conversation. My acknowledgements, madam!" bowed the Colonel, with true Southern courtesy.

"Maria, my dear, you look careworn; are you indisposed?" inquired Franks of his wife, who during conversation sat silent.

"Not physically, Colonel," replied she, "but——"

Just at this moment a servant, throwing open the door, announced dinner.

Besides a sprightly black boy of some ten years of age, there was in attendance a prepossessing, handsome maid-servant, who generally kept, as much as the occasion would permit, behind the chair of her mistress. A mutual attachment appeared to exist between them, the maid apparently disinclined to leave the mistress, who seemed to keep her as near her person as possible.

Now and again the fat cook, Mammy Judy, would appear at the door of the dining room bearing a fresh supply for the table, who with a slight nod of the head, accompanied with an affectionate smile and the word "Maggie," indicated a tie much closer than that of mere fellow servants.

Maggie had long been the favorite maid-servant of her mistress, having attained the position through merit. She was also nurse and foster-mother to the two last children of Mrs. Franks, and loved them, to all appearance, as her own. The children reciprocated this affection, calling her "mammy."

Mammy Judy, who for years had occupied this position, ceded it to her daughter; she preferring, in consequence of age, the less active life of the culinary department.

The boy Tony would frequently cast a comic look upon Mrs. Ballard, then imploringly gaze in the face of his mistress. So intent was he in this, that twice did his master admonish him by a nod of the head.

"My dear," said the Colonel, "you are dull today; pray tell me what makes you sad?"

"I am not bodily afflicted, Colonel Franks, but my spirit is heavy," she replied.

"How so? What is the matter?"

"That will be best answered at another time and place, Colonel."

Giving his head an unconscious scratch accompanied with a slight twitch of the corner of the mouth, Franks seemed to comprehend the whole of it.

On one of her Northern tours to the watering places—during a summer season some two years previous, having with her Maggie the favorite—Mrs. Franks visited the family of the Judge, at which time Mrs. Ballard first saw the maid. She was a dark mulatto of a rich, yellow, autumn-like complexion, with a matchless, cushion-like head of hair, neither straight nor curly, but handsomer than either.

Mrs. Franks was herself a handsome lady of some thirty-five summers, but ten years less in appearance, a little above medium height, between the majestic and graceful, raven-black hair, and dark, expressive eyes. Yet it often had been whispered that in beauty the maid equalled if not excelled the mistress. Her age was twenty-eight.

The conduct of Mrs. Franks toward her servant was more like that of an elder sister than a mistress, and the mistress and maid sometimes wore dresses cut from the same web of cloth. Mrs. Franks would frequently adjust the dress and see that the hair of her maid was properly arranged. This to Mrs. Ballard was as unusual as it was an objectionable sight, especially as she imagined there was an air of hauteur in her demeanor. It was then she determined to subdue her spirit.

Acting from this impulse, several times in her absence, Mrs. Ballard took occasion to administer to the maid severities she had never experienced at the hands of her mistress, giving her at one time a severe slap on the cheek, calling her an "impudent jade."

At this, Mrs. Franks, on learning, was quite surprised; but on finding that the maid gave no just cause for it, took no further notice of it, designedly evading the matter. But before leaving, Mrs. Ballard gave her no rest until she gave her the most positive assurance that she would part with the maid on her next visit to Natchez. And thus she is found pressing her suit at the residence of the Mississippi planter.

WALT WHITMAN (1819–1892)

First published gay-themed poetry in America.

Walt Whitman was born in Long Island, New York, in 1819 to Walter, a carpenter and luckless house builder, and Louisa, a devout Quaker. He attended elementary school in Brooklyn, apprenticed in jobs including printing and journalism, and worked as a teacher in Long Island from 1836 to 1841. He traveled extensively, became editor of several periodicals and newspapers, and published short stories, poems, as well as a serialized novel without much notice. In 1855 he self-published the first edition of *Leaves of Grass*, a loosely connected series of poems in free verse narrated by a mythic poetic persona to present an epic, largely inclusive image of America as both concrete and imagined reality. In 1862 Whitman traveled to Virginia to tend to his brother George, who had been wounded in the Civil War. There he saw large numbers of wounded soldiers and volunteered to help. In 1865 Whitman was fired from a post in the Department of the Interior in Washington because of the alleged indecency of *Leaves of Grass*. He was immediately rehired into another government position where he remained until 1873 when he suffered a mild paralytic stroke. He spent the final years of his life in Camden, New Jersey, where he received illustrious visitors, commissioned a biography, continued to write, and prepared his poems for posterity. He died on March 26, 1892.

The "Calamus" poems were published first in the 1860 edition of *Leaves of Grass*. In the collection, Whitman tried to present an original and specifically American voice to a country whose dominant culture was still attached to European literary traditions and critical standards. Of the original forty-five poems, thirty-nine appear in later editions of *Leaves of Grass*, which Whitman revised several times.

In "Here the Frailest Leaves of Me," Whitman said these poems "expose me more than all my other poems." The love Whitman celebrates in these poems is both specific, frequently for a male lover, but also generic in the form of his social project of communal "comradeship" leading to a shared American identity. The specificity of the lines, "something fierce and terrible in me eligible to burst forth, / I dare not tell it in words, not even in these songs," has startled readers since their first publication. They have also greatly moved many readers and influenced subsequent writers who sought to express especially homosexual love under conditions where such expression was condemned and criminalized. The "Calamus" poems give voice to a reality that both laws and social conventions of his time denigrated, punished, and outlawed. Whitman, who cared greatly about his legacy and reputation, later denied that the "Calamus" poems could have a homosexual meaning. While critics usually hesitate to speculate on Whitman's sexuality, in contemporary scholarship the poems are considered a starting point for gay literature in America and the veiled expression of Whitman's imagination under conditions that prohibited and condemned same-sex love. The celebration of communal comradeship exists side by side with the poem's unabashed declaration of the poet's specific, and in today's language, gay love for other men. By aligning his experience of loving men with the project of imagining America as an all-encompassing truly democratic place, Whitman opened a space for subsequent writers and readers who now have a precedent and validation of their own desires, even if the existence of gay people would be consolidated into a social, and ultimately political and legal identity, only decades later.

From LEAVES OF GRASS, "CALAMUS" [1860]

NOT HEAVING FROM MY RIBB'D BREAST ONLY.

Not heaving from my ribb'd breast only,
Not in sighs at night, in rage, dissatisfied with myself,
Not in those long-drawn, ill-supprest sighs,
Not in many an oath and promise broken,
Not in my wilful and savage soul's volition,
Not in the subtle nourishment of the air,
Not in this beating and pounding at my temples and wrists,
Not in the curious systole and diastole within which will one day cease,
Not in many a hungry wish told to the skies only,

Not in cries, laughter, defiances, thrown from me when alone far in
    the wilds,
Not in husky pantings through clinch'd teeth,
Not in sounded and resounded words, chattering words, echoes, dead
    words,
Not in the murmurs of my dreams while I sleep,
Nor the other murmurs of these incredible dreams of every day,
Nor in the limbs and senses of my body that take you and dismiss you
    continually—not there,
Not in any or all of them O adhesiveness! O pulse of my life!
Need I that you exist and show yourself any more than in these songs.

Of the Terrible Doubt of Appearances.

Of the terrible doubt of appearances,
Of the uncertainty after all, that we may be deluded,
That may-be reliance and hope are but speculations after all,
That may-be identity beyond the grave is a beautiful fable only,
May-be the things I perceive, the animals, plants, men, hills, shining
    and flowing waters,
The skies of day and night, colors, densities, forms, may-be these are
    (as doubtless they are) only apparitions, and the real something
    has yet to be known,
(How often they dart out of themselves as if to confound me and
    mock me!
How often I think neither I know, nor any man knows, aught of
    them,)
May-be seeming to me what they are (as doubtless they indeed but
    seem) as from my present point of view, and might prove (as of
    course they would) nought of what they appear, or nought anyhow,
    from entirely changed points of view;
To me these and the like of these are curiously answer'd by my lovers,
    my dear friends,
When he whom I love travels with me or sits a long while holding me
    by the hand,
When the subtle air, the impalpable, the sense that words and reason
    hold not, surround us and pervade us,
Then I am charged with untold and untellable wisdom, I am silent, I

require nothing further,
I cannot answer the question of appearances or that of identity
    beyond the grave,
But I walk or sit indifferent, I am satisfied,
He ahold of my hand has completely satisfied me.

When I Heard at the Close of the Day.

When I heard at the close of the day how my name had been receiv'd
    with plaudits in the capitol, still it was not a happy night for me
    that follow'd,
And else when I carous'd, or when my plans were accomplish'd, still I
    was not happy,
But the day when I rose at dawn from the bed of perfect health,
    refresh'd, singing, inhaling the ripe breath of autumn,
When I saw the full moon in the west grow pale and disappear in the
    morning light,
When I wander'd alone over the beach, and undressing bathed,
    laughing with the cool waters, and saw the sun rise,
And when I thought how my dear friend my lover was on his way
    coming, O then I was happy,
O then each breath tasted sweeter, and all that day my food nourish'd
    me more, and the beautiful day pass'd well,
And the next came with equal joy, and with the next at evening came
    my friend,
And that night while all was still I heard the waters roll slowly
    continually up the shores,
I heard the hissing rustle of the liquid and sands as directed to me
    whispering to congratulate me,
For the one I love most lay sleeping by me under the same cover in the
    cool night,
In the stillness in the autumn moonbeams his face was inclined
    toward me,
And his arm lay lightly around my breast—and that night I was happy.

I Saw in Louisiana a Live Oak Growing

I saw in Louisiana a live-oak growing,
All alone stood it and the moss hung down from the branches,

Without any companion it grew there uttering joyous leaves of dark
    green,
And its look, rude, unbending, lusty, made me think of myself,
But I wonder'd how it could utter joyous leaves standing alone there
    without its friend near—for I knew I could not,
And I broke off a twig with a certain number of leaves upon it, and
    twined around it a little moss,
And brought it away—and I have placed it in sight in my room,
It is not needed to remind me as of my own dear friends,
(For I believe lately I think of little else than of them,)
Yet it remains to me a curious token—it makes me think of manly
    love;
—For all that, and though the live-oak glistens there in Louisiana
    solitary in a wide flat space,
Uttering joyous leaves all its life without a friend a lover near,
I know very well I could not.

City of Orgies.

City of orgies, walks and joys,
City whom that I have lived and sung in your midst will one day
    make you illustrious,
Not the pageants of you, not your shifting tableaus, your spectacles,
    repay me,
Not the interminable rows of your houses, nor the ships at the
    wharves,
Nor the processions in the streets, nor the bright windows with goods
    in them,
Nor to converse with learn'd persons, or bear my share in the soiree
    or feast;
Not those, but as I pass O Manhattan, your frequent and swift flash of
    eyes offering me love,
Offering response to my own—these repay me,
Lovers, continual lovers, only repay me.

I Hear It Was Charged Against Me.

I hear it was charged against me that I sought to destroy institutions,
But really I am neither for nor against institutions,

(What indeed have I in common with them?—Or what with the
    destruction of them?)
Only I will establish in the Mannahatta, and in every city of These
    States, inland and seaboard,
And in the fields and woods, and above every keel little or large, that
    dents the water,
Without edifices, or rules, or trustees, or any argument,
The institution of the dear love of comrades.

WE TWO BOYS TOGETHER CLINGING.

We two boys together clinging,
One the other never leaving,
Up and down the roads going, North and South excursions making,
Power enjoying, elbows stretching, fingers clutching,
Arm'd and fearless, eating, drinking, sleeping, loving,
No law less than ourselves owning, sailing, soldiering, thieving,
    threatening,
Misers, menials, priests alarming, air breathing, water drinking, on
    the turf or the sea-beach dancing,
Cities wrenching, ease scorning, statutes mocking, feebleness chasing,
Fulfilling our foray.

HERE THE FRAILEST LEAVES OF ME.

Here the frailest leaves of me, and yet my strongest-lasting,
Here I shade and hide my thoughts—I myself do not expose them,
And yet they expose me more than all my other poems.

A GLIMPSE.

A glimpse through an interstice caught,
Of a crowd of workmen and drivers in a bar-room around the stove
    late of a winter night, and I unremark'd seated in a corner,
Of a youth who loves me and whom I love, silently approaching and
    seating himself near, that he may hold me by the hand,
A long while amid the noises of coming and going, of drinking and
    oath and smutty jest,
There we two, content, happy in being together, speaking little,
    perhaps not a word.

Earth, My Likeness.

Earth, my likeness,
Though you look so impassive, ample and spheric there,
I now suspect that is not all;
I now suspect there is something fierce in you eligible to burst forth,
For an athlete is enamour'd of me, and I of him,
But toward him there is something fierce and terrible in me eligible to
    burst forth,
I dare not tell it in words, not even in these songs.

Sometimes with One I Love.

Sometimes with one I love I fill myself with rage for fear I effuse
    unreturn'd love,
But now I think there is no unreturn'd love, the pay is certain one way
    or another,
(I loved a certain person ardently and my love was not return'd,
Yet out of that I have written these songs.)

Among the Multitude.

Among the men and women the multitude,
I perceive one picking me out by secret and divine signs,
Acknowledging none else, not parent, wife, husband, brother, child,
    any nearer than I am,
Some are baffled, but that one is not—that one knows me.

Ah lover and perfect equal,
I meant that you should discover me so by faint indirections,
And I when I meet you mean to discover you by the like in you.

O You Whom I Often and Silently Come.

O you whom I often and silently come where you are that I may be
    with you,
As I walk by your side or sit near, or remain in the same room with
    you,
Little you know the subtle electric fire that for your sake is playing
    within me.

THEODORE WINTHROP (1828–1861)

First published American queer novel.

Theodore Winthrop was an author, lawyer, and world traveler. He was born into two well-known New England families in New Haven, one of whom counted Governor Winthrop of the colonial Massachusetts Bay Colony among their ancestors. He attended Yale College, where his uncle was President. After extensive travels in Europe, Great Britain, and the United States, he settled in Long Island. He joined the Union Army in 1861 where he was quickly appointed major and started reporting on the war for the *Atlantic Monthly*. During one of the war's first battles, he was shot and killed—the first high-ranking casualty of the Civil War on the Union side. Very quickly after the highly publicized death of such a prominent person, four of his unpublished novels about key moments in American history were rushed into print, as well as some of his poetry and prose pieces. *Cecil Dreeme* is set on the campus of New York University in New York City, where Winthrop was once a lodger. The Gothic novel was a success, partly due to its provocative subject matter which includes blackmail, switched identities, debauchery, and plenty of gender confusion.

Some histories of gay literature identify Bayard Taylor's novel *Joseph and His Friend: A Story of Pennsylvania* (1870) to be America's first gay-themed novel, where a male friendship found in many fictional texts of the time deserves the term "love" in its serious implications. But *Cecil Dreeme* is the chronologically earlier text and opens up a wider lens on the range of sexual and gender expressions in American literature. Critics refer to it as an example of both early gay fiction, as well as, sometimes, a "queer/trans novel." There is no straight line that leads from *Cecil Dreeme* to today's queer-themed fiction or the academic fields of queer and gender studies, almost as if the unresolved aspects of the novel had simply awaited today's enlightened readers and terminology to decode and name them. Rather, Winthrop's novel gives us dynamic terms to talk about same-sex relationships that are neither fully modern nor stuck in a remote, unspeakable past. The novel foreshadows our present circumstances, including the idea of sexuality as a political identity. Gender and sexuality in the novel also serve as an invitation to today's readers to imagine new ways of living and thereby establish their place in the world anew.

From CECIL DREEME [1861]

CHAPTER 20

A NOCTURE

NIGHT! NIGHT IN the great city!

Night! when the sun, the eye of God, leaves men to their own devices; when the moon is so faint, and the stars so far away in the infinite, that their inspection and record are forgotten; when Light, the lawgiver and orderer of human life, withdraws, and mankind are free to break or obey the commands daylight has taught them.

Night! when the gas-lights, relit, reawaken harmful purposes, that had slept through all the hours of honest sunshine in their lairs; when the tigers and tigresses take their stand where their prey will be sure to come; when the rustic in the peaceful country, with leaves whispering and crickets singing around him, sees a glow on the distant horizon, and wonders if the bad city beneath it be indeed abandoned of its godly men, and burning for its crimes. Night! the day of the base, the guilty, and the desolate!

Every evening, when it was possible, of that late winter and wintry spring, I abandoned club, parlor, and ball-room, and all the attractions of the brilliant world, to wander with Cecil Dreeme about the gas-lit city, and study the side it showed to night. And yet the phenomena of vice and crime, my companion refused to consider fit objects of curiosity. Vice and crime were tacitly avoided by us. Dreeme's nature repelled even the thought of them. I was happy to know one solitary man whose mind the consciousness of evil could not make less virgin.

It chanced one evening, a fortnight after our conversation when Dreeme gave me the picture, that walking as usual, and quite late, we passed the Opera-House. Some star people were giving an extra performance on an off night. The last act of an heroic opera was just beginning. Dreeme hummed the final air,—a noble burst of triumph over a victory bought by a martyrdom.

"Your song makes me hungry to hear more," said I.

"I have been almost starving for music," he rejoined.

"Come in, then. You can take your stand in the lobby, with your mysterious cloak about you, and slouched hat over your eyes. I defy your best friend or worst foe to know you."

"No, no!" said he, nervously; "in the glare of a theatre I should excite suspicion. I should be seen."

"And pounced upon and hurried off to durance vile?" said I, lightly enough; for I began at last to fancy that his panic of concealment was the sole disorder of a singularly healthy brain. "Well, I will not urge it. I cannot spare you. I am selfish. I should soon go to the bad without my friend and Mentor."

"It is strange," said Dreeme, bitterly, "that I, with a soul white as daylight, should be compelled to lurk about like a guilty thing,—to be as one dead and buried."

"I thank the mystery that secludes you for my benefit, Dreeme," I said. "I dread the time when you will find a thousand friends, and many closer than I."

He dropped his cloak and took my arm. It was the first time he had given me this slight token of intimacy. We had been very distant in our personal intercourse. I am not a man to slap another on the back, shake him by the shoulder, punch him in the ribs, or indulge in any rude play or coarse liberties. Yet there is a certain familiarity among men, by which we, after our roughish and unbeautiful fashion, mean as much tenderness for our friends as women do by their sweet embraces and caresses. Nothing of this kind had ever passed between Dreeme and me. His reserve and self-dependence had made me feel that it would be an impertinence to offer even that kind of bodily protection which a bigger man holds ready for a lesser and slighter.

It surprised me, then, a little, when Dreeme, for the first time, took my arm familiarly.

"You have been a kind friend to me, Mr. Byng," said he; "there are not many men in the world who would have treated my retirement with such delicate forbearance and good faith."

"Do not give me too much credit. I have been a selfish friend. I know that I am a facile person, something of the chameleon; I need the fairer colors in contact with me to keep me from becoming an ugly brown reptile. Having this adaptability of character, I have had very close relations with many of the best and noblest; but of all the men I have ever known, your society charms me most penetratingly. All the poetry in my nature being latent, I need precisely you to bring it to the surface. The feminine element is largely developed in you, as a poetic artist. It precisely supplies the want which a sisterless and motherless man, like myself, has always felt. Your influence over me is inexpressibly bland and soothing. You certainly are my good spirit. I like you so much, that I have been quite content with your isolation; I get you all to myself. These walks with you, since that famous oyster supper, the very day of my return home, have been the chief feature of my life. I count my hour with you as the pay for my scuffle with the world. A third party would spoil the whole! What would become of our confidence, our intimate exchange of thought on every possible subject, if there were another fellow by, who might be a vulgarian or a muff? What could we do with a chap to whom we should have to explain our metaphysics, give page and line for our quotations, interpret our puns, translate our allusions, analyze our intuitions, define our God? Such a companion would take the sparkle and the flash of this rapid and unerring sympathy out of our lives. No, Dreeme, this isolation of yours suits me; and since you continue to tolerate my society, I must suit you. We form a capital exclusive pair, close as any of the historic ones,—Orestes and Pylades, for example,—to close my long discourse classically."

"Do not compare us to those ill-omened two. Orestes was ordained to slay his parent for her sin," my friend rejoined, in an uneasy tone.

"It was a judicial murder,—the guiltless execution of a decree of fate. And all turned out happily at last, you remember. Orestes became king of Argos, and gave his sister in marriage to his Pylades, the faithful. Who knows but when your tragic duty is over, whatever it be, and you have brought the guilty to justice, you will resume your proper crown, and find a sister for me, your Pylades, the faithful? If my present flame should not smile, that would be admirable. Your sister for me would make our brotherhood actual."

"My sister for you!" said Dreeme, with an accent almost of horror; and I could feel, by his arm in mine, that a strong shudder ran through him.

We had by this time passed from the side-front of the Opera-House, where this conversation began, had walked along Quatorze Street, and turned up into the Avenue. Quatorze Street, as only a total stranger need be informed, is named in triumphant remembrance of the minikin monarch whom we defeated in the old French war. The crossing of Quatorze Street and the Avenue was, at that time, the very focus of fashion. Within half a mile of that corner, Everybody lived—Everybody who was not Nobody.

It was mid-March. Lent was in full sigh. Balls were over until Easter. Fasting people cannot take violent exercise. One can dance on full, but not on meagre diet, on turkey, not on fish. But in default of balls, Mrs. Bilkes, still a leader of fashion, had her Lent evenings. They were The Thing, so Everybody agreed, and this evening was one of them. I had deserted for my walk with Dreeme.

Mrs. Bilkes's house was just far enough above Quatorze Street, on the Avenue, to be in the van of the upward march of fashion. Files of carriages announced that all the world was with her that evening. The usual band discoursed the usual music within; but wanting the cadence of dancers' feet to enliven them, those Lenten strains came dolefully forth.

We were passing this mansion when Dreeme had last spoken. Before I had time to ask him what meant his agitation at the thought of me for possible brother-in-law, the factotum of the Bilkes party, the well-known professional, hailed me from the steps, where he stood in authority; for by the bright light from the house he could easily recognize me.

"What, Mr. Byng! You won't drop in upon us? They're packed close as coffins inside, but there's always room for another like yourself. Better come in,—Mrs. Bilkes will take on tremendous if she finds I let you go by without stopping."

I paused a moment, half disgusted, half amused by the privileged man's speech. As I did so, a gentleman coming down the steps addressed me. And it is such trivial pauses as these that bid us halt till Destiny overtakes our unconscious steps.

I turned with a slight start, for I had not observed the new-comer as an acquaintance until he was at my side.

It was Densdeth.

He looked, with his keen, hasty glance, at my companion. He seemed to recognize him as a stranger. He did not bow, but turned to me, and said,—

"What, Byng! Are you not going in? It is very brilliant. All the fair penitents are there, keeping Lent, in their usual severe simplicity of penitential garb. I asked Matilda Mildood if I should give her a bit of partridge and some chicken-salad. 'I'm quite ashamed of you, Mr. Densdeth,' says Matilda, with the air of one resolutely mortifying the flesh; 'don't you remember it's

Lent. Oysters and lobster-salad, if you please, and a little terrapin, if there is any."

While Densdeth made this talk, he glanced again at my companion. Dreeme had withdrawn his arm, and stood a little apart, half turned away from us, avoiding notice, as usual.

"Don't throw away your cigar, Byng," continued Densdeth, taking out his case, and stepping toward the lamp-post, to make, as it seemed to me, a very elaborate selection. "Give me a light first. Will you try one of mine?"

"No, thank you. I have had my allowance."

Densdeth took my cigar to light his. The slight glow was sufficient to illuminate his face darkly. Its expression seemed to me singularly cruel and relentless. It was withal scornful and triumphant. Something evidently had happened which gave Densdeth satisfaction. Whom had he vanquished to-night?

The cigar would not draw.

"Bah!" said Densdeth, tearing it in two, with his white-gloved hands, with a manner of dainty torture, as if he were inflicting an indignity upon a foe. "Bah!" said he, taking out another cigar, with even more elaborate selection, and as he did so glancing, quick and sharp, at my friend, who had retreated from the lamp. "I don't allow cigars, any more than other creatures, to baffle me. Excuse me, Byng, for detaining you. The second trial must succeed; if not, I'll try a third time,—*that* always wins. Thanks!"

He lighted his cigar. Again by the glow I observed the same relentless, triumphant look.

Densdeth turned down the Avenue. I rejoined Dreeme. He took my arm again and clung to it almost weakly.

"What is the matter, Dreeme?" I asked, my tenderness for him all awake.

No answer, but a nervous pressure on my arm.

"You are tired. Shall we turn back?"

"Not the way that man has gone," said he.

"Why not? What do you fear?"

"I heard him name himself Densdeth. I saw his face—that cruel face of his. Mr. Byng,—my dear friend, Robert Byng,—that man is evil to the core. You call me your Mentor, your good influence; take my warning! Obey me, and shun him, as you would a fiend. You say that I have a fresh nature; believe that my instinct of aversion for a villain is unerring."

"Is not this prejudice?" said I, somewhat moved by his panic, but still fancying so much alarm idle.

"It might before have been prejudice, derived from your own account of him; but now I have seen him, face to face."

"A glance merely, and in a dusky light."

"Yes, but one look at that face of his sears it into the heart."

"You seem to have been as inquisitive about him as he about you. He studied your back pretty thoroughly. In fact, I believe it was to observe you that he made such parade of breaking up his delinquent cigar. He evidently meant to know for what comrade I was abandoning the charms of the Bilkes *soirée*."

"I shudder at the thought of such a man's observation. What ugly fate brought me here?"

Dreeme turned, and looked back.

I involuntarily did the same.

The Avenue, at that late hour, was nearly deserted of promenaders. As far away as two blocks behind us, I noticed the spark of a cigar, and as the smoker passed a gas-light, I could see him take the cigar from his lips with a white-gloved hand. He even seemed to brandish it triumphantly.

"He is following us!" cried Dreeme.

The painter whirled me about a corner, and dragged me, almost at a run, along several humbler streets. At last we turned into one of the avenues by the North River, far away from the beat of any guest of Mrs. Bilkes.

There Dreeme paused, and spoke.

"Good exercise I have given you by my panic," said he, with a forced laugh. "How absurd I have been! Pardon me! You are aware how nervous I get, being so much shut up alone. And then, you know, I was only hurrying you away from your devil."

"Strange fellow you are, Dreeme! I suppose this very strangeness is one element of your control over me. You excite my curiosity in degree, though not in kind, quite as much as Densdeth does. And now that you and he are brought together, I hope these two mysterious personages will explain each other by some flash of hostile electricity. I wait for light from the meeting of the thunder-clouds."

"It must be very late," said Dreeme in a weary tone. "What a dismal part of the city! This squalor sickens me. These rows of grog-shops infect me with utter hopelessness. Sin—sin everywhere, and the sorrow that never can be divorced from sin! How can we escape? How can we save others? These nocturnal wanderings of ours have told me of a breadth and a depth of misery that years of a charitable lifetime would never have revealed. If

I ever have opportunities for action and influence, I shall know my duty, and how to do it. I see, Mr. Byng, as I have before told you, that you do not thoroughly share my sympathy for poverty and suffering and crime."

"Perhaps not fully. My heart is not so tender as yours. I cannot seem to make other people's distress my personal business, as you do. I endure the misfortunes of strangers with reasonable philosophy. Suffering, like pain, I suppose is to be borne heroically, until it passes off. Every man has his hard times."

"You are not cruel," said Dreeme, "but you talk cruelly on a subject you hardly understand. Wait until the hours of your own bitterness come, and you will learn the precious lesson of sympathy! You will soften to others, and most to those who suffer for no fault of theirs,—the wronged, driven to despair by wrong-doing in those they love,—the erring, visited with what we name ruin, for some miserable mistake of inexperience. But let us hasten home! I have never felt so sick at heart, so doubtful of the future, so oppressed by the 'weary weight of all this unintelligible world,' as I do at this moment."

"Dreeme, are you never to take your future into your own hands, and live a healthy, natural life, like other men? Think of yourself! Do not be so wretched with other people's faults! You cannot annihilate the troubles that have made you unhappy; but do not brood over them. Be young, and live young, in sunshine and gayety."

"Be young!" said he, more drearily than ever.

"Yes; make me your confidant! Face down your difficulties! If you do not trust my experience, and think me too recent in the country to give you practical help, there is my friend, Mr. Churm. He will be here to-morrow from a journey. Churm is true as steel. Trust him! He and I will pull you through."

"I trust no one but you. Do not press me yet. I am generally contented, as you know, with my art and your society. Only to-night the sight of that bad man has discomposed me."

"Discomposed is a mild term," said I, as I unlocked the outer door of Chrysalis.

"Well, I am composed now. But I wish," said he in a trepidating way, that belied his words, "that you would see me safe to my door."

I did so, and we parted, closer friends than ever.

Densdeth, Cecil Dreeme, Emma Denman,—these three figures battled strangely in my dreams.

MARÍA AMPARO RUIZ DE BURTON (1832–1895)

First novel published in English by a Mexican American author.

María Amparo Ruiz de Burton was born on the Baja peninsula in Mexico, south of today's state of California, the heiress and granddaughter of Don Jose Manuel Ruiz, commandant of the presidio in Baja. A famously determined and intelligent woman, she married a respected army officer, Henry Stanton Burton, who evacuated her and her family from Baja after California became part of the U.S. following the conclusion of the Mexican War in 1848. In 1859 her husband reported to the Union Army and the family moved to Virginia. They participated in East Coast social life before the Civil War started and attended the inauguration of President Lincoln in 1861. In 1869 Ruiz de Burton's husband died of malaria contracted at the end of the Civil War, leaving her a thirty-nine-year-old widow with two young children. She returned to California where she managed two estates. She became embroiled in protracted legal battles over land claims that were not resolved by the time of her death in 1895.

Ruiz de Burton published two English-language novels, *Who Would Have Thought It?* (1872) and *The Squatter and the Don* (1885), in which she criticized the hypocrisy of dominant Anglo society on the East Coast and its racist treatment of Latinxs, especially during the battles over land rights between native-born Californians and newcomers after the 1848 Treaty of Guadalupe Hidalgo. The treaty granted the United States the formerly Mexican territories of present-day Arizona, California, Colorado, Nevada, Utah, Wyoming, New Mexico, and Texas, and technically assured land rights to current inhabitants. Instead, in practice, it led to fierce battles between Mexican Americans and Anglos trying to push them off their land.

Although published long before the term Mexican American entered the vocabulary, Ruiz de Burton's novels are considered the first known texts of Mexican American literature. Only retrospectively can we locate the book as a point of origin for Latinx literature in the U.S. today. Once its existence in the public sphere is recognized, however, the entire landscape of American culture before and after its publication is transformed. *Who Would Have Thought It?* lets us see a longer presence of Latinx culture in the United States. The opening chapter from *Who Would Have Thought It?* captures Ruiz de Burton's sharp irony, ear for dialogue, and sense of pacing, up to the moment when Mr. Norval brings home from New England a mysterious girl, clad in a red shawl, who will expose the moral fault lines of everyone she meets.

From WHO WOULD HAVE THOUGHT IT? [1872]

CHAPTER I.
THE ARRIVAL

"WHAT WOULD THE good and proper people of this world do if there were no rogues in it,—no social delinquents? The good and proper, I fear, would perish of sheer inanity,—of hypochondriac lassitude, or, to say the least, would grow very dull for want of convenient whetstones to sharpen their wits. Rogues are useful."

So saying, the Rev. Mr. Hackwell scrambled up the steep side of a crazy buggy, which was tilting ominously under the pressure of the Rev. Mr. Hammerhard's weight, and sat by him. Then the Rev. Hackwell spread over the long legs of his friend Hammerhard a well-worn buffalo-robe, and tucked the other end carefully under his own graceful limbs, as if his wise aphorism upon rogues had suggested to him the great necessity of taking good care of himself and friend, all for the sake of the good and dull of this world.

"May I inquire whether present company suggested the philosophical query and highly moral aphorism? and if so, whether I am to be classed with the dull good, or the useful whetstones?" asked Mr. Hammerhard the reverend.

Mr. Hackwell smiled a smile which seemed to say, "Ah, my boy! you know full well where we ought to be classed; "but he answered,—

"I was thinking of Dr. Norval."

"Of Dr. Norval! And in what category?"

"In that of a whetstone, of course."

Mr. Hammerhard looked at his friend, and waited for him to explain his abstruse theory more clearly.

"I was thinking," Mr. Hackwell continued, "how, in default of real rogues (there being none such in our community, eh, Ham? ahem!), our good and proper people have made a temporary whetstone of Dr. Norval's back. Which fact goes to prove that a social delinquent—real or supposed—is a necessity to good people. As for the charity of the thing, why should people who have all the other virtues care to have charity?"

"An excellent text for next Sunday," said Mr. Hammerhard, laughing.

Mr. Hackwell joined in the laugh, and with a series of pulls and jerks to the reins, he began to turn slowly the big head of a yellow horse of a Gothic build and slow motion, in the direction of the railroad depot, for the two divines were going to meet Dr. Norval, who was expected to arrive from California in the six P.M. train from New York that evening.

The yellow beast hung down his big head, put out his tongue, shut tight his left eye, and started, eye opened wide, as if he had been in the habit of wearing an eyeglass, which he had just dropped as he started.

Hi! hi! hi! went the crazy buggy, as if following the big-headed beast just to laugh at him, but in reality only squeaking for want of oiling and from great old age.

"Confound the brute! He squints and lolls his tongue out worse than ever!" exclaimed Mr. Hack well. "And the rickety vehicle fairly laughs at us! Hear it!"

Hi! hi! creaked the buggy very opportunely.

"Look here, Ham, it is your turn to grease the wheels now. I greased them last time," added Hackwell.

"Greasing the wheels won't prevent the crazy, dilapidated concern from squeaking and going to pieces, any more than your sermons prevent some members of your congregation from gossiping and going to the devil," answered Mr. Hammerhard, sententiously.

"I wish I could send them there in this wagon,—all, all, the palsied beast, and the rotten wagon, and the penurious Yankees, that won't give us a decent conveyance," said Mr. Hackwell.

"All the rich people of our town belong to your congregation,—all the rich and the good. Make them shell out, Hack. You are the fashion," Hammerhard observed.

"Yes, that is the reason I drive this fashionable turn-out. No, they won't give except it is squeezed out of them. They are *so good,* you know. My only hope is in Dr. Norval."

"Because he is a whetstone?" asked Ham.

"Exactly. Because he is the only man who don't pretend to be a saint. Because he is the only one in this village who has a soul, but makes no parade of the trouble it gives him to save it."

"His virtuous wife and Mrs. Cackle will save his soul for him. You would think so if you had heard Mrs. Cackle's conversation to-day with my wife.

"The old lady gave us a hash of it well spiced. We went over the vast field of Mrs. Norval's virtues, and the vaster one of the doctor's errors, all of which have their root in the doctor's most unnatural liking for foreigners. That liking was the cause of the doctor's sending his only son Julian to be educated in Europe,—as if the best schools on earth were not in New England,—and Heaven knows what might have become of Julian if his heroic mother had not sent for him. He might have been a Roman Catholic, for all we know. That liking was also the cause of the doctor's sending Isaac to be a good-for-nothing clerk in sinful Washington, among foreigners, when he could have remained in virtuous New England to be a useful farmer. And finally, impelled by that liking, the doctor betook himself to California, which is yet full of 'natives.' 'And as a just retribution for such perverse liking, the doctor was wellnigh' roasted by the natives,' said the old lady. Whereupon, in behalf of truth, I said, 'Not by the natives, madam. The people called "the natives" are mostly of Spanish descent, and are not cannibals. The wild Indians of the Colorado River were doubtless the ones who captured the doctor and tried to make a meal of him.' 'Perhaps so' said the old lady, visibly disappointed. 'To me they are all alike,—Indians, Mexicans, or Californians,—they are all horrid. But my son Beau says that our just laws and smart lawyers will soon "freeze them out." That as soon as we take their lands from them they will never be heard of any more, and then the Americans, with God's help, will have all the land that was so righteously, acquired through a just war and a most liberal payment in money.' Ain't that patriotism and Christian faith for you?" added Mr. Hackwell.

"For yourself, since it comes from one of the pillars of your congregation," answered Mr. Hammerhard, laughing, Mr. Hackwell too joining in the laugh, and touching up the horse, which tripped as he always did when pretending to trot, and the quickened motion caused the crazy vehicle to join in also with a series of squeaks, which made Mr. Hackwell's blood curdle, and set his teeth on edge, although a philosopher.

Whilst the two divines thus beguiled their way to the depot, the subject of their conversation—Mrs. Cackle—made hers laboriously towards home, thinking what pretext she could invent to be at Dr. Norval's when he arrived.

"I would give worlds to know his version of his conduct. Maybe—like Mr. Hackwell—he won't admit that the native Californians are savages; of course not, being foreigners. Mrs. Norval, though, will soon show him we ain't to be fooled."

Hi! hi! hi! she heard; and the squint and the lolling tongue of the parson's horse passed by her, as if in derisive triumph.

"The aggravating beast! "exclaimed Mrs. Cackle,—meaning the horse,—just as Mr. Hackwell bowed to her most politely. "Going for the doctor?" said she to the divines, as if she thought the turn-out needed physic; but the answer was lost in the squeaking of the wagon. "I know they are. I'll go and let Mrs. Norval know it," said the old lady, and walked briskly on.

Jack Sprig—Miss Lavinia Sprig's poodle—sat bolt upright upon Mrs. Norval's front doorsteps, watching the shadows of coming events whilst supper was cooking, as Mrs. Cackle came sneaking by the picket-fence. Jack was happy, sporting a new blue ribbon around his white neck, and the fragrance of broiled chicken and roasted turkey came gratefully to his nostrils, whilst to his memory came the triumphant recollection that *he* had helped to catch that turkey who was now roasting, and who had been his bitter enemy, pecking at him unmercifully whenever he dared venture into the chicken-yard. Jack wagged his tail, thinking the turkey could peck never more, when lo! the round face of Mrs. Cackle, like a red full moon in heated atmosphere, peered over the picket fence. Jack's tail dropped. Then a growl arose to his swelling throat. Would that he could put Mrs. Cackle beside the turkey! And who has not felt like Jack? He was a good hater, and ever since he could remember there had existed between himself and Mrs. Cackle a "magnetism of repulsion," of such peculiar strength that, after going to the very extreme, it curled back on itself, and from a repulsion came out an attraction, which made Mrs. Cackle's feet almost dance with longing to kick Jack, and made Jack's mouth water to bite the well-fed calves of Mrs. Cackle.

"There is that miserable poodle, with his wool all washed up white, adorned with a new ribbon!" exclaimed Mrs. Cackle, holding to the pickets to catch breath, for she had walked fast. "That old maid Lavvy Sprig, I suppose, has decked her thousand cats and her million canary-birds all with ribbons, like her odious poodle." And Mrs. Cackle looked towards the house; but she saw no decked cats there, though the hall-door and all the windows were open. In a few moments, however, she espied Ruth Norval—eldest daughter of Dr. Norval—sitting by one of the parlor windows, rocking herself in a chair, reading a fashion magazine.

"There is Ruth, as usual, studying the fashions. If her father's funeral was coming, she would do the same," said Mrs. Cackle, and peered at the other window. "Who is there?" said she, putting her fat chin over the pickets to take a better view. She then distinguished a face so flattened against the window-pane that it had lost all human shape. But she rightly conjectured that the face belonged to Mattie Norval—youngest daughter of Dr. Norval—inasmuch as Mrs. Norval was too dignified to go and mash her face against the window-glass, and Lavinia's high nose would have presented the same obstruction as her sister's dignity. Mrs. Cackle saluted the flattened mass, but it "gave no token," only it looked more flattened than ever, as now Mattie riveted her gaze more intently in the direction of the railroad depot, saying to her sister Ruth,—

"Don't look up, Rooty; study the fashions. There is old Cackler's moon-face on the pickets saluting, but I don't see it. 'Deed I don't. I am looking down the road."

"Tell your mother I heard the whistle bawled out the old lady, holding to the pickets.

"I wish she had heard the last trumpet," said Ruth. "Don't answer her, Mattie; she wants to be invited in. Why don't she go home? I see all the young Cacklers in their '*setting-room*,'—as she very properly calls it,—all watching for papa's coming, to begin their cackling."

"Ruth, I have told you not to make puns on Mrs. Cackle's name. It is very unkind to do so, and in very bad taste," said Mrs. Norval, from the corner.

"In bad taste!" replied Ruth. "La, ma! the exquisite Mr. Hackwell makes puns all the time. I asked him why he kept 'The Comic Blackstone' among his theological books, and he answered, 'In abjuring all that pertains to the worldly profession of the law, I permitted myself the privilege of keeping this innocent punster. And the 'innocent punster' Mr. Hackwell the divine keeps between Kant and Calvin,—above Martin Luther, ma!"

"Here he is!" screamed Mattie, interrupting her sister, and all flocked to the window. A light wagon, followed by another so heavily loaded that four strong horses could hardly pull it up, approached the gate.

"What upon earth is he bringing now?" exclaimed Mrs. Norval, looking at the light wagon in alarm.

"More rocks and pebbles, of course; but I don't know where he is to put them: the garret is full now," said Ruth, looking at the large wagon.

"He will store them away in the barn-loft, where he keeps his bones and petrified woods. He brings quite a load. It is a government wagon," added Lavinia, also looking at the large wagon.

"I don't mean the boxes in the large wagon. I mean the—the—that—the red shawl," stammered Mrs. Norval. And now the three other ladies noticed for the first time a figure wrapped in a bright plaid shawl, leaning on the doctor's breast, and around which he tenderly encircled his arm.

From THE SQUATTER AND THE DON
A NOVEL DESCRIPTIVE OF CONTEMPORARY OCCURRENCES IN
CALIFORNIA [1885]

CHAPTER II
THE DON'S VIEW OF THE TREATY OF GUADALUPE HIDALGO.

IF THERE HAD been such a thing as communicating by telephone in the days of '72, and there had been those magic wires spanning the distance between William Darrell's house in Alameda County and that of Don Mariano Alamar in San Diego County, with power to transmit the human voice for five hundred miles, a listener at either end would have heard various discussions upon the same subject, differentiated only by circumstances. No magic wires crossed San Francisco Bay to bring the sound of voices to San Diego, but the law of necessity made the Squatter and the Don, distant as they were—distant in every way, without reckoning the miles between them—talk quite warmly of the same matter. The point of view was of course different, for how could it be otherwise? Darrell thought himself justified, and *authorized*, to "take up lands," as he had done before. He had had more than half of California's population on his side, and though the "*Squatter's Sovereignty*" was now rather on the wane, and the "*squatter vote*" was no longer the power, still, the squatters would not abdicate, having yet much to say about election times.

But Darrell was no longer the active squatter that he had been. He controlled many votes yet, but in his heart he felt the weight which his wife's sad eyes invariably put there when the talk was of litigating against a Mexican land title.

This time, however, Darrell honestly meant to take no land but what belonged to the United States. His promise to his wife was sincere, yet his coming to Southern California had already brought trouble to the Alamar rancho.

Don Mariano Alamar was silently walking up and down the front piazza of his house at the rancho; his hands listlessly clasped behind and his head slightly bent forward in deep thought. He had pushed away to one side the many arm-chairs and wicker rockers with which the piazza was furnished. He wanted a long space to walk. That his meditations were far from agreeable, could easily be seen by the compressed lips, slight frown, and sad gaze of his mild and beautiful blue eyes. Sounds of laughter, music and dancing came from the parlor; the young people were entertaining friends from town with their usual gay hospitality, and enjoying themselves heartily. Don Mariano, though already in his fiftieth year, was as fond of dancing as his sons and daughters, and not to see him come in and join the quadrille was so singular that his wife thought she must come out and inquire what could detain him. He was so absorbed in his thoughts that he did not hear her voice calling him—

"What keeps you away? Lizzie has been looking for you; she wants you for a partner in the lancers," said Doña Josefa, putting her arm under that of her husband, bending her head forward and turning it up to look into his eyes.

"What is the matter?" she asked, stopping short, thus making her husband come to a sudden halt. "I am sure something has happened. Tell me."

"Nothing, dear wife. Nothing has happened. That is to say, nothing new."

"More squatters?" she asked. Señor Alamar bent his head slightly, in affirmative reply.

"More coming, you mean?"

"Yes, wife; more. Those two friends of squatters Mathews and Hager, who were here last year to locate claims and went away, did not abandon their claims, but only went away to bring proselytes and their families, and a large invoice of them will arrive on to-morrow's steamer. The worst of it all is, that among the new comers is that terrible and most dangerous squatter William Darrell, who some years ago gave so much trouble to the Spanish people in Napa and Sonoma Counties, by locating claims there. John Gasbang wrote to Hogsden that besides Darrell, there will be six or seven other men bringing their families, so that there will be more rifles for my cattle."

"But, didn't we hear that Darrell was no longer a squatter, that he is rich and living quietly in Alameda?"

"Yes, we heard that, and it is true. He is quite well off, but Gasbang and Miller and Mathews went and told him that my rancho had been rejected, and that it is near enough to town to become valuable, as soon as we have a railroad. Darrell believed it, and is coming to locate here."

"Strange that Darrell should believe such men; I suppose he does not know how low they are."

"He ought to know them, for they were his teamsters when he crossed the plains in '48. That is, Miller, Mathews, Hughes and Hager, were his teamsters, and Gasbang was their cook—the cook for the hired men. Mrs. Darrell had a colored woman who cooked for the Darrell family; she despised Gasbang's cooking as we despise his character, I suppose."

Doña Josefa was silent, and holding to her husband's arm, took a turn with him up and down the piazza.

"Is it possible that there is no law to protect us; to protect our property; what does your lawyer say about obtaining redress or protection; is there no hope?" she asked, with a sigh.

"Protection for our land, or for our cattle, you mean?"

For both, as we get it for neither," she said.

"In the matter of our land, we have to await for the attorney general, at Washington, to decide."

"Lizzie was telling Elvira, yesterday, that her uncle Lawrence is a friend of several influential people in Washington, and that George can get him to interest himself in having your title decided."

"But, as George is to marry my daughter, he would be the last man from whom I would ask a favor."

"What is that I hear about not asking a favor from me?" said George Mechlin, coming out on the piazza with Elvira on his arm, having just fin-ished a waltz—"I am interested to know why you would not ask it."

"You know why, my dear boy. It isn't exactly the thing to bother you with my disagreeable business."

"And why not? And who has a better right? And why should it be a bother to me to help you in any way I can? My father spoke to me about a dismissal of an appeal, and I made a note of it. Let me see, I think I have it in my pocket now,"—said George, feeling in his breast pocket for his memoran-dum book,—"yes, here it is,—'For uncle to write to the attorney general about dismissing the appeal taken by the squatters in the Alamar grant, against Don Mariano's title, which was approved.' Is that the correct idea? I only made this note to ask you for further particulars."

"You have it exactly. When I give you the number of the case, it is all that you need say to your uncle. What I want is to have the appeal dismissed, of course, but if the attorney general does not see fit to do so, he can, at least, remand back the case for a new trial. Anything rather than this killing suspense. Killing literally, for while we are waiting to have my title settled, the *settlers* (I don't mean to make puns), are killing my cattle by the hundred head, and I cannot stop them."

"But are there no laws to protect property in California?" George asked.

"Yes, some sort of laws, which in my case seem more intended to help the law-breakers than to protect the law-abiding," Don Mariano replied.

"How so? Is there no law to punish the thieves who kill your cattle?"

"There are some enactments so obviously intended to favor one class of citizens against another class, that to call them laws is an insult to law, but such as they are, we must submit to them. By those laws any man can come to my land, for instance, plant ten acres of grain, without any fence, and then catch my cattle which, seeing the green grass without a fence, will go to eat it. Then he puts them in a '*corral*' and makes me pay damages and so much per head for keeping them, and costs of legal proceedings and many other trumped up expenses, until for such little fields of grain I may be obliged to pay thousands of dollars. Or, if the grain fields are large enough to bring more money by keeping the cattle away, then the settler shoots the cattle at any time without the least hesitation, only taking care that no one sees him in the act of firing upon the cattle. He might stand behind a bush or tree and fire, but then he is not seen. No one can swear that they saw him actually kill the cattle, and no jury can convict him, for although the dead animals may be there, lying on the ground shot, still no one saw the settler kill them. And so it is all the time. I must pay damages and expenses of litigation, or my cattle get killed almost every day."

"But this is infamous. Haven't you—the cattle owners—tried to have some law enacted that will protect your property?" George asked. "It seems to me that could be done."

"It could be done, perhaps, if our positions were reversed, and the Spanish people—'*the natives*'—were the planters of the grain fields, and the Americans were the owners of the cattle. But as we, the Spaniards, are the owners of the Spanish—or Mexican—land grants and also the owners of the cattle ranchos, our State legislators will not make any law to protect cattle. They make laws '*to protect agriculture*' (they say proudly), which means to drive to the wall all owners of cattle ranchos. I am told that at this session of the legislature a law more strict yet will be passed, which will be ostensibly 'to protect agriculture,' but in reality to destroy cattle and ruin the native Californians. The agriculture of this State does not require legislative protection. Such pretext is absurd."

"I thought that the rights of the Spanish people were protected by our treaty with Mexico," George said.

"Mexico did not pay much attention to the future welfare of the children she left to their fate in the hands of a nation which had no sympathies for us," said Doña Josefa, feelingly.

"I remember," calmly said Don Mariano, "that when I first read the text of the treaty of Guadalupe Hidalgo, I felt a bitter resentment against my people; against Mexico, the mother country, who abandoned us—her children—with so slight a provision of obligatory stipulations for protection. But afterwards, upon mature reflection, I saw that Mexico did as much as could have been reasonably expected at the time. In the very preamble of the treaty the spirit of peace and friendship, which animated both nations, was carefully made manifest. That spirit was to be the *foundation* of the relations between the conqueror and conquered. How could Mexico have foreseen then that when scarcely half a dozen years should have elapsed the trusted conquerors would, '*In Congress Assembled*,' pass laws which were to be retroactive upon the defenceless, helpless, conquered people, in order to despoil them? The treaty said that our rights would be the same as those enjoyed by all other American citizens. But, you see, Congress takes very good care not to enact retroactive laws for Americans; laws to take away from American citizens the property which they hold *now*, already, with a recognized legal title. No, indeed. But they do so quickly enough with us—with us, the Spano-Americans, who were to enjoy equal rights, mind you, according to the treaty of peace. This is what seems to me a breach of faith, which Mexico could neither presuppose nor prevent."

"It is nothing else, I am sorry and ashamed to say," George said. "I never knew much about the treaty with Mexico, but I never imagined we had acted so badly."

"I think but few Americans know or believe to what extent we have been wronged by Congressional action. And truly, I believe that Congress itself did not anticipate the effect of its laws upon us, and how we would be despoiled, we, the conquered people," said Don Mariano, sadly.

"It is the duty of law-givers to foresee the effect of the laws they impose upon people," said Doña Josefa.

"That I don't deny, but I fear that the conquered have always but a weak voice, which nobody hears," said Don Mariano. "We have had no one to speak for us. By the treaty of Guadalupe Hidalgo the American nation pledged its honor to respect our land titles just the same as Mexico would have done. Unfortunately, however, the discovery of gold brought to California the riff-raff of the world, and with it a horde of land-sharks, all possessing the privilege of voting, and most of them coveting our lands, for which they very quickly began to clamor. There was, and still is, plenty of good government land, which any one can take. But no. The forbidden fruit is the sweetest. They do not want government land. They want the land of the Spanish people, because we 'have too much,' they say. So, to win their votes, the votes of the squatters, our representatives in Congress helped to pass laws declaring all lands in California open to pre-emption, as in Louisiana, for instance. Then, as a coating of whitewash to the stain on the nation's honor, a 'land commission' was established to examine land titles. Because, having pledged the national word to respect our rights, it would be an act of despoliation, besides an open violation of pledged honor, to take the lands without some pretext of a legal process. So then, we became obliged to present our titles before the said land commission to be examined and approved or rejected. While these legal proceedings are going on, the squatters locate their claims and raise crops on our lands, which they convert into money to fight our titles. But don't let me, with my disagreeable subject spoil your dance. Go back to your lancers, and tell Lizzie to excuse me," said Don Mariano.

Lizzie would not excuse him. With the privilege of a future daughter-in-law, she insisted that Don Mariano should be her partner in the lancers, which would be a far pleasanter occupation than to be walking up and down the porch thinking about squatters.

Don Mariano therefore followed Lizzie to their place in the dance. Mercedes sat at the piano to play for them. The other couples took their respective positions.

The well-balanced mind and kindly spirit of Don Mariano soon yielded to the genial influences surrounding him. He would not bring his trouble to mar the pleasure of others. He danced with his children as gaily as the gayest. He insisted that Mr. Mechlin, too, should dance, and this gentleman graciously yielded and led Elvira through a quadrille, protesting that he had not danced for twenty years.

SUSETTE LA FLESCHE / INSHATA THEUMBA
(1854–1903)

First published nonlegend short story by a Native American author.

Susette La Flesche was born in Bellevue, Nebraska, in 1854, into an affluent and acculturated family as part of the Omaha tribe in the year the Omaha gave up their Nebraska hunting grounds. Assuming that compliance would be safer than resistance, they agreed to move to a northeastern Nebraska reservation. Susette was the oldest daughter of Joseph La Flesche, the last recognized chief of the Omaha, known as "Iron Eyes." She grew up on the Omaha Reservation where she attended the Presbyterian Mission Boarding Day School. In 1869 she attended the Elizabeth Institute for Young Ladies, a private school at Elizabeth, New Jersey, to further her education. After some struggles with the Indian Commissioner, La Flesche became the first American Indian teacher on the Omaha reservation.

In 1877, the Ponca Tribe, of which Iron Eye's mother was a member, was dislocated to Indian Territory. Susette accompanied her father when he went to inspect the conditions there. After their return, Susette worked with Thomas H. Tibbles of the *Omaha Herald* to publicize the Ponca's plight. In a trial in 1879, Susette was Standing Bear's interpreter, which made her nationally known as "Bright Eyes," the English translation of her name, Inshata Theumba. The landmark ruling in "Standing Bear vs. Crook" (1879) stated that American Indians had certain rights as "persons" under the law. She married Tibbles and became a well-known speaker on behalf of Indian rights, traveling with Standing Bear and working as his interpreter to parts of the United States, England, and Scotland. In 1891 they traveled to South Dakota to inquire about the Battle of Wounded Knee and problems of Native Americans at the reservation there. From 1893 to 1895, the Tibbles in 1881 lived in Washington D.C. Bright Eyes wrote, lectured, and advocated for Indian concerns before various government committees.

Thomas Tibbles and Bright Eyes moved to Bancroft in 1902 to live among the Omaha, where she died in 1903 at the age of forty-nine. She was eulogized in the U.S. Senate and has been inducted into the National Woman's Hall of Fame, where she is honored as the first woman to speak out for the cause of Native Americans in national political settings.

"Nedawi" is considered the first nonlegend fictional story published by a Native American. The remarkably subtle and moving tale recounts a young girl's afternoon when she is charged to watch her little brother while the rest of her family carries out various tasks. In the course of a few hours she makes several choices that lead to deeper lessons about her role in her circle of friends, in her family, in the community, and in the wider world. The story was first published in *St. Nicholas* magazine.

NEDAWI
(AN INDIAN STORY FROM REAL LIFE) [1881]

"NEDAWI!" CALLED HER mother, "take your little brother while I go with your sister for some wood." Nedawi ran into the tent, bringing back her little red blanket, but the brown-faced, roly-poly baby, who had been having a comfortable nap in spite of being all the while tied straight to his board, woke with a merry crow just as the mother was about to attach him, board and all, to Nedawi's neck. So he was taken from the board instead, and, after he had kicked in happy freedom for a moment, Nedawi stood in front of her mother, who placed Habazhu on the little girl's back, and drew the blanket over him, leaving his arms free. She next put into his hand a little hollow gourd, filled with seeds, which served as a rattle; Nedawi held both ends of the blanket tightly in front of her, and was then ready to walk around with the little man.

Where should she go? Yonder was a group of young girls playing a game of *konci*, or dice. The dice were five plum-seeds, scorched black, and had little stars and quarter-moons instead of numbers. She went over and stood by the group, gently rocking herself from side to side, pretty much as white children do when reciting the multiplication table. The girls would toss up the wooden bowl, letting it drop with a gentle thud on the pillow beneath, the falling dice making a pleasant clatter which the baby liked to hear. The stakes were a little heap of beads, rings, and bracelets. The laughter and exclamations of the girls, as some successful toss brought down the dice three stars and two quarter-moons (the highest throw), made Nedawi wish that she, too, were a young girl, and could win and wear all those pretty things. How gay she would look! Just then, the little glittering heap caught baby's eye. He tried to wriggle out of the blanket to get to it, but Nedawi held tight. Then he set up a yell. Nedawi walked away very reluctantly, because she wanted to stay and see who would win. She went to her mother's tent, but found it deserted. Her father and brothers had gone to the chase. A herd of buffalo had been seen that morning, and all the men in the tribe had gone, and would not be back till night. Her mother, her sister, and the women of the household had gone to the river for wood and water. The tent looked enticingly cool, with the sides turned up to let the breeze sweep through, and the straw mats and soft robes seemed to invite her to lie down on them and dream the afternoon away, as she was too apt to do. She did not yield to the temptation, however, for she knew Mother would not like it, but walked over to her cousin Metai's tent. She found her cousin "keeping house" with a number of little girls, and stood to watch them while they put up little tents, just large enough to hold one or two girls.

"Nedawi, come and play," said Metai. "You can make the fire and cook. I'll ask Mother for something to cook."

"But what shall I do with Habazhu?" said Nedawi.

"I'll tell you. Put him in my tent, and make believe he's our little old grandfather."

Forthwith he was transferred from Nedawi's back to the little tent. But Habazhu had a decided objection to staying in the dark little place, where he could not see anything, and crept out of the door on his hands and knees. Nedawi collected a little heap of sticks, all ready for the fire, and went off to get a fire-brand to light it with. While she was gone, Habazhu crawled up to a bowl of water which stood by the intended fire-place, and began dabbling in it with his chubby little hands, splashing the water all over the sticks prepared for the fire. Then he thought he would like a drink. He tried to lift the bowl in both hands, but only succeeded in spilling the water over himself and the fire-place.

When Nedawi returned, she stood aghast; then, throwing down the brand, she took her little brother by the shoulders and, I am sorry to say, shook him violently, jerked him up, and dumped him down by the door of the little tent from which he had crawled. "You bad little boy!" she said. "It's too bad that I have to take care of you when I want to play."

You see, she was no more perfect than any little white girl who gets into a temper now and then. The baby's lip quivered, and he began to cry. Metai said to Nedawi: "I think it's real mean for you to shake him, when he doesn't know any better."

Metai picked up Baby and tried to comfort him. She kissed him over and over, and talked to him in baby language. Nedawi's conscience, if the little savage could be said to have any, was troubling her. She loved her baby brother dearly, even though she did get out of patience with him now and then.

"I'll put a clean little shirt on him and pack him again," said she, suddenly. Then she took off his little wet shirt, wrung it out, and spread it on the tall grass to dry in the sun. Then she went home, and, going to a pretty painted skin in which her mother kept his clothes, she selected the red shirt, which she thought was the prettiest. She was in such a hurry, however, that she forgot to close and tie up the skin again, and she carelessly left his clean shirts lying around as she had laid them out. When Baby was on her back again, she walked around with him, giving directions and overseeing the other girls at their play, determined to do that rather than nothing.

The other children were good-natured, and took her ordering as gracefully as they could. Metai made the fire in a new place, and then went to ask her mother to give her something to cook. Her mother gave her a piece of dried buffalo meat, as hard as a chip and as brittle as glass. Metai broke it up into small pieces, and put the pieces into a little tin pail of water, which she hung over the fire. "Now," she said, "when the meat is cooked and the soup is made, I will call you all to a feast, and Habazhu shall be the chief."

They all laughed. But alas for human calculations! During the last few minutes, a shy little girl, with soft, wistful black eyes, had been watching them from a little distance. She had on a faded, shabby blanket and a ragged dress.

"Metai," said Nedawi, "let's ask that girl to play with us; she looks so lonesome."

"Well," said Metai, doubtfully, "I don't care; but my mother said she didn't want me to play with ragged little girls."

"My father says we must be kind to poor little girls, and help them all we can; so I'm going to play with her if you don't," said Nedawi, loftily.

Although Metai was the hostess, Nedawi was the leading spirit, and had her own way, as usual. She walked up to the little creature and said, "Come and play with us, if you want to." The little girl's eyes brightened, and she laughed. Then she suddenly drew from under her blanket a pretty bark basket, filled with the most delicious red and yellow plums. "My brother picked them in the woods, and I give them to you," was all she said. Nedawi managed to free one hand, and took the offering with an exclamation of delight, which drew the other girls quickly around. Instead of saying "Oh! Oh!" as you would have said, they cried "Hin! Hin!" which expressed their feeling quite as well, perhaps.

"Let us have them for our feast," said Metai, taking them.

Little Indian children are taught to share everything with one another, so it did not seem strange to Nedawi to have her gift looked on as common property. But, while the attention of the little group had been concentrated on the matter in hand, a party of mischievous boys, passing by, caught sight of the little tents and the tin pail hanging over the fire. Simultaneously, they set up a war-whoop and, dashing into the deserted camp, they sent the tent-poles scattering right and left, and snatching up whatever they could lay hands on, including the tin pail and its contents, they retreated. The little girls, startled by the sudden raid on their property, looked up. Rage possessed their little souls. Giving shrieks of anger, they started in pursuit. What did Nedawi do? She forgot plums, baby, and everything. The ends of the blanket slipped from her grasp, and she darted forward like an arrow after her companions.

Finding the chase hopeless, the little girls came to a stand-still, and some of them began to cry. The boys had stopped, too; and seeing the tears flow, being good-hearted boys in spite of their mischief, they surrendered at discretion. They threw back the articles they had taken, not daring to come near. They did not consider it manly for big boys like themselves to strike or hurt little girls, even though they delighted in teasing them, and they knew from experience that they would be at the mercy of the offended party if they went near enough to be touched. The boy who had the dinner brought the little pail which had contained it as near as he dared, and setting it down ran away.

"You have spilt all our soup. There's hardly any of it left. You bad boys!" said one of the girls.

They crowded around with lamentations over their lost dinner. The boys began to feel remorseful.

"Let's go into the woods and get them some plums to make up for it."

"Say, girls, hand us your pail, and we'll fill it up with plums for you."

So the affair was settled.

But, meanwhile, what became of the baby left so unceremoniously in the tall grass? First he opened his black eyes wide at this style of treatment. He was not used to it. Before he had time, however, to make up his mind whether to laugh or cry, his mother came to the rescue. She had just come home and thrown the wood off her back, when she caught sight of Nedawi dropping him. She ran to pick him up, and finding him unhurt, kissed him over and over. Some of the neighbors had run up to see what was the matter. She said to them:

"I never did see such a thoughtless, heedless child as my Nedawi. She really has 'no ears.' I don't know what in the world will ever become of her. When something new interests her, she forgets everything else. It was just like her to act in this way."

Then they all laughed, and one of them said:

"Never mind—she will grow wiser as she grows older," after which consoling remark they went away to their own tents.

It was of no use to call Nedawi back. She was too far off.

Habazhu was given over to the care of the nurse, who had just returned from her visit. An hour or two after, Nedawi came home.

"Mother!" she exclaimed, as she saw her mother frying bread for supper, "I am so hungry. Can I have some of that bread?"

"Where is your little brother?" was the unexpected reply.

Nedawi started. Where *had* she left him? She tried to think.

"Why, mother, the last I remember I was packing him, and—and, oh, Mother! you *know* where he is. Please tell me."

"When you find him and bring him back to me, perhaps I shall forgive you," was the cold reply.

This was dreadful. Her mother had never treated her in that way before. She burst into tears, and started out to find Habazhu, crying all the way. She knew that her mother knew where baby was, or she would not have taken it so coolly; and she knew also that her mother expected her to bring him home. As she went stumbling along through the grass, she felt herself seized and held in somebody's strong arms, and a great, round, hearty voice said:

"What's the matter with my little niece? Have all her friends deserted her that she is wailing like this? Or has her little dog died? I thought Nedawi was a brave little woman."

It was her uncle Two Crows. She managed to tell him, through her sobs, the whole story. She knew, if she told him herself, he would not laugh at her about it, for he would sympathize in her troubles, though he was a great tease. When she ceased, he said to her: "Well, your mother wants you to be more careful next time, I suppose; and, by the way, I think I saw a little boy who looked very much like Habazhu, in my tent."

Sure enough, she found him there with his nurse. When she got home with them, she found her mother,—her own dear self,—and, after giving her a big hug, she sat quietly down by the fire, resolved to be very good in the future. She did not sit long, however, for soon a neighing of horses, and the running of girls and children through the camp to meet the hunters, proclaimed their return. All was bustle and gladness throughout the camp. There had been a successful chase, and the led horses were laden with buffalo meat. These horses were led by the young girls to the tents to be unpacked, while the boys took the hunting-horses to water and tether in the grass. Fathers, as they dismounted, took their little children in their arms, tired as they were. Nedawi was as happy as any in the camp, for her seventeen-year-old brother, White Hawk, had killed his first buffalo, and had declared that the skin should become Nedawi's robe, as soon as it was tanned and painted.

What a pleasant evening that was to Nedawi, when the whole family sat around a great fire, roasting the huge buffalo ribs, and she played with her little brother Habazhu, stopping now and then to listen to the adventures of the day, which her father and brothers were relating! The scene was truly a delightful one, the camp-fires lighting up the pleasant family groups here and there, as the flames rose and fell. The bit of prairie where the tribe had camped had a clear little stream running through it, with shadowy hills around, while over all hung the clear, star-lit sky. It seemed as if nature were trying to protect the poor waifs of humanity clustered in that spot. Nedawi felt the beauty of the scene, and was just thinking of nestling down by her father to enjoy it dreamily, when her brothers called for a dance. The little drum was brought forth, and Nedawi danced to its accompaniment and her brothers' singing. She danced gravely, as became a little maiden whose duty it was to entertain the family circle. While she was dancing, a little boy, about her own age, was seen hovering near. He would appear, and, when spoken to, would disappear in the tall, thick grass.

It was Mischief, a playmate of Nedawi's. Everybody called him "Mischief," because mischief appeared in every action of his. It shone from his eyes and played all over his face.

"You little plague," said White Hawk; "what do you want?"

For answer, the "little plague" turned a somersault just out of White Hawk's reach. When the singing was resumed, Mischief crept quietly up behind White Hawk, and, keeping just within the shadow, mimicked Nedawi's grave dancing, and he looked so funny that Nedawi suddenly laughed, which was precisely Mischief's object. But before he could get out of reach, as he intended, Thunder, Nedawi's other brother, who had been having an eye on him, clutched tight hold of him, and Mischief was landed in front of the fire-place, in full view of the whole family. "Now," said Thunder, "you are my prisoner. You stay there and dance with Nedawi." Mischief knew there was no escape, so he submitted with a good grace. He went through all sorts of antics, shaking his fists in the air, twirling suddenly around and putting his head close to the ground, keeping time with the accompaniment through it all.

Nedawi danced staidly on, now and then frowning at him; but she knew of old that he was irrepressible. When Nedawi sat down, he threw into her lap a little dark something and was off like a shot, yelling at the top of his voice, either in triumph at his recent achievements or as a practice for future war-whoops.

"Nedawi, what is it?" said her mother.

Nedawi took it to the fire, when the something proved to be a poor little bird.

"I thought he had something in his hand when he was shaking his fist in the air," said Nedawi's sister, Nazainza, laughing.

"Poor little thing!" said Nedawi; "it is almost dead."

She put its bill into the water, and tenderly tried to make it drink. The water seemed to revive it somewhat.

"I'll wrap it up in something warm," said Nedawi, "and may be it will sing in the morning."

"Let me see it," said Nedawi's father.

Nedawi carried it to him.

"Don't you feel sorry for it, daughter?"

"Yes, Father," she answered.

"Then take it to the tall grass, yonder, and put it down where no one will step on it, and, as you put it down, say: 'God, I give you back your little bird. As I pity it, pity me.'"

"And will God take care of it?" said Nedawi, reverently, and opening her black eyes wide at the thought.

"Yes," said her father.

"Well, I will do as you say," said Nedawi, and she walked slowly out of the tent.

Then she took it over to the tall, thick grass, and making a nice, cozy little nest for it, left it there, saying just what her father had told her to say. When she came back, she said:

"Father, I said it."

"That was right, little daughter," and Nedawi was happy at her father's commendation.

Nedawi always slept with her grandmother and sister, exactly in the middle of the circle formed by the wigwam, with her feet to the fire-place. That place in the tent was always her grandmother's place, just as the right-hand side of the tent was her father's and mother's, and the left-hand her brothers'. There never was any confusion. The tribe was divided into bands, and every band was composed of several families. Each band had its chief, and the whole tribe was ruled by the head-chief, who was Nedawi's father. He had his own particular band besides. Every tent had its own place in the band, and every band had its own particular place in the great circle forming the camp. Each chief was a representative, in council, of the men composing his band, while over all was the head-chief. The executive power was vested in the "soldiers' lodge," and when decisions were arrived at in council, it was the duty of its soldiers to execute all its orders, and punish all violations of the tribal laws. The office of "town-crier" was held by several old men, whose duty it was "to cry out" through the camp the announcements of councils, invitations to feasts, and to give notice of anything in which the whole tribe were called on to take part.

Well, before Nedawi went to sleep this evening, she hugged her grandmother, and said to her:

"Please tell me a story."

Her grandmother said:

"I cannot, because it is summer. In the winter I will tell you stories."

"Why not in summer?" said Nedawi.

"Because, when people tell stories and legends in summer, the snakes come around to listen. You don't want any snakes to come near us to-night, do you?"

"But," said Nedawi, "I have not seen any snakes for the longest times, and if you tell it right softly they wont hear you."

"Nedawi," said her mother, "don't bother your grandmother. She is tired and wants to sleep."

Thereupon Grandmother's heart felt sorry for her pet, and she said to Nedawi:

"Well, if you will keep still and go right to sleep when I am through, I will tell you how the turkeys came to have red eyelids.

"Once upon a time, there was an old woman living all alone with her grandson, Rabbit. He was noted for his cunning and for his tricks, which he played on every one. One day, the old woman said to him, 'Grandson, I am hungry for some meat.' Then the boy took his bow and arrows, and in the evening he came home with a deer on his shoulders, which he threw at her feet, and said, 'Will that satisfy you?' She said, 'Yes, grandson.' They lived on that meat several days, and when it was gone, she said to him again, 'Grandson, I am hungry for some meat.' This time he went without his bow and arrows, but he took a bag with him. When he got into the woods, he called all the turkeys together. They gathered around him, and he said to them: 'I am going to sing to you, while you shut your eyes and dance. If one of you opens his eyes while I am singing, his eyelids shall turn red.' Then they all stood in a row, shut their eyes, as he had told them, and began to dance, and this is the song he sang to them while they danced:

"'Ha! wadamba thike
Inshta zhida, inshta zhida,
Imba theonda,
Imba theonda.'"

[The literal translation is:

"Ho! he who peeps
Red eyes, red eyes,
Flap your wings,
Flap your wings."]

"Now, while they were dancing away, with their eyes shut, the boy took them, one by one, and put them into his bag. But the last one in the row began to think it very strange that his companions made no noise, so he gave one peep, screamed in his fright, 'They are making 'way with us!' and fled away. The boy took his bag of turkeys home to his grandmother, but ever after that the turkeys had red eyelids."

Nedawi gave a sigh of satisfaction when the story was finished, and would have asked for more, but just then her brothers came in from a dance which they had been attending in some neighbor's tent. She knew her lullaby time had come. Her brothers always sang before they slept either love or dancing songs, beating time on their breasts, the regular beats making a sort of accompaniment for the singing. Nedawi loved best of all to hear her father's war-songs, for he had a musical voice, and few were the evenings when she had gone to sleep without hearing a lullaby from her father or brothers. Among the Indians, it is the fathers who sing, instead of the mothers. Women sing only on state occasions, when the tribe have a great dance, or at something of the sort. Mothers "croon" their babies to sleep, instead of singing.

Gradually the singing ceased, and the brothers slept as well as Nedawi, and quiet reigned over the whole camp.

SOPHIA ALICE CALLAHAN (1868–1894)

First published novel by a Native American woman author.

Sophia Alice Callahan was born in Texas, the daughter of Samuel Benton Callahan and Sarah Elizabeth Callahan. Her father was one-eighth Muscogee and very active in tribal affairs throughout his life. He served in the Muscogee House of Kings from 1868–1872 and in 1901 as justice of the Muscogee nation's supreme court.

By 1886 Sophia Callahan was teaching in Okmulgee, Indian Territory. In 1888 she attended the Wesleyan Female Institute in Staunton, Virginia, for ten months and became a Methodist teacher for the Muscogee (Creek) Nation in Oklahoma at the Muscogee Council's Harrell National Institute. She also edited a journal associated with Harrell, and in 1891 finished *Wynema*, her first and only novel. She taught at additional schools but hoped to complete her own education in Virginia. After prolonged suffering from pleurisy, an inflammation of the lungs, she died at age twenty-six in 1894.

Wynema tells the story of two women—Genevieve Weir, a non-Indian teacher from a Southern family, and the student Wynema Harjo, a full-blooded Muscogee child who becomes her closest friend. The story is told from alternating distinctive points of view, non-Indian and Indian. While the plot of a woman whose moral and physical strength is tested by difficult circumstances is familiar from fiction of the time, Callahan places it in the context of issues about women's and Indians' rights. The storyline of a woman seeking happiness without surrendering her sense of self in marriage is here told from a previously unheard of point of view. Genevieve ends her engagement with a man whose views of Indians and women she does not support. Wynema falls in love with Genevieve's brother and both women return to Muscogee Nation. The excerpted chapters center on the Massacre at Wounded Knee, which took place at the Pine Ridge Indian Reservation in 1890, and which greatly affected Callahan.

From WYNEMA: A CHILD OF THE FOREST [1891]

TO THE INDIAN TRIBES OF NORTH AMERICA
Who have felt the wrongs and oppression of their pale-faced brothers, I
lovingly dedicate this work, praying that it may serve to open the eyes and
heart of the world to our afflictions, and thus speedily issue into existence
an era of good feeling and just dealing toward us and our more oppressed
brothers.

THE AUTHOR

CHAPTER XXI
CIVILIZATION OR SAVAGE BARBARITY

A DARK FIGURE with a babe in her arms creeps stealthily from a tent into the
dark night. Softly and stealthily it steps until it reaches the outskirts of the
reservation, where it is met by other dark figures, some with the papoose,
some without. When these figures are out of hearing distance, they run rapidly and joyously toward the tepees of the defiant Indians. Sixteen miles! Ah,
that is nothing to one going on a mission of love. Patriotism has inspired
men to greater deeds. Paul Revere and Philip Sheridan have been made
famous for a terrible ride; these dark figures, running, sliding and falling
along the dark road in the bitter night, will not be known to the world, for
theirs was only a walk for love. They reached the tents of the rebels.

"Miscona," exclaimed her husband reproachfully, hardly believing his
eyes. "And the papoose! You must go back, Miscona. It is not safe here," said
he throwing his arms about them. "We are to battle to-morrow. Yes, to-morrow's sun, when he opens his great eye, will see the rebel band of Indians
surrounding their white tyrants, and before he closes it the ground will be
strewn with the dead bodies of our enemies, or of us. We have arranged our
skirmish so that it will seem at first that our numbers are smaller than they
are. Then when the enemy engages this brave few, the others will rush up
from all sides, with a mighty whoop, and surround them. This is our plan,
whether it is a good one remains to be proved. How many women came
with you?"

"About forty, and many of them carried the papoose."

"Well, you must start back to-morrow. It will be dangerous for you to
remain here."

But "man proposes and God disposes,"—in this instance, the Indian proposes, the Government disposes. It was reported by scouts sent out for that purpose, to the commander of the troops stationed on the reservation, that the Indians were plotting war and were planning to surround them on the following day. So the general sent a detachment to meet the "hostiles," and surprise them, and to capture all unharmed if possible. But, instead of this, the Indians were slaughtered like cattle, shot down like dogs. Surprised at the sudden apparition of white soldiers drawn up in line of battle, when they supposed the soldiers to be in their camps miles distant, their presence of mind deserted them, and it was with difficulty that Wildfire rallied his forces. To add to this consternation, on turning about toward his camps, he beheld the women who had followed them to battle, instead of going to the reservation as they had promised and started to do. It was useless to motion them back, for on they came, their faces speaking with noiseless eloquence. "We have lived with you; we will die with you." Up they rushed into the line of battle where they more unfitted the men for fighting.

"Good and gracious Father, Miscona! You have lost the battle for me," groaned the chieftain.

"It is a lost cause. You will die and I will die by your side, my husband," she replied resolutely.

Then came the dust and smoke and din of battle, the hurrying forward of the foes to the onset.

"Indians, I command you to go into the reservation quietly or, by God, you die here in your tracks!" shouted the commander.

"We shall die, then," shouted Wildfire in return; "but we will never enter the reservation alive!"

Oh! the terrible, terrible battle! Old Chikena in giving the circumstances relating to it to Wynema, always closed her eyes and shuddered. Everywhere could be seen Wildfire fighting and urging his troops on, and everywhere, the iron-clad hand of the white soldiers beating down his Indian adversary—yes, and not only the men, but the helpless, defenseless women and children. The command was, "No quarter! Kill them every one."

In the midst of the one-sided battle, Wildfire was slain, felled to the ground, and by his side, as was afterwards found, his devoted Miscona—only an Indian squaw, so it did not matter.

The Indians, seeing their leader slain, fled precipitately to the camps, followed for some distance by their adversaries, who, finally drew up in line and marched back to quarters. On the night following the battle came a terrible blizzard—wind so piercingly cold that it freezes the very marrow in the bones of one so unfortunate as to be exposed to it. Out on the battle-field, with no covering but the open sky lay the bodies of the dying and dead Indians, left there by friends and foes. Over here are the bodies of Wildfire and Miscona, free at last, and the little papoose sweetly sleeping between them. Over there lies a warrior, groaning and murmuring—and everywhere is blood, blood! Over everything, around everything, on everything. Oh! the awful sight!

A dark form is seen presently gliding among them administering to the wants of the dying as best she can. It is an Indian squaw, watching over the battle-field, guarding the dead and dying. Like Rizpah of old, on the Gibeah plain, she took her distant station and watched to see that nothing came near to harm her beloved dead.

During the forenoon of the following day, two men rode on the ghastly scene, astonished at the almost numberless dead and wounded bodies strewn over the plain; astonished to see women and children slain among the number, for it has ever been the policy of a strong, brave nation to protect the helpless, the weak, the defenseless.

Alighting and walking among the dead, they saw what at first they had not noticed, the form of the Indian woman kneeling among the wounded. Carl Peterson walked up to where she knelt and addressed her.

"Woman, why are you here, and whence did you come?"

She raised her head mournfully, her face dripping with tears, and started as she recognized the speaker; "Carl Peterson!" she exclaimed.

"Yes, and is this Chikena, the happy wife of the brave Great Wind, when I last saw her?" he asked. "What are you doing on this field of battle?"

"Ah! The times have changed for poor Chikena," she answered, weeping. "Here lies the dead body of the brave Great Wind, and yonder lies his son. Dead! Dead! I am all alone in the world—the only one left of my tribe. Why did not the Great Father take me too?"

"How long have you been here, poor soul?" Carl asked sympathetically. "And have you been here all alone?"

"Yes, all alone since they left me with my dead. The pale-faces killed our brave Wildfire and his beautiful Miscona—yonder they lie in each other's arms—and then our people fled back to their tents, the soldiers pursuing until they reached the creek. I did not leave, for I did not care what became of me—my loved ones were gone and I staid to protect them. But, oh, the bitter, bitter night! The cold wind swept by me and tortured me with its keen, freezing breath; but I drew my blanket more closely about me and defiantly watched my dead. The wolves came to take them but I lighted a fire and kept the wolves at bay. Then the wounded groaned with their wounds and the cold, and I dragged as many of them together as I could and covered them with my blanket. Then, uncovered, in the bitter cold, how I walked and heaped the fire higher and longed for the coming of day! When day broke I went about among the dead, washed their wounds and ministered to their wants as I could; and so I have been doing since. On my rounds I found three little papooses, about three months old, all wrapped up snugly in their dead mothers' bosoms. I took them, wrapped them in the blankets of the ones they will never know, and yonder they lie, sleeping sweetly."

Carl went to the tents of the Indians, informed them concerning the state of affairs, gathered together wagons for the dead and stretchers for the dying and wounded, and repaired to the scene we had just quitted. There the Indians gathered together their dead and buried them, and took the wounded back to their tents.

The two friends with Chikena and the babies returned to the reservation, there to await the termination of the Indian war of the Northwest.

With a few slight skirmishes, the papers say, only the death of a few "Indian bucks," the war of the Northwest ended.

"But," you ask, my reader, "did not the white people undergo any priva-tions? Did not the United States army lose two brave commanders and a number of privates?" Oh, yes. So the papers tell us; but I am not relating the brave (?) deeds of the white soldier. They are already flashed over the world by electricity; great writers have burned the midnight oil telling their story to the world. It is not my province to show how brave it was for a great, strong nation to quell a riot caused by the dancing of a few 'bucks'—for *civilized* soldiers to slaughter indiscriminately, Indian women and children. Doubtless it was brave, for so public opinion tells us, and it cannot err. But what will the annals of history handed down to future generations disclose to them? Will history term the treatment of the Indians by the United States Government, right and honorable? Ah, but that does not affect my story! It is the Indian's story—his chapter of wrongs and oppression.

CHAPTER XXII
IS THIS RIGHT?

"Wynema, this is a friend of ours whom we found in the Sioux country. Can you speak the language? If so, she will tell you all, and I should like for you to interpret for my benefit. Ask her to tell you about the 'starving time,' as the Indians call the time when they lived on one cent per day," said Robin one day, some weeks after his return home. He had been to Keithly College and had brought Chikena home with him that she might see the "squaw and papoose," as he laughingly called Wynema and Genevieve.

"Very well, dear," Wynema replied. "I learned to speak the Sioux language when quite a child. We had an old Sioux woman who lived with us until I was almost grown, when she died. And thus I became familiar with the language."

Then Wynema took the old woman's hand and kissed her softly, remembering the dear ones she had left behind in the burying-ground of the battle-field; and she spoke words of sympathy, leading her to talk of her troubles.

"My husband wishes to hear of your sufferings during the time you came near starving, before the Indian war. Can you tell me while I interpret?"

This is the story she told Wynema and Robin as they sat by the window of the pleasant sitting-room of Hope Seminary.

"There was a time when my people had plenty of land, plenty of cattle and plenty of everything; but after awhile the pale-faces came along, and by partly buying, partly seizing our lands by force, drove us very far away from our fertile country, until the Government placed us on a reservation in the Northwest, where the cold wind sweeps away our tents and almost freezes us. Then the great and powerful Government promised us to supply us with bountiful rations, in return for our lands it had taken. It was the treaty with us. But one day the agent told us the Government was poor, very poor, and could not afford to feed us so bountifully as in the past. So he gave us smaller rations than before, and every day the portion of each grew smaller, until we felt that we were being starved; for our crops failed and we were entirely dependent on the Government rations. Then came the days when one cent's worth daily was issued to each of us. How we all sickened and grew weak with hunger! I saw my boy, my Horda, growing paler and weaker every day, and I gave him my portion, keeping him in ignorance of it, for he would not have taken it had he known. Our chiefs and warriors gathered around the medicine man and prayed him to ask the Great Father what we should do to avert this evil. So the medicine man prayed to the Great Father all night, in his strange, murmuring way; and the next morning he told us to gather together and dance the holy dance to the Great Father and to sing while we danced, 'Great Father, help us! By thy strong arm aid us! Of thy great bounty give us that we may not die.' We were to dance thus until dawn, when the Messiah would come and deliver us. Many of our men died dancing, for they had become so weak from fasting that they could not stand the exertion. Then the great Government heard of our dances, and fearing trouble, sent out troops to stop us."

"Strange the great Government did not hear of your starving too, and send troops to stop *that*," remarked Robin, per parenthesis.

"The our great chief, Sitting Bull, told us the Government would starve us if we remained on the reservation; but if we would follow him, he would lead us to a country teeming with game, and where we could hunt and fish at our pleasure. We followed him to the Bad Lands where we struck our tents, as we were tired, intending to resume our march after we had rested. But one day we saw a cloud of dust, and there rode up a crowd of Indian police with Buffalo Bill at their head. They called out our chief and ordered him to surrender, then arrested him. Sitting Bull fired several shots, instructed his men how to proceed to recapture him, but all to no avail, for the police were backed by the pale-faced soldiers; and they killed our chief, his son, and six of the bravest warriors. Thus began the war of which your husband has already told you. It ended in Indian submission—yes, a submission extorted by blood."

"Buffalo Bill is the assumed name of the man who went about everywhere, taking a crowd of Indians with him and showing them, is he not?" asked Wynema of her husband.

"Yes, he was at the exposition at New Orleans with a band of Indians whom he was then 'showing,' and thus gaining means for subsistence for himself."

"It is strange he would lead a police force against the people who have helped him to gain a livelihood. Do you suppose the Indians who traveled with him became wealthy thereby?" ironically.

"Oh, yes. Very," he answered in the same tone. "Some of the Indians went from near us, and when they came back their friends and neighbors had to make up a 'pony purse' to give them a start. One trip with this 'brave' man was sufficient, though I never heard one of them express a desire to go again."

"There is an old man in the Territory, now, if he has not died recently, who traveled a great deal with Buffalo Bill, and I have never heard anything of the fortune he made. He is old and poor, and goes about doing what odd jobs he can get to do, and his friends almost entirely maintain him. It seems to me that gratitude, alone, to this benighted people who have served him would have rendered him at least *neutral*. If I could not have been for them, I most certainly would not have taken so prominent a part against them," Wynema said indignantly.

"Robin, there was such a scathing criticism of the part the United States Government has taken against the Indians of the Northwest, in the *St. Louis Republic*. I put the paper away to show you, but it has gotten misplaced. The substance of the article was this: the writer commended the Government on its slaughter of the Indians, and recommended that the dead bodies of the savages be used for fertilizers instead of the costly guano Mr. Blaine had been importing. He said the Indians alive were troublesome and expensive, for they would persist in getting hungry and cold; but the Indians slaugh-tered would be useful, for besides using their carcasses for fertilizers, the land they are now occupying could then be given as homes to the 'homeless whites.' I don't believe I ever read a more sarcastic, ironical article in any newspaper. I should like to shake hands with the writer, for I see he is a just, unprejudiced, thinking man, who believes in doing justice even to an Indian 'buck.' But here are more papers with dots from the battle-field; yet you know more and better about this than the writers of these articles, for you were all around and among the Indians, as well as the soldiers."

"Yes; but I should like to read their story and know their opinion. Good!" said he, reading; "Hear this from the *Cherokee Telephone* and interpret, for Chikena can understand:"

"The papers of the states are discussing the Indian war in the Northwest, its causes, etc. Here is what the matter is in a nutshell: Congress, the Secretary of the Interior, the Army and the Indian agents, have vied with each other in shameful dealings with these poor creatures of the plains. They buy their lands—for half price—make treaties and compacts with them in regard to pay, provisions, etc., then studiously turn and commence to lay plans to evade their promises and hold back their money to squander, and withhold the provisions agreed to be furnished. It must be remem-bered that these Indians buy, aye, more than pay for all the United States Government lets them have—they have given the Government an acre of land for every pound of beef, sugar, coffee and flour they have ever received. The Government has neglected to comply with treaties with these people—hence the war. They would rather die by the sword and bullet than to see their wives and children perish by degrees. Remember, too, that for every acre of land the United States Government holds to-day, which it acquired from the Indians of any tribe, from the landing of Columbus, it has not paid five cents on an average. The Government owes the Indians of North America justly to-day, ten times more than it will ever pay them. Search history and you will find that these are facts and figures and not mere sentimentalism. Newspaper editors in the states, who speak so vainly of the kindness of the Government to the Indians of this country, should post themselves a little, and each and every one could write a page of history on the United States Government's treatment of the Indians, as black and damnable as hell itself."

"Phew! That's pretty strong isn't it?" said Robin, finishing and looking up. "What does Chikena say?"

"She says it is all so. I am glad the editors of newspapers are denouncing the right parties.

CARL SADAKICHI HARTMANN (1867–1944)

First published play by an Asian American author.

The poet, playwright, critic, graphic artist, dancer, editor, art historian, screenwriter, and actor Carl Sadakichi Hartmann was born on the artificial traders' island of Dejima in the bay of Nagasaki, Japan, to a German father, Carl Hermann Oskar Hartmann, and a Japanese mother, Osada Hartmann, who died when he was a toddler. After spending his childhood with a brother and his father's well-off family in Germany, he was enrolled in a naval academy at age thirteen but ran away to Paris. His enraged father sent him to live with relatives in Philadelphia in 1882. At age seventeen he introduced himself to Walt Whitman, who became a formative influence and led Hartmann to think of himself as an American artist, although extensively schooled in Europe and with strong affinities for Japanese culture. He became a U.S. citizen in 1894 and worked as an art critic for several papers and magazines, some of which he also edited. He published *Conversations with Walt Whitman* in 1895. From the late 1890s Hartmann published a range of poetry and promoted Whitman's free verse as well as French symbolism. He became an early and immensely influential champion of photography as an art form and published over six hundred and fifty essays, many for *Camera Notes* and later *Camera Work*, edited or founded by Alfred Stieglitz, and others under the pseudonym Sydney Allan. Among his works are a long-time standard two-volume textbook, *History of American Art*, books on Japanese art, American painter James McNeill Whistler, and other subjects. He lived in New York City, in an artists' colony in New York state, and spent time as the foreign correspondent for American publications in Paris and London, where he befriended and later corresponded with poets Stéphane Mallarmé and Algernon Swinburne, and musician Franz Liszt. In the 1920s he moved with his second wife and children to California, where he staged a symphony of smells—a concert of perfumes—still considered a landmark event in performance art. He also directed plays and acted in the Hollywood epic film, *The Thief of Baghdad*. In his seventies he moved to a shack on the Morongo Indian reservation in the Southern California desert near one of his daughters. Starting in 1942 he was frequently investigated and interrogated by local and federal officials and because of his Japanese and German heritage accused of being a spy, and he barely escaped internment due to health conditions. He died during a visit to one of his daughters in St. Petersburg, Florida, in 1944.

At age twenty-three, Hartmann produced his "erotic play," *Christ*, in Boston. It told the story of Christ with Jesus portrayed as an ordinary commoner grappling with the decision whether to live a life of tangible experiences or devote himself to the cause of universal love. The audiences were horrified, as were the police and the New England Society for the Suppression of Vice, who closed the theater, banned the play and publicly burned copies of it. Hartmann was briefly jailed for what New York's *The Sun* called "the most daring of all decadent productions."

From CHRIST, A DRAMATIC POEM IN THREE ACTS [1893]

This Work
Is Dedicated To Those
Who Have
Misjudged, Humiliated, or Injured
Me
During My Past Life.

INTRODUCTION

I have written this book because the "great Pan" is not dead yet. Sensuality rules the world as heretofore, and optimists like myself must seize every opportunity to awaken mankind from its Bacchanalian revery.

I am fully aware that mankind cannot be reformed by the medium of printed sheets of paper; therefore this book is written merely: to cultivate a consideration for the severe contagious malady of humanity, with the hope of arousing an interest in individual liberty in regard to religion and morality.

In this drama I allow myself a freedom of expression, which will be understood only by the few who are able to rise with me to the height from which I regard man and the universe. Full of contradictions as life itself, it can scarcely be thoroughly appreciated before it has been performed on the stage, with appropriate dramatic music and scenic effects.

Whatever nation gives an ideal representation of my drama "Christ" can claim of having a National Dramatic Art.

THE AUTHOR.

PERSON REPRESENTED

JESHUA.
MOTHER MARIA, his mother.
MAGDALEN, his sister.
BROTHERS AND SISTERS to Jeshua.
AN OLD HERMIT.
TUBAL CAIN, a money-dealer.
HANNAH, a pilgrimess.
EVA, a young widow.
AHOLIBAH, young girl of the village
TABEA, young girl of the village
HAGAR, young girl of the village
ELLOSAR, a poet
OTHNIEL, young man of the village
REUBEN, young man of the village
SEMAJA, young man of the village
MEN, WOMEN, CHILDREN, TEMPLE-GUARD, etc.
CARUS MAXIMUS, a Roman centurion.
ROMAN SOLDIERS.
ZENOBIA, a foreign queen.
PRINCE PARSONDES.
CAMILLUS, a Greek, her steward.
ATMA, a dancing-woman.
CORTEGE of Zenobia and Parsondes, stewards, male and female attendants, body-guard, amazons, musicians, palanquin-bearers, etc.

SYNOPSIS.

Act I. Before Maria's Cottage, First Day, Evening.
Act II. 1.—Interior of Maria's Cottage, Second Day, Dawn.
2.—Among the Sandhills, Second Day, Noon.

3.—Before Maria's Cottage, Second Day, Afternoon.
Act III. Zenobia's Camp in the Desert, Third Day, Night.

Place: A Village in Palestine.
Time: August, 20 A. D.

ACT 1

SCENE: *To the left Mother Maria's cottage. A road leads across the stage. In the background a well. View on the sandhills.*

TUBAL CAIN, *enters with Mother Maria.* Nobody is impatient with his creditors, Mother Maria. As I have said before, my demands you must meet. Old Tubal Cain may be pot-bellied and bandy-legged, but he is not such a fool as to wait until the next festive year, he, he!

MOTHER MARIA, *leaning on a staff.* You only open your mouth to speak evil.

TUBAL CAIN. The poor can easily be generous. The rich have to be brutal now and then. Yet we two will remain friends, won't we, Mother Maria?

MOTHER MARIA. The desire of gain has no true friends.

TUBAL CAIN. Yet its power is omnipotent—How is Jeshua? It seems to me that he brings nothing but bitterness upon her who bore him.

MOTHER MARIA. True, he never lends a helping hand in all our distress, and yet he is my favorite son. Sorrow is often the comfort of old age.

TUBAL CAIN. He does not labor, aye? Labor warms the body; he who does not work deserves his poverty.

MOTHER MARIA. He was born for something better. I, his own mother, have never understood the motive of his life. He is different to other human beings.

TUBAL CAIN. No matter whether a goat be white or black, it should give the same amount of milk. That is an old saying. Things learnt in childhood are not forgotten.

MOTHER MARIA. Then remember your mother; she never spoke an unkind word to anyone.

TUBAL CAIN. I remember my mother well, he, he. When a child, I laughingly grasped with my little fingers for the glittering coins, which she was clinking in her hand to please me. Gold rules this world. An ass who denies it.

MOTHER MARIA. Cursed be the man who first brought gold among his fellow men. It dries up every source of kindness and affection.

TUBAL CAIN. Mammon is a lust of possession, and so is love. Like all human efforts it contains as much good as evil. Without these gerahs we would have no temple in Jerusalem, no caravans bringing to us the luxuries of the East and West—no progress could take place. And those who willingly denounce wealth in words would be the very ones to misuse it, if they could, he, he.

MOTHER MARIA. But to what purpose do you toil and struggle? Your gold creates no beneficial influence. Avarice is no enjoyment.

TUBAL CAIN. If you would but consent to make my dwelling yours, you would value my frugality.

MOTHER MARIA. Be silent—not another word!

TUBAL CAIN. I or another man, what is the difference as long as one is wholesome?

MOTHER MARIA. To insult a woman is an easy task, Tubal Cain.

TUBAL CAIN. Gossip says so, not I. I like you; that's all. I like stout women. Yes, I do, he, he.

MOTHER MARIA. I have loved but once.

TUBAL CAIN. But he was not your husband?

MOTHER MARIA. To the carpenter I was married against my will. It was adultery. I have loved but once. The sun shone hot upon me, but the golden light did not linger upon my head. Like a day of pleasure, it quickly passed. *As to herself.* One evening, standing out there in the desert, I mourned and longed for him who had left me for a hermit's life. I felt as if I were alone—alone in this wide, barren world. All springs of nature were at rest; neither bird nor insect seemed to live. All bright colors were lost in the darkness pervading the silent, desolate plain. Time itself stood still, as if hesitating to lift the veil from the immensity of that lonely, immeasurable stretch of sand, where hitherto, only the spirits of perished nations swayed in deep lament. It was a silence which my presence seemed to desecrate. An inexpressible fear came over me—a dream of heavenly love stormed o'er my trembling frame. I saw my lover's pale, wan face in clouds of raining light, and my maternal fruitfulness embraced the seed of Jeshua. *She stands at the garden gate, in Titanic gloom after her short summer life, like the personification of the Jewish race—a picture, stern and sombre, like the Arabian desert.*

TUBAL CAIN. Nature cannot be overcome. We all admire purity. It is our body that causes disturbances. We all err through our temperament. Yes, yes, Mother Maria, love is a burden.

MOTHER MARIA. It is a cruelty to women wherever unlawful maternity is proclaimed a crime. As long as a woman's body glows with the warmth of youth, men will be desirous to test her amativeness. To him it becomes the memory of a radiant hour of joy; while the woman is obliged to suckle a being of whom she owns nothing but the burden and the shame.

TUBAL CAIN. You speak of free copulation, I of marriage.

MOTHER MARIA. Wedlock is but free copulation sanctioned by the law, nothing more. Leave me for tonight, good Tubal Cain.

Turns to exit.

TUBAL CAIN, *shrugs his shoulders; aside.* How I would like to pet her haunches!

Exits slowly.

JESHUA, *enters robed in dull red.* Mother, what are your dealings with this man?

MOTHER MARIA. Those which necessity demand. *Looks at Jeshua with a yearning expression.*

JESHUA. Mother?

MOTHER MARIA. My son, why do you act so strangely? People speak of you in a slandering way. They say that you intend renouncing the Mosaic laws. Remember, you are a Jew, even if your father was a stranger to this land. Do not take vengeance upon me and my great sin by casting aside the religion of my forefathers.

JESHUA. Mother, have I ever said a word of reproach to you?

MOTHER MARIA. No, Jeshua.

JESHUA. Why then, Mother, must our roads always cross each other?

MOTHER MARIA. I would do anything, my son, to please you. (*Aside.*) Can I do nothing to draw him to me?

Exits.

JESHUA. Shall I ever be understood? The world is so wide, and I am alone! The world is so wide!—oh, years without fulfillment! how I suffer, wasting my energies of youth! In hours of adversity I also grow faithless like the rest.

Occupies himself in the garden.

ELLOSAR, *enters in conversation with Othniel, Reuben, and Semaja.*Day for
　　day, my whole being concentrates itself in a long, lascivious, lambent
　　breath of longing! How can these amorous sighs be satisfied? Youth is
　　troublesome enough without sterility.

OTHNIEL. Virgins, for various reasons, are as inconvenient as lewds.
　　Childless widows and cunning jades seem most commendable.

REUBEN. The guide through all sexual temptations should be health, and
　　health alone.

SEMAJA. Oh, let nature have its way; we can in nowise improve upon it.

Points to Eva.

A wind-stirred garment reveals to men all there is and can ever be.

ELLOSAR. True enough. I feel as if dewdrops should impearl her lanugi-
　　nous chalice of hope. Oh, garden of defloration, what loveless denuda-
　　tions have swept through thy mystic realms!

JESHUA. Innocence in manly strength should consecrate each sexual kiss
　　with salutary gentleness.

OTHNIEL, *to Semaja.* In such company, it were best to be a hermaphrodite.

ELLOSAR. Virtue can only be based on knowledge and conviction. The
　　innocent and ignorant can neither be chaste nor sensual.

JESHUA. Self-denial in love's desire, however fierce or faint it may be!

ELLOSAR. Dear friend, you speak of self-denial and know not what it is.
　　The pregnant lines in which a woman is created would also weave a
　　magic web around your soul while resting in a virgin's arm.

Jeshua smiles.

OTHNIEL. Oh, abstinent Essenian! For you must know that Jeshua is more
　　modest than a sister of Ammon behind her curtain.

ELLOSAR. And you, wanton Saducee, cannot let a woman pass without
　　insulting and undressing her in your imagination.

OTHNIEL. Can you?

REUBEN, *musingly.* Jeshua and Othniel are two entirely different represen-
　　tatives of life, and yet alike. Neither will fathom fatherhood.

SEMAJA, *to Jeshua.* And do you never feel as if you should purify yourself
　　in the ardent glow of a deep delight?

Jeshua remains silent.

REUBEN. You see how natures differ. Othniel, you never knew restraint without dictation. Look at the Arabs, how they breed their horses. They do not allow the stallion to touch the mare after conception, while husbands molest their wives a few hours before delivery.

OTHNIEL. Should they mount their neighbor's mare, perhaps?

ELLOSAR. If men and women would practice purity in married life, what a glorious religion would rise from the present chaos! Science and philosophy, music and poetry, all arts, all noble, unselfish actions would be the children of one mother: Health.

OTHNIEL. When will that be?

ELLOSAR. The future will proudly assert that the seminal fluid of a perfect father is the very essence of life, and that upon the wombs of perfect mothers the happiness of the world depends. Sexual intercourse could be a religion! The wife, trembling with the hopes of maternity, embraces with all her trust and feminine grandeur her husband, who presses all his strength, his manliness, and ideal thought into her sacred body. Such a connection between body and body, soul and soul, is worthy of god— the creation of life, the eternity of nature, divinity itself!

OTHNIEL. If you were god, how different the world would be. *Murmurs.* For my part, Aholibah suits my loins well enough.

SEMAJA. Such idle imaginings remain a blank to me.

REUBEN. It is a pastime. But who comes there?

SEMAJA. The old centurion, who has half persuaded me to join the Roman army.

CARUS MAXIMUS, *enters with soldiers and a crowd of villagers.* Flock around the Roman eagle, boys! Show courage! Take the chance I offer you. Ovations and trophies shall be yours. Do not hesitate; enter a life of liberty! Nothing more glorious than a life of war!

JESHUA. Will mankind never lead a peaceful life?

CARUS MAXIMUS. Never, youth. War is a necessity; peace unnatural. What would become of man if he could not endure the sight of blood and death? What would become of valor, vigor, vassalage? They soon would have to sound retreat, and power would fall to the vafrous. I spent many years at Augustus' imperial court, unrolled many a parchment scroll, witnessed the devotions of many creeds, gazed at the triumphs of beauty in Rome and in foreign lands, but nothing met my eye that could rival this keen-edged sword. Rather a scabrous gladiator than a decrepit sage! To me, he is a god who knows no fear! Who will enlist?

SEMAJA. Put down my name! I have nothing to lose and much to gain.

YOUNG MEN. Also mine!—And mine!—Would I had no filial piety to perform!—Alas, that I am still so young!

CARUS MAXIMUS. Brave, my boys! You will never repent it. Blow the bugle! strike the drum! We march tomorrow. Now go, and enjoy the last evening at home; and let sweethearts and sisters decorate my future heroes with garlands of flowers.

> *Exits with soldiers and young men, who shout and embrace each other.*
> *Young girls and women come with jars and vessels to the well,*
> *Tabea and Hagar among them.*

OLD HERMIT, *crosses the stage.* I once dreamed like you, my boys. I also loved the burning sun; now, I prefer a clear and mellow evening. The feeling of approaching darkness and melancholy solitude of night, puts my mind at rest. All your strength, imagination, ardent zeal of youth, will arrive at the same goal. And as annihilation knows of no restraint, the nations which you conquer, as well as the Roman empire which you serve, will perish. At last all humanity will decay. Sun and stars will extinguish; like this day, the earth will sink into oblivion.

TABEA. She will soon be here. I long to see her.

AHOLIBAH, *enters with Eva; a mysterious, sensual smile plays continually about Aholibah's lips, she is dressed in green and black.* Are you speaking of the foreign queen? I am craving to know, how many of her suitors the enchantress has killed.

TABEA. Her camp equipments passed by this morning. At least thirty camels, accompanied by hundreds of slaves.

HAGAR. Why are some people so poor and others so rich?

AHOLIBAH. There is no greater harlot living; they say, she changes her lovers as we change our robes.

TABEA. That takes away all my pleasure of seeing her.

AHOLIBAH. You need not stay. The loom and spindle are waiting for you at home. *Aside.* Oh, if I could but lead her wild, unrestrained life! Oh, that there are thousands of men longing for us, and that we dare not satisfy them and ourselves. The thought drives me mad. Why is this forbidden and that not allowed? If it is wrong, why am I so created that at certain moments I feel like throwing myself into the arms of the lowest man?

EVA. Hush!

MOTHER MARIA, *sings inside the cottage.* Unhappy children, having lost a parent still mother-naked, children growing up in ignorance and want, children bred without a kind word or kiss. Toil along, toil along! Unhappy lovers, young widows and widowers, parents sitting at the empty cradle, beggars, all diseased and deformed beings, poets and artists without success, Toil along, toil along! Unhappy mortals, struggling with poverty, sickness and sorrow, repentant sinners, all human beings who have a crime on their conscience, Toil along, toil along, oh, toil along!

ELLOSAR. Look at the last greeting of the setting sun! What color-dreams weave over the distant hills! The evening star steals softly into the trembling air.

The templeguard is heard singing.

Heaven on earth! That my art could hold this picture for eternity! But before we have comprehended it, it fades in its magic flight.

OTHNIEL. Ellosar, write a song on these colors, so hot and so wild!

REUBEN. The golden dust can be seen, but not grasped.

ELLOSAR. Always denying?

REUBEN. Always searching for truth.

ELLOSAR. And never admiring when it reveals itself.

TABEA. How wide the meshes of the spider's web are. A sure sign of bad weather.

AHOLIBAH. I dissolve in pain.

The languid voluptuousness of Southern climes takes possession of her body. Eva in profound silence watches the sunset. Jeshua comes into the garden and saws wood.

TABEA. Look at Jeshua.

AHOLIBAH. He pretends to be above curiosity.

EVA. Jeshua always acts as he feels.

OTHNIEL, *to Aholibah.* You spoke quite differently about him last summer, if I do not err?

AHOLIBAH. We sometimes change and know not why.

HAGAR. In my life, nothing changes. One day is like the other, full of pain.

Hannah enters barefooted; she perceives, Jeshua, and stands as if in a dream; the languid voluptuousness of Southern climes takes for a moment possession of her soul.

TABEA. Queer I could never understand Jeshua.

OTHER GIRLS. Nor I!—Nor I!

AHOLIBAH. What is there strange about it? Is he not the son of Mother
  Maria? Sons take after their mother. *Aside.* God forgive me for saying
  this. How I have loved that man! Milk exuded from my nipples from
  very joy, when I thought of him. And he rejected me!

EVA. Jeshua deserves everyone's love.

TABEA. There they come!

> *Music is heard, slaves appear waving perfumed kerchiefs and strewing
> flowers, carmine, and gold dust on the road. Coins are thrown among the
> crowd, who shout Hosanna!*

JESHUA. So everybody is saluted, whether friend or foe, as long as
  curiosity is satisfied.

> *Enter Camillus and attendants, some on horse back. Zenobia, dressed in
> striped black and golden yellow, is borne on a palanquin. Prince Parsondes
> rides in a chariot. The village girls hail them with palm leaves.*

PRINCE PARSONDES. What a vile place!

ZENOBIA. We shall linger here over night.

PRINCE PARSONDES. In your embrace the humblest spot on earth con-
  verts into a place of bliss.

MURMURING OF THE CROWD. Isn't she just splendid!—She looks
  like the queen of abomination!—What sumptuous, saturated brilliancy!—What merciless glare and glitter!—Not half as dazzling as I
  thought!—Observe the luring glances of her emerald eye!—I wonder if
  the vermilion of her lips is real!—How grey those many-colored tunics
  look!—Will I be able to hallow her after-image by my art?

ZENOBIA. How they stare at me! I am used to the shouting of multitudes.
  Soulless creatures, insipid fools, they envy me, and do not know that I
  am the unhappiest creature of them all. In my mighty passion I absorb
  all other ones. I stand smiling in the arena of the world, and shed my
  heart-blood unseen, in the carmine and gold dust of my poetry.

> *Suddenly perceives Jeshua, and stares at him.
> Hannah anxiously watches the queen.*

CAMILLUS. What ails you, my queen?

ZENOBIA. Find out the name of yonder swain.

CAMILLUS, *aside.* May the gods of your forefathers preserve you from her luring smiles, young Jew.

ZENOBIA. I have never met the man of whom I desired children until now. Embracing him I could fall into eternal slumber. And mine he will be. An ocean of light surrounds me. Oh, could I but throw myself into its clear and steady flames, that it might purify and burn up all that is foul within me!

AHOLIBAH. She has cast an eye upon the coyish dreamer. Ha! wait now and see, if he can resist that virulent demon of passion.

HANNAH. I knew it, I knew it!

> *Zenobia and procession exit; the crowd follows them. A few remain, speaking about the event, then slowly disperse in different directions. Only Hannah and Jeshua remain on the stage. It grows dark during the following scene.*

HANNAH, *slowly approaches Jeshua, and whispers with sisterly affection.* Beware! Beware!

> *Long pause.*

JESHUA. Who are you?

HANNAH. A part of you. All else I love in you. Take what I am, it is yours!

JESHUA. Who are you?

HANNAH. I know no more, I simply feel that I belong to you, and to nobody else on earth.

> *They gaze at each other for a long while, then embrace.*

JESHUA. The first long, slumbering kiss confirms all that god and the heavens decreed.

HANNAH, *quivering with bliss.* Hold me fast!

> *Pause.*

JESHUA. Also upon us lingers the silent sadness known to all who listen to the woeful song of life and death. We soar above the dust and bitterness of human cares. When our lips meet, they touch—

HANNAH. Infinitude.

JESHUA. Infinitude. Our Love is as healthy and strong as the noon of summer days. Ages may sink into the past, yet our friendship would not change, not even with death, for we would continue—

HANNAH. Beyond.

JESHUA. Beyond. The waves of our mind meet on the vibrating ocean of air, and wandering to and fro, from soul to soul, call forth responsive thoughts.

BOTH, *as in a trance, hardly audible, Hannah speaking more softly than Jeshua, like music accompanying a song.* Our Love fills the world with the thunder of unearthly joy! We penetrate into all the kindred parts of the universe. Like eagles, we cleave the ambient realms of dark and darker blue, and break the dreariness of Northern darkness as inconstant lights. We sweep over vast, variegated plains, and sink with the roaring waters into the depth of the wild, unresting sea! How glorious is our Love! We float with the jubilating songs of nightingales on the silver beams of night. We rest on the lips of lovers; we bloom with the flowers that fade unseen, and smile through the mist of tears at morn. We rest on Nature's bosom, and dream her naked dream of grace; we feel the burning passion of all mankind, and the body becomes as sacred as the soul! How old and new is our Love! We are buried by hurricanes that crush the homes of peaceful men; we drown in seas of blood shed for a future state of joy. And, with enthusiasm's blazing flames our Love soars to the suns of heaven, and falls into the sunless gulfs of hell. We leap into the boundlessness of space, and taste, in the rapture of one moment, the eternity of time! We laugh at the violence of fate; we laugh at wealth, wisdom, beauty, power. We sink into each other's arms. Dark immensity of night surround us! We are in Love!

> *In their kisses, body and soul are trembling in a rapturous embrace.*

The heavens open! The widening infinite! Spirits of heaven and hell, they cast their sickles upon earth, and stars are falling from the clouds, and earthquakes split the realms, and still we cry for Love, more Love! And from the unfathomed depth of this restless world rise thousands of gigantic visions. We tremble in the laments of life; we feel the holy agony, the godlike sufferings of the past; and our bodies crumble into dust, while our souls mount to those wonderful, brooding stars, which flame through the sky in endless variation.

> *An old hermit enters.*

Oh, everchanging orbs of God, you are the symbol of Love! Myriads of falling stars, that whirl around each other, you are like the maddening yearning of humanity itself; the nameless longing of life and Love to throw itself into another life and Love, until you dash together in the fury of a glorious, overwhelming light!

Meteors shoot across heaven.

OLD HERMIT. Oh, world of fire-balls, destined to be embodied in one star, in you mankind can read, night for night, the secret of the universe, how glowing suns transform into cold and glittering stars of ice, till they collide to become once more the ardent suns of time and space. And like creation's cycling course the stars form circles, rolling forth in endless chains to nothingness. The fires of the universe prophecy their destiny in your immortal Love,

Extends his arms to Hannah and Jeshua.

when at last, in the far distant future, all the ambitious suns of heaven tumble into one mighty, burning giant star, who will shed a light of redemption over the final union of hostile elements, sleeping mysteriously and motionless in the dark immensity of time. Then Love, the one colossal soul of the departed worlds, will dreamingly begin a new existence for decillions of ages to come.

The old hermit exits, the lovers remain as petrified, in an embrace expressing the triumph of purity in Love. The stars are sparkling like diamonds on the turquoise vault. After a long pause, the curtain drops.

SUI SIN FAR / EDITH MAUDE EATON (1865–1914)

First stories published by an Asian American writer in the United States.

Sui Sin Far, 水仙花, or Edith Maude Eaton, was born to a British father and Chinese mother who immigrated with their children from England first to the U.S. and then to Montreal in 1872. She grew up in Montreal and worked as a stenographer, typist, and free-lance journalist who published articles on the local laws and practices that limited the civil rights and social standing of Chinese Canadians and Chinese Americans. Many Chinese Canadians and Chinese Americans contacted her to ask her to write about difficulties created by racist laws and attitudes. Although she could have "passed" for a white woman under her Western name, she adopted the name Sui Sin Far ("Water Lily" in Cantonese) and, during this time of intense Sinophobia, she chose to align herself with Chinese Americans. After working as a journalist in the British colony of Jamaica, Far moved for health reasons in 1898 to the United States, where she settled first in San Francisco and then in Seattle's small but growing Chinatown. Sui Sin Far died in 1914 in Montreal.

With her stories, many of which feature Chinese American characters grappling with assimilation, cultural differences, and social conditions, she becomes one of the first authors to present a positive image of Chinese American life for general readers. She is considered the first Asian American author to publish fiction in America. But her stories are more than social commentary about the increasingly hostile attitudes toward Asians and the racist laws affecting them, including the Chinese Exclusion Act of 1882, renewed in 1902, which barred Asian immigration into the United States. Additional laws and ordinances during the following decades restricted not only immigration but also Asian Americans' rights in the country. Her stories have been recognized by scholars for their literary merit. Her sense of irony, deft character descriptions, and dynamic dialogue in situations specific to the Asian American and Asian Canadian communities render moral dilemmas with universal resonance. The stories achieve a level of authenticity missing from most writings about the Chinese American communities of the time. Through her fiction she creates space for readers to imagine Asian Americans' lives in the United States in a more authentic light.

Of the stories included here, "Mrs. Spring Fragrance" is Far's best-known publication. The witty and compelling protagonist is a woman with her own mind who cleverly navigates the political injustices facing Chinese Americans as well as the emotional terrain of her own life. In "The Land of the Free," Far dramatizes the traumatic scenario of a baby who is seized from the arms of his young Chinese American parents by border agents when he and his mother arrive in San Francisco after a stay in China. The expertly paced and harrowing story of the parents' struggle to regain their baby captures the human toll of policies and attitudes that shaped the lives of Asian Americans but remained largely unspoken in fiction written by white authors at the time. The stories first appeared in 1909 and 1910, and then in a 1912 collection, *Mrs. Spring Fragrance,* which the *New York Times* reviewed: "Miss Eaton has struck a new note in American fiction." Her first story published in the United States, "The Gamblers," appeared in 1896 under the name of Sui Seen Far, in the *Fly Leaf,* in Boston.

The Gamblers [1896]

The rain splashed in his face, soaked through his garments, ran down his back and trickled though his wide sleeves in an almost vindictive manner. But he shambled on indifferently, slowly and heavily, apparently totally unconscious of physical discomfort. Looking into that bald face one could not penetrate its placidity, and even the eyes seemed expressionless. The small, well-shaped hands did not look as if they were accustomed to manual labor; nevertheless his clothing consisted of the ordinary blue blouse and pantaloons of a working Chinaman, and it was a very dilapidated Yankee hat around which he had wound his queue. The peculiar means by which he prevented the last mentioned part of his costume from being blown off by the wind and rain attracted some little attention from the passers-by; but to jocose remarks and amused smiles he paid no heed.

Ah Lin was proceeding to a gambling resort, and his thoughts were not with the scenes and faces about him.

When he reached his destination, he slipped a key from out of his sleeve and admitted himself into a large low room furnished with a long table, a couch and some wooden chairs. Two men sat on the couch, and about a dozen were grouped around the table—all Chinamen. There was but one small window in the place, and the day being dull, the gloom of the room seemed to make palpable and visible by the light of two oil lamps. On the window ledge was a pipe, a small lamp and a tiny porcelain cup full of jellified opium.

One of the Chinamen arose, took the pipe, dipped a pin into the opium, turned it around until a quantity of the sticky drug adhered to it, then inserted it into the pipe, held the pipe over the flame of the lamp, and drew two or three long breaths. Here was peace and a foretaste of oblivion—a vapor was seen to exhale out of his mouth and nose.

Ah Lin walked up to the smoker, and the two held a short confab.

"Well," said Ah Lih at length, "I have fifty cents left; with twenty-five cents I can draw a lot, and with the balance I will see if I can win half a dollar on a red cord stick."

"All right," returned the smoker, "and I'll do the same; but first let us worship the tiger."

In a corner of the room on a small table stood a wooden image of a tiger with wings grasping an immense cash between its paws.

Ah Lin and Hom Lock lighted some sticks of incense and bowed themselves before the image—the Chinaman's gambling god.

Some of those who were at the head of the centre table called to Ah Lin, and tried to prevail upon him to stake some money in a game which was played by means of a round board with a hole in the centre through which a slender stick was passed and fastened underneath to a larger board. The top piece of wood was designed to be moved around like a wheel; it was marked off into many parts upon which cabalistic figures were painted. Ah Lin had no inclination to spin the wheel, and turned to another man who sat near holding three sticks in his hand. Those three sticks were three lots; three ends projected outwards; three ends were grasped and hidden by the man's hand, hanging down from which was a red tassel or string professedly attached to one of the sticks. The sport consisted in guessing which stick had the red string.

Ah Lin ventured twenty-five cents on one of the lots of sticks, but lost. The head gambler pocketed the twenty-five cents and Ah Lin moved silently away. If he had won he would have received his quarter back with another quarter added.

At the other end of the table was a deep earthen vessel, and around it were grouped the major part of the men in the room. One man was tying up small bundles containing sums of money from one cent up to twenty-five dollars. Each package was marked with a sign word. When his task was completed, the man cast all the bundles into the vessel, and in a loud voice announced that all who wished could cast lots and for twenty-five cents have the chance of making twenty-five dollars.

A number, including Ah Lin, paid twenty-five cents and marked their names on a list of signs. Then the vessel and its contents were shaken up. All in turn were then invited to take at hazard from its portentous belly, the parcel for which they had staked. As he opened his, Ah Lin's face turned grey; it contained but one cent.

"What have you got?" asked Hom Lock, in an excited whisper, leaning over Ah Lin's shoulder. "Just one cent, eh? Well, I have the twenty-five dollars—the Tiger favors me—he's a great God."

There was a crash; the lamps were knocked down and extinguished. Ah Lin had leapt across the table and was dragging the Gambling God around the room, striking it repeatedly with a stick.

"It's a great God, isnt' it," he yelled. "See how it likes to be insulted. Oh, it's a great big God."

"It's a great God," shouted Hom Lock; there was a knife in his hand; he pressed close to Ah Lin.

Ah Lin saw the knife, and something slipped from his sleeve and two knives gleamed—then disappeared.

Some one struck a light. The owner of the place picked up the fallen God and placed it on the table. It calmly looked down upon two dead men.

IN THE LAND OF THE FREE [1909]

I

"SEE, LITTLE ONE—the hills in the morning sun. There is thy home for years to come. It is very beautiful and thou wilt be very happy there."

The Little One looked up into his mother's face in perfect faith. He was engaged in the pleasant occupation of sucking a sweetmeat; but that did not prevent him from gurgling responsively.

"Yes, my olive bud; there is where thy father is making a fortune for thee. Thy father! Oh, wilt thou not be glad to behold his dear face. 'Twas'for thee I left him."

The Little One ducked his chin sympathetically against his mother's knee. She lifted him on to her lap. He was two years old, a round, dimple-cheeked boy with bright brown eyes and a sturdy little frame.

"Ah! Ah! Ah! Ooh! Ooh! Ooh!" puffed he, mocking a tugboat steaming by.

San Francisco's waterfront was lined with ships and steamers, while other craft, large and small, including a couple of white transports from the Philippines, lay at anchor here and there off shore. It was some time before the *Eastern Queen* could get docked, and even after that was accomplished, a lone Chinaman who had been waiting on the wharf for an hour was detained that much longer by men with the initials U.S.C. on their caps, before he could board the steamer and welcome his wife and child.

"This is thy son," announced the happy Lae Choo.

Hom Hing lifted the child, felt of his little body and limbs, gazed into his face with proud and joyous eyes; then turned inquiringly to a customs officer at his elbow.

"That's a fine boy you have there," said the man.

"Where was he born?"

"In China," answered Hom Hing, swinging the Little One on his right shoulder, preparatory to leading his wife off the steamer.

"Ever been to America before?"

"No, not he," answered the father with a happy laugh.

The customs officer beckoned to another. "This little fellow," said he, "is visiting America for the first time."

The other customs officer stroked his chin reflectively.

"Good day," said Hom Hing.

"Wait!" commanded one of the officers. "You cannot go just yet."

"What more now?" asked Hom Hing.

"I'm afraid," said the first customs officer, "that we cannot allow the boy to go ashore. There is nothing in the papers that you have shown us—your wife's papers and your own—having any bearing upon the child."

"There was no child when the papers were made out," returned Hom Hing. He spoke calmly; but there was apprehension in his eyes and in his tightening grip on his son.

"What is it? What is it?" quavered Lae Choo, who understood a little English.

The second customs officer regarded her pityingly.

"I don't like this part of the business," he muttered.

The first officer turned to Horn Ming and in an official tone of voice, said:

"Seeing that the boy has no certificate entitling him to admission to this country you will have to leave him with us."

"Leave my boy! " exclaimed Hom Hing.

"Yes; he will be well taken care of, and just as soon as we can hear from Washington he will be handed over to you."

"But," protested Hom Hing, "he is my son."

"We have no proof," answered the man with a shrug of his shoulders; "and even if so we cannot let him pass without orders from the Government."

"He is my son," reiterated Hom Hing, slowly and solemnly. "I am a Chinese merchant and have been in business in San Francisco for many years. When my wife told to me one morning that she dreamed of a green tree with spreading branches and one beautiful red flower growing thereon, I answered her that I wished my son to be born in our country, and for her to prepare to go to China. My wife complied with my wish. After my son was born my mother fell sick and my wife nursed and cared for her; then my father, too, fell sick, and my wife also nursed and cared for him. For twenty moons my wife care for and nurse the old people, and when they die they bless her and my son, and I send for her to return to me. I had no fear of trouble. I was a Chinese merchant and my son was my son."

"Very good, Hom Hing," replied the first officer. "Nevertheless, we take your son."

"No, you not take him; he my son too."

It was Lae Choo. Snatching the child from his father's arms she held and covered him with her own.

The officers conferred together for a few moments; then one drew Hom Hing aside and spoke in his ear.

Resignedly Hom Hing bowed his head, then approached his wife.

"'Tis the law," said he, speaking in Chinese, "and 'twill be but for a little while—until tomorrow's sun arises."

"You, too," reproached Lae Choo in a voice eloquent with pain. But accustomed to obedience she yielded the boy to her husband who in turn delivered him to the first officer. The Little One protested lustily against the transfer; but his mother covered her face with her sleeve and his father silently led her away. Thus was the law of the land complied with.

II

DAY WAS BREAKING. Lae Choo, who had been awake all night, dressed herself, then awoke her husband.

"'Tis the morn," she cried. "Go, bring our son."

The man rubbed his eyes and arose upon his elbow so that he could see out of the window. A pale star was visible in the sky. The petals of a lily in a bowl on the windowsill were unfurled.

"'Tis not yet time," said he, laying his head down again.

"Not yet time. Ah, all the time that I lived before yesterday is not so much as the time that has been since my little one was taken from me."

The mother threw herself down beside the bed and covered her face.

Hom Hing turned on the light, and touching his wife's bowed head with a sympathetic hand inquired if she had slept.

"Slept!" she echoed, weethrepingly. "Ah, how could I close my eyes with my arms empty of the little body that has filled them every night for more than twenty moons! You do not know—man—what it is to miss the feel of the little fingers and the little toes and the soft round limbs of your little one. Even in the darkness his darling eyes used to shine up to mine, and often have I fallen into slumber with his pretty babble at my ear. And now, I see him not; I touch him not; I hear him not. My baby, my little fat one!"

"Now! Now! Now!" consoled Hom Hing, patting his wife's shoulder reassuringly; "there is no need to grieve so; he will soon gladden you again. There cannot be any law that would keep a child from its mother!"

Lae Ghoo dried her tears.

"You are right, my husband," she meekly murmured. She arose and stepped about the apartment, setting things to rights. The box of presents she had brought for her California friends had been opened the evening before; and silks, embroideries, carved ivories, ornamental lacquer-ware, brasses, camphorwood boxes, fans, and chinaware were scattered around in confused heaps. In the midst of unpacking the thought of her child in the hands of strangers had overpowered her, and she had left everything to crawl into bed and weep.

Having arranged her gifts in order she stepped out on to the deep balcony. The star had faded from view and there were bright streaks in the western sky. Lae Choo looked down the street and around. Beneath the flat occupied by her and her husband were quarters for a number of bachelor Chinamen, and she could hear them from where she stood, taking their early morning breakfast. Below their dining-room was her husband's grocery store. Across the way was a large restaurant. Last night it had been resplendent with gay colored lanterns and the sound of music. The rejoicings over "the completion of the moon," by Quong Sum's firstborn, had been long and loud, and had caused her to tie a handkerchief over her ears. She, a bereaved mother, had it not in her heart to rejoice with other parents. This morning the place was more in accord with her mood. It was still and quiet. The revellers had dispersed or were asleep.

A roly-poly woman in black sateen, with long pendant earrings in her ears, looked up from the street below and waved her a smiling greeting. It was her old neighbor, Kuie Hoe, the wife of the gold embosser, Mark Sing. With her was a little boy in yellow jacket and lavender pantaloons. Lae Choo remembered him as a baby. She used to like to play with him in those days when she had no child of her own. What a long time ago that seemed! She caught her breath in a sigh, and laughed instead.

"Why are you so merry?" called her husband from within.

"Because my Little One is coming home," answered Lae Choo. "I am a happy mother—a happy mother."

She pattered into the room with a smile on her face.

***

The noon hour had arrived. The rice was steaming in the bowls and a fragrant dish of chicken and bamboo shoots was awaiting Hom Hing. Not for one moment had Lae Choo paused to rest during the morning hours; her activity had been ceaseless. Every now and again, however, she had raised her eyes to the gilded clock on the curiously carved mantelpiece. Once, she had exclaimed:

"Why so long, oh I why so long?" Then apostrophizing herself: "Lae Choo, be happy. The Little One is coming! The Little One is coming!" Several times she burst into tears: and several times she laughed aloud.

Hom Hing entered the room; his arms hung down by his side.

"The Little One!" shrieked Lae Choo.

"They bid me call tomorrow."

With a moan the mother sank to the floor.

The noon hour passed. The dinner remained on the table.

III

THE WINTER RAINS were over: the spring had come to California, flushing the hills with green and causing an ever-changing pageant of flowers to pass over them. But there was no spring in Lae Choo's heart, for the Little One remained away from her arms. He was being kept in a mission. White women were caring for him, and though for one full moon he had pined for his mother and refused to be comforted he was now apparently happy and contented. Five moons or five months had gone by since the day he had passed with Lae Choo through the Golden Gate; but the great Government at Washington still delayed sending the answer which would return him to his parents.

***

Hom Hing was disconsolately rolling up and down the balls in his abacus box when a keen-faced young man stepped into his store.

"What news?" asked the Chinese merchant.

"This!" The young man brought forth a typewritten letter. Hom Hing read the words:

> "Re Chinese child, alleged to be the son of Hom Hing, Chinese merchant, doing business at 425 Clay Street, San Francisco. Same will have attention as soon as possible."

Hom Hing returned the letter, and without a word continued his manipulation of the counting machine.

"Have you anything to say?" asked the young man.

"Nothing, They have sent the same letter fifteen times before. Have you not yourself showed it to me?"

"True!" The young man eyed the Chinese merchant furtively. He had a proposition to make and he was pondering whether or not the time was opportune.

"How is your wife?" he inquired solicitously—and diplomatically.

Hom Hing shook his head mournfully.

She seems less every day," he replied. "Her food she takes only when I bid her and her tears fall continually. She finds no pleasure in dress or flowers and cares not to see her friends. Her eyes stare all night. I think before another moon she will pass into the land of spirits."

"No!" exclaimed the young man, genuinely startled.

"If the boy not come home I lose my wife sure," continued Hom Hing with bitter sadness. "It's not right," cried the young man indignantly. Then he made his proposition.

The Chinese father's eyes brightened exceedingly.

"Will I like you to go to Washington and make them give you the paper to restore my son?" cried he. "How can you ask when you know my heart's desire?"

"Then," said the young fellow, "I will start next week. I am anxious to see this thing through if only for the sake of your wife's peace of mind."

"I will call her. To hear what you think to do will make her glad," said Hom Hing.

He called a message to Lae Choo upstairs through a tube in the wall.

In a few moments she appeared, listless, wan, and hollow-eyed; but when her husband told her the young lawyer's suggestion she became as one electrified; her form straightened, her, eyes glistened; the color flushed to her cheeks.

"Oh," she cried, turning to James Clancy, "You are a hundred man good!"

The young man felt somewhat embarrassed; his eyes shifted a little under the intense gaze of the Chinese mother.

"Well, we must get your boy for you," he responded. "Of course"—turning to Hom Hing—"it will cost a little money. You can't get fellows to hurry the Government for you without gold in your pocket."

Hom Hing stared blankly for a moment. Then: "How much do you want, Mr. Clancy?" he asked quietly.

"Well, I will need at least five hundred to start with."

Hom Hing cleared his throat.

"I think I told to you the time I last paid you for writing letters for me and seeing the Custom boss here that nearly all I had was gone!"

"Oh, well then we won't talk about it, old fellow. It won't harm the boy to stay where he is, and your wife may get over it all right."

"What that you say?" quavered Lae Choo.

James Clancy looked out of the window.

"He says," explained Hom Hing in English, "that to get our boy we have to have much money."

"Money! Oh, yes."

Lae Choo nodded her head.

"I have not got the money to give him."

For a moment Lae Choo gazed wonderingly from one face to the other;

then, comprehension dawning upon her, with swift anger, pointing to the lawyer, she cried: "You not one hundred man good; you just common white man."

"Yes, ma'am," returned James Clancy, bowing and smiling ironically.

Hom Hing pushed his wife behind him and addressed the lawyer again: "I might try," said he, "to raise something; but five hundred—it is not possible."

"What about four?"

"I tell you I have next to nothing left and my friends are not rich."

"Very well!"

The lawyer moved leisurely toward the door, pausing on its threshold to light a cigarette.

"Stop, white man; white man, stop!"

Lae Choo, panting and terrified, had started forward and now stood beside him, clutching his sleeve excitedly.

"You say you can go to get paper to bring my Little One to me if Hom Hing give you five hundred dollars?"

The lawyer nodded carelessly; his eyes were intent upon the cigarette which would not take the fire from the match.

"Then you go, get paper. If Hom Hing not can give you five hundred dollars—I give you perhaps what more that much."

She slipped a heavy gold bracelet from her wrist and held it out to the man. Mechanically he took it.

"I go get more!"

She scurried away, disappearing behind the door through which she had come.

"Oh, look here, I can't accept this," said James Clancy, walking back to Hom Hing and laying down the bracelet before him.

"It's all right," said Hom Hing, seriously, "pure China gold. My wife's parent give it to her when we married."

"But I can't take it anyway," protested the young man.

"It is all same as money. And you want money to go to Washington," replied Hom Hing in a matter of fact manner. "See, my jade earrings—my gold buttons—my hairpins—my comb of pearl and my rings—one, two, three, four, five rings; very good—very good—all same much money. I give them all to you. You take and bring me paper for my Little One."

Lae Choo piled up her jewels before the lawyer.

Hom Hing laid a restraining hand upon her shoulder. "Not all, my wife," he said in Chinese. He selected a ring—his gift to Lae Choo when she dreamed of the tree with the red flower. The rest of the jewels he pushed toward the white man.

"Take them and sell them," said he. "They will pay your fare to Washington and bring you back with the paper."

For one moment James Clancy hesitated. He was not a sentimental man; but something within him arose against accepting such payment for his services.

"They are good, good," pleadingly asserted Lae Choo, seeing his hesitation

Whereupon he seized the jewels; thrust them into his coat pocket, and walked rapidly away from the store.

IV

LAE CHOO FOLLOWED after the missionary woman through the mission nursery school. Her heart was beating so high with happiness that she could scarcely breathe. The paper had come at last—the precious paper which gave Hom Hing and his wife the right to the possession of their own child. It was ten months now since he had been taken from them—ten months since the sun had ceased to shine for Lae Choo.

The room was filled with children,—most of them wee tots, but none so wee as her own. The mission woman talked as she walked. She told Lae Choo that little Kim, as he had been named by the school, was the pet of the place, and that his little tricks and ways amused and delighted everyone. He had been rather difficult to manage at first and had cried much for his mother; "but children so soon forget, and after a month he seemed quite at home and played around as bright and happy as a bird."

"Yes," responded Lae Choo. "Oh, yes, yes!"

But she did not hear what was said to her. She was walking in a maze of anticipatory joy.

"Wait here, please," said the mission woman, placing Lae Choo in a chair. "The very youngest ones are having their breakfast."

She withdrew for a moment—it seemed like an hour to the mother— then she reappeared leading by the hand a little boy dressed in blue cotton overalls and white-soled shoes. The little boy's face was round and dimpled and his eyes were very bright.

"Little One, ah, my Little One!" cried Lae Choo.

She fell on her knees and stretched her hungry arms toward her son.

But the Little One shrunk from her and tried to hide himself in the folds of the white woman's skirt.

"Go'way, go'way!" he bade his mother.

MRS. SPRING FRAGRANCE [1910]

WHEN MRS. SPRING Fragrance first arrived in Seattle, she was unacquainted with even one word of the American language. Five years later her husband, speaking of her, said: "There are no more American words for her learning." And everyone who knew Mrs. Spring Fragrance agreed with Mr. Spring Fragrance.

Mr. Spring Fragrance, whose business name was Sing Yook, was a young curio merchant. Though conservatively Chinese in many respects, he was at the same time what is called by the Westerners, "Americanized." Mrs. Spring Fragrance was even more "Americanized."

Next door to the Spring Fragrances lived the Chin Yuens. Mrs. Chin Yuen was much older than Mrs. Spring Fragrance; but she had a daughter of eighteen with whom Mrs. Spring Fragrance was on terms of great friendship. The daughter was a pretty girl whose Chinese name was Mai Gwi Far (a rose) and whose American name was Laura. Nearly everybody called her Laura, even her parents and Chinese friends. Laura had a sweetheart, a youth named Kai Tzu. Kai Tzu, who was American-born, and as ruddy and stalwart as any young Westerner, was noted amongst baseball players as one of the finest pitchers on the Coast. He could also sing, "Drink to me only with thine eyes," to Laura's piano accompaniment.

Now the only person who knew that Kai Tzu loved Laura and that Laura loved Kai Tzu, was Mrs. Spring Fragrance. The reason for this was that, although the Chin Yuen parents lived in a house furnished in American style, and wore American clothes, yet they religiously observed many Chinese customs, and their ideals of life were the ideals of their Chinese forefathers. Therefore, they had betrothed their daughter, Laura, at the age of fifteen, to the eldest son of the Chinese Government school-teacher in San Francisco. The time for the consummation of the betrothal was approaching.

Laura was with Mrs. Spring Fragrance and Mrs. Spring Fragrance was trying to cheer her.

"I had such a pretty walk today," said she. "I crossed the banks above the beach and came back by the long road. In the green grass the daffodils were blowing, in the cottage gardens the currant bushes were flowering, and in the air was the perfume of the wallflower. I wished, Laura, that you were with me."

Laura burst into tears. "That is the walk," she sobbed, "Kai Tzu and I so love; but never, ah, never, can we take it together again."

"Now, Little Sister," comforted Mrs. Spring Fragrance, "you really must not grieve like that. Is there not a beautiful American poem written by a noble American named Tennyson, which says:

"'Tis better to have loved and lost,
Than never to have loved at all?"

Mrs. Spring Fragrance was unaware that Mr. Spring Fragrance, having returned from the city, tired with the day's business, had thrown himself down on the bamboo settee on the veranda, and that although his eyes were engaged in scanning the pages of the *Chinese World,* his ears could not help receiving the words which were borne to him through the open window.

"'Tis better to have loved and lost,
Than never to have loved at all,"

repeated Mr. Spring Fragrance. Not wishing to hear more of the secret talk of women, he arose and sauntered around the veranda to the other side of the house. Two pigeons circled around his head. He felt in his pocket, for a li-chi which he usually carried for their pecking. His fingers touched a little box. It contained a jadestone pendant, which Mrs. Spring Fragrance had particularly admired the last time she was down town. It was the fifth anniversary of Mr. and Mrs. Spring Fragrance's wedding day.

Mr. Spring Fragrance pressed the little box down into the depths of his pocket.

A young man came out of the back door of the house at Mr. Spring Fragrance's left. The Chin Yuen house was at his right.

"Good evening," said the young man. "Good evening," returned Mr. Spring Fragrance. He stepped down from his porch and went and leaned over the railing which separated this yard from the yard in which stood the young man.

"Will you please tell me," said Mr. Spring Fragrance, "the meaning of two lines of an American verse which I have heard?"

"Certainly," returned the young man with a genial smile. He was a star student at the University of Washington, and had not the slightest doubt that he could explain the meaning of all things in the universe.

"Well," said Mr. Spring Fragrance, "it is this:

"'Tis better to have loved and lost,
Than never to have loved at all."

"Ah!" responded the young man with an air of profound wisdom. "That, Mr. Spring Fragrance, means that it is a good thing to love anyway—even if we can't get what we love, or, as the poet tells us, lose what we love. Of course, one needs experience to feel the truth of this teaching."

The young man smiled pensively and reminiscently. More than a dozen young maidens "loved and lost" were passing before his mind's eye.

"The truth of the teaching!" echoed Mr. Spring Fragrance, a little testily. "There is no truth in it whatever. It is disobedient to reason. Is it not better to have what you do not love than to love what you do not have?"

"That depends," answered the young man, "upon temperament."

"I thank you. Good evening," said Mr. Spring Fragrance. He turned away to muse upon the unwisdom of the American way of looking at things.

Meanwhile, inside the house, Laura was refusing to be comforted.

"Ah, no! no!" cried she. "If I had not gone to school with Kai Tzu, nor talked nor walked with him, nor played the accompaniments to his songs, then I might consider with complacency, or at least without horror, my approaching marriage with the son of Man You. But as it is—oh, as it is—!"

The girl rocked herself to and fro in heartfelt grief.

Mrs. Spring Fragrance knelt down beside her, and clasping her arms around her neck, cried in sympathy:

"Little Sister, oh, Little Sister! Dry your tears—do not despair. A moon has yet to pass before the marriage can take place. Who knows what the stars may have to say to one another during its passing? A little bird has whispered to me—"

For a long time Mrs. Spring Fragrance talked. For a long time Laura listened. When the girl arose to go, there was a bright light in her eyes.

II

MRS. SPRING FRAGRANCE, in San Francisco, on a visit to her cousin, the wife of the herb doctor of Clay Street, was having a good time. She was invited everywhere that the wife of an honorable Chinese merchant could go. There was much to see and hear, including more than a dozen babies who had been born in the families of her friends since she last visited the city of the Golden Gate. Mrs. Spring Fragrance loved babies. She had had two herself, but both had been transplanted into the spirit land before the completion of even one moon. There were also many dinners and the-atre-parties given in her honor. It was at one of the theatre-parties that Mrs. Spring Fragrance met Ah Oi, a young girl who had the reputation of being the prettiest Chinese girl in San Francisco, and the naughtiest. In spite of gossip, however, Mrs. Spring Fragrance took a great fancy to Ah Oi and invited her to a tête-à-tête picnic on the following day. This invitation Ah Oi joyfully accepted. She was a sort of bird girl and never felt so happy as when out in the park or woods.

On the day after the picnic Mrs. Spring Fragrance wrote to Laura Chin Yuen thus:

MY PRECIOUS LAURA,—May the bamboo ever wave. Next week I accompany Ah Oi to the beauteous town of San José. There will we be met by the son of the Illustrious Teacher, and in a little Mission, presided over by a benevolent American priest, the little Ah Oi and the son of the Illustrious Teacher will be joined together in love and harmony—two pieces of music made to complete one another.

The Son of the Illustrious Teacher, having been through an American Hall of Learning, is well able to provide for his orphan bride and fears not the displeasure of his parents, now that he is assured that your grief at his loss will not be inconsolable. He wishes me to waft to you and to Kai Tzu—and the little Ah Oi joins with him—ten thousand rainbow wishes for your happiness.

My respects to your honorable parents, and to yourself, the heart of your loving friend,

JADE SPRING FRAGRANCE

To Mr. Spring Fragrance, Mrs. Spring Fragrance also indited a letter:

GREAT AND HONORED MAN,—Greeting from your plum blos-som,* who is desirous of hiding herself from the sun of your presence for a week of seven days more. My honorable cousin is preparing for the Fifth Moon Festival, and wishes me to compound for the occasion

---

* The plum blossom is the Chinese flower of virtue. It has been adopted by the Japanese, just in the same way as they have adapted the Chinese national flower, the chrysanthemum.

some American "fudge," for which delectable sweet, made by my clumsy hands, you have sometimes shown a slight prejudice. I am enjoying a most agreeable visit, and American friends, as also our own, strive benevolently for the accomplishment of my pleasure. Mrs. Samuel Smith, an American lady, known to my cousin, asked for my accompaniment to a magniloquent lecture the other evening. The subject was "America, the Protector of China!" It was most exhilarating, and the effect of so much expression of benevolence leads me to beg of you to forget to remember that the barber charges you one dollar for a shave while he humbly submits to the American man a bill of fifteen cents. And murmur no more because your honored elder brother, on a visit to this country, is detained under the roof-tree of this great Government instead of under your own humble roof. Console him with the reflection that he is protected under the wing of the Eagle, the Emblem of Liberty. What is the loss of ten hundred years or ten thousand times ten dollars compared with the happiness of knowing oneself so securely sheltered? All of this I have learned from Mrs. Samuel Smith, who is as brilliant and great of mind as one of your own superior sex.

For me it is sufficient to know that the Golden Gate Park is most enchanting, and the seals on the rock at the Cliff House extremely entertaining and amiable. There is much feasting and merry-making under the lanterns in honor of your Stupid Thorn.

I have purchased for your smoking a pipe with an amber mouth. It is said to be very sweet to the lips and to emit a cloud of smoke fit for the gods to inhale.

Awaiting, by the wonderful wire of the telegram message, your gracious permission to remain for the celebration of the Fifth Moon Festival and the making of American "fudge," I continue for ten thousand times ten thousand years,

Your ever loving and obedient woman,

JADE

P.S. Forget not to care for the cat, the birds, and the flowers. Do not eat too quickly nor fan too vigorously now that the weather is warming.

Mrs. Spring Fragrance smiled as she folded this last epistle. Even if he were old-fashioned, there was never a husband so good and kind as hers.

Only on one occasion since their marriage had he slighted her wishes. That was when, on the last anniversary of their wedding, she had signified a desire for a certain jadestone pendant, and he had failed to satisfy that desire.

But Mrs. Spring Fragrance, being of a happy nature, and disposed to look upon the bright side of things, did not allow her mind to dwell upon the jadestone pendant. Instead, she gazed complacently down upon her bejeweled fingers and folded in with her letter to Mr. Spring Fragrance a bright little sheaf of condensed love.

III

MR. SPRING FRAGRANCE sat on his doorstep. He had been reading two letters, one from Mrs. Spring Fragrance, and the other from an elderly bachelor cousin in San Francisco. The one from the elderly bachelor cousin was a business letter, but contained the following postscript:

> Tsen Hing, the son of the Government schoolmaster, seems to be much in the company of your young wife. He is a good-looking youth, and pardon me, my dear cousin;—but if women are allowed to stray at will from under their husbands' mulberry roofs, what is to prevent them from becoming butterflies?

"Sing Foon is old and cynical," said Mr. Spring Fragrance to himself. "Why should I pay any attention to him? This is America, where a man may speak to a woman and a woman listen, without any thought of evil."

He destroyed his cousin's letter and re-read his wife's. Then he became very thoughtful. Was the making of American fudge sufficient reason for a wife to wish to remain a week longer in a city where her husband was not?

The young man who lived in the next house came out to water the lawn.

"Good evening," said he. "Any news from Mrs. Spring Fragrance?"

"She is having a very good time," returned Mr. Spring Fragrance.

"Glad to hear it. I think you told me she was to return the end of this week."

"I have changed my mind about her," said Mr. Spring Fragrance. "I am bidding her remain a week longer, as I wish to give a smoking party during her absence. I hope I may have the pleasure of your company."

"I shall be delighted," returned the young fellow. "But, Mr. Spring Fragrance, don't invite any other white fellows. If you do not I shall be able to get in a scoop. You know, I'm a sort of honorary reporter for the *Gleaner*."

"Very well," absently answered Mr. Spring Fragrance.

"Of course, your friend the Consul will be present. I shall call it 'A high-class Chinese stag party!'

In spite of his melancholy mood, Mr. Spring Fragrance smiled.

"Everything is 'high-class' in America," he observed.

"Sure!" cheerfully assented the young man. "Haven't you ever heard that all Americans are princes and princesses, and just as soon as a foreigner puts his foot upon our shores, he also becomes of the nobility—I mean, the royal family."

"What about my brother in the Detention Pen?" dryly inquired Mr. Spring Fragrance.

"Now, you've got me," said the young man, rubbing his head. "Well, that is a shame—'a beastly shame,' as the Englishman says. But understand, old fellow, we that are real Americans are up against that—even more than you. It is against our principles."

"I offer the real Americans my consolations that they should be compelled to do that which is against their principles."

"Oh, well, it will all come right some day. We're not a bad sort, you know. Think of the indemnity money returned to the Dragon by Uncle Sam."

Mr. Spring Fragrance puffed his pipe in silence for some moments. More than politics was troubling his mind.

At last he spoke. "Love," said he, slowly and distinctly, "comes before the wedding in this country; does it not?"

"Yes, certainly."

Young Carman knew Mr. Spring Fragrance well enough to receive with calmness his most astounding queries.

"Presuming," continued Mr. Spring Fragrance—"presuming that some friend of your father's, living—presuming—in England—has a daughter that he arranges with your father to be your wife. Presuming that you have never seen that daughter, but that you marry her, knowing her not. Presuming that she marries you, knowing you not.—After she marries you and knows you, will that woman love you?"

"Emphatically, no," answered the young man.

"That is the way it would be in America that the woman who marries the man like that—would not love him?"

"Yes, that is the way it would be in America. Love, in this country, must be free, or it is not love at all."

"In China, it is different!" mused Mr. Spring Fragrance.

"Oh, yes, I have no doubt that in China it is different."

"But the love is in the heart all the same," went on Mr. Spring Fragrance.

"Yes, all the same. Everybody falls in love sometime or another. Some"—pensively—"many times."

Mr. Spring Fragrance arose.

"I must go down town," said he.

As he walked down the street he recalled the remark of a business acquaintance who had met his wife and had had some conversation with her: "She is just like an American woman."

He had felt somewhat flattered when this remark had been made. He looked upon it as a compliment to his wife's cleverness; but it rankled in his mind as he entered the telegraph office. If his wife was becoming as an American woman, would it not be possible for her to love as an American woman—a man to whom she was not married? There also floated in is memory the verse which his wife had quoted to the daughter of Chin Yuen. When the telegraph clerk handed him a blank, he wrote this message:

> "Remain as you wish, but remember that 'Tis better to have loved and lost, than never to have loved at all."

∗∗∗

When Mrs. Spring Fragrance received this message, her laughter tinkled like falling water. How droll! How delightful! Here was her husband quoting American poetry in a telegram. Perhaps he had been reading her American poetry books since she had left him! She hoped so. They would lead him to understand her sympathy for her dear Laura and Kai Tzu. She need no longer keep from him their secret. How joyful! It had been such a hardship to refrain from confiding in him before. But discreetness had been most necessary, seeing that Mr. Spring Fragrance entertained as old-fashioned notions concerning marriage as did the Chin Yuen parents. Strange that that should be so, since he had fallen in love with her picture before *ever* he had seen her, just as she had fallen in love with his! And when the marriage veil was lifted and each beheld the other for the first time in the flesh, there had been no disillusion—no lessening of the respect and affection, which those who had brought about the marriage had inspired in each young heart.

Mrs. Spring Fragrance began to wish she could fall asleep and wake to

find the week flown, and she in her own little home pouring tea for Mr.
Spring Fragrance.

IV

MR. SPRING FRAGRANCE was walking to business with Mr. Chin Yuen. As
they walked they talked.

"Yes," said Mr. Chin Yuen, "the old order is passing away, and the new
order is taking its place, even with us who are Chinese. I have finally consented to give my daughter in marriage to young Kai Tzu."

Mr. Spring Fragrance expressed surprise. He had understood that the
marriage between his neighbor's daughter and the San Francisco school-
teacher's son was all arranged.

"So 'twas," answered Mr. Chin Yuen; "but it seems the young renegade,
without consultation or advice, has placed his affections upon some
untrustworthy female, and is so under her influence that he refuses to fulfil
his parents' promise to me for him."

"So!" said Mr. Spring Fragrance. The shadow on his brow deepened.

"But," said Mr. Chin Yuen, with affable resignation, "it is all ordained by
Heaven. Our daughter, as the wife of Kai Tzu, for whom she has long had
a loving feeling, will not now be compelled to dwell with a mother-in-law
and where her own mother is not. For that, we are thankful, as she is our
only one and the conditions of life in this Western country are not as in
China. Moreover, Kai Tzu, though not so much of a scholar as the teacher's
son, has a keen eye for business and that, in America, is certainly much
more desirable than scholarship. What do you think?"

"Eh! What!" exclaimed Mr. Spring Fragrance. The latter part of his companion's remarks had been lost upon him.

That day the shadow which had been following Mr. Spring Fragrance
ever since he had heard his wife quote, "'Tis better to have loved," etc.,
became so heavy and deep that he quite lost himself within it.

At home in the evening he fed the cat, the bird, and the flowers. Then,
seating himself in a carved black chair—a present from his wife on his
last birthday—he took out his pipe and smoked. The cat jumped into his
lap. He stroked it softly and tenderly. It had been much fondled by Mrs.
Spring Fragrance, and Mr. Spring Fragrance was under the impression that
it missed her. "Poor thing!" said he. "I suppose you want her back!" When

he arose to go to bed he placed the animal carefully on the floor, and thus apostrophized it:

"O Wise and Silent One, your mistress returns to you, but her heart she leaves behind her, with the Tommies in San Francisco."

The Wise and Silent One made no reply. He was not a jealous cat.

Mr. Spring Fragrance slept not that night; the next morning he ate not. Three days and three nights without sleep and food went by.

There was a springlike freshness in the air on the day that Mrs. Spring Fragrance came home. The skies overhead were as blue as Puget Sound stretching its gleaming length toward the mighty Pacific, and all the beautiful green world seemed to be throbbing with springing life.

Mrs. Spring Fragrance was never so radiant.

"Oh," she cried light-heartedly, "is it not lovely to see the sun shining so clear, and everything so bright to welcome me?"

Mr. Spring Fragrance made no response. It was the morning after the fourth sleepless night.

Mrs. Spring Fragrance noticed his silence, also his grave face.

"Everything—everyone is glad to see me but you," she declared, half seriously, half jestingly.

Mr. Spring Fragrance set down her valise. They had just entered the house.

"If my wife is glad to see me," he quietly replied, "I also am glad to see her!"

Summoning their servant boy, he bade him look after Mrs. Spring Fragrance's comfort.

"I must be at the store in half an hour," said he, looking at his watch. "There is some very important business requiring attention."

"What is the business?" inquired Mrs. Spring Fragrance, her lip quivering with disappointment.

"I cannot just explain to you," answered her husband.

Mrs. Spring Fragrance looked up into his face with honest and earnest eyes. There was something in his manner, in the tone of her husband's voice, which touched her.

"Yen," said she, "you do not look well. You are not well. What is it?"

Something arose in Mr. Spring Fragrance's throat which prevented him from replying.

"O darling one! O sweetest one!" cried a girl's joyous voice. Laura Chin Yuen ran into the room and threw her arms around Mrs. Spring Fragrance's neck.

"I spied you from the window," said Laura, "and I couldn't rest until I told you. We are to be married next week, Kai Tzu and I. And all through you, all through you—the sweetest jade jewel in the world!"

Mr. Spring Fragrance passed out of the room.

"So the son of the Government teacher and little Happy Love are already married," Laura went on, relieving Mrs. Spring Fragrance of her cloak, her hat, and her folding fan.

Mr. Spring Fragrance paused upon the doorstep.

"Sit down, Little Sister, and I will tell you all about it," said Mrs. Spring Fragrance, forgetting her husband for a moment.

When Laura Chin Yuen had danced away, Mr. Spring Fragrance came in and hung up his hat.

"You got back very soon," said Mrs. Spring Fragrance, covertly wiping away the tears which had begun to fall as soon as she thought herself alone.

"I did not go," answered Mr. Spring Fragrance. "I have been listening to you and Laura."

"But if the business is very important, do not you think you should attend to it?" anxiously queried Mrs. Spring Fragrance.

"It is not important to me now," returned Mr. Spring Fragrance. "I would prefer to hear again about Ah Oi and Man You and Laura and Kai Tzu."

"How lovely of you to say that!" exclaimed Mrs. Spring Fragrance, who was easily made happy. And she began to chat away to her husband in the friendliest and wifeliest fashion possible. When she had finished she asked him if he were not glad to hear that those who loved as did the young lovers whose secrets she had been keeping, were to be united; and he replied that indeed he was; that he would like every man to be as happy with a wife as he himself had ever been and ever would be.

"You did not always talk like that," said Mrs. Spring Fragrance slyly. "You must have been reading my American poetry books!"

"American poetry!" ejaculated Mr. Spring Fragrance almost fiercely, "American poetry is detestable, *abhorrable*!"

"Why! why!" exclaimed Mrs. Spring Fragrance, more and more surprised.

But the only explanation which Mr. Spring Fragrance vouchsafed was a jadestone pendant.

YONE NOGUCHI (1875–1947)

First Japanese author to publish a book of poems in America.

Poet and critic Yone (Yonejirō) Noguchi was the first Japanese-born writer to publish poetry in English in America. Noguchi, known for popularizing haiku, a traditional Japanese poetic genre, was born in 1875 in Tsushima, Japan and studied at Keio Gijuku University in Tokyo. In 1893, he moved to San Francisco, California, where he worked as a journalist, house servant, and assistant for legendary California writer, Joaquín Miller, who had a formative influence on him. His first poems appeared in the July 1896 issue of *The Lark*, San Francisco, which was actually printed in 1897. That year *The Lark's* editor, Gellett Burgess, and publisher William Doxey published Noguchi's first book of poetry, *Seen and Unseen, or Monologues of a Homeless Snail*. In 1897 Doxey also published Noguchi's *The Voice of the Valley*, inspired by his trip to Yosemite. In 1900 he moved first to Chicago and then to the East Coast, where he rewrote the first draft of his novel with the help of an editor, Léonie Gilmour, while consulting with other writers, including Onoto Watanna. In 1904 Noguchi published an invitation to American poets to try writing Japanese haiku, or hokku, as he preferred to call them.

He had several romantic relationships while in America. A correspondence he had begun while still in California with the poet Charles Warren Stoddard became a romantic relationship when they met in 1900. At Stoddard's house he met and fell in love with *Washington Post* journalist Ethel Armes, to whom he became engaged while he was simultaneously in a common-law marriage with Léonie Gilmour. In 1904 Gilmour separated from Noguchi, who returned to Japan, while she moved to Los Angeles. Noguchi's engagement to Armes ended when it became known that Léonie Gilmour had given birth to Noguchi's son, future sculptor Isamu Noguchi. After a brief reconciliation in Japan, Gilmour and Noguchi separated permanently. Noguchi married a Japanese woman, Matsu Takeda.

Noguchi published several volumes of English-language poetry, including *The Pilgrimage* (1909), which contained haiku, and two novels. He became an esteemed professor at Keio University in Tokyo and lectured on Japanese poetry at prestigious English and American universities. He published a critical essay on Watanna's work although he probably did not realize that the Anglo Chinese author's Japanese heritage was an invention.

Noguchi finally reconciled with his estranged son Isamu in 1946. The author of over a hundred books, one third of them in English, and many articles, he died in Japan on July 13, 1947. His influence on American letters can be measured by the popularity of the haiku as a poetic form, which influenced American poets including Ezra Pound. He also encouraged the poet W. B. Yeats to study Noh drama, which led Yeats to try new forms.

From SEEN AND UNSEEN [1897]

LIKE A PAPER LANTERN

"Oh, my friend, thou wilt not come back to me this night!"
I am lonely in this lonely cabin, alas, in the friendless Universe, and
    the snail at my door hides stealishly his horns.
"Oh, for my sake, put forth thy honourable horns!"
To the Eastward, to the Westward? Alas, where is
    Truthfulness?— Goodness?—Light?
The world enveils me; my body itself this night enveils my soul.
Alas, my soul is like a paper lantern, its pastes wetted off under the
    rainy night, in the rainy world.

TO AN UNKNOWN POET

When I am lost in the deep body of the
    mist on the hill,
The world seems built with me as its
    pillar!
Am I the god upon the face of the deep, deepless
    deepness in the Beginning?

WHERE WOULD I GO?

Gliding downward the peace-buried, silence-toned Somewhere,

driven by the gray Melody of the monotonous-rhymed rivulet,—
Eternal chant of perennial spirits,
My soul wrapped in warm darkness, I lost drowsily the memory of times.
Roaming about the harmless sky through the chattering atoms, accompanied by the White Musician—the mountain breeze, more snowy than powdered marble—under poetry-stringed harp,
My weightless soul, round-formed, forgot the fancies of my shuddering passion.
But for the remembering, (nay, for the remembering even in forgetting) the mother,—where would I go?
Ever looking up to the high sky, heart-filled I breathe the Western airs under heavy tears.
My shy soul was consoled then, as if I had drunk my mother's sweet breath, love-frozen, out of the far West.

Alone

Alone!
Though the heaven above breaks down; though the earth spreads around—apart, alone, not even with my own shadow in the world of darkness; with only my withered soul, housed in the tear-rusted body,
As a motherless wind in breathless vale, as a funeral bell stealing down into the unvisible world by a dream-muffled path.
Alone with my own loneliness, with my own reverie.
Alone in this ghost-raining night, my cabin walls dying like formless corpses into the darkness of vacuity.
Alone in this boundless universe, closing my mortal eyes; yet, under the radiant darkness, I am ever awake to the sheeted memory of the past.
Alas, my almost decayed soul picked by the incessant tear-rains, my one desire is to be myself as nothing.

The Boatman

The boatman who waits for a guest at the ferry of night, cries:
"The boat leaves for the City of Wonder!"

"Please, burn a lantern to light the water of night:
Darkness, I am afraid, will bite my bones!"

"My guest, any lantern should be of no use:
Sliding through the darkest loneliness and thought,
You can reach the city of Wonder for the first time.
Oh, my guest, you must not be afraid of night!
Until you are baptized in solitude, my guest,
No ticket for the City of Wonder will be sold to you."

MY UNIVERSE

We roam out,—
Selfless, will-less, virtueless, viceless, passionless, thoughtless, as
     drunken in Dreamland of Dawn, or of Nothing, into visible
     darkness—this world that seems like Being.
We go back again,—
Contentless; despairless,—a thing but of Nothing
Into this unvisible world, or visible, nothing-formed world, as storm-
     winged winds die stealishly away, in the open spiritless face of the
     field.
What about Goodness?
Like the winds above, formless-formed, driving mystery-iced clouds
     into a mountain-mouth.
What about Wisdom?
Like winds, matron-faced, scattering flower seeds around an
     unexpecting land.
The world is round; no-headed, no-footed, having no left side, no right
     side!
And to say *Goodness* is to say *Badness*:
And to say *Badness* is to say *Goodness*.
The world is so filled with names; often the necessity is forgotten,
     often the difference is unnamed!
The Name is nothing!
East is West,
West is East:
South is North,
North is South:
The greatest robber seems like saint:
The cunning man seems like nothing-wanted beast!
Who is the real man in the face of God?

One who has fame not known,
One who has Wisdom not applauded,
One who has Goodness not respected:
One who has n't loved Foolishness strongly!
The good man stands in the world like an unknown god in
    Somewhere; where Goodness, Badness, Wisdom, Foolishness meet
    face to face at the divisionless border between them.

From Japanese Hokkus [1920]

I

What is life? A voice,
A thought, a light on the dark,—
Lo, crow in the sky.

II

Sudden pain of earth
I hear in the fallen leaf.
"Life's autumn," I cry.

III

The silence-leaves from Life,
Older than dream or pain,—
Are they my passing ghost?

IV

Is it not the cry of a rose to be saved?
Oh, how could I
When I, in fact, am the rose!

V

But the march to Life . . .
Break song to sing the new song!
Clouds leap, flowers bloom.

VI

Fallen leaves! Nay, spirits?
Shall I go downward with thee
By a stream of Fate?

VII

Speak not again, Voice!
The silence washes off sins:
Come not again, Light!

VIII

Is it too late to hear a nightingale?
Tut, tut, tut, . . . some bird sings,—
That's quite enough, my friend.

IX

I shall cry to thee across the years?
Wilt thou turn thy face to respond
To my own tears with thy smile?

X

Where the flowers sleep,
Thank God! I shall sleep, to-night.
Oh, come, butterfly!

XI

My Love's lengthened hair
Swings o'er me from Heaven's gate:
Lo, Evening's shadow!

XII

Is there anything new under the sun?
Certainly there is.
See how a bird flies, how flowers smile!

WINNIFRED EATON / ONOTO WATANNA (1875–1954)

First published novel by an Asian American writer.

Winnifred Eaton was the daughter of an English trader and merchant, Edward Eaton. Her Chinese mother, Achuen Amoy, had been born in China and sold as a child to a Chinese acrobat whose performing company toured China, the United States, and Europe starting in 1851. In 1861 Amoy was baptized "Grace" and adopted by English missionaries who moved to Shanghai, where Edward and she, now Grace "Lotus Blossom" Trefusis, married in 1863. A year later they returned to England. In the early 1870s, the family left England to live first in Hudson, New York, and then Montreal, Canada, where Winnifred was born, one of fourteen children. Her father struggled to earn enough as a painter to support the large family, yet her parents remained committed to providing an intellectually stimulating environment for their children.

Eaton published her first story at age twenty (but claiming she was fourteen) in a Montreal newspaper that had already published pieces by her sister, Edith Maude, who became known also under the name Sui Sin Far. Soon Eaton placed articles in popular magazines in the United States, notably the *Ladies' Home Journal*. At twenty-one she moved to Kingston, Jamaica, to work as a writer and reporter for the Jamaican newspaper, *The Kingston,* and after five months relocated to Chicago, Illinois, where she worked as a typist while writing short stories. She decided to publish stories and novels under the pseudonym of an invented, somewhat Japanese-sounding name Onoto Watanna, possibly to escape the strong anti-Chinese sentiment in American culture and to benefit from the public's thirst for Japanese-themed things. Under that name, she published the controversial *Miss Numé of Japan* and became the first writer of Asian descent to reach a mainstream American audience. She would write more than sixteen novels, short stories, ethnographic pieces and poems. She married journalist

Bertrand Whitcomb Babcock in 1901, and parlayed her success with a best-selling second novel that year, *A Japanese Nightingale*, into a Broadway play and film (1919). She had a screenwriting career from 1921–1930 during which time she worked as a writer, editor and literary advisor, under the names Winnifred Eaton Reeve, Winnifred Reeve, Winnifred Eaton Babcock, or Winnifred Babcock, at major studios, among them Universal and Metro-Goldwyn-Mayer. She divorced in 1917, gained custody of her three surviving children, and married businessman Francis Reeve. They moved to his ranch in Alberta, Canada, but Eaton returned to New York at least once to revive her writing career. She lost much of her money in the 1929 stock market crash and, after reconciling with Reeve who had had an adulterous affair in 1931, returned to Calgary, Canada, to live with her family. After World War II Eaton expressed regret for having posed as a Japanese American author. She died in 1954.

Miss Numè of Japan. A Japanese Romance is the fast-paced, gripping story of two couples, Japanese and American, who switch partners in a series of dramatic and romantic incidents. As a writer of Anglo and Chinese descent who assumed a Japanese identity and published stories under a Japanese-sounding pseudonym dealing with interracial romances, Eaton is not easily subsumed into histories of Asian American literature.

From MISS NUMÈ OF JAPAN: A JAPANESE-AMERICAN ROMANCE [1899]

CHAPTER I.
PARENTAL AMBITIONS.

WHEN ORITO, SON of Takashima Sachi, was but ten years of age, and Numè, daughter of Watanabe Omi, a tiny girl of three, their fathers talked quite seriously of betrothing them to each other, for they had been great friends for many years, and it was the dearest wish of their lives to see their children united in marriage. They were very wealthy men, and the father of Orito was ambitious that his son should have an unusually good education, so that when Orito was seventeen years of age, he had left the public school of Tokyo and was attending the Imperial University. About this time, and when Orito was at home on a vacation, there came to the little town where they lived, and which was only a very short distance from Tokyo, certain foreigners from the West, who rented land from Sachi and became neighbors to him and to Omi.

Sachi had always taken a great deal of interest in these foreigners, many of whom he had met quite often while on business in Tokyo, and he was very much pleased with his new tenants, who, in spite of their barbarous manners and dress, seemed good-natured and friendly. Often in the evening he and Omi would walk through the valley to their neighbors' house, and listen to them very attentively while they told them of their home in America, which they said was the greatest country in the world. After a time the strange men went away, though neither Sachi nor Omi forgot them, and very often they talked of them and of their foreign home. One day Sachi said very seriously to his friend:

"Omi, these strangers told us much of their strange land, and talked of the fine schools there, where all manner of learning is taught. What say you that I do send my unworthy son, Orito, to this America, so that he may see much of the world, and also become a great scholar, and later return to crave thy noble daughter in marriage?"

Omi was fairly delighted with this proposal, and the two friends talked and planned, and then sent for the lad.

Orito was a youth of extreme beauty. He was tall and slender; his face was pale and oval, with features as fine and delicate as a girl's. His was not merely a beautiful face; there was something else in it, a certain impassive look that rendered it almost startling in its wonderful inscrutableness. It was not expressionless, but unreadable—the face of one with the noble blood of the Kazoku and Samourai—pale, refined, and emotionless.

He bowed low and courteously when he entered, and said a few words of gentle greeting to Omi, in a clear, mellow voice that was very pleasing. Sachi's eyes sparkled with pride as he looked on his son. Unlike Orito, he was a very impulsive man, and without preparing the boy, he hastened to tell him at once of their plans for his future. While his father was speaking Orito's face did not alter from its calm, grave attention, although he was unusually moved. He only said, "What of Numè, my father?"

Sachi and Omi beamed on him.

"When you return from this America I will give you Numè as a bride," said Omi.

"And when will that be?" asked Orito, in a low voice.

"In eight years, my son, and you shall have all manner of learning there, which cannot be acquired here in Tokyo or in Kyushu, and the manner of learning will be different from that taught anywhere in Japan. You will have a foreign education, as well as what you have learned here at home. It shall be thorough, and therefore it will take some years. You must prepare at once, my son; I desire it."

Orito bowed gracefully and thanked his father, declaring it was the chief desire of his life to obey the will of his parent in all things.

Now Numè was a very peculiar child. Unlike most Japanese maidens, she was impetuous and wayward. Her mother had died when she was born, and she had never had any one to guide or direct her, so that she had grown up in a careless, happy fashion, worshiped by her father's servants, but depending entirely upon Orito for all her small joys. Orito was her only companion and friend, and she believed blindly in him. She told him all her little troubles, and he in turn tried to teach her many things, for, although their fathers intended to betroth them to each other as soon as they were old enough, still Numè was only a little girl of ten, whilst Orito was a tall man-youth of nearly eighteen years. They loved each other very dearly; Orito loved Numè because she was one day to be his little wife, and because she was very bright and pretty; whilst Numè loved big Orito with a pride that was pathetic in its confidence.

That afternoon Numè waited long for Orito to come, but the boy had gone out across the valley, and was wandering aimlessly among the hills, trying to make up his mind to go to Numè and tell her that in less than a week he must leave her, and his beautiful home, for eight long years. The next day a great storm broke over the little town, and Numè was unable to go to the school, and because Orito had not come she became very restless and wandered fretfully about the house. So she complained bitterly to her father that Orito had not come. Then Omi, forgetting all else save the great future in store for his prospective son-in-law, told her of their plans. And Numè listened to him, not as Orito had done, with quiet, calm face, for hers was stormy and rebellious, and she sprang to her father's side and caught his hands sharply in her little ones, crying out passionately:

"No! no! my father, do not send Orito away."

Omi was shocked at this display of unmaidenly conduct, and arose in a dignified fashion, ordering his daughter to leave him, and Numè crept out, too stunned to say more. About an hour after that Orito came in, and discovered her rolled into a very forlorn little heap, with her head on a cushion, and weeping her eyes out.

"You should not weep, Numè," he said. "You should rather smile, for see, I will come back a great scholar, and will tell you of all I have seen—the people I have met—the strange men and women." But at that Numè pushed him from her, and declared she wanted not to hear of those barbarians, and flashed her eyes wrathfully at him, whereat Orito assured her that none of them would be half as beautiful or sweet as his little Numè—his plum blossom; for the word Numè means plum blossom in Japanese. Finally Numè promised to be very brave, and the day Orito left she only wept when no one could see her.

And so Orito sailed for America, and entered a great college called "Harvard." And little Numè remained in Japan, and because there was no Orito now to tell her thoughts to, she grew very subdued and quiet, so that few would have recognized in her the merry, wayward little girl who had followed Orito around like his very shadow. But Numè never forgot Orito for one little moment, and when every one else in the house was sound asleep, she would lie awake thinking of him.

CHAPTER II.
CLEO.

"No use looking over there, my dear. Takie has no heart to break—never knew a Jap that had, for that matter—cold sort of creatures, most of them."

The speaker leaned nonchalantly against the guard rail, and looked half-amusedly at the girl beside him. She raised her head saucily as her companion addressed her, and the willful little toss to her chin was so pretty and wicked that the man laughed outright.

"No need for *you* to answer in words," he said. "That wicked, willful look of yours bodes ill for the Jap's—er—heart."

"I would like to know him," said the girl, slowly and quite soberly. "Really, he is very good-looking."

"Oh! yes—I suppose so—for a Japanese," her companion interrupted.

The girl looked at him in undisguised disgust for a moment.

"How ignorant you are, Tom!" she said, impatiently; "as if it makes the slightest difference *what* nationality he belongs to. Mighty lot *you* know about the Japanese."

Tom wilted before this assault, and the girl took advantage to say: "Now, Tom, I want to know Mr.—a—a—Takashima. *What* a name! Go, like the dear good boy you are, and bring him over here."

Tom straightened his shoulders.

"I utterly, completely, and altogether *refuse* to introduce you, young lady, to any other man on board this steamer. Why, at the rate you're going there won't be a heart-whole man on board by the time we reach Japan."

"But you said Mr. Ta—Takashima—or 'Takie,' as you call him, had no heart."

"True, but you might create one in him. I have a great deal of confidence in you, you know."

"Oh! Tom, *don't* be ridiculous now. Horrid thing! I believe you just want to be coaxed."

Tom's good-natured, fair face expanded in a broad smile for a moment. Then he tried to clear it.

"*Always* disliked to be coaxed," he choked.

"Hem!" The girl looked over into the waters a moment, thinking. Then she rose up and looked Tom in the face.

"Tom, if you don't I'll go over and speak to him without an introduction."

"Better try it," said Tom, aggravatingly. "Why, you'd shock him so much he wouldn't get over it for a year. You don't know these Japs as I do, my dear—dozens of them at our college—awfully strict on subject of etiquette, manners, and all that folderol."

"Yes, but I'd tell him it was an American custom."

"Can't fool Takashima, my dear. Been in America eight years now—knows a thing or two, I guess."

Takashima, the young Japanese, looked over at them, with the unreadable, quiet gaze peculiar to the better class Japanese. His eyes loitered on the girl's beautiful face, and he moved a step nearer to them, as a gentleman in passing stood in front, and for a moment hid them from him.

"He is looking at us now," said the girl, innocently.

Tom stared at her round-eyed for a moment.

"How on earth do you know that? Your head is turned right from him."

Again the saucy little toss of the chin was all the girl's answer.

"He's right near us now. Tom, please, please—now's your chance," she added, after a minute.

The Japanese had come quite close to them. He was still looking at the girl's face, as though thoroughly fascinated with its beauty. A sudden wind came up from the sea and caught the red cape she wore, blowing it wildly about her. It shook the rich gold of her hair in wondrous soft shiny waves about her face, as she tried vainly to hold the little cap on her head. It was a sudden wild wind, such as one often encounters at sea, lasting only for a moment, but in that moment almost lifting one from the deck. The girl, who had been clinging breathlessly to the railing, turned toward

Takashima, her cheeks aflame with excitement, and as the violent gust subsided, they smiled in each other's faces.

Tom relented.

"Hallo! Takie—you there?" he said, cordially. "Thought you'd be laid up. You're a pretty good sailor, I see." Then he turned to the girl and said very solemnly and as if they had never even discussed the subject of an intro-duction, "Cleo, this is my old college friend, Mr. Takashima—Takie, my cousin, Miss Ballard."

"Will you tell me why," said the young Japanese, very seriously, "you did not want that I should know your cousin?"

"Don't mind Tom," the girl answered, with embarrassment, as that gen-tleman threw away his cigar deliberately; and she saw by his face that he intended saying something that would mislead Takashima, for he had often told her of the direct, serious and strange questions the Japanese would ask, and how he was in the habit of leading him off the track, just for the fun of the thing, and because Takashima took everything so seriously.

"Why—a—" said Tom, "the truth of the matter is—my cousin is a—a flirt!"

"Tom!" said the girl, with flaming cheeks.

"A flirt!" repeated the Japanese, half-musingly. "Ah! I do not like a flirt—that is not a nice word," he added, gently.

"Tom is just teasing me," she said; and added, "But how did you know Tom did not want you to know me?"

"I heard you tell him that you want to know me, and I puzzle much myself why he did not want."

"I was sorry for you in advance, Takie," said Tom, wickedly, and then seeing by the girl's face that she was getting seriously offended, he added: "Well, the truth is—er—Cleo—is—a so—young, don't you know. One can't introduce their female relatives to many of their male friends. You under-stand. That's how you put it to me once."

"Yes!" said Takashima, "I remember that I tell you of that. Then I am most flattered to know your relative."

As Tom moved off and left them together, feeling afraid to trust him-self for fear he would make things worse, he heard the gentle voice of the Japanese saying very softly to the girl:

"I am most glad that you do not flirt. I do not like that word. Is it American?"

Tom chuckled to himself, and shook his fist, in mock threat, at Cleo.

YONE NOGUCHI (1875–1947)

First novel published by a Japanese author in America.

The American Diary of a Japanese Girl was first published in two installments in a magazine in 1901, and then republished as a novel, with illustrations by Genjiro Yeto, in 1902. Marketed as the authentic diary of an eigh-
teen-year-old female visitor to the United States, most readers assumed that
the book was the real-life confessional diary by a young Japanese woman
although many such books and stories were known to be fabrications. The
story of a young Japanese woman offering her candid first impressions of
the United States while reflecting on mundane matters as well as racial
prejudices, social customs, and the prospects of love intrigued readers.
Noguchi deployed some American stereotypes about Japanese women
found in works like Gilbert and Sullivan's 1880s opera *Mikado,* John Luther
Long's *Madame Butterfly* (1898), Onoto Watanna's *Miss Numé of Japan,* and
A Japanese Nightingale in order to cleverly undermine such caricatures. The
Japanese woman's love interest in a white man can be read in the context
of common state laws against interracial marriage, which was first ruled
unconstitutional in a 1948 California Supreme Court decision. Noguchi
treats his heroine with a deep sense of irony, which perhaps places the
novel more into the tradition of subversive modernist fiction than of Asian
American literature.

From THE AMERICAN DIARY OF A JAPANESE GIRL [1902]

BEFORE I SAILED
TOKIO, SEPT. 23RD

My new page of life is dawning.
A trip beyond the seas—Meriken Kenbutsu—it's not an ordinary event.

It is verily the first event in our family history that I could trace back for six centuries.

My to-day's dream of America—dream of a butterfly sipping on golden dews—was rudely broken by the artless chirrup of a hundred sparrows in my garden.

"Chui, chui! Chui, chui, chui!"

Bad sparrows!

My dream was silly but splendid.

Dream is no dream without silliness which is akin to poetry.

If my dream ever comes true!

24th—The song of gay children scattered over the street had subsided. The harvest moon shone like a yellow halo of "Nono Sama." All things in blessed Mitsuho No Kuni—the smallest ant also—bathed in sweet inspiring beams of beauty. The soft song that is not to be heard but to be felt, was in the air.

'Twas a crime, I judged, to squander lazily such a gracious graceful hour within doors.

I and my maid strolled to the Konpira shrine.

Her red stout fingers—like sweet potatoes—didn't appear so bad tonight, for the moon beautified every ugliness.

Our Emperor should proclaim forbidding woman to be out at any time except under the moonlight.

Without beauty woman is nothing. Face is the whole soul. I prefer death if I am not given a pair of dark velvety eyes.

What a shame even woman must grow old!

One stupid wrinkle on my face would be enough to stun me.

My pride is in my slim fingers of satin skin.

I'll carefully clean my roseate finger-nails before I'll land in America.

Our wooden clogs sounded melodious, like a rhythmic prayer unto the sky. Japs fit themselves to play music even with footgear. Every house with a lantern at its entrance looked a shrine cherishing a thousand idols within.

I kneeled to the Konpira god.

I didn't exactly see how to address him, being ignorant what sort of god he was.

I felt thirsty when I reached home. Before I pulled a bucket from the well, I peeped down into it. The moonbeams were beautifully stealing into the waters.

My tortoise-shell comb from my head dropped into the well.

The waters from far down smiled, heartily congratulating me on going to Amerikey.

25th—I thought all day long how I'll look in 'Merican dress.

26th—My shoes and six pairs of silk stockings arrived.

How I hoped they were Nippon silk!

One pair's value is 4 yens.

Extravagance! How dear!

I hardly see any bit of reason against bare feet.

Well, of course, it depends on how they are shaped.

A Japanese girl's feet are a sweet little piece. Their flatness and artlessness manifest their pathetic womanliness.

Feet tell as much as palms.

I have taken the same laborious care with my feet as with my hands. Now they have to retire into the heavy constrained shoes of America.

It's not so bad, however, to slip one's feet into gorgeous silk like that.

My shoes are of superior shape. They have a small high heel.

I'm glad they make me much taller.

A bamboo I set some three Summers ago cast its unusually melancholy shadow on the round paper window of my room, and whispered, "Sara! Sara! Sara!" It sounded to me like a pallid voice of sayonara.

(By the way, the profuse tips of my bamboo are like the ostrich plumes of my new American hat.)

"Sayonara" never sounded before more sad, more thrilling.

My good-bye to "home sweet home" amid the camellias and white chrysanthemums is within ten days. The steamer "Belgic" leaves Yokohama on the sixth of next month. My beloved uncle is chaperon during my American journey.

27th—I scissored out the pictures from the 'Merican magazines.

(The magazines were all tired-looking back numbers. New ones are serviceable in their own home. Forgotten old actors stray into the villages for an inglorious tour. So it is with the magazines. Only the useless numbers come to Japan, I presume.)

The pictures—Meriken is a country of woman; that's why, I fancy, the pictures are chiefly of woman—showed me how to pick up the long skirt. That one act is the whole "business" of looking charming on the street. I apprehend that the grace of American ladies is in the serpentine curves of the figure, in the narrow waist.

Woman is the slave of beauty.

I applied my new corset to my body. I pulled it so hard.

It pained me.

28th—My heart was a lark.

I sang, but not in a trembling voice like a lark, some slices of school song.

I skipped around my garden.

Because it occurred to me finally that I'll appear beautiful in my new costume.

I smiled happily to the sunlight whose autumnal yellow flakes—how yellow they were!—fell upon my arm stretched to pluck a chrysanthemum.

I admit that my arm is brown.

But it's shapely.

29th—English of America—sir, it is light, unreserved and accessible—grew dear again. My love of it returned like the glow in a brazier that I had watched passionately, then left all the Summer days, and to which I turned my apologetic face with Winter's approaching steps.

Oya, oya, my book of Longfellow under the heavy coat of dust!

I dusted the book with care and veneration as I did a wee image of the Lord a month ago.

The same old gentle face of 'Merican poet—a poet need not always to sing, I assure you, of tragic lamentation and of "far-beyond"—stared at me from its frontispiece. I wondered if he ever dreamed his volume would be opened on the tiny brown palms of a Japan girl. A sudden fancy came to me as if he—the spirit of his picture—flung his critical impressive eyes at my elaborate cue with coral-headed pin, or upon my face.

Am I not a lovely young lady?

I had thrown Longfellow, many months ago, on the top shelf where a grave spider was encamping, and given every liberty to that reticent, studious, silver-haired gentleman Mr. Moth to tramp around the "Arcadie."

Mr. Moth ran out without giving his own "honourable" impression of the popular poet, when I let the pages flutter.

Large fatherly poet he is, but not unique. Uniqueness, however, has become commonplace.

Poet of "plain" plainness is he—plainness in thought and colour. Even his elegance is plain enough.

I must read Mr. Longfellow again as I used a year ago reclining in the Spring breeze,—"A Psalm of Life," "The Village Blacksmith," and half a dozen snatches from "Evangeline" or "The Song of Hiawatha" at the least. That is not because I am his devotee—I confess the poet of my taste isn't he—but only because he is a great idol of American ladies, as I am often told, and I may suffer the accusation of idiocy in America, if I be not charming enough to quote lines from his work.

30th—Many a year I have prayed for something more decent than a marriage offer.

I wonder if the generous destiny that will convey me to the illustrious country of "woman first" isn't the "something."

I am pleased to sail for Amerikey, being a woman.

Shall I have to become "naturalized" in America?

The Jap "gentleman"—who desires the old barbarity—persists still in fancying that girls are trading wares.

When he shall come to understand what is Love!

Fie on him!

I never felt more insulted than when I was asked in marriage by one unknown to me.

No Oriental man is qualified for civilisation, I declare.

Educate man, but—beg your pardon—not the woman!

Modern gyurls born in the enlightened period of Meiji are endowed with quite a remarkable soul.

I act as I choose. I haven't to wait for my mamma's approval to laugh when I incline to.

Oct. 1st—I stole into the looking glass—woman loses almost her delight in life if without it—for the last glimpse of my hair in Japan style.

Butterfly mode!

I'll miss it adorning my small head, while I'm away from home.

I have often thought that Japanese display Oriental rhetoric—only oppressive rhetoric that palsies the spirit—in hair dressing. Its beauty isn't animation.

I longed for another new attraction on my head.

I felt sad, however, when I cut off all the paper cords from my hair.

I dreaded that the American method of dressing the hair might change my head into an absurd little thing.

My lengthy hair languished over my shoulders.

I laid me down on the bamboo porch in the pensive shape of a mermaid fresh from the sea.

The sportive breezes frolicked with my hair. They must be mischievous boys of the air.

I thought the reason why Meriken coiffure seemed savage and without art was mainly because it prized more of natural beauty.

Naturalness is the highest of all beauties.

Sayo shikaraba! Let me learn the beauty of American freedom, starting with my hair!

Are you sure it's not slovenliness?

Woman's slovenliness is only forgiven where no gentleman is born.

2nd—Occasional forgetfulness, I venture to say, is one of woman's charms.

But I fear too many lapses in my case fill the background.

I amuse myself sometimes fancying whether I shall forget my husband's name (if I ever have one).

How shall I manage "shall" and "will"? My memory of it is faded.

I searched for a printed slip, "How to use Shall and Will." I pressed to explore even the pantry after it.

Afterward I recalled that Professor asserted that Americans were not precise in grammar. The affirmation of any professor isn't weighty enough. But my restlessness was cured somehow.

"This must be the age of Jap girls!" I ejaculated.

I was reading a paper on our bamboo land, penned by Mr. Somebody.

The style was inferior to Irving's. I have read his gratifying "Sketch Book." I used to sleep holding it under my wooden pillow.

Woman feels happy to stretch her hand even in dream, and touch something that belongs to herself. "Sketch Book" was my child for many, many months.

Mr. Somebody has lavished adoring words over my sisters.

Arigato! Thank heavens!

If he didn't declare, however, that "no sensible musume will prefer a foreign raiment to her kimono!"

He failed to make of me a completely happy nightingale.

Shall I meet the Americans in our flapping gown?

I imagined myself hitting off a tune of "Karan Coron" with clogs, in circumspect steps, along Fifth Avenue of somewhere. The throng swarmed around me. They tugged my silken sleeves, which almost swept the ground, and inquired, "How much a yard?" Then they implored me to sing some Japanese ditty.

I'll not play any sensational rôle for any price.

Let me remain a homely lass, though I express no craft in Meriken dress.

Do I look shocking in a corset?

"In Pekin you have to speak Makey Hey Rah" is my belief.

3rd—My hand has seldom lifted anything weightier than a comb to adjust my hair flowing down my neck.

The "silver" knife (large and sharp enough to fight the Russians) dropped and cracked a bit of the rim of the big plate.

My hand tired.

My uncle and I were seated at a round table in a celebrated American restaurant, the "Western Sea House."

It was my first occasion to face an orderly heavy Meriken table d'hote.

Its fertile taste was oily, the oppressive smell emetic.

Must I make friends with it?

I am afraid my small stomach is only fitted for a bowl of rice and a few cuts of raw fish.

There is nothing more light, more inviting, than Japanese fare. It is like a sweet Summer villa with many a sliding shoji from which you smile into the breeze and sing to the stars.

Lightness is my choice.

When, I wondered, could I feel at home with American food!

My uncle is a Meriken "toow." He promised to show me a heap of things in America.

He is an 1884 Yale graduate. He occupies the marked seat of the chief secretary of the "Nippon Mining Company." He has procured leave for one year.

What were the questionable-looking fragments on the plate?

Pieces with pock-marks!

Cheese was their honourable name.

My uncle scared me by saying that some "charming" worms resided in them. Pooh, pooh!

They emitted an annoying smell. You have to empty the choicest box of tooth powder after even the slightest intercourse with them.

I dare not make their acquaintance—no, not for a thousand yens.

I took a few of them in my pocket papers merely as a curiosity.

Shall I hang them on the door, so that the pest may not come near to our house?

(Even the pest-devils stay away from it, you see.)

4th—The "Belgic" makes one day's delay. She will leave on the seventh. "Why not one week?" I cried.

I pray that I may sleep a few nights longer in my home. I grow sadder, thinking of my departure.

My mother shouldn't come to the Meriken wharf. Her tears may easily stop my American adventure.

I and my maid went to our Buddhist monastery.

I offered my good-bye to the graves of my grandparents. I decked them with elegant bunches of chrysanthemums.

When we turned our steps homeward the snowy-eyebrowed monk—how unearthly he appeared!—begged me not to forget my family's church while I am in America.

"Christians are barbarians. They eat beef at funerals," he said.

His voice was like a chant.

The winds brought a gush of melancholy evening prayer from the temple.

The tolling of the monastery bell was tragic.

"Goun! Goun! Goun!"

5th—A "chin koro" barked after me.

The Japanese little doggie doesn't know better. He has to encounter many a strange thing.

The tap of my shoes was a thrill to him. The rustling of my silk skirt—such a volatile sound—sounded an alarm to him.

I was hurrying along the road home from uncle's in Meriken dress.

What a new delight I felt to catch the peeping tips of my shoes from under my trailing koshi goromo.

I forced my skirt to wave, coveting a more satisfactory glance.

Did I look a suspicious character?

I was glad, it amused me to think the dog regarded me as a foreign girl.

Oh, how I wished to change me into a different style! Change is so pleasing.

My imitation was clever. It succeeded.

When I entered my house my maid was dismayed and said:

"Bikkuri shita! You terrified me. I took you for an ijin from Meriken country."

"Ho, ho! O ho, ho, ho!"

I passed gracefully (like a princess making her triumphant exit in the fifth act) into my chamber, leaving behind my happiest laughter and shut myself up.

I confess that I earned the most delicious moment I have had for a long time.

I cannot surrender under the accusation that Japs are only imitators, but I admit that we Nippon daughters are suited to be mimics.

Am I not gifted in the adroit art?

Where's Mr. Somebody who made himself useful to warn the musumes?

Then I began to rehearse the scene of my first interview with a white lady at San Francisco.

I opened Bartlett's English Conversation Book, and examined it to see if what I spoke was correct.

I sat on the writing table. Japanese houses set no chairs.

(Goodness, mottainai! I sat on the great book of Confucius.)

The mirror opposite me showed that I was a "little dear."

6th—It rained.

Soft, woolen Autumn rain like a gossamer!

Its suggestive sound is a far-away song which is half sob, half odor. The October rain is sweet sad poetry.

I slid open a paper door.

My house sits on the hill commanding a view over Tokio and the Bay of Yedo.

My darling city—with an eternal tea and cake, with lanterns of festival—looked up to me through the gray veil of rain.

I felt as if Tokio were bidding me farewell.

Sayonara! My dear city!

AMEEN RIHANI (1876–1940)

First novel published by an Arab American in the United States.

Ameen Rihani was a poet, writer, diplomat and intellectual, who wrote and published in both English and Arabic. He was born in 1876 in Lebanon and spent his teenage years in New York, where, with his friend and fellow Lebanese-born author Kahlil Gibran, he contributed to the literary and cultural circles of the time. He was a popular writer in the United States during his lifetime and remains widely read in the Middle East to this day. *The Book of Khalid*, published in 1911, is one of several works in which Rihani introduces American readers to Arab history and culture. It is the first Arab American novel published in the United States and is today considered the foundation of Arab American literature.

"What the Arabs always said of Andalusia, Khalid and Shakib said once of America: a most beautiful country with one single vice—it makes foreigners forget their native land." Rihani's novel, *The Book of Khalid*, counters beautifully and slyly that sentence found in the novel when his characters recall their native lands. It recounts the travails, hopes, and desires of two young men from Lebanon, Khalid and Shakib, who immigrate at the beginning of the twentieth century to the Little Syria neighborhood in Lower Manhattan in New York. They sail across the Atlantic, pass through Ellis Island and make their lives by working and contributing to the political and cultural world of New York City. They are armed with the particular perspective of young Arab men with a deep interest in philosophy, keen observation, and a sense of humor. After some years the two protagonists return to Lebanon where, inspired by their American experiences, they become social and political revolutionaries in a conflict with the ruling Ottoman Empire. Told with compassion, irony and wit, and a particular kind of wisdom, Rihani's book inspired Kahlil Gibran, who provided the first illustrations for the novel, to write his global bestseller *The Prophet* (1923).

From THE BOOK OF KHALID [1911]

From CHAPTER II
THE CITY OF BAAL

[…] AND NOW, WARMING himself on the fire of his first ideal, Khalid will seek the shore and launch into unknown seas towards unknown lands. From the City of Baal to the City of Demiurgic Dollar is not in fact a far cry. It has been remarked that he always dreamt of adventures, of long journeys across the desert or across the sea. He never was satisfied with the seen horizon, we are told, no matter how vast and beautiful. His soul always yearned for what was beyond, above or below, the visible line. And had not the European tourist alienated from him the love of his mare and corrupted his heart with the love of gold, we might have heard of him in Mecca, in India, or in Dahomey. But Shakib prevails upon him to turn his face toward the West. One day, following some tourists to the Cedars, they behold from Dahr'ul-Qadhib the sun setting in the Mediterranean and make up their minds to follow it too. "For the sundown," writes Shakib, "was more appealing to us than the sunrise, ay, more beautiful. The one was so near, the other so far away. Yes, we beheld the Hesperian light that day, and praised Allah. It was the New World's bonfire of hospitality: the sun called to us, and we obeyed."

CHAPTER III
VIA DOLOROSA

IN THEIR BAGGY, lapping trousers and crimson caps, each carrying a bundle and a rug under his arm, Shakib and Khalid are smuggled through the port of Beirut at night, and safely rowed to the steamer. Indeed, we are in a country where one can not travel without a passport, or a password, or a little pass-money. And the boatmen and officials of the Ottoman Empire can better read a gold piece than a passport. So, Shakib and Khalid, not having the latter, slip in a few of the former, and are smuggled through. One more longing, lingering glance behind, and the dusky peaks of the Lebanons, beyond which their native City of Baal is sleeping in peace, recede from view. On the high sea of hope and joy they sail; "under the Favonian wind of enthusiasm, on the friendly billows of boyish dreams," they roll. Ay, and they sing for joy. On and on, to the gold-swept shores of distant lands, to the generous cities and the bounteous fields of the West, to the Paradise of the World—to America.

We need not dwell too much with our Scribe, on the repulsive details of the story of the voyage. We ourselves have known a little of the suffering and misery which emigrants must undergo, before they reach that Western Paradise of the Oriental imagination. How they are huddled like sheep on deck from Beirut to Marseilles; and like cattle transported under hatches across the Atlantic; and bullied and browbeaten by rough disdainful stewards; and made to pay for a leathery gobbet of beef and a slice of black flint-like bread: all this we know. But that New World paradise is well worth these passing privations.

The second day at sea, when the two Baalbekian lads are snug on deck, their rugs spread out not far from the stalls in which Syrian cattle are shipped to Egypt and Arab horses to Europe or America, they rummage in their bags—and behold, a treat! Shakib takes out his favourite poet Al-Mutanabbi, and Khalid, his favourite bottle, the choicest of the Ksarah distillery of the Jesuits. For this whilom donkey-boy will begin by drinking the wine of these good Fathers and then their—blood! His lute is also with him; and he will continue to practise the few lessons which the bulbuls of the poplar groves have taught him. No, he cares not for books. And so, he uncorks the bottle, hands it to Shakib his senior, then takes a nip himself, and, thrumming his lute strings, trolls a few doleful pieces of Arabic song. "In these," he would say to Shakib, pointing to the bottle and the lute, "is real poetry, and not in that book with which you would kill me." And Shakib, in stingless sarcasm, would insist that the music in Al-Mutanabbi's lines is just a little more musical than Khalid's thrumming. They quarrel about this. And in justice to both, we give the following from the *Histoire Intime.*

"When we left our native land," Shakib writes, "my literary bent was not shared in the least by Khalid. I had gone through the higher studies which, in our hedge-schools and clerical institutions, do not reach a very remarkable height. Enough of French to understand the authors tabooed by our Jesuit professors,—the Voltaires, the Rousseaus, the Diderots; enough of Arabic to enable one to parse and analyse the verse of Al-Mutanabbi; enough of Church History to show us, not how the Church wielded the sword of persecution, but how she was persecuted herself by the pagans and barbarians of the earth;—of these and such like consists the edifying curriculum. Now, of this high phase of education, Khalid was thoroughly immune. But his intuitive sagacity was often remarkable, and his humour, sweet and pathetic. Once when I was reading aloud some of the Homeric effusions of Al-Mutanabbi, he said to me, as he was playing his lute, 'In the heart of this,' pointing to the lute, 'and in the heart of me, there be more poetry than in that book with which you would kill me.' And one day, after wandering clandestinely through the steamer, he comes to me with a gesture of surprise and this: 'Do you know, there are passengers who sleep in bunks below, over and across each other? I saw them, billah! And I was told they pay more than we do for such a low passage—the fools! Think on it. I peeped into a little room, a dingy, smelling box, which had in it six berths placed across and above each other like the shelves of the reed man-chons we build for our silk-worms at home. I wouldn't sleep in one of them, billah! even though they bribe me. This bovine fragrance, the sight of these fine horses, the rioting of the wind above us, should make us forget the bru-tality of the stewards. Indeed, I am as content, as comfortable here, as are their Excellencies in what is called the Salon. Surely, we are above them—at least, in the night. What matters it, then, if ours is called the Fourth Class and theirs the Primo. Wherever one is happy, Shakib, there is the Primo.'"

But this happy humour is assailed at Marseilles. His placidity and stolid indifference are rudely shaken by the sharpers, who differ only from the boatmen of Beirut in that they wear pantaloons and intersperse their Arabic with a jargon of French. These brokers, like rapacious bats, hover around the emigrant and before his purse is opened for the fourth time, the trick is done. And with what ceremony, you shall see. From the steamer the emigrant is led to a dealer in frippery, where he is required to doff his baggy trousers and crimson cap, and put on a suit of linsey-woolsey and a hat of hispid felt: end of First Act; open the purse. From the dealer of frippery, spick and span from top to toe, he is taken to the hostelry, where he is detained a fortnight, sometimes a month, on the pretext of having to wait for the best steamer: end of Second Act; open the purse. From the hos-telry at last to the steamship agent, where they secure for him a third-class passage on a fourth-class ship across the Atlantic: end of Third Act; open the purse. And now that the purse is almost empty, the poor emigrant is permitted to leave. They send him to New York with much gratitude in his heart and a little trachoma in his eyes. The result being that a month later they have to look into such eyes again. But the purse of the distressed emi-grant now being empty,—empty as his hopes and dreams,—the rapacious bats hover not around him, and the door of the verminous hostelry is shut in his face. He is left to starve on the western shore of the Mediterranean.

Ay, even the droll humour and stolidity of Khalid, are shaken, aroused, by the ghoulish greed, the fell inhumanity of these sharpers. And Shakib from his cage of fancy lets loose upon them his hyenas of satire. In a squib describing the bats and the voyage he says: "The voyage to America is the Via Dolorosa of the emigrant; and the Port of Beirut, the verminous hostelries of Marseilles, the Island of Ellis in New York, are the three stations thereof. And if your hopes are not crucified at the third and last station, you pass into the Paradise of your dreams. If they are crucified, alas! The gates of the said Paradise will be shut against you; the doors of the hostelries will be slammed in your face; and with a consolation and a vengeance you will throw yourself at the feet of the sea in whose bosom some charitable Jonah will carry you to your native strands."

And when the emigrant has a surplus of gold, when his capital is such as can not be dissipated on a suit of shoddy, a fortnight's lodging, and a passage across the Atlantic, the ingenious ones proceed with the Fourth Act of *Open Thy Purse*. "Instead of starting in New York as a peddler," they say, unfolding before him one of their alluring schemes, "why not do so as a merchant?" And the emigrant opens his purse for the fourth time in the office of some French manufacturer, where he purchases a few boxes of trinketry,—scapulars, prayer-beads, crosses, jewelry, gewgaws, and such like,—all said to be made in the Holy Land. These he brings over with him as his stock in trade.

Now, Khalid and Shakib, after passing a fortnight in Marseilles, and going through the Fourth Act of the Sorry Show, find their dignity as merchants rudely crushed beneath the hatches of the Atlantic steamer. For here, even the pleasure of sleeping on deck is denied them. The Atlantic Ocean would not permit of it. Indeed, everybody has to slide into their stivy bunks to save themselves from its rising wrath. A fortnight of such unutterable misery is quite supportable, however, if one continues to cherish the Paradise already mentioned. But in this dark, dingy smelling hole of the steerage, even the poets cease to dream. The boatmen of Beirut and the sharpers of Marseilles we could forget; but in this grave among a hundred and more of its kind, set over and across each other, neither the lute nor the little that remained in that Ksarah bottle, could bring us any solace.

We are told that Khalid took up his lute but once throughout the voyage. And this when they were permitted one night to sleep on deck. We are also informed that Khalid had a remarkable dream, which, to our Scribe at least, is not meaningless. And who of us, thou silly Scribe, did not in his boyhood tell his dreams to his mother, who would turn them in her interpretation inside out? But Khalid, we are assured, continued to cherish the belief, even in his riper days, that when you dream you are in Jannat, for instance, you must be prepared to go through Juhannam the following day. A method of interpretation as ancient as Joseph, to be sure. But we quote the dream to show that Khalid should not have followed the setting sun. He should have turned his face toward the desert.

They slept on deck that night. They drank the wine of the Jesuits, repeated, to the mellow strains of the lute, the song of the bulbuls, intoned the verses of Al-Mutanabbi, and, wrapping themselves in their rugs, fell asleep. But in the morning they were rudely jostled from their dreams by a spurt from the hose of the sailors washing the deck. Complaining not, they straggle down to their bunks to change their clothes. And Khalid, as he is doing this, implores Shakib not to mention to him any more that New-World paradise. "For I have dreamt last night," he continues, "that, in the multicoloured robes of an Arab amir, on a caparisoned dromedary, at the head of an immense multitude of people, I was riding through the desert. Whereto and wherefrom, I know not. But those who followed me seemed to know; for they cried, 'Long have we waited for thee, now we shall enter in peace.' And at every oasis we passed, the people came to the gate to meet us, and, prostrating themselves before me, kissed the fringe of my garment. Even the women would touch my boots and kiss their hands, exclaiming, 'Allahu akbar!' And the palm trees, billah! I could see bending towards us that we might eat of their fruits, and the springs seemed to flow with us into the desert that we might never thirst. Ay, thus in triumph we marched from one camp to another, from one oasis to the next, until we reached the City on the Hills of the Cedar Groves. Outside the gate, we were met by the most beautiful of its tawny women, and four of these surrounded my camel and took the reins from my hand. I was then escorted through the gates, into the City, up to the citadel, where I was awaited by their Princess. And she, taking a necklace of cowries from a bag that hung on her breast, placed it on my head, saying, 'I crown thee King of—' But I could not hear the rest, which was drowned by the cheering of the multitudes. And the cheering, O Shakib, was drowned by the hose of the sailors. Oh, that hose! Is it not made in the paradise you harp upon, the paradise we are coming to? Never, therefore, mention it to me more."

This is the dream, at once simple and symbolic, which begins to worry Khalid. "For in the evening of the day he related it to me," writes Shakib, "I found him sitting on the edge of his bunk brooding over I know not what. It was the first time he had the blues. Nay, it was the first time he looked pensive and profound. And upon asking him the reason for this, he said, 'I am thinking of the paper-boats which I used to sail down the stream in Baalbek, and that makes me sad.'"

How strange! And yet, this first event recorded by our Scribe, in which Khalid is seen struggling with the mysterious and unknown, is most significant. Another instance, showing a latent phase, hitherto dormant, in his character, we note. Among the steerage passengers is a Syrian girl who much resembles his cousin Najma. She was sea-sick throughout the voyage, and when she comes out to breathe of the fresh air, a few hours before they enter the harbour of New York, Khalid sees her, and Shakib swears that he saw a tear in Khalid's eye as he stood there gazing upon her. Poor Khalid! For though we are approaching the last station of the Via Dolorosa, though we are nearing the enchanted domes of the wonder-working, wealth-worshipping City, he is inexplicably sad.

And Shakib, directly after swearing that he saw a tear in his eye, writes the following: "Up to this time I observed in my friend only the dominating traits of a hard-headed, hard-hearted boy, stubborn, impetuous, intractable. But from the time he related to me his dream, a change in his character was become manifest. In fact a new phase was being gradually unfolded. Three things I must emphasise in this connection: namely, the first dream he dreamt in a foreign land, the first time he looked pensive and profound, and the first tear he shed before we entered New York. These are keys to the secret chamber of one's soul."

And now, that the doors, by virtue of our Scribe's open-sesames, are thrown open, we enter, *bismillah*.

CHAPTER IV
ON THE WHARF OF ENCHANTMENT

NOT IN OUR make-up, to be sure,—not in the pose which is preceded by the tantaras of a trumpet,—do the essential traits in our character first reveal themselves. But truly in the little things the real self is exteriorised. Shakib observes closely the rapid changes in his co-adventurer's humour, the shadowy traits which at that time he little understood. And now, by applying his palm to his front, he illumines those chambers of which he speaks, and also the niches therein. He helps us to understand the insignificant points which

mark the rapid undercurrents of the seemingly sluggish soul of Khalid. Not
in vain, therefore, does he crystallise for us that first tear he shed in the harbour of Manhattan. But his gush about the recondite beauty of this pearl of
melancholy, shall not be intended upon the gustatory nerves of the Reader.
This then we note—his description of New York harbour.

"And is this the gate of Paradise," he asks, "or the port of some subterres-
trial city guarded by the Jinn? What a marvel of enchantment is everything
around us! What manifestations of industrial strength, what monstrosities
of wealth and power, are here! These vessels proudly putting to sea; these
tenders scurrying to meet the Atlantic greyhound which is majestically
moving up the bay; these barges loading and unloading schooners from
every strand, distant and near; these huge lighters carrying even railroads
over the water; these fire-boats scudding through the harbour shrilling their
sirens; these careworn, grim, strenuous multitudes ferried across from one
enchanted shore to another; these giant structures tickling heaven's sides;
these cable bridges, spanning rivers, uniting cities; and this superterres-
trial goddess, torch in hand—wake up, Khalid, and behold these wonders.
Salaam, this enchanted City! There is the Brooklyn Bridge, and here is the
Statue of Liberty which people speak of, and which are as famous as the
Cedars of Lebanon."

But Khalid is as impassive as the bronze goddess herself. He leans over
the rail, his hand supporting his cheek, and gazes into the ooze. The stolidity of his expression is appalling. With his mouth open as usual, his lips
relaxed, his tongue sticking out through the set teeth,—he looks as if his
head were in a noose. But suddenly he braces up, runs down for his lute,
and begins to serenade—Greater New York?

"On thee be Allah's grace,
Who hath the well-loved face!"

No; not toward this City does his heart flap its wings of song. He is
on another sea, in another harbour. Indeed, what are these wonders as
compared with those of the City of Love? The Statue of Eros there is more
imposing than the Statue of Liberty here. And the bridges are not of iron
and concrete, but of rainbows and—moonshine! Indeed, both these lads
are now on the wharf of enchantment; the one on the palpable, the sensu-
ous, the other on the impalpable and unseen. But both, alas, are suddenly,
but temporarily, disenchanted as they are jostled out of the steamer into
the barge which brings them to the Juhannam of Ellis Island. Here, the

unhappy children of the steerage are dumped into the Bureau of Emigration as—such stuff! For even in the land of equal rights and freedom, we have a right to expect from others the courtesy and decency which we ourselves do not have to show, or do not know.

These are sturdy and adventurous foreigners whom the grumpy officers jostle and hustle about. For neither poverty, nor oppression, nor both together can drive a man out of his country, unless the soul within him awaken. Indeed, many a misventurous cowering peasant continues to live on bread and olives in his little village, chained in the fear of dying of hunger in a foreign land. Only the brave and daring spirits hearken to the voice of discontent within them. They give themselves up to the higher aspirations of the soul, no matter how limited such aspirations might be, regardless of the dangers and hardship of a long sea voyage, and the precariousness of their plans and hopes. There may be nothing noble in renouncing one's country, in abandoning one's home, in forsaking one's people; but is there not something remarkable in this great move one makes? Whether for better or for worse, does not the emigrant place himself above his country, his people and his Government, when he turns away from them, when he goes forth propelled by that inner self which demands of him a new life?

And might it not be a better, a cleaner, a higher life? What say our Masters of the Island of Ellis? Are not these straggling, smelling, downcast emigrants almost as clean inwardly, and as pure, as the grumpy officers who harass and humiliate them? Is not that spirit of discontent which they cherish, and for which they carry the cross, so to speak, across the sea, deserving of a little consideration, a little civility, a little kindness?

Even louder than this Shakib cries out, while Khalid open-mouthed sucks his tongue. Here at the last station, where the odours of disinfectants are worse than the stench of the steerage, they await behind the bars their turn; stived with Italian and Hungarian fellow sufferers, uttering such whimpers of expectancy, exchanging such gestures of hope. Soon they shall be brought forward to be examined by the doctor and the interpreting officer; the one shall pry their purses, the other their eyes. For in this United States of America we want clear-sighted citizens at least. And no cold-purses, if the matter can be helped. But neither the eyes, alas, nor the purses of our two emigrants are conformable to the Law; the former are filled with granulations of trachoma, the latter have been emptied by the sharpers of Marseilles. Which means that they shall be detained for the present; and if within a fortnight nothing turns up in their favour, they shall certainly be deported.

Trachoma! a little granulation on the inner surface of the eyelids, what additional misery does it bring upon the poor deported emigrant? We are asked to shed a tear for him, to weep with him over his blasted hopes, his strangled aspirations, his estate in the mother country sold or mortgaged,— in either case lost,—and his seed of a new life crushed in its cotyledon by the physician who might be short-sighted himself, or even blind. But the law must be enforced for the sake of the clear-sighted citizens of the Republic. We will have nothing to do with these poor blear-eyed foreigners.

And thus our grievous Scribe would continue, if we did not exercise the prerogative of our Editorial Divan. Rather let us pursue our narration. Khalid is now in the hospital, awaiting further development in his case. But in Shakib's, whose eyes are far gone in trachoma, the decision of the Board of Emigration is final, irrevocable. And so, after being detained a week in the Emigration pen, the unfortunate Syrian must turn his face again toward the East. Not out into the City, but out upon the sea, he shall be turned adrift. The grumpy officer shall grumpishly enforce the decision of the Board by handing our Scribe to the Captain of the first steamer returning to Europe—if our Scribe can be found! For this flyaway son of a Phœnician did not seem to wait for the decision of the polyglot Judges of the Emigration Board.

And that he did escape, we are assured. For one morning he eludes the grumpy officer, and sidles out among his Italian neighbours who were per- mitted to land. See him genuflecting now, to kiss the curbstone and thank Allah that he is free. But before he can enjoy his freedom, before he can sit down and chuckle over the success of his escapade, he must bethink him of Khalid. He will not leave him to the mercy of the honourable Agents of the Law, if he can help it. Trachoma, he knows, is a hard case to cure. And in ten days, under the care of the doctors, it might become worse. Straightway, therefore, he puts himself to the dark task. A few visits to the Hospital where Khalid is detained—the patients in those days were not held at Ellis Island—and the intrigue is afoot. On the third or fourth visit, we can not make out which, a note in Arabic is slipt into Khalid's pocket, and with a significant Arabic sign, Shakib takes himself off.

The evening of that very day, the trachoma-afflicted Syrian was absent from the ward. He was carried off by Iblis,—the porter and a few Greenbacks assisting. Yes, even Shakib, who knew only a few English monosyllables, could here make himself understood. For money is one of the two universal languages of the world, the other being love. Indeed, money and love are as eloquent in Turkey and Dahomey as they are in Paris or New York.

And here we reach one of those hedges in the *Histoire Intime* which we must go through in spite of the warning-signs. Between two paragraphs, to be plain, in the one of which we are told how the two Syrians established themselves as merchants in New York, in the other, how and wherefor they shouldered the peddling-box and took to the road, there is a crossed paragraph containing a most significant revelation. It seems that after giving the matter some serious thought, our Scribe came to the conclusion that it is not proper to incriminate his illustrious Master. But here is a confession which a hundred crosses can not efface. And if he did not want to bring the matter to our immediate cognisance, why, we ask, did he not re-write the page? Why did he not cover well that said paragraph with crosses and arabesques? We do suspect him here of chicanery; for by this plausible recantation he would shift the responsibility to the shoulders of the Editor, if the secret is divulged. Be this as it may, no red crosses can conceal from us the astounding confession, which we now give out. For the two young Syrians, who were smuggled out of their country by the boatmen of Beirut, and who smuggled themselves into the city of New York (we beg the critic's pardon; for, being foreigners ourselves, we ought to be permitted to stretch this term, smuggle, to cover an Arabic metaphor, or to smuggle into it a foreign meaning), these two Syrians, we say, became, in their capacity of merchants, smugglers of the most ingenious and most evasive type.

We now note the following, which pertains to their business. We learn that they settled in the Syrian Quarter directly after clearing their merchandise. And before they entered their cellar, we are assured, they washed their hands of all intrigues and were shrived of their sins by the Maronite priest of the Colony. For they were pious in those days, and right Catholics. 'Tis further set down in the *Histoire Intime*:

"We rented a cellar, as deep and dark and damp as could be found. And our landlord was a Teague, nay, a kind-hearted old Irishman, who helped us put up the shelves, and never called for the rent in the dawn of the first day of the month. In the front part of this cellar we had our shop; in the rear, our home. On the floor we laid our mattresses, on the shelves, our goods. And never did we stop to think who in this case was better off. The safety of our merchandise before our own. But ten days after we had settled down, the water issued forth from the floor and inundated our shop and home.

It rose so high that it destroyed half of our capital stock and almost all our furniture. And yet, we continued to live in the cellar, because, perhaps, every one of our compatriot-merchants did so. We were all alike subject to these inundations in the winter season. I remember when the water first rose in our store, Khalid was so hard set and in such a pucker that he ran out capless and in his shirt sleeves to discover in the next street the source of the flood. And one day, when we were pumping out the water he asked me if I thought this was easier than rolling our roofs in Baalbek. For truly, the paving-roller is child's play to this pump. And a leaky roof is better than an inundated cellar."

However, this is not the time for brooding. They have to pump ahead to save what remained of their capital stock. But Khalid, nevertheless, would brood and jabber. And what an inundation of ideas, and what questions!

"Think you," he asks, "that the inhabitants of this New World are better off than those of the Old?—Can you imagine mankind living in a huge cellar of a world and you and I pumping the water out of its bottom?—I can see the palaces on which you waste your rhymes, but mankind live in them only in the flesh. The soul I tell you, still occupies the basement, even the sub-cellar. And an inundated cellar at that. The soul, Shakib, is kept below, although the high places are vacant."

And his partner sputters out his despair; for instead of helping to pump out the water, Khalid stands there gazing into it, as if by some miracle he would draw it out with his eyes or with his breath. And the poor Poet cries out, "Pump! the water is gaining on us, and our shop is going to ruin. Pump!" Whereupon the lazy, absent-minded one resumes pumping, while yearning all the while for the plashing stone-rollers and the purling eaves of his home in Baalbek. And once in a pinch,—they are labouring under a peltering rain,—he stops as is his wont to remind Shakib of the Arabic saying, "From the dripping ceiling to the running gargoyle." He is labouring again under a hurricane of ideas. And again he asks, "Are you sure we are better off here?"

And our poor Scribe, knee-deep in the water below, blusters out curses, which Khalid heeds not. "I am tired of this job," he growls; "the stone-roller never drew so much on my strength, nor did muleteering. Ah, for my dripping ceiling again, for are we not now under the running gargoyle?" And he reverts into a stupor, leaving the world to the poet and the pump.

For five years and more they lead such a life in the cellar. And they do not move out of it, lest they excite the envy of their compatriots. But instead of sleeping on the floor, they stretch themselves on the counters. The rising tide teaches them this little wisdom, which keeps the doctor and Izräil away. Their merchandise, however,—their crosses, and scapulars and prayer-beads,—are beyond hope of recovery. For what the rising tide spares, the rascally flyaway peddlers carry away. That is why they themselves shoulder the box and take to the road. And the pious old dames of the suburbs, we are told, receive them with such exclamations of joy and wonder, and almost tear their coats to get from them a sacred token. For you must remember, they are from the Holy Land. Unlike their goods, they at least are genuine. And every Saturday night, after beating the hoof in the country and making such fabulous profits on their false Holy-Land gewgaws, they return to their cellar happy and content.

"In three years," writes our Scribe, "Khalid and I acquired what I still consider a handsome fortune. Each of us had a bank account, and a check book which we seldom used.... In spite of which, we continued to shoulder the peddling box and tramp along.... And Khalid would say to me, 'A peddler is superior to a merchant; we travel and earn money; our compatriots the merchants rust in their cellars and lose it.' To be sure, peddling in the good old days was most attractive. For the exercise, the gain, the experience— these are rich acquirements."

And both Shakib and Khalid, we apprehend, have been hitherto most moderate in their habits. The fact that they seldom use their check books, testifies to this. They have now a peddleress, Im-Hanna by name, who occupies their cellar in their absence, and keeps what little they have in order. And when they return every Saturday night from their peddling trip, they find the old woman as ready to serve them as a mother. She cooks *mojadderah* for them, and sews the bed-linen on the quilts as is done in the mother country.

"The linen," says Shakib, "was always as white as a dove's wing, when Im-Hanna was with us."

And in the Khedivial Library Manuscript we find this curious note upon that popular Syrian dish of lentils and olive oil.

"*Mojadderah*," writes Khalid, "has a marvellous effect upon my humour and nerves. There are certain dishes, I confess, which give me the blues. Of these, fried eggplants and cabbage boiled with corn-beef on the American system of boiling, that is to say, cooking, I abominate the most. But *mojadderah* has such a soothing effect on the nerves; it conduces to cheerfulness, especially when the raw onion or the leek is taken with it. After a good round pewter platter of this delicious dish and a dozen leeks, I feel as if I could do the work of all mankind. And I am then in such a beatific state of mind that I would share with all mankind my sack of lentils and my pipkin of olive oil. I wonder not at Esau's extravagance, when he saw a steaming mess of it. For what is a birthright in comparison?"

That Shakib also shared this beatific mood, the following quaint picture of their Saturday nights in the cellar, will show.

"A bank account," he writes, "a good round dish of *mojadderah*, the lute for Khalid, Al-Mutanabbi for me,—neither of us could forego his hobby,—and Im-Hanna, affectionate, devoted as our mothers,—these were the joys of our Saturday nights in our underground diggings. We were absolutely happy. And we never tried to measure our happiness in those days, or gauge it, or flay it to see if it be dead or alive, false or real. Ah, the blessedness of that supreme unconsciousness which wrapped us as a mother would her babe, warming and caressing our hearts. We did not know then that happiness was a thing to be sought. We only knew that peddling is a pleasure, that a bank account is a supreme joy, that a dish of *mojadderah* cooked by Im-Hanna is a royal delight, that our dour dark cellar is a palace of its kind, and that happiness, like a bride, issues from all these, and, touching the strings of Khalid's lute, mantles us with song."

SELECTED ADDITIONAL READINGS

For scholarly and critical discussions on authors and texts, consult: jstor.com (digital library of academic journals, books and primary sources); the MLA (Modern Language Association) International Bibliography database; Oxford Academic Journals open access platform, all available via public and academic libraries. The suggestions below provide background information and are meant to be starting points for additional reading.

Anne Bradstreet. For a discussion of Bradstreet in her historical moment, see Rosamond Rosenmeier, *Anne Bradstreet Revisited* (1991); Charlotte Gordon, *Mistress Bradstreet: The Untold Life of America's First Poet* (2005). For discussions of Bradstreet's poetry, see Emily Stipes Watts, *The Poetry of American Women from 1632 to 1945* (1977); Susan Castillo and Ivy Schweitzer, *The Literatures of Colonial America: An Anthology* (2001). For discussions of Bradstreet's status in the canon of poetry, see John Berryman, *Homage to Mistress Bradstreet* (1959); Adrienne Rich, "Anne Bradstreet and Her Poetry" [originally published 1967; with 1979 postscript] in *The Works of Anne Bradstreet 1612-1672*, Jeannine Hensley, ed. (2010); Alan Golding, *From Outlaw to Classic: Canons in American Poetry* (1995); Elaine Showalter, *A Jury of Her Peers: American Women Writers from Anne Bradstreet to Annie Proulx* (2009); Louisa Hall, "The Influence of Anne Bradstreet's Innovative Errors," *Early American Literature* (2015). For a discussion of women's writing in general, with specific discussion of Bradstreet, see Wendy Martin and Sharone Williams, eds., *Routledge Introductions to American Literature: Routledge Introduction to American Women Writers* (2016).

William Hill Brown. For a discussion of the status of Brown's novel as the first American novel, see Jeffrey Rubin-Dorsky, "The Early American Novel," in Emory Elliott, Cathy Davidson, Patrick O'Donnell, Valerie Smith, Christopher Wilson, eds., *The Columbia History of the American Novel* (1991); Cathy N. Davidson, *Revolution and the Word: The Rise of the Novel in America* (2004). For a critical reading of Brown's novel, see Karen A. Weyler, "The Sentimental Novel and the Seductions of Postcolonial Imitation," in J. Gerald Kennedy and Leland S. Person, eds., *The Oxford History of the Novel in English: Volume 5: The American Novel to 1870* (2014).

William Wells Brown. For a general discussion of William Wells Brown, see William Edward Farrison, *William Wells Brown: Author and Reformer* (1969); Curtis W. Wilson, *William Wells Brown and Martin R. Delany: A Reference Guide* (2000); Henry Louis Gates, Jr., and Evelyn Brooks Higginbotham, eds., *African American National Biography* (2008); Ezra Greenspan, *William Wells Brown: An African American Life* (2014). For discussions of *Clotel*, see John Ernest, *Resistance and Reformation in Nineteenth Century African-American Literature: Brown, Wilson, Jacobs, Delany, Douglass, and Harper* (1995); Rafia Zafar, *We Wear the Mask: African Americans Write American Literature, 1760-1870* (1997); Robert Reid-Pharr, *Conjugal Union: The Body, the House, and the Black American* (1999); Ivy Wilson, *Specters of Democracy: Blackness and the Aesthetics of Politics in the Antebellum U.S.* (2011). For discussions of *The Escape: A Leap for Freedom*, see W. Edward Farrison, "Brown's First Drama," *College Language Association Journal*, vol. 2: 2 (1958); Garff B. Wilson, *Three Hundred Years of American Drama and Theatre: From Ye Bare and Ye Cubb to Chorus Line* (1982); James Vernon Hatch, *Black Theatre USA* (1996); Harry J. Elam Jr and David Krasner, eds., *African American Performance and Theater History: A Critical Reader* (2001); John Ernest, ed., William Wells Brown, *The Escape: A Leap for Freedom* (reprint 2001); Linda M. Carter, "William Wells Brown," in Emmanuel S. Nelson, ed., *African American Dramatists: An A-to-Z Guide* (2004).

Sophia Alice Callahan. For discussions of Callahan, see Caroline Thomas Foreman and Muriel H. Wright, "S. Alice Callahan: Author of *Wynema: A Child of the Forest*," *Chronicles of Oklahoma* 33 (1955); A. LaVonne Brown Ruoff, "Early Native American Women Authors: Jane Johnston Schoolcraft, Sarah Winnemucca, S. Alice Callahan, E. Pauline Johnson, and Zitkala-Sa," in Karen Kilcup, ed., *Nineteenth-Century American Women Writers: A Critical Reader* (1998); "S. Alice Callahan," in Sharon M. Harris, Heidi Jacobs, and Jennifer Putzi, eds., *American Prose Writers 1870-1920* (2000); Karen Kilcup, ed., *Native American Women's Writing c.1800-1924: An Anthology* (2012). For specific discussions of the novel, see A. LaVonne Brown Ruoff, "Editor's Introduction," S. *Alice Callahan, Wynema: A Child of the Forest* (1997). For additional readings on Native American literature, see entry under John Rollin Ridge.

Rose Terry Cooke. On "My Visitation," see Elizabeth Ammons, ed., *"How Celia changed her mind" and Selected Stories by Rose Terry Cooke* (1968); Susan Koppelman, ed., *Two Friends and other Nineteenth-Century Lesbian Stories by American Women Writers* (1994); Ralph J. Poole, "Body Rituals: The (Homo)Erotics of Death in Elizabeth Stuart Phelps, Rose Terry Cooke, and Edgar Allan Poe," in Karen Kilcup, ed., *Soft Canons: American Women Writers and Masculine Tradition*

(1999); Kathryn R. Kent , *Making Girls into Women: American Women's Writing and the Rise of Lesbian Identity* (2003); Charles L. Crow, ed., *American Gothic: From Salem Witchcraft to H .P . Lovecraft* (2013). For discussions of how to classify gay and lesbian writing before and after the invention of corresponding social categories, see Lillian Faderman, *Surpassing the Love of Men: Romantic Friendship and Love between Women from the Renaissance to the Present* (1981); Caroll Smith-Rosenberg, *Disorderly Conduct. Visions of Gender in Victorian America* (1985); Terry Castle, *The Literature of Lesbianism* (2003); Kristin M. Comment, "When it ceases to be silly it becomes actually wrong": The Cultural Contexts of Female Homoerotic Desire in Rose Terry Cooke's "My Visitation," in *Legacy* (2009); Natasha Hurley, *Circulating Queerness: Before the Gay and Lesbian Novel* (2018); Travis Foster, "Nineteenth Century Queer Literature," in Scott Herring, ed., *The Cambridge Companion to American Gay and Lesbian Literature* (2015).

Martin Delany. Most writings on Delany focus on his nonfiction and political writings; good introductions are Nell Irvin Painter's profile of Delany in Leon F. Litwack and August Meier, eds., *Black Leaders of the Nineteenth Century* (1988); Jane Campbell, *Mythic Black Fiction: The Transformation of History* (1986); Robert S. Levine, *Martin Robinson Delany: A Documentary Reader* (2003). For discussions of Delany's novel *Blake*, see Ernest John, *Resistance and Reformation in Nineteenth Century African-American Literature: Brown, Wilson, Jacobs, Delany, Douglass, and Harper* (1995); Robert Reid-Pharr, "Violent Ambiguity: Martin Delany, Bourgeois Sadomasochism, and the Production of a Black National Masculinity," in Marcellus Blount and George Philbert Cunningham, eds., *Representing Black Men* (1996).

Frederick Douglass. The Library of Congress has made available searchable online versions of newspapers edited by Douglass. There are several major biographies of Frederick Douglass, including Nathan Irvin Huggins, *Slave and Citizen: The Life of Frederick Douglass (1980)*; William McFeely, *Frederick Douglass* (1991); John Stauffer, *Giants: The Parallel Lives of Frederick Douglass and Abraham Lincoln* (2009); David Blight, *Frederick Douglass: Prophet of Freedom* (2018). For specific discussions of "The Heroic Slave," see Frances Smith Foster, *Witnessing Slavery: The Development of Antebellum Slave Narratives* (1994); Ivy Wilson, *Specters of Democracy: Blackness and the Aesthetics of Politics in the Antebellum U.S.* (2011). A scholarly edition, including contemporary accounts of the historical slave rebellion fictionalized by Douglass and recent criticism, is Robert S. Levine, John Stauffer, and John R. McKivigan, eds., *Frederick Douglass, The Heroic Slave: A Cultural and Critical Edition* (2015).

Sui Sin Far/Edith Maude Eaton. Sui Sin Far's collection *Mrs. Spring Fragrance* has received critical attention especially since her stories were first mentioned in Frank Chin, Jeffrey Chan, Lawson Fusao Inada and Shawn Wong, eds., *Aiiieeeee! An*

Anthology of Asian American Writers (1974). For discussions of Sin Far/Eaton as a writer, see Amy Ling, *Between Worlds: Women Writers of Chinese Ancestry* (1990); Elizabeth Ammons, *Conflicting Stories: American Women Writers at the Turn into the Twentieth Century* (1991); Annette White-Parks, *Sui Sin Far–Edith Maude Eaton: A Literary Biography* (1995); Xiao-huang Yin, "The Voice of a Eurasian," in Yin, *Chinese American Literature since the 1850s* (2000); Mary Chapman, *Becoming Sui Sin Far: Early Fiction, Journalism, and Travel Writing by Edith Maude Eaton* (2016). For a discussion of the works of both Eaton sisters in relation to Asian American literature, see Viet Thanh Nguyen, *Race and Resistance: Literature and Politics in Asian America* (2002). For a discussion of her literary writings, see the introduction and materials in Amy Ling and Annette White-Parks, eds., *Mrs. Spring Fragrance and Other Writings* (1995).

Jupiter Hammon. For information on the recently discovered "An Essay on Slavery," see Cedrick May and Julie McCown, "'An Essay on Slavery': An Unpublished Poem by Jupiter Hammon," in *Early American Literature* (2015). For a comprehensive account and critical introduction to Hammon's work, see Sondra A. O'Neale, *Jupiter Hammon and the Biblical Beginnings of African-American Literature* (1993); Cedrick May, *The Collected Works of Jupiter Hammon, Poems and Essays* (2017). For a discussion of Hammon in the context of early African American writing, see Rosemary Fithian Guruswamy, "'Thou Hast the Holy Word': Jupiter Hammon's Regards to Phillis Wheatley," in Vincent Carretta and Phillip Gould, eds., *Genius in Bondage: Literature of the Early Black Atlantic* (2001); Vincent Carretta, *Unchained Voices: An Anthology of Black Authors in the English-Speaking World of the Eighteenth Century* (2003).

Frances Ellen Watkins Harper. Useful discussions of Harper's poetry and fiction are Hazel V. Carby, *Reconstructing Womanhood: The Emergence of the Afro-American Woman Novelist* (1987); Mary Helen Washington, *Invented Lives: Narratives of Black Women, 1860-1960* (1987); Frances Smith Foster, *A Brighter Coming Day: A Frances Ellen Watkins Harper Reader* (1990); Frances Foster Smith, *Written by Herself: Literary Production by African American Women, 1746-1892* (1993); John Ernest, *Resistance and Reformation in Nineteenth-Century African-American Literature* (1995); Janet Gray, *Race and Time: American Women's Poetics from Antislavery to Racial Modernity* (2004); Mary Loeffelholz, *From School to Salon: Reading Nineteenth-Century American Women's Poetry* (2004); Gene Andrew Jarrett, *African American Literature Beyond Race* (2006). Harper's role in the abolitionist and suffragist movements is discussed in Melba Joyce Boyd, *Discarded Legacy: Politics and Poetics in the Life of Frances E. W. Harper, 1825-1911* (1994); Martha P. Jones, *Vanguard: How Black Women Broke Barriers, Won the Vote, and Insisted on Equality for All* (2020).

Carl Sadakichi Hartmann. Many of Hartmann's numerous writings on art, photography, and cinema, including essays and reviews published in Alfred Stieglitz's *Camera Work* and *Camera Notes*, are held by the University of California at Riverside. Hartmann also published hundreds of articles for a German-language newspaper, *New York Staats-Zeitung*, under various pseudonyms. For an edition of his critical writings, see Jane Weaver, ed., *Sadakichi Hartmann: Critical Modernist. Collected Art Writings* (1991); for a literary sketch, see Luc Sante, *Low Lives: Lures and Snares of Old New York* (2003). For a full biography see George Knox, *The Life and Times of Sadakichi Hartmann 1867-1944* (1970); James S. Peter, *Sadakichi Hartmann: Alien Son* (2017).

George Moses Horton. For a discussion of Horton's writings, see Amanda Page, "George Moses Horton," in William L. Andrews, ed., *The North Carolina Roots of African American Literature: An Anthology* (2006); Carole Lynn Stewart, "George Moses Horton's Freedom: A Temperate Republicanism and a Critical Cosmopolitanism," in Stewart, *Temperance and Cosmopolitanism: African American Reformers in the Atlantic World* (2018). For biographical information on Horton, see Sherman, Joan R. "Horton, George Moses" in Henry Louis Gates, Jr. and Evelyn Brooks Higginbotham, eds., *African American Lives* (2004). A full account of his life and work is Joan Sherman, *The Black Bard of North Carolina: George Moses Horton and his Poetry* (1997).

Robert Hunter. For a discussion of the play in its historical context, see Brooks McNamara, "Robert Hunter and *Androboros*," *Southern Speech Journal* (1964); Michael Warner, *The Letters of the Republic: Publication and the Public Sphere in Eighteenth-Century America* (1990). For a discussion of the play's role in American public life, law and politics, see Peter A. Davis, *From Androboros to the First Amendment. A History of America's First Play* (2015).

Iroquois Creation Myth. Transcribed 1816 by John Norton/Teyoninhokarawen in *The Journal of Major John Norton*. For extensive information on Norton, see Carl F. Klinck and James J. Talman, eds., *The Journal of Major John Norton, 1816* (1970); Jarold Ramsey, *Reading the Fire: The Traditional Indian Literatures of America* (1999). On Norton's heritage and status as a Native American, see Carl Benn, "Missed Opportunities and the Problem of Mohawk Chief John Norton's Cherokee Ancestry," in *Ethnohistory* (2012). For discussions of the status of Native American literature in relation to print culture, see Elizabeth Cook-Lynn, "The American Indian Fiction Writer: 'Cosmopolitanism, Nationalism, The Third World, and Native Sovereignty.'" *Wicazo Sa Review* 9:2 (1993); Wasiyatawin Angela Wilson and Michael Yellow Bird, *For Indigenous Eyes Only: A Decolonization Handbook* (2005).

Susette LaFlesche/Inshata Theumba. For biographical information, see Norma Kidd Green, *Iron Eye's Family: The Children of Joseph LaFlesche* (1969); Dorothy

Clarke Wilson, *Bright Eyes: The Story of Susette LaFlesche, An Omaha Indian* (1974); Jerry E. Clark and Martha Ellen Webb, "Susette and Susan LaFlesche: Reformer and Missionary," in James A. Clifton, ed., *Being and Becoming Indian: Biographical Studies of North American Frontiers* (1989); Marion Marsh Brown, *Susette La Flesche: Advocate for Native American Rights* (1992). For commentary on the story, see Bernd Peyer, *The Singing Spirit. Early Short Stories by North American Indians* (1991). For LaFlesche's commentary on the status of Native Americans, see her introduction to William Justin Harsha, ed., *Ploughed Under: The Story of an Indian Chief Told by Himself* (1881). For additional readings on Native American literature, see entry under John Rollin Ridge.

Yone (Yonejirō) Noguchi. For a discussion of Noguchi's early literary writings in English, see Gerald W. Haslam, "Three Exotics: Yone Noguchi, Shiesei Tsuneishi, and Sadakichi Hartmann," *College Language Association Journal* 19: 3 (1976). Many of Noguchi's academic publications are available in online versions and libraries. For an overview of Noguchi's career and life, see Masayo Duus, *The Life of Isamu Noguchi: Journey without Borders* (2004); Amy Sueyoshi, *Queer Compulsions: Race, Nation, and Sexuality in the Affairs of Yone Noguchi* (2012); Edward Marx, *Yone Noguchi: The Stream of Fate* (2019). On Noguchi's role in introducing haiku to America, see Yoshinobu Hakutani, ed., *Selected English Writings of Yone Noguchi: An East-West Literary Assimilation* (1990); Edward Marx, "A Slightly-Open Door: Yone Noguchi and the Invention of English Haiku," *Genre* 39: 3 (2006).

Samson Occom. For Samson Occom in his historical context, see DeLoss W. Love, *Samson Occom and the Christian Indians of New England* (1899; reprinted 2000); Frederick E. Hoxie, Ronald Hoffman, and Peter J Albert, eds., *Native Americans and the Early Republic* (1999); Ivy Schweitzer, *Samson Occom and the Brotherton Indians* (2012); Dana D. Nelson, "(I speak like a fool but I am constrained): Samson Occom's *Short Narrative* and economies of the racial self," in Helen Jaskoski, ed., *Early Native American Writing: Critical Essays* (2010). For an extensive discussion of Occom's hymns in particular, including their provenance and authentication, see Joanna Brooks, *American Lazarus: Religion and the Rise of African-American and Native American Literatures* (2003), which includes all of Occom's original hymns and unattributed hymns first published in Occom's *Collection of Divine Hymns and Spiritual Songs* (1774).

Lucy Terry Prince. For a detailed discussion of the historical context and the definition of African American literature (including a discussion of Terry, Wheatley, Hammon and other authors), see Bruce D. Dickson, Jr., *The Origins of African American Literature, 1680-1865* (2001). For biographical information on Terry, see David R. Proper, *Lucy Terry Prince: Singer of History* (1997). For a discussion of the poem in its context, see Frances Smith Foster, *Written by Herself: Literary*

Production by African American Women 1746-1892 (1993); Sharon M. Harris, *Executing Race: Early American Women's Narratives of Race, Society, and the Law* (2005); April C. E. Langley, *The Black Aesthetic Unbound: Theorizing the Dilemma of Eighteenth Century African American Literature* (2010).

John Rollin Ridge/Yellow Bird. For a biography of Ridge, see James W. Parins, *John Rollin Ridge. His Life and Words* (1991). For approaches to the novel, see John Lowe, "'I am Joaquín!': Space and freedom in Yellow Bird's *The Life and Adventures of Joaquín Murieta, the Celebrated California Bandit*," in Helen Jaskoski, ed., *Early Native American Writing: Critical Essays* (2010). For discussions of Rollin's poetry, see Robert Dale Parker, *Changing is Not Vanishing: A Collection of American Indian Poetry to 1930* (2011). For general discussions of Ridge in the context of Native American literature, see A. Lavonne Brown Ruoff, *American Indian Literatures: An Introduction, Bibliographic Review, and Selected Bibliography* (1991); Louis Owens, *Other Destinies: Understanding the American Indian Novel* (1994); Lawana Trout, *Native American Literature: An Anthology* (1998); Robert Dale Parker, *The Invention of Native American Literature* (2002); Joy Porter and Kenneth M. Roemer, *Cambridge Companion to Native American Literature* (2010).

Ameen Rihani. Todd Fine published a scholarly edition of *The Book of Khalid* in 2016 that offers critical essays on Rihani and Arab-American literature, the novel in the context of Rihani's other writings, Rihani's relationship and collaboration with Khalil Gibran, and biographical information. For discussions of Rihani, see Aida N. Imangulijeva, *Gibran, Rihani, & Naimy: East-West Interactions in Early-Twentieth-Century Arab Literature* (2009). For discussions of Arab American literature, see Waïl Hassan, *Immigrant Narratives: Orientalism and Cultural Translation in Arab-American and Arab-British Literature* (2011); Lisa Suhair Majaj, "Arab-American Literature: Origins and Developments," in *American Studies Journal* 52 (2008). For background on the immigration of Lebanese to the United States fictionalized in Rihani's book, see Akram Fouad Khater, *Inventing Home: Emigration, Gender, and the Middle Class in Lebanon, 1870-1920* (2001).

Susanna Haswell Rowson. For a reading of Rowson's novel, *Charlotte Temple: A Tale of Truth*, in the context of other publications in the early republic, see Bryan Waterman, "Introduction: Reading Early America with Charles Brockden Brown," *Early American Literature* 44.2 (2009). For interpretations of Rowson's novel in the context of her other writings and her historical moment, see Marion Rust, *Prodigal Daughters: Susanna Rowson's Early American Women* (2008); Marion Rust, "Charles Brockden Brown, Susanna Rowson, and the Early American Sentimental Gothic," in J. Gerald Kennedy and Leland S. Person, eds., *The Oxford History of the Novel in English: The American Novel to 1870* (2014); Patricia L. Parker, "Susanna Rowson," in Angela Vietto and Amy E. Winans, eds., *American Women Prose Writers to 1820* (1999).

María Amparo Ruiz de Burton. For additional information on Ruiz de Burton and her role in the tradition of Chicano/Hispanic Literature, see Ramón Gutiérrez and Padilla Genaro, eds., *Recovering the U.S. Hispanic Literary Heritage* (1993); Rosaura Sánchez and Beatrice Pita, eds., *Conflicts of Interest: The Letters of María Amparo Ruiz de Burton* (2001); Amelia María de la Luz Montes and Anne Elizabeth Goldman, eds., *María Amparo Ruiz de Burton: Critical and Pedagogical Perspectives* (2004). To place her work into a wider historical context see Nicolás Kanellos, *Hispanic Literature of the United States: A Comprehensive Reference* (2003); John-Michael Rivera, *The Emergence of Mexican America: Recovering Stories of Mexican Peoplehood in U. S. Culture* (2006); Lene Johannessen, *Threshold Time: Passage of Crisis in Chicano Literature* (2008); Marissa K. López, *Chicano Nations: The Hemispheric Origins of Mexican American Literature* (2011); Rodrigo Lazo and Jesse Alemán, eds., *The Latino Nineteenth Century* (2016).

"S." For discussions of the identity of "S," see Dickson Bruce, Jr., *The Origins of African American Literature, 1680-1865* (2001); Frances Smith Foster, "Forgotten Manuscripts: How Do You Solve a Problem Like Theresa?" *African American Review* 40.4 (2006). For discussions of the story, its author, and the historical context, see Jean Lee Cole, "Theresa and Blake: Mobility and Resistance in Antebellum African American Serialized Fiction," *Callaloo* 34.1 (Winter 2011); Marlene L. Daut, *Tropics of Haiti: Race and the Literary History of the Haitian Revolution in the Atlantic World, 1789-1865* (2016). On public readership and African American literary societies and newspapers, including *Freedom's Journal* where the story was first serialized, see Elizabeth McHenry and Donald E. Pease, *Forgotten Readers: Discovering the Lost History of African American Literary Societies* (2002).

Jane Johnston Schoolcraft, also known as Bamewawagezhikaquay (Ojibwe name). The authoritative text on Schoolcraft's life and work is Robert Dale Parker, *The Sound the Stars Make Rushing Through the Sky: The Writings of Jane Johnston Schoolcraft* (2007). For additional information see also Basil Johnston, *Ojibway Heritage* (1976); George L. Cornell, "The Imposition of Western Definitions of Literature on Indian Oral Traditions," in Thomas King, Cheryl Calver, and Helen Hoy, eds., *The Native in Literature* (1987); William M. Clements, *Native American Verbal Art: Texts and Contexts* (1996); LaVonne Brown A. Ruoff, "Early Native American Women Authors: Jane Johnston Schoolcraft, Sarah Winnemucca, S. Alice Callahan, E. Pauline Johnson, and Zitkala-Sa," in Karen L. Kilcup, ed., *Nineteenth-Century American Women Writers: A Critical Reader* (1998); Paula Bernat Bennett, *Poets in the Public Sphere: The Emancipatory Project of American Women's Poetry, 1800-1900* (2003). For additional readings on Native American literature, see entry under John Rollin Ridge.

Mercy Otis Warren. For discussions of Warren's contribution to American politics and culture, see Rosemarie Zagarri, *A Woman's Dilemma: Mercy Otis Warren* *and the American Revolution* (2015); Jeffrey H. Richards, "Mercy Otis Warren," in Angela Vietto and Amy E. Winans, eds., *American Women Prose Writers to 1820* (1999); Leopold Lippert, "Virtual Theatricality, Transatlantic Representation, and Mercy Otis Warren's Revolutionary Plays," *Approaching Transnational America in Performance*, Birgit M. Bauridl and Pia Wiegmink, eds., (2016).

Onoto Watanna/Winnifred Eaton. An extensive online database, *The Winnifred Eaton Archive* (winnifredeatonarchive.org), founded by Jean Lee Cole and further developed by Mary Chapman, holds many of Eaton's writings from different phases of her career as well as scholarship on Eaton and her sister, Sui Sin Far/Maude Eaton. For Eaton/Watanna's life story, see Diana Birchall, *Onoto Watanna: The Story of Winnifred Eaton* (2006); Amy Ling, *In Between Worlds: Women Writers of Chinese Ancestry* (1990). A briefer biographical sketch is Lisa Botshon, "Winnifred Eaton (1875-1954)," in Emmanuel S. Nelson, ed., *Asian American Novelists: A Bio-Bibliographical Critical Sourcebook* (2000). For a discussion of Eaton's literary works, see Jean Lee Cole, *The Literary Voices of Winnifred Eaton: Redefining Ethnicity and Authenticity* (2002); Dominika Ferens, *Edith and Winnifred Eaton: Chinatown Missions and Japanese Romances* (2002); Susan L. Blake, "Behind the Mask of Coquetry: The Trickster Narrative in *Miss Numè of Japan: A Japanese-American Romance*," in Susan Strehle and Mary Paniccia Carden, eds., *Double Plots: Romance and History* (2003). For a discussion of the works of both Eaton sisters in relation to Asian American literature, see Viet Thanh Nguyen, *Race and Resistance: Literature and Politics in Asian America* (2002).

Phillis Wheatley. For interpretations of Wheatley's writings, see Dorothy Porter, ed., *Early Negro Writing, 1760-1837* (1971/1995); Frances Smith Foster, *Written by Herself: Literary Production by African American Women 1746-1892* (1993); Robert Reid-Pharr, *Conjugal Union: The Body, the House, and the Black American* (1999); John C. Shields, *Phillis Wheatley's Poetics of Liberation: Backgrounds and Contexts* (2008); Kathrynn Seidler Engberg, *The Right to Write: The Literary Politics of Anne Bradstreet and Phillis Wheatley* (2009); Rowan Ricardo Phillips, *When Blackness Rhymes with Blackness* (2010); Vincent Carretta, *Phillis Wheatley: Biography of a Genius in Bondage* (2014).

Walt Whitman. All of Whitman's writings, as well as photographs, contemporary reviews, and other materials are available online at *The Walt Whitman Archive*, edited by Matt Cohen, Ed Folsom and Kenneth M. Price. There are several key biographies: Gay Wilson Allen, *The Solitary Singer* (1967); Justin Kaplan, *Walt Whitman: A Life* (1980); Davis S. Reynolds, *Walt Whitman's America: A Cultural Biography* (1995); Gary Schmidgall, *Walt Whitman: A Gay Life* (1998); Ed Folsom and Kenneth M. Price, *Re-scripting Walt Whitman: An Introduction to His Life and Work* (2005). Selected critical interpretations include: Betsy Erkkila, *Whitman the*

Political Poet (1989); Kenneth M. Price, *Whitman and Tradition* (1990); Michael Moon, *Disseminating Whitman: Revision and Corporeality in 'Leaves of Grass'* (1991); Ed Folsom, *Walt Whitman's Native Representations* (1994); David Haven Blake, *Walt Whitman and the Culture of American Celebrity* (2006); David Haven Blake and Michael Robertson, eds., *Walt Whitman, Where the Future Becomes Present* (2008); Matt Miller, *Collage of Myself: Walt Whitman and the Making of Leaves of Grass* (2010); Ivy Wilson, *Whitman Noir: Black America and the Good Gray Poet* (2014). For commentary on the "Calamus" poems, see Betsy Erkkila, ed. *Walt Whitman's Songs of Male Intimacy and Love: "Live Oak, with Moss" and "Calamus"* (2011); *Live Oak, With Moss* (2019), introduction by Karen Karbiener and illustrations by Brian Selznick. For a discussion of definitions of "gay" or "queer" literature, see Scott Herring, *The Cambridge Companion to American Gay and Lesbian Literature* (2015).

Harriet E. Wilson. For discussions of Wilson's novel, see Ann DuCille, *The Coupling Convention: Sex, Text, and Tradition in Black Women's Fiction* (1994); Ernest John, *Resistance and Reformation in Nineteenth Century African-American Literature: Brown, Wilson, Jacobs, Delany, Douglass, and Harper* (1995); Xiomara Santamarina, *Belabored Professions: Narratives of African American Working Womanhood* (2005); P. Gabrielle Foreman and Reginald H. Pitts, *Activist Sentiments: Reading Black Women in the Nineteenth Century* (2009); Karen Kilcup, *Soft Canons: American Women Writers and Masculine Tradition* (2012). For a general discussion of the rise of the African American novel, see Maurice S. Lee, "The 1850s: The First Renaissance of Black Letters," in Gene Andrew Jarrett, ed., *A Companion to African American Literature* (2010).

Theodore Winthrop. For information on Winthrop and the circumstances of the novel's creation and posthumous publication, see Elbridge Colby, *Theodore Winthrop* (1965); Peter Coviello, *Peculiar Tendernesses: Cecil Dreeme and the Queer Nineteenth Century* (2016). For more context on same-sex relationships in nineteenth century American fiction, see Peter Coviello, *Intimacy in America: Dreams of Affiliation in Antebellum Literature* (2005); Axel Nissen, *Manly Love: Romantic Friendship in American Fiction* (2009); Christopher Looby, ed., *The Man Who Thought Himself a Woman and Other Queer Nineteenth-Century Short Stories* (2017).

BIBLIOGRAPHY OF FIRST PUBLICATIONS

Iroquois Creation Myth, First publication in John Norton, *Journal of a Voyage, of a Thousand Miles, Down the Ohio; From the Grand River, Upper Canada;—Visit to the Country of the Cherokees:—Through the States of Kentucky and Tennessee: and an Account of the Five Nations, Etc. from an Early Period, to the Conclusion of the late War Between Great Britain & America*, 1818. Manuscript in Dukes of Northumberland (Alnwick Castle; Great Britain).

Anne Bradstreet, *The Tenth Muse, lately Sprung up in America, or Several Poems Compiled with Great Variety of Wit and Learning, Full of Delight, Wherein especially is Contained a Complete Discourse and Description of the Four Elements, Constitutions, Ages of Man, Seasons of the Year, together with an exact Epitome of the Four Monarchies, viz., The Assyrian, Persian, Grecian, Roman, Also a Dialogue between Old England and New, concerning the late troubles. With divers other pleasant and serious Poems, By a Gentlewoman in those parts* (London: Stephen Bowtell, 1650).

Robert Hunter, *Androboros* (New York: Printed at Monoropolis, 1714 [date of actual publication 1715]).

Lucy Terry Prince, "Bars Fight." Composed after 1746; first publication in Josiah Gilbert Holland, *History of Western Massachusetts* (Springfield, Mass.: S. Bowles and Company, 1855).

Jupiter Hammon, "An Evening Thought: Salvation by Christ, with Penentential Cries: Composed by Jupiter Hammon, a Negro belonging to Mr Lloyd of Queen's Village, on Long-Island, the 25th of December, 1760," printed 1760 in New York. "An Essay on Slavery, with submission to Divine providence, knowing that God Rules over all things—Written by Jupiter Hammon." In Cedrick May and Julie McCown, "'An Essay on Slavery': An Unpublished Poem by Jupiter Hammon," *Early American Literature* 48 (2), 2013.

Mercy Otis Warren, *The Adulateur, A Tragedy, Acted in Upper Servia.* in *Massachusetts Spy*, March/April 1772, Boston and Worcester, Massachusetts.

Phillis Wheatley, *Poems on Various Subjects, Religious and* Moral (London: A. Bell; Boston: Cox and Berry, 1773)

Samson Occom, "Throughout the Saviour's Life We Trace," in Samson Occom, *A Choice Collection of Hymns and Spiritual Songs* (New London, Connecticut: Timothy Green, 1774). "A Morning Hymn, or, Now the Shades of Night are Gone," in John Curtis, ed., *A New Collection of Hymns and Spiritual Songs, from Various Authors* (Newark, New Jersey: Daniel Dodge, 1797). "The Slow Traveller, or, O Happy Souls How Fast You Go" [written 1773], in Joshua Smith, ed., *Divine Hymns, or, Spiritual Songs* (Exeter, New Hampshire: Henry Ranlet, 1791). "Come All My Young Companions, Come" first published in Smith, *Divine Hymns, or, Spiritual Songs* (Troy, New York, 1803). All hymns reprinted in Joanna Brooks, *The Collected Writings of Samson Occom, Mohegan: Leadership and Literature in Eighteenth-Century Native America* (New York: Oxford University Press, 2006).

William Hill Brown, *The Power of Sympathy* (Boston: Isaiah Thomas and Company, 1789).

Susanna Rowson, *Charlotte Temple, A Tale of Truth* (Philadelphia: Matthew Carey, 1794).

Jane Johnston Schoolcraft, "Pensive Hours." Dated 1820; in Henry Rowe Schoolcraft, ed., *The Literary Voyager; The Muzzeniegun* (manuscript magazine), Sault Ste. Marie, Michigan, 1826/27, and edited by Philip P. Mason, Michigan State University Press, 1962. "Invocation. *To my Maternal Grand-father on hearing his descent from Chippewa ancestors misrepresented.*" Dated 1823; in *Southern Literary Messenger,* 1860; reprinted in Parker, ed., *The Sounds the Stars Make Rushing Through the Sky* (2007). "The Contrast." Dated 1823; in Henry Rowe Schoolcraft, ed., *The Literary Voyager; The Muzzeniegun*; also in Henry Rowe Schoolcraft, *Indian Melodies* (New York: Elam Bliss 1830). "To the Pine Tree on first seeing it on returning from Europe" in Parker, ed., *The Sound the Stars Make Rushing Through the Sky* (2007). "To my ever beloved and lamented Son William Henry." Dated 1827; in *Literary Voyager; The Muzzeniegun* (1827) and in Henry Rowe Schoolcraft, *Personal Memoirs of a Residence of Thirty Years with the Indian Tribes on the American Frontiers* (Philadelphia: Lippincott, Grambo, 1851). "Language Divine!" Dated 1816; in *The Literary Voyager; The Muzzeniegun,* Sault Ste. Marie, Michigan, 1826/27. "Resignation" Dated 1826; in *The Literary Voyager; The Muzzeniegun,* Sault Ste. Marie, Michigan, 1826/27. All of Johnston's known poems have been published in Robert Dale Parker, ed., *The Sound the Stars Make Rushing Through the Sky. The Writings of Jane Johnston Schoolcraft* (Philadelphia: University of Pennsylvania Press, 2007).

"S," "Theresa: A Haytien Tale." In *Freedom's Journal,* New York, January 18, 1828.

George Moses Horton, "On Liberty and Slavery," "Love," "The Slave's Complaint," "On hearing of the intention of a gentleman to purchase the Poet's freedom," in *The Hope of Liberty. Containing a Number of Poetical Pieces* (Raleigh, North Carolina: J. Gales and Son, 1829). "On an Old Deluded Suitor," "Division of an Estate," in *The Poetical Works of George M. Horton. The Colored Bard of North Carolina, To Which is Prefixed the Life of the Author, Written by Himself* (Hillsborough: D. Heartt, 1845).

William Wells Brown, *Clotel, or, The President's Daughter: A Narrative of Slave Life in the United States* (London: Partridge and Oakey, 1853). First American edition serialized as *Miralda; or, The Beautiful Quadroon. A Romance of American Slavery, Founded on Fact*, in the *Weekly Anglo African* (New York), December 1860-March 1861.

Frederick Douglass, *The Heroic Slave*, in Julia Griffiths, ed., *Autographs for Freedom* (Boston: John P. Jewett; Cleveland, Ohio: Jewett, Proctor and Worthington; London: Low and Company, 1853).

John Rollin Ridge/Cheesquatalawny/Yellow Bird, *The Life and Adventures of Joaquín Murieta.* (San Francisco: Frederick McCrellish, 1854). "An Indian's Grave," in *Arkansas State Democrat*, 6 August 1847. "Reflections Irregular," in *Arkansas State Democrat*, 28 January 1848. "Mount Shasta," "The Stolen White Girl," in John Rollin Ridge, *Poems* (San Francisco: Henry Payot, 1868). Ridge's poems are published in Robert Dale Parker, ed., *Changing is not Vanishing. A Collection of American Indian Poetry to 1930* (Philadelphia: University of Pennsylvania Press, 2011).

William Wells Brown, *The Escape: or a Leap to Freedom* (Boston: R. F. Wallcut, 1858).

Rose Terry Cooke, "My Visitation," *Harper's New Monthly Magazine*, July 1858.

Harriet E. Wilson, *Our Nig; or, Sketches from the Life of a Free Black, In A Two-Story White House, North* (Boston: George C. Rand and Avery, 1859).

Frances Ellen Watkins Harper, "The Two Offers," published in two installments in the *Anglo-African Magazine*, New York, 1859. "Learning to Read" in Frances E. Watkins Harper, *Sketches of Southern Life* (Philadelphia: Merrihew and Son, 1873).

Martin Delany, *Blake, or the Huts of America.* The first of two serialized versions was published in the *Anglo-African Magazine*, January 1859-March 1860; the second version in the *Weekly Anglo-African* in 1861-62. The first complete publication in 1970, with an introduction by Floyd J. Miller, was published in Boston by Beacon Press.

Walt Whitman "Calamus." In Walt Whitman, *Leaves of Grass* (Boston: Thayer and Eldridge, 1860).

Theodore Winthrop, *Cecil Dreeme* (Boston: Ticknor and Fields, 1861).

María Amparo Ruiz de Burton, *Who Would Have Thought It?* (Philadelphia: J.B. Lippincott and Co., 1872). *The Squatter and the Don* (San Francisco: Samuel Carson and Co., 1885).

Susette La Flesche, "Nedawi," in *St. Nicholas Magazine,* (New York: Scribners, January 18, 1881).

Sophia Alice Callahan, *Wynema, A Child of the Forest* (Philadelphia, Chicago, Kansas City, and Oakland: H.J. Smith & Co., 1891).

Carl Sadakichi Hartmann, *Christ* (New York, 1893).

Sui Sin Far/Maude Eaton, "The Gamblers" (author's name Sui Seen Far), in *Fly Leaf,* February 1896, Boston. "In the Land of the Free," in *The Independent,* 1909. "Spring Fragrance," in *Hampton's Magazine,* January 1910, New York.

Yone Noguchi, "Where Would I Go?" "Alone," "My Universe," "Like a Paper Lantern," in *The Lark,* San Francisco, July 1896 [publication 1897] and in *Seen and Unseen, or, Monologues of a Homeless Snail* (San Francisco: Gelett Burgess & Porter Garnett, 1897). "Japanese Hokkus," in Yone Noguchi, *Japanese Hokkus* (Boston: Four Seas 1920).

Winnifred Eaton/Onoto Watanna, *Miss Numè of Japan: A Japanese-American Romance* (New York: Rand, McNally, 1899).

Yone Noguchi, *The American Diary of a Japanese Girl* (serialized in *Frank Leslie's Illustrated Monthly Magazine,* New York, 1901).

Ameen Rihani, *The Book of Khalid* (New York: Dodd, Mead and Company, 1911).

ABOUT THE EDITORS

ULRICH BAER holds a B.A. from Harvard and a Ph.D. from Yale. A widely published author, he is University Professor at New York University, and has been awarded Guggenheim, Getty, and Alexander von Humboldt fellowships. He has written and edited numerous books, including *110 Stories: New York Writes After September 11; The Shoshana Felman Reader; The Rilke Alphabet; Spectral Evidence: The Photography of Trauma; Remnants of Song: Poetry and the Experience of Modernity in Charles Baudelaire and Paul Celan,* and edited and translated Rainer Maria Rilke's *The Dark Interval, Letters on Life, and Letters to a Young Poet.* He hosts leading writers and artists to talk about big ideas and great books on his *Think About It* podcast. In the Warbler Press *Contemplations* series, he has published: *Nietzsche, Rilke, Dickinson, Wilde,* and *Shakespeare on Love.*

SMARAN DAYAL is a Ph.D. candidate in Comparative Literature at New York University, working on a dissertation on Afrofuturist and postcolonial science fiction. He holds a B.A. in English and American Studies from the University of Freiburg, an M.A. in American Studies from the Humboldt University, Berlin, and an M.Phil. in Comparative Literature from NYU. He is one of the co-organizers of the NYU Postcolonial, Race and Diaspora Studies Colloquium, and co-translator of the book *The Queer Intersectional in Contemporary Germany* (2018).

Printed in the USA
CPSIA information can be obtained
at www.ICGtesting.com
LVHW041603040823
754191LV00005B/515

9 781735 778983